## BY HUGH THOMAS

# WORLD
# WITHOUT
# END

# WORLD WITHOUT END

*Spain, Philip II, and the First Global Empire*

## HUGH THOMAS

RANDOM HOUSE
NEW YORK

Published in the United States by Random House, an imprint and
division of Penguin Random House LLC, New York.

RANDOM HOUSE and the HOUSE colophon are registered trademarks
of Penguin Random House LLC.

Originally published in 2014 in the United Kindom by Allen Lane,
an imprint of Penguin Books.

Library of Congress Cataloging-in-Publication Data

Thomas, Hugh.
World without end : Spain, Philip II, and the first global empire / Hugh Thomas.
pages cm
Originally published: London, England : Allen Lane, 2014.
Includes bibliographical references and index.
ISBN 978-0-8129-9811-5
eBook ISBN 978-0-8129-9812-2
1. Philip II, King of Spain, 1527–1598. 2. America—Discovery and exploration—
Spanish. 3. Spain—Colonies—America—History—16th century. 4. Spain—
Colonies—Asia—History—16th century. I. Title.
F1411.T463 2015
946'.043—dc23    2014045880

Printed in the United States of America on acid-free paper

randomhousebooks.com

2 4 6 8 9 7 5 3 1

First U.S. Edition

*Here I cannot forbear to commend the patient virtue of the Spaniards. We seldom or never find any nation hath endured so many misadventures and miseries as the Spaniards have done in their Indian discoveries. Yet persisting in their enterprises, with invincible constancy, they have annexed to their kingdom so many goodly provinces as bury the remembrance of all dangers past. Tempests and shipwrecks, famines, overthrows, mutinies, heat and cold, pestilence and all manner of diseases both old and new, together with extreme poverty and want of all things needful have been the enemies, wherewith every one of their most noble discoveries, at one or other, hath encountered. Many years have passed over some of their heads in the search of not so many leagues: yea, more than one have spent their labour, their wealth and their lives in search of a golden kingdom without getting further notice of it than what they had at their setting forth. All which notwithstanding, the third, the fourth and fifth undertakers have not been disheartened. Surely they are worthily rewarded with those treasures and paradises, which they enjoy, and well deserve to hold them quietly, if they hinder not the like virtue in others, which (perhaps) will not be found.*

*[. . .]*

*Since the fall of the Roman empire (omitting that of the Germans which had neither greatness nor continuance) there hath been no state fearful in the East but that of the Turk; nor in the West any prince that hath spread his wings far over his nest but the Spaniards who since the time that Ferdinand expelled the Moors out of Granada have made many attempts to make themselves masters of all Europe.*

Sir Walter Raleigh, *The History of the World*

# Contents

### BOOK THREE
## The Imperial Backcloth

### BOOK FOUR
## The East in Fee

# List of Illustrations

# List of Maps

Several of these maps derive from the admirable *Atlas de Historia de España*, edited by Fernando García de Cortazar, Barcelona, 2005, especially maps 3 and 4.

# Introduction

With this book, I complete a trilogy about the Spanish empire in the Americas begun in 2003 with *Rivers of Gold*, and continued in 2010 with *The Golden Age*. The present book brings the history up to 1598, the year of the death of the long-lasting Spanish king Philip II, when administrators, colonists, clergymen, and other officials were doing what they could to manage a large political empire, rather than expand it. The vast undertaking would last for another two hundred and more years; in the case of Cuba, Puerto Rico, and the Philippine islands and some other places, three hundred. But by 1598 the men of empire had mostly become guardians, not conquerors.

The present volume includes chapters where I try and consider life in one or other of the conquered territories; and there are the chapters of adventure in which I discuss new conquests. The two are the same in some cases, as, for example, in chapter 11 about Chile. There are also chapters where I talk of the arrangements made in the mother country, Spain, for the control of the new imperial territories.

Books play a part in this story, as Irving Leonard pointed out years ago in his admirable study *Books of the Brave*, first published in 1949.[1] The number of persons inspired by chivalrous novels to go and seek their fortunes in the new world is considerable. Antonio Pigafetta, the Italian chronicler of Magellan's journey around the world declared: 'When I was in Spain in 1509, certain people whom I met and several books which I read, revealed to me the marvels of the ocean sea and there and then I resolved to see such marvels with my own eyes.'[2] The reflections on this subject of the German Philipp von Hutten are quoted in this book's immediate predecessor, *The Golden Age*: 'I could not die in peace without having seen the Indies.'[3] Bernal

Díaz del Castillo, who came from Medina del Campo in Castile, wrote in *Historia verdadera de la conquista de la Nueva España* that he thought a distant sight of Mexico/Tenochtitlan reminded him of a depiction he remembered from the marvellously successful novel *Amadís de Gaula*,[4] which is a little odd since there are no scenes of great cities in *Amadís* that I can find. But Bernal Díaz differs, and it is worth recalling that he must have known the author, or re-writer, of *Amadís*, Garci Rodríguez de Montalvo, since, astonishingly, they came from the same town, where their houses were not far from one another. Rodríguez de Montalvo was a councillor (*regidor*) in Medina del Campo, as was Díaz's father.

Díaz's famous chronicle, like Montalvo's *Amadís*, was characteristic of the age and would not have been thought of a hundred years earlier. For the European sixteenth century had yielded one surprising innovation from which much of the rest of its history flowed. That was printing, and the possibility of the widespread dissemination of both texts and copies of pictures. Reading became transformed from being the privilege of a small elite, able to afford handwritten copies, to something which most educated people could access by way of printed pamphlets and books. The effect was similar to the achievement of the radio in the twentieth century in widening the appreciation of music. In Spain, the new era began with such novels as Joanot Martorell and Martí Joan de Galba's *Tirant lo Blanch*, published in 1490 in Valencia, and *Amadís de Gaula*, whose first identifiable publication was in Saragossa in 1508. With these works 'a wide public awoke to the realization that a book could also be a means of entertainment'.[5] In this new world, people looked to the chivalrous novel as a sort of modern-day tourist guide: beyond the next cape, *Sergas de Esplandián* might have suggested, in the book of that name, there were sure to be Amazons.

These chivalrous novels influenced behaviour in many ways. Fernando de Ávalos, marquis of Pescara in Italy, the husband of Michelangelo's friend Vittoria Colonna, read many chivalrous novels in his youth before embarking on his own valiant career.[6] Saint Ignatius Loyola, founder of the Jesuit order, was accustomed to read those 'vayne Treatises' to relieve the boredom during his recovery in 1522 from a broken leg at the siege of Pamplona.[7] Equally, Saint Teresa of Ávila describes how she fell 'into the habit of reading them [chivalrous novels] and it seemed that it was not wrong to spend many hours of the day and nights in such vain exercise, though concealed from my father. I became so utterly absorbed in this that if I did not have a new book, I did not feel I could be happy.'[8] Surely this reading influenced Saint Teresa's own life and her own book, *El Castillo interior o las Moradas (The Castle of the Soul)*. Irving Leonard recalls a priest who not only knew of the deeds of Amadís and other heroes but believed that they were true merely because he had seen them in print.[9]

The conquest of the Americas also appears to have been in some ways the last crusade. The role of the Catholic Church in the unfolding of this great drama was as great as it had been in the earlier adventures of Christianity. We can recognize the role of the Franciscan, Dominican and Augustinian orders, and then the Jesuits, in this age of imperial conquest. Christianity gave the Spanish empire an ideology. But it also provided that empire with a purpose and an essential discipline.

I am grateful to the following for their help: Mr Stuart Proffitt of Penguin Books, and his successive assistants Shan Vahidy and Donald Futers; Mr Andrew Wylie, Ms Sarah Chalfant, James Pullen, and others at Wylie Inc.; I can only describe Stuart Proffitt's work on my text of volume 3 as marvellous, to use Columbus's favourite word. He has been meticulous, imaginative, learned and interesting, as well as wise.

I also thank Ana Bustelo at Planeta, Barcelona; Gloria Gutiérrez and Carmen Balcells, at the Agencia Carmen Balcells; Guillaume Villeneuve, my excellent French translator; Agnès Hirtz and Jean-Louis Barré at Robert Laffont, Inc.; and the following with whom I stayed or consulted: Mr and Mrs John Hemming; Sir John Elliott; Damian and Paloma Fraser in Mexico; the late Carlos Fuentes; Marita Martínez del Río de Redo; Enrique Krauze; Dr Kwasi Kwarteng, MP; Professor Enriqueta Vila Vilar; Dr Juan Gil and Professor Consuelo Varela; the Duke and Duchess of Segorbe; Gerarda de Orleans; Rafael Atienza, Marquis of Salvatierra; the Marquis of Tamarón; Don Gonzalo Anes, Marquis of Castrillón, director of the Royal Academy of History in Spain; Don Vicente Lleó; Don Rafael Manzano; the director of the Archivo de Indias in Seville; Don Antonio Sánchez, director of the Museo de las Ferias, in Medina del Campo; and Don Miguel-Angel Cortés, Member of Parliament for Valladolid.

My assistants, Teresa Velasco, then Cecilia Calamante and finally

Carlota Ribeiro Sanches, did much on different volumes of this work and I shall always be grateful to them for their care. Teresa Alzugaray has, as in the past, helped me with sixteenth-century Spanish script.

I should also mention certain books which have been an inspiration as well as a great help. These include the *Dictionary of Spanish National Biography*, of which masterpiece of book production I am one of the first to benefit (references are to *DBE*, or *Diccionario Biográfico Español*). There is also the *Colección de documentos inéditos relativos al descubrimiento, conquista y organización de las antiguas posesiones españolas en América y Oceania*, 42 volumes, Madrid 1864–84, to which I have alluded in the notes by the abbreviation 'CDI'. I have also benefited from Marcel Bataillon, *Érasme en Espagne*; Manuel Ollé, *La empresa de China*; Manuel Fernández Álvarez, *Felipe II y su tiempo*; Sir John Elliott, *Imperial Spain*; James Lockhart, *The Men of Cajamarca* and *Spanish Peru*; Sir Nicholas Cheetham, *New Spain*; Irving Leonard, *Books of the Brave*; Geoffrey Parker, *Philip II*; Fernand Braudel, *The Mediterranean in the Age of Philip II*; Manuel Giménez Fernández, *Bartolomé de las Casas*; John Hemming, *The Search for El Dorado*; Ludwig von Pastor, *History of the Papacy*; and Robert Ricard, *The Spiritual Conquest of Mexico*.

On the subject of King Philip, I have used several important biographies: those of the late Manuel Fernández Álvarez (*Felipe II y su tiempo*), Madrid 1998; Geoffrey Parker, whose *Philip II* (Boston 1978) is illuminating; and Henry Kamen, whose comparable biography I also enjoyed. These books helped me greatly in writing volume I. I had the pleasure many years ago also of meeting in Rome the late Orestes Ferrara, who wrote a remarkable life in the 1940s when an exile from Cuba (*Philippe II*, Paris 1961). Two novels of the epoch helped me greatly in ways that I explain 'sobre la marcha', as the Spaniards would put it: *Amadís de Gaula* of 1508; and *Tirant lo Blanch* of 1490.

I am also most grateful to my wife, Vanessa, for her help and patience in reading and correcting an early version of my text; as well as my children, Íñigo, Isambard and Isabella, for their support. I thank also my son-in-law Dr Georgios and my grandson Alexander Varouxakis.

Hugh Thomas, 31 January 2014

# Prologue: A Journey to Paris

*La Reine manda au Roi qu'elle conjurait de ne plus courir,*
*qu'il avait si bien fait qu'il devait être content et qu'elle le sup-*
*pliait de revenir auprès d'elle.*

Madame de la Fayette, *La Princesse de Clèves*.
This was Queen Catherine de' Medici appealing
to King Henry II not to go on with his joust.

A treaty of peace made in 1559, between France on the one hand and Spain in alliance with the Holy Roman Empire on the other, heralded what we have come to think of as modern times. The pact was made in the shadow of the two military victories by the latter, allies who came together in the north-east of France, in battles at Saint Quentin (1557) and at Gravelines (1558). Subsequent financial exhaustion had forced France to seek a settlement. They were victories of one nation state, Spain, against another such, namely France, though Spain could count on the ancient edifice of the Holy Roman Empire, which meant Germany, as an ally.

The negotiations for the treaty were embarked upon in 1558 in the twelfth-century monastery of Cercamp in the north of France and were completed in the nearby town of Le Cateau-Cambrésis. There were also discussions at Cambrai. These places had been for a long time in the Flemish county of Hainault, and so part of the inheritance of the Dukes of Burgundy. Cambrai had been the seat of a previous peace treaty, the so-called 'Paix des Dames' of 1530, and had, for several generations before that, been known for a fine white linen cloth known as 'cambric'. That seemed a good omen.

At Cambrai, in 1558, the great men of all the countries concerned –
all the major countries of Europe in fact – had assembled. For Spain,
there was the grand figure of the third Duke of Alba, an aristocrat
who was an effective military commander, courtier, and diplomat. It
was Alba who had really won the battle of Mühlberg for the Emperor
Charles in 1547, a triumph commemorated superbly by Titian in one
of his most famous equestrian portraits. In attendance at Cambrai
also was Philip II's chief secretary, Ruy Gómez, a courtier who had
come to Spain with the king's Portuguese mother when she became
queen-empress and who had recently been given the Neapolitan title
of 'Prince of Éboli'.

Other prominent leaders in the very international Spanish delegation were the Bishop of Arras, the future Cardinal Granvelle; a learned
lawyer, Virgilius van Aytta of Zwichen, who had been president of the
Privy Council of the Netherlands; and William, Prince of Orange, a
rich young Dutch nobleman who was at the time conducting a flirta-
tion with a Flemish girl, Eva Elincx, a liaison which persuaded the
austere Alba that the prince was a man of straw. Count Egmont,
another of the imperial delegates, was also an outstanding leader. He
came from an ancient family of Hainault which had played a part in
the golden years of Burgundian self-assertion in the fifteenth century.
The count had himself married a sister of the Elector Palatine of the
Rhine and had participated in the Emperor Charles's disastrous
expedition to Algiers in 1541. A knight of the Golden Fleece since
1546, Egmont was good-natured, charming, easy-going and brave,
and a fine commander of cavalry. But he could also be rash and intemperate. He had commanded the German – or Burgundian – cavalry,
the 'Schwartzreitern', which had won the day for Spain at the battles
of both Saint Quentin and Gravelines.

The French at the peace negotiations were led by the Constable of
the country, the peace-loving Anne,[1] Duke of Montmorency, supported by the more warlike and intelligent Cardinal of Lorraine,
brother of the Duke of Guise, an able soldier who had recently captured Calais from the English. These princely French eminences were
supported by Jean de Morvilliers and Sébastien de L'Aubespine, men
of letters who acted as secretaries (L'Aubespine would soon be French
ambassador in the Low Countries).[2]

Of Montmorency, the Venetian ambassador, Martín de Cavalli, wrote to the Doge: 'If there is peace, the Constable is the most important man in France; if there is war, he is a prisoner, deprived of all importance.'[3] As usual Venetian ambassadors' reports give the best outside view of what was happening in the courts to which they were accredited.

These delegations included the ablest men in Europe. Alba and Montmorency made common cause in the diplomacy in 1559. The former was the most reliable of the courtiers of King Philip, who both admired and feared him. The latter was known as a skilful negotiator.[4]

In these negotiations, which culminated in signatures on 2 and 3 April 1559, many territories and frontiers were at stake, including most of Italy. So too were small garrison towns (known as *presidios*) such as Talamona, Orbetello, Porto-Ercole, and Santo Stefano, imperial possessions which made it possible for Spain to interrupt commerce between Genoa and Naples.[5] Marriages and inheritances were also to be discussed. Would the new queen of England, Elizabeth, marry King Philip, the widower of her sister Mary? What, too, of the pretty but very young daughter to Henry II of France, Elisabeth of Valois? Would she perhaps marry the heir to the Spanish throne, Charles ('Don Carlos'). Or would she perhaps prefer his father, Philip? The Duke of Alba wrote a letter from Le Quesnoy, a fortified town between Cambrai and Paris, that it did not seem right for his king not to have married again when he had only one son.[6] Meantime the future of Calais was settled in a curious way. If Queen Elizabeth of England were to marry, and have a son, and if that son were to marry a daughter of the king of France or even a daughter of the Dauphin, that son would have Calais. But if that solution did not please Queen Elizabeth, she would receive back the town in eight years' time. Some 500,000 crowns were to be paid in Venice as a security for the gifts.[7]

The Italians accepted what Stendhal several hundred years later would refer to as the 'Spanish despotism',[8] because they both needed protection against the Turks and coveted American silver.[9] But France too retained some Italian footholds. She had five of these in Piedmont including Turin, Pinerolo, and Savignano, as well as the marquisate of Saluzzo. But these places were nothing in comparison to the parts of Corsica and Siena which were abandoned to the Doge of Genoa and to the Grand Duke of Tuscany, both of whom were in effect Spanish vassals.

Alba, Gómez, the Prince of Orange and the Count of Egmont all went on from Cambrai to the French capital. Before that, they had attended a meeting in Brussels of the chapter of the Golden Fleece, the chivalrous order which had been founded by Philip the Good in Burgundy in the fifteenth century and which his descendants maintained as if it were the highest order of chivalry. The Duke of Alba, however, had, as it turned out, a new role in Paris: he was to marry the French princess Elisabeth by proxy on behalf of King Philip.

The wedding which was to mark the end of the war was planned for 22 June, and was held on a platform mounted before the west front of the cathedral of Notre-Dame. Alba was dressed in cloth of gold surmounted by an imperial crown, the new queen-to-be was decked out with jewels. After the ceremony, the duke gave Elisabeth a jewel box full of precious stones with a cameo of the king on it, on King Philip's behalf.[10] He went to the queen's bedroom, placed his arm and a leg across the bed, and then left. The girl became known as 'the Queen of Peace' because of her marriage to Philip. A second wedding was next held, between Marguerite, Henry II's sister, and the Duke of Savoy, Emmanuel Philibert. The latter, unlike King Philip, was present in person, being the first Savoyard to become a significant European statesman.

Tournaments followed. There was also a hunt in Chantilly during which King Henry told the Netherlands Prince of Orange that the Duke of Alba wanted to set about the extermination of heresy with a joint Spanish-French army, beginning in that 'plague spot, the Netherlands'. He chose the wrong confidant, for Orange, though taciturn, was horrified.[11]

A special joust was arranged in the Rue Saint-Antoine, that famous street in Paris which leads from the Louvre to the Bastille, a journey from palace to prison often taken in the past by the most unexpected people, including the most noble of aristocrats. King Henry II of France excelled at jousting.[12] The street was left especially unpaved for the great occasion. Rich hangings bearing the arms of Spain, France, and Savoy covered nearby balconies, and statues, symbolizing the benefits of peace, were placed between the columns of the palaces.

Two days of jousting were successful. On 30 June the king, wearing the black and white colours of his famous *maîtresse en titre*, Diane de Poitiers, and riding a horse named 'Malheureux', had several triumphs. Diane was there to cheer. The queen, Catherine de' Medici, who, despite the display of the colours of her rival, was watching, begged Henry to cease combat on account of the heat, but he insisted on going through with the three challenges for which the rulebook provided. He engaged successfully the dukes of Savoy and of Guise, but then faced a challenge from a young Huguenot, Gabriel de Montgomery, Count of Lorges, captain of the king's Scotch guard.[13] The first collision between the two was indecisive and perhaps the joust should have ended there. But Henry refused to put up his lance, exclaiming 'I want my revenge', for Montgomery had almost unhorsed him. He then charged the count again, in a collision so violent that both wooden lances shattered and both contestants fell. Montgomery remounted, but Henry lay for a time unconscious and bleeding. A splinter of wood four inches long protruded from the royal visor. Montgomery begged to be punished for his apparent crime, but the king, recovering – as it seemed – forgave him. Henry was then taken to the nearby royal palace, the rambling 'Maison Royale des Tournelles', so called because of its many little towers, built at the end of the fourteenth century by the Chancellor of France, Pierre d'Orgemont. The king was there attended by the great Belgian surgeon, Ambroise Paré, sent from Brussels by Philip II, and also by the anatomist, André Vesalius, the doctor of the century who served both the Emperor Charles and his son King Philip.[14] To be able to count on two such great men associated with two opposing monarchs surely meant that Europe really was at peace. But though he seemed to rally after the attention of those distinguished physicians, King Henry died on 10 July.[15] He was in the prime of life, being only forty-one years old, and he left four small sons, none of whom was ready to rule a kingdom.

Power in France, therefore, passed to Henry's grieving widow, the clever Catherine de' Medici, great-granddaughter of Lorenzo the Magnificent in Florence. She maintained her rule for nearly thirty years. Among her first acts as Regent was to knock down the palace where the king died, the Maison Royale des Tournelles.[16] She herself

left for the Louvre where she lived henceforth. In the place of the former there would first be established a market for horses, and
then – from April 1612 – there was established the Place Royale, now
known as the Place des Vosges. Victor Hugo would say that the world
owed that attractive square, where he lived himself, to the lance of
Montgomery.[17]

The Duke of Alba wrote to King Philip about this tragedy the day
after Henry's death.[18] The late king of France had admired Philip and
told his courtiers so, despite their war. Henry's daughter Elisabeth,
who as already mentioned was known as 'the Queen of Peace' in
Spain because of her marriage to Philip, proved a political success for
France, since her betrothal prevented a Spanish marriage to another
Elizabeth, the new queen of England, such as Philip had proposed (to
be rejected in October 1558).[19]

'The French seek to display great courtesy towards your majesty in
conversation,' Alba had written a month before. 'Those who surround
the king cannot say three words without two of them mentioning the
love and friendship which the Christian king [King Henry] bears Your
Majesty and the help which he will bring him in all his enterprises. It
is perhaps the truth because it corresponds to reason. It is also possible that they are offering to participate in Your Majesty's enterprises
in the hope of preventing him from causing the failure of any of their
own.'[20]

King Philip, for his part, had returned from Brussels to his kingdom
by August 1559.[21] Thenceforth, except for two years in Lisbon in the
1580s, after he had reduced Portugal to a Spanish satrapy, he remained
in Spain for the rest of his long life, after a while living chiefly at the
monastery-palace he would build at El Escorial (he could not move
there completely until 1571), a village in the Guadarrama mountains
which was built to celebrate his victories over France in 1558, which
caused Philip to think of himself and to conduct himself as the 'gendarme of Europe'.[22]

This role as 'gendarme' seemed to be guaranteed by an army of
about 50,000 to 60,000 men.[23] But King Philip was already the gendarme of the Americas too. The Venetian ambassador Antonio Tiepolo
thought that Philip was the 'arbiter of the world'.[24] In 1560 his status
did indeed seem to be a global one.

# BOOK ONE

# Old Spain

# I

# King Philip II the Enlightened Despot

*Philip, by the Grace of God, King of Castile, of Leon, Aragón, of the two Sicilies, of Jerusalem, of Navarre, of Granada, of Toledo, of Valencia, of Galicia, of Mallorca, of Seville, of Sardinia, of Córdoba, of Murcia, of Jaén, of the Algarves, of Algeciras, of Gibraltar, of the Canary Isles, of the Isles of the Indies, and of the mainland of the Ocean sea, Archduke of Austria, Duke of Burgundy, of Brabant, and of Milan, Count of Barcelona, of Flanders and of Tyrol, Lord of Biscay and of Molina, Duke of Athens and of Neopatria, Count of the Roussillon and of Cerdagne, Marquis of Oristan and Gociano . . .*

The style of the monarch in accepting
Ercilla's dedication of his poem *La Araucana*, 1569

The new queen of Spain, the 'Queen of Peace', Elisabeth of Valois, arrived in Pamplona, in January 1560, just after King Philip too had returned to Spain after his many journeys in his northern European domains. The new queen, still only fourteen years old, had a dark and Italian complexion, recalling her Medici forbears. She was vivacious and attractive, but not exactly beautiful, or so the Venetian ambassador thought.[1] Both parties seemed pleased to be married, even though King Philip was twenty years older than his new bride. Elisabeth wrote to her mother, Catherine, kindly of the king. Balls, hunts, jousting, bullfights, marked the moment. The new monarchs went to Toledo for the Carnival in 1560, and stayed in the Alcázar there. There were more celebrations. They also visited Aranjuez, where Philip set in motion elaborate plans for the reconstruction of the garden. The king now abandoned his mistress, Eufrasia de Guzmán, who, being pregnant, perhaps with a royal baby, quickly married Antonio Luis de León, the third Prince of Ascoli, an appropriate Neapolitan. Her daughter by the king afterwards lived happily at the court in Spain.[2] Eufrasia herself founded a convent for Recoletos Augustinians.

One significant consequence of the Spanish military victories in Flanders was a commission to the architect, Juan Bautista de Toledo, to plan in memory of these triumphs a new religious house, a large Jeronymite monastery, in the foothills of the Guadarrama mountains. This became the great foundation of the Escorial.

Bautista de Toledo, as we have seen (in *The Golden Age*), had learned his trade in Italy, first in Rome and then in Naples, working for the powerful viceroy, Pedro de Toledo, Marquis of Villafranca, who was responsible for confirming Spanish power in the Mediterranean. That marquis did much to beautify Naples.[3] He was helped by Bautista de Toledo, who had also worked alongside Michelangelo in the Vatican. The collaboration betweeen Italy and Spain in these golden years was thus immensely positive.

In 1560 Philip was thirty-two years old, having been born in Valladolid in the town house of Bernardino Pimentel, the count-duke of Benavente, in May 1527. The Benaventes lived just next to the great Dominican church of San Pablo which his father Charles, and others, treated as a cathedral. He had been christened Philip (Felipe) after his philandering grandfather, Philip the Handsome, of the Netherlands, who had used the title of King Philip I after his marriage to Juana la Loca, queen of Spain in her own right. The youthful Duke of Alba, an adviser to the Emperor Charles on so many matters, as he would become to Philip too, had wanted him to be named Fernando after his successful grandfather, Fernando the Catholic. But Philip he always was.

Philip's mother was the beautiful, strong-minded and unbending Empress Isabel, daughter of King Manuel the Fortunate, King of Portugal. She was a first cousin of her husband, the Emperor Charles, and was usually surrounded by Portuguese friends and courtiers.[4]

Philip's chief political guide, however, was a Spanish nobleman, Pedro González de Mendoza,[5] son of the famous Duke of Infantado who was seen as the grandfather, or at least the senior member, of the Spanish aristocracy. There was also Juan de Zúñiga, who, as well as being a decisive authority, passed on to Philip his own passion for hunting. Zúñiga, born in 1488, was son of Pedro de Zúñiga y Velasco, Count of Miranda, and thus a member of a great family of Extremadura.[6] He was a first cousin of Juana, the second wife of the great conqueror Hernando Cortés.[7]

As a young man, Zúñiga had been a friend and supporter of the loose-living King Philip I, and was in Flanders from 1506 to 1517 with a minor post in the royal household. He became *camarlengo*, lord of the bedchamber, to the young Prince Charles, the future emperor, in 1511, and then his *camarero*, or chamberlain. By 1520 he was Charles's chief adviser, and *el ayo del príncipe*, the tutor of the prince. He was for a long time in Charles's confidence: in 1522 Charles sent Zúñiga to Portugal as ambassador to try and subvert the rebel leaders who had taken refuge in that country.[8] He was also called on to work out in Lisbon the details of Charles's wedding with Isabel. He took the side of Bartolomé de Las Casas in his famous argument with Archbishop Rodríguez de Fonseca as to how to treat Indians in 1519[9] and later seemed a great friend of Charles's omnipotent secretary, Francisco de los Cobos.

Despite this mutual trust, in 1541 in a secret instruction for Philip, Charles argued that Zúñiga was jealous both of Cobos and of the Duke of Alba because he was distressed to have too few grants at his disposal. (The emperor also thought that his wife and his many children exhausted him.) All the same, Charles accepted that Philip 'could have no more faithful counsellor than Don Juan'.[10] Cobos once wrote that 'Don Juan de Zúñiga is working hard for himself. I do not mean that he is acting against me, lest I make myself suspect by such a comment. But I think that he wants complete control without regard for the ... rest of us and to ... do all he can to make himself the only counsellor – to such an extent that his ambition becomes obvious. The sternness and rigour with which he brought up the Prince was turned into sweetness and gentleness, all of it arising from flattery to help him attain his goal.'[11] Another view of Zúñiga comes from the dissolute but clever courtier Enríquez de Guzmán, who thought him a friend: 'he is truly honourable'.[12]

Zúñiga married into a family of royal advisers, for his wife was Estefanía de Requesens, daughter of Lluis de Requesens, commander of the Spanish fleet which had served the 'Gran Capitán' (Gonzalo Fernández de Córdoba) in his victories in Italy, and who had also been bailiff-general to the king in Barcelona. Estefanía was something of a foster-mother to Philip, who would usually stay with her when he went to Barcelona. Her son, Luis de Requesens, was a playmate of the king as a child and would be often with him later in life, serving him as ambassador to Rome in the 1550s and as governor-general in the Low Countries in the 1570s. When they were young, Luis was teased at court for his Catalan accent. But he was the most loyal of King Philip's followers.

From April 1535, when he was just seven, Philip had his own household independent of that of the queen. There he was educated. The Emperor Charles, who spent so much time outside Spain, his chief kingdom, for a long time received enthusiastic reports of his son's progress.[13] The dour Bishop Silíceo (Juan Martínez de Guijarro) wrote in March 1540 that Philip had 'improved considerably in speaking Latin and speaks no other language during class'.[14] Actually, he never spoke Latin adequately, any more than his father had done. He paid more attention to music, which all Habsburgs loved, to popular songs, and to both Moorish and French dancing. Luis Narváez of Granada[15] became his music teacher and taught him the *vihuela*, a large primitive guitar.[16] Philip's sisters also loved dancing and they taught him many songs. As early as 1540, however, hunting was 'what he was most inclined to', since when walking in the countryside Philip could think of his projects, his fears, and his dreams (this again was Silíceo's judgement).

We do not know whether Philip ever played or sang, but he had an ear for music and an interesting collection of instruments, including ten clavichords, thirteen *vihuelas*, and sixteen bagpipes.[17] He had 219 *cantorales* or choir books made, so that each chorister in his service would have his own copy. He disliked the great Palestrina, much preferring the old-fashioned plainsong. But Palestrina's *Liber Secundus Missarum* (Missa Papae Marcelli), published in 1567, was dedicated to Philip.[18] Many musicians were part of the royal household, perhaps as many as

150 – a figure far exceeding the equivalents in France, England, or even the Vatican.

Silíceo was a gaunt enemy of Spanish Jews and was soon to be named Bishop of Cartagena because, the Emperor Charles rather curiously thought, 'he had given in to you [Philip] too much'. Juan Cristóbal Calvete de Estrella succeeded Silíceo as Philip's teacher of Latin and the polemicist Ginés de Sepúlveda, the trenchant enemy of Las Casas, would teach him history and geography – a dangerous brew for such prejudiced hands. Calvete, only four years older than Philip, found books for him, and accompanied him on his state visits to Italy, Germany, and the Netherlands in 1549 and then to England in 1554 to marry Queen Mary.[19] Calvete later became the first biographer of the successful proconsul in Lima, Pedro de la Gasca.[20]

The resourceful adventurer Enríquez de Guzmán thought, no doubt exhibiting in his memoir a sycophantic desire to please, that at fourteen Philip was 'most elegant in his gesture, with the most charming disposition, with a very wise understanding, pious, honest and balanced', who 'knew how to arrange everything in its right place'.[21] He added that Philip was handsome in the face, though of short stature, 'learned, affable and exceedingly grave, like an emperor and grown man'.[22]

After the early death of the Empress Isabel in 1539 in childbirth, and the departure again for Germany of the Emperor Charles, Philip was once more placed under the control of Zúñiga. Philip's household in 1543 had a staff of 110, including a clerk, physician, porters, and stable boys, as well as eleven chaplains (headed by Silíceo who had returned from Cartagena). There were also the men of the bedchamber and kitchen staff who were, as so often in those days, hostile to fish, but always provided meat, bread, chicken, and eggs. There would be lettuce and endives and, once a week, fruit – oranges in winter, pears in summer. Sometimes as a young man there would be beer on Philip's table, but rarely after 1551, when wine (often *cazalla* from the Sierra Morena, such as drunk by the conquistadors) began to be served lavishly. Philip had the service of about seventy pages, all sons of the nobility. Later his staff increased to 1,500 officials, dominated and largely chosen by the Duke of Alba as master of the household (*majordomo*). But this household also effectively made up the entire central civil service in Spain.

Cobos wrote to the emperor about Philip in 1543 that:

> Philip is already so great a king that his knowledge and capacity have outstripped his years [he was then sixteen], for he seems to have achieved the impossible by his great understanding and his lofty comprehension. His diversions are a complete and constant devotion to work and to the affairs of the kingdom. He is always thinking about matters of good government and justice, without leaving any room for . . . idleness or flattery or any vice. His discussions are always about these matters, being held with mature men of the highest repute. When necessary to have meetings, he listens to the opinions of all present with the greatest gravity and attention . . . he is often closeted with me for hours at a time . . . After that, he does the same with the president of the Council, Fernando de Valdés, the archbishop of Seville and grand inquisitor, to talk of justice. Then he would be with the Duke of Alba to discuss war.

He added, 'I am astonished at his prudent, well-considered recommendations.'[23]

The admirable French historian Bartolomé Bennassar considered Valdés the 'prototype' of Grand Inquisitors.[24] Valdés was an Asturian, born in the little town of Salas, thirty miles west of Oviedo, on the way to Galicia. He began to work for the Inquisition as early as 1524. In 1539 he was the successor to Cardinal Tavera as president of the Council of Castile, and in 1547 Valdés became president of the Council of the Inquisition. Perhaps because he was on good terms with Cobos, he was considered a possible Regent to the kingdom when Philip, as well as his father Charles, left the country in 1554. Valdés remained Grand Inquisitor till his death in his eighties in 1568. He had by then found an ideally prejudiced theologian as a disciple, namely Melchor Cano.

Long before the triumph of Valdés, Philip had experienced another personal tragedy. In the summer of 1545 his young first wife and first cousin, María Manuela of Portugal, died aged eighteen, giving birth to the young Prince Charles ('Don Carlos'). Like Philip's mother, she had been an infanta of Portugal. Alonso de Ulloa said that she died because her ladies-in-waiting, María de Mendoza and the Duchess of Alba, went to an *auto-de-fe* and her Lutheran and Portuguese servants gave her a lemon on which she choked. More likely, however, she died from a puerperal fever, deriving from an infection of the womb: the most frequent type of death for suffering pregnant women in those days.[25]

Philip's second wife was Mary Tudor of England, a bride much desired for his son by the Emperor Charles because he saw that as a way of absorbing England. That Philip went through with such an unpromising match demonstrates Charles's influence. Mary, who was eleven years older than Philip, had made it evident that she did not want any intimacy with him. Yet he must surely have felt the need to have more royal princes of his blood to ensure the succession.

The marriage was far from beneficial to either party. But Philip was proclaimed King of England at his wedding feast at Winchester in 1554, a declaration usually forgotten.[26]

After Mary's death in 1558 from what appears to have been a malignant growth, Philip seems to have enjoyed several months of agreeable solitude in Flanders. The Venetian ambassador to Madrid, Federico Badoaro,[27] an invaluable observer, recalled that the king suffered now from a bad stomach and 'for that reason, he has begun recently on advice of doctors to make frequent outings ... he eats excessively of sweets and pastries and abstains from fruit and similar things which have a tendency to create ill humours'.

Another Venetian diplomat, Antonio Tiepolo, a cousin of the painter, wrote that Philip was short in stature, with a round face, very blue eyes ('the bigot blue eyes' of Richard Ford's famous if prejudiced description), prominent lips, and 'a rosy skin like an English sailor'.[28] His habits, thought Ambassador Badoaro:

> were of a tranquil nature. But he was dissipated with women, likes to go out in disguise at night [a frequent occupation of the Spanish nobility at that time] and enjoys all kinds of gaming ... he tends more to gentle reactions ... than to anger and displays an especial courtesy to ambassadors ... He frequently tells amusing jokes and enjoys listening to them. But though jesters are admitted at meal times, he does not give himself over to laughter then so much as in his own rooms where the laughter is unconfined ... He pays great attention to what is said to him but normally does not look at those speaking to him and keeps his eyes down, raising them only to look from side to side. He replies

succinctly to all questions put to him . . . and his efforts are directed not so much as to increase his possessions by war as to preserve them by peace. The Emperor governed entirely according to his own views but, in contrast, the King governs according to the views of others, though he has no esteem for any nation other than Spain. He consorts only with Spaniards.[29]

Philip was always fascinated by architecture and took great interest in the planning or reconstruction of his palaces, above all the monastery of the Escorial, where he would soon be spending much time in rooms which echoed his father's lodging in the monastery of Yuste.[30] Another Venetian, Miguel Suriano, wrote that Philip:

did not like crowds at all, though he was tranquil and always in control of himself. He lacked neither humour nor vivacity, but he always spoke in a low voice. When people addressed him, they were always asked to speak first, and he listened to the end. He was always quiet and courteous. Though like his father, he liked to dress in black, he was not specially gloomy in dress. He was, however, preoccupied by the need for personal cleanliness. Thus he had a new suit every month. He abhorred vanity in all things.[31]

The solemn historian of the Papacy, Ludwig von Pastor, for whom no detail was too inconsiderable and no generalization too gross, gave a more negative judgement of Philip at this time: 'instead of acting, the King was for ever thinking things over, trying to gain time and put off a decision. His instinctive absolutism was shown in his mania for undertaking the personal direction of the smallest detail of government. Stern, laconic, inaccessible, the only decision the King comes to is to be forever undecided.'[32] That judgement was unfair, though Philip was certainly often the victim of self-doubt. Thus, early in 1569, he would write a sad letter to Cardinal Diego de Espinosa, the President of the Royal Council:

So many things are going wrong that they cannot fail to cause me pain and exhaustion and . . . were it not for the business of Granada [the war against the Moriscos][33] which cannot be abandoned I do not know what I would do . . . I am certainly no good for the world of today. I know very well that I should be in some other station of life, one not so exalted as the one that God has given me, which is terrible . . . Pray God that in heaven, we shall be treated better.[34]

Such reflections are unusual to find in royal personages. Philip acted very much in the shadow of his mother the empress and, after the death of his French queen, Elisabeth of Valois, he would tell his chamberlain, the Marquis of Landrada, a Fleming, that 'spending must be done as it was in the time of my mother' – that is, economically.

Philip was very well travelled, for during his reign he spent fourteen months in England, fifteen months in Germany, two years and four months in Portugal, as well as five years in the Netherlands and quite long spells in Italy and France. It is difficult to think of another monarch who had such experience except for his father Charles, or of a modern head of state who has been so widely experienced in the life of other countries.

The Venetian Badoaro, who has already been quoted, reported of Philip that 'he rises very early and attends to business or correspondence till midday. Then he always eats at the same time and almost always the same type and same amount of food. He drinks wine from average-sized glasses which he drains twice. In general, his health is good. But he sometimes suffers from a little gout.' The gout would increase and in the end give him continual discomfort.

Three or four times a week Philip would go to the country in a carriage to hunt game or rabbits with a crossbow. In the early 1560s, he would visit Queen Elisabeth three times a day: in the morning before Mass; before he began his work; and at night. The ambassador noted that, as in many modern bedrooms, 'the King and Queen had two beds separated by a palm's width but, because of the curtains which cover them, they appear one bed'. Philip went to Mass daily, but received communion only four times a year.

His religiosity was obvious. Out of the forty-two books beside 'his bed all but one was religious'.[35] 'God's service and mine' was a favourite phrase of his. Philip's best-loved saint seems to have been Our Lady of Monserrat and, for that reason, he loved Catalonia (also perhaps because he was fond of Estefanía de Requesens). He had much respect, too, for Our Lady of the Pilar in Saragossa. He was interested in episcopal appointments and took great care over them. He almost

always supported the Inquisition but paid for Dr Martín de Azpilcueta,[36] a celebrated moralist as well as a canon lawyer, to go to Rome
to defend Archbishop Carranza who in 1558 had published what was
deemed a dubious work on the catechism. Philip had an impressive
collection of over 6,000 holy relics.

Philip's confessors were usually fat men: for example, the Franciscan Bernardo de Fresneda,[37] later Bishop of Cuenca and Archbishop
of Saragossa, who was his chief confessor from 1553 until 1577. After
him, there was an austere Dominican, Diego Rodriguez de Chaves.[38]
As with Charles V's confessors, they often gave their opinion on matters and issues other than religious ones.

The king possessed about a hundred pieces of sculpture, mostly
antique, and most of them marble or bronze. Among these were twelve
white marble Roman emperors sent him by Cardinal Ricci, and
another twelve, also of emperors, sent by the pious and harsh Pope
Pius V, Antonio Ghislieri, the last pontiff to be canonized. Philip owned
some bronzes collected by the historian Diego Hurtado de Mendoza
who, when he died in 1575, left all his treasures to the king. The most
celebrated of the objects in Philip's collection was a white marble
Christ on the Cross, the work of Benvenuto Cellini, the great sculptor
of the popes from the valley of the Mugello in Tuscany, which was sent
to him by Francesco de' Medici, the second Grand Duke of Tuscany.[39]
The king also bought some excellent pictures in the Low Countries,
including some famous ones by Hieronymus Bosch, Joachim Patinir
(including the wonderful crossing by Charon of the River Styx), and
Roger van der Weyden. They are the basis for the magnificent Flemish
galleries in the Museo del Prado and the Escorial.

Even more important were the Titians which Philip commissioned
in 1559, including *Diana and Actaeon* and *Diana and Callisto*. There
are also paintings in the series which Titian called his *Poesié*.[40] When
he died, Philip had a collection of over a thousand pictures, in addition to the 500 mainly Flemish works which he had inherited.[41]
Titian's most recent biographer, the admirable Sheila Hale, calls the
Spanish king 'the most generous, liberating and sensitive patron of
Titian's entire career'.[42] Philip built up other collections, of coins,
watches and astrolabes, arms as well as armour in a style which was

wholly unknown among his contemporary monarchs, interested though they often were in a *schatzkammer*.

Philip was a book collector. In 1553 he owned 812 books. In 1576 he had 4,545. In 1598, at his death, he had as many as 14,000 books, including works in Greek, Hebrew, and Arabic. This was the second largest private library in the world, being only a little smaller than that in Seville of Fernando Colón, who is supposed to have possessed 15,000 books.

Philip himself toyed with literature. He probably wrote *The Order of Creatures* (1560) and *The Diversity of Nature*, which are both volumes of what we would call natural history, and he may have also written some sonnets.

Like many of his time, he thought that, if one found the right formula, one could make gold from lead, and he himself experimented to that end, having dabbled improbably in innumerable sciences. Philip established an academy of mathematics in Salamanca and provided money for four professorial chairs. Teaching was to be in Spanish, not Latin, as it was in other universities. Philip was thus an enlightened despot.

Philip was often gregarious and welcoming. Thus when in 1564 he made a formal entry into Barcelona at Carnival time, he mixed with everyone. He wanted to cast off the melancholy which had affected him during his four and a half months in the gloomy town of Monzón, where he had had to attend the Cortes of Aragón. Later, he went down to Valencia where there were many balls, banquets, and tourneys. But he disagreed with his father Charles's ideas about travelling constantly through his realms and, after his return from the Low Countries in 1558, did as little of it as he could. 'Travelling in one's kingdoms is neither useful nor decent,' he told his son and eventual successor, Philip III, in 1598. He was probably mistaken in that judgement, since the Emperor Charles V, like his predecessors the Catholic kings, learned much about provincial problems and personalities from lodging in unexpected places.

His greatest enemy could not reproach Philip with any act which was not directly or indirectly inspired by a sense of responsibility for his subjects. Being naturally mistrustful, however, he unfortunately had no confidence in the two cleverest men in his family, his half-brother, the dashing Don Juan, an illegitimate son of the emperor,[43] and his nephew, Alexander Farnese, the brilliant general who was son of Margaret of Parma.[44] Philip seems too to have preferred his secretaries to be people of no very clear personality, such as Ruy Gómez de Silva (the Prince of Éboli) and, later, Mateo Vázquez.

Philip's cautious personality affected his way of governing. In this respect he was the reverse of his father, who took risks which sometimes turned out to be disastrous, or anyway unhelpful. Philip devoted a great deal of care to the institutions through which he administered his realm, which became larger every year. But when talking of those institutions we must remember that Philip as a boy was always accompanied by caged birds and was happy to do anything 'provided that he could do it in the country', said Zúñiga.[45] He had no bodyguards. He liked being addressed as '*señor*', not 'your majesty' as his father had desired to be known. He disliked bullfighting but never condemned it, knowing that it was a popular fiesta.[46]

When at Salamanca, before his first marriage to María of Portugal, Philip would often listen to lectures. He probably heard some by the great theologian Francisco de Vitoria, the father of international law.

Thus, considering Philip's place in history, one should recognize his unusual love of art. He was a contradictory person, being an intellectual who greatly liked the country, and who was a hunter as well as a collector. His contradictions were as striking as his interests.

# 2

# King Philip the Bureaucrat Monarch

*The love which I have always had for these realms, the head-piece of my monarchy where I was born, where I was brought up, and where I began to govern in the lifetime of the Emperor my lord . . . has obliged me to come back and see them and help them, so leaving my patrimonial estates in Flanders and Italy even though they are of course important. My love and respect prefers you.*

Philip II in 1558[1]

Like Frederick the Great in eighteenth-century Prussia, Philip II preferred to have all information, and all news, given to him in written form. In keeping with this desire, in 1566 he commissioned a survey of Spain, the *Relación topográfica*, based on answers by local authorities to fifty-seven questions. It was much the most complete survey made to that date by any European monarch about his own realm. In 1570, Philip also commissioned a good landscape painter, Anton van den Wyngaerde, of Brussels, to make sketches of the chief towns of Castile.[2] He also invited Francisco Domínguez,[3] a botanist from Portugal, to make a similarly elaborate survey of New Spain, his settled dependency in the New World, and appointed Juan López de Velasco to be the cosmographer-historian of America.[4] In 1576, Philip issued forty-nine questions which were to be answered by all officials in America. This series of 'geographical relations' began to be published the following year.

As early as 1560, Philip began to think of establishing Madrid as the capital of his realm.[5] He had seen the royal palaces of other monarchs in northern Europe; he had made sketches of such places; and, as we have seen, he had already sent for the architect Bautista de Toledo. The king's decisions in this regard derived from his sense that it would be more efficient to have all the governmental papers available in one place: anyone who likes documents likes them to have a home. Philip as Regent in 1545 also took the first steps to convert the fortress of Simancas into a national archive. Emperor Charles's chief secretary, Francisco de los Cobos, was the father of that intelligent idea.

The portraits of King Philip are numerous. There was Titian's Prince Philip in armour of 1550, now in the Prado, and the same painter's delightful portrait of Philip offering his son Fernando to heaven after the victory of Lepanto in 1571 over the forces of the Ottoman empire. This painting is both allegorical and human as well as physical. It is surely unusual to see pictures which thus have two qualities. In addition, there was Antonio Moro's King Philip in armour of 1557, in the Escorial (the 'Saint Quentin portrait'). There is a fine anonymous head in white marble in the Museum of Sculpture in Valladolid, probably dating from about 1550, in which Philip is wearing the golden fleece. In 1565 the Italian Sofonisba de Cremona executed a remarkable portrait of Philip II with a rosary, also in the Prado,[6] and in 1550 the Valencian Alonso Sánchez Coello painted Philip II in armour, now in the Stirling Maxwell Collection in Edinburgh. There is another Sánchez Coello portrait of Philip in black, aged sixty,[7] painted in 1587, in the Palazzo Pitti in Florence. Finally, there is the Madrid painter Juan Pantoja de la Cruz's Philip when he was old in 1597, now in the Escorial.[8] The king is thus easy to recall at every stage of his long life.

Philip's secretaries were the equivalent of ministers in modern times. The first of these was Gonzalo Pérez, an invaluable adviser, who had been Latin secretary to the Erasmian private secretary to the emperor, Alfonso de Valdés, before 1532. He was recommended by Cobos. The twentieth-century English historian Henry Kamen wrote that Pérez was 'a gruff and bossy career priest'. He was also a humanist and a *converso* (a converted Jew) in origin.[9] He held various minor ecclesiastical appointments before joining Philip's entourage in 1543. In the same year, Pérez was named secretary of the Council of State, where he was the only university-trained courtier in those days. Pérez remarked: 'I have been ill these past few days but that has not prevented me from attending to business punctually, since decisions are taken so slowly that even a cripple could keep up with them. Truly, with sixteen councillors who are so different in background and in other things, I do not see how we can agree. I believe, though, that, in the end, H. M. will see the light and realise what should be done.' Four years later, Pérez remarked of his master's working habits: 'In many things, H. M. makes, and will make mistakes, because he discusses matters with several people, now with one, then with another, hiding something from one, but revealing it to others, and so it is not surprising that differing and even contradictory judgments emerge . . . This cannot fail to cause great harm . . .' Philip once wrote to Pérez about a paper submitted to him: 'To be candid, I do not understand a word of this. I do not know what I should do. Should I send it to someone for comment and, if so, to whom? Time is slipping away. Tell me what you advise.'[10] The king was thus often candid in his comments about himself and his own work.

Pérez died in 1566, after Philip had been king for ten years. His place was filled first by his charming, feline, and ambitious son, Antonio, and then by a nominee of the Duke of Alba, Gabriel de Zayas.[11]

Another important secretary was Ruy Gómez, Prince of Éboli, the head of the Portuguese family of Silva which imaginatively claimed to trace its descent from the Roman royal house of Alba Longa. His mother had come to Castile in the entourage of the Empress Isabel; his uncle was Ruiz Téllez de Meneses, the *majordomo* of the empress; he himself had held the empress's train as a page at her wedding in 1526; and he had been a childhood playmate of Philip. Self-effacing but with a strong personality, Éboli was always loyal to the king. His success derived from his capacity to achieve everything by means of good manners.[12] No persecution or act of violence can be attributed to him. His power depended on, first, his ease of access to the king, as *sumiller* (chamberlain), which made him responsible for both waking Philip and wishing him 'good night'; second, to his long association with the monarch, even though he himself was ten years older; and third, to his post as *contador mayor*, chief accountant, which enabled him to control payments.

Éboli was reliable. His famously one-eyed yet beautiful wife, Ana, was not so, though she was a Mendoza, being a great granddaughter of the cardinal archbishop who was said to have been the third monarch of Castile in the days of Fernando and Isabel.[13] She was well informed about people and places. Éboli seems to have been pushed to one side by the king in 1564 to become chamberlain to Don Carlos, Philip assuring Éboli that the trust he had in him was such that he could not afford having any less responsible person in control of his son. Nevertheless, Éboli was disconsolate. He died in 1573. About that time, his wife had become the *confidante* (at the least) of Antonio Pérez.

There were other important officials or advisers: first and foremost, Fernando, the third Duke of Alba.[14] In 1559, Alba was fifty-two years old. He already had been powerful in the reign of the emperor, who, after the victory at Mühlberg, looked on him as his only trustworthy general, and who asked him to be *majordomo* of the court, a position which he retained under Philip, and which gave him effective control of the royal household. Charles then entrusted him with the task of introducing the rigorous Burgundian ceremonial into the court, which he did efficiently though he disliked it. Alba always had good Italian connections, for his uncle Pedro, Marquis of Villafranca, was for many years viceroy of Naples, and Pedro's daughter, Leonor, married Cosimo de' Medici, the first Grand Duke of Tuscany. Another uncle, Juan, was a busy cardinal in Rome.

Alba had the reputation of being an unbending aristocrat who did not shy away from hard decisions, and he did not mollify that reputation by his advice to Queen Catherine of France in 1565 to execute all the Protestant leaders. He certainly was inclined to be harsh. But the duke also had many human qualities. He was known to share all the discomforts experienced by his soldiers, so he was a popular commander. He was friendly with all kinds of undisciplined people, such as the courtier and memorialist Enríquez de Guzmán. In his youth Alba had been a friend, as well as a patron, of Garcilaso de la Vega, the poet of courtly knighthood, who represented him (unflatteringly) as the shepherd Albanio in his second eclogue.[15] In his old age, Alba combined a remarkable grandeur with an untroubled informality of spirit.

Alba himself had an unusual childhood since his father, Don García, was killed (gloriously) in Gelves in north Africa in 1510, and so he was brought up by his uncle Fadrique, the second duke. Alba's tutor was the poet Juan Boscán Almogáver (Joan Bosch), an intimate friend of Garcilaso de la Vega. Bosch's translation of Castiglione's *The Courtier* made it one of the most important books of the Renaissance in Spain, and Alba was influenced by it. In addition, unusually for a Spanish aristocrat, the duke had learned a number of languages – Italian and Latin, also some German and French. He was also exceptional among noblemen in his knowledge of the arts.[16] Like his master, Alba was a bibliophile and, in his correspondence, we find references to a present of a Bible, as well as to a painting on copper of the Archangel Gabriel. He handled most of the royal correspondence with the Netherlands in the 1570s. In 1580 he recommended that secretaries to the king should be well paid to avoid the possibility of corruption.[17]

Another important adviser in the 1560s was Cardinal Diego de Espinosa, who came from Las Posadas near Segovia and was from a noble family in reduced circumstances. Born in 1512, he had a long career on judicial councils before becoming auditor of the Inquisition at Granada and then president of the Royal Council in 1565. For the next few years everything at court seemed to revolve around the haughty Espinosa. He became *inquisidor* (Grand Inquisitor) in 1568. Philip promoted him because of his efficiency, even though he could be discourteous and offhand to grandees. In 1572 he died of apoplexy, leaving Philip his competent secretary Mateo Vázquez.

Vázquez was Philip's chief secretary for most of his last years. He had no imagination and no capacity for innovation, but he was efficient. He suited his monarch perfectly. He had begun life in the court as a chaplain of the house of Castile before moving to serve Espinosa. After Espinosa's death, Vázquez wrote to Philip in 1573 in a realistic style. 'It does not appear,' he said, 'that Your Majesty has a secretary, with the result that there is a great deal of unavoidable reading and writing. From this employment of time, and from this effort, we must fear that damage to health which befalls most people who deal with papers.' Vázquez thereupon suggested that he should himself deal with all incoming correspondence intended for the king. Much duplication of reading could, he thought, thereby be avoided. Thereafter Vázquez himself would make a report about any proposals made to the king in correspondence. Philip would pronounce, and Vázquez would write everything down.

Philip's last great minister was Antoine Perrenot, Count of Granvelle, the son of Nicholas Perrenot the first lord of Granvelle, who came from a modest Burgurdian family. Nicholas was probably the son of a blacksmith of Ornans in the lovely valley of the Loue in the Doubs. He began his labours as a Latinist and a doctor of law at the parliament of Dôle, and then entered the service of the Archduchess Margaret, the ruler of the Netherlands and Charles's Much-loved aunt. The first Granvelle was imperial ambassador to France, and for a time was in Spain as the archduchess's agent. He was then the chief informant of Martín de Salinas, the ambassador of King Ferdinand, Charles V's patient brother, the monarch of Austria. When Granvelle died in 1550, the emperor said that he seemed to 'have lost his soul'.

The first Granvelle was in every sense succeeded by his son Antoine who, as titular Bishop of Arras, seems to have written Philip's noble speech at the ceremony of the abdication of his father. He was from then on continually used as an adviser by Philip. He was an artistic adviser as well as a political one, for he introduced the Flemish painter Antonio Moro to the king. Antoine, the second Count of Granvelle, then became chief adviser of Margaret de Farnese of Parma, the Regent of the Netherlands. The nobles there resented Granvelle, about whom, complaining, Counts Egmont and Horn (Philip de Montmorency) sent a letter to Philip in 1562. They also dispatched another nobleman, Horn's brother, the Baron de Montigny (Floris de Montmorency), to Spain to represent them.[18] Granvelle then went to Besançon in eastern France, allegedly to see his sick mother, but for several years he virtually retired. Then in 1572 he returned to become viceroy of Naples. From there he remarked in relation to his instructions from Madrid: 'If one had to wait for death, one would like it to come from Spain, for then it would never arrive.' He remained afterwards a close adviser on Philip's foreign policy, being able to dictate fluently in five languages.

At the beginning of Philip's reign there were in the Kingdom of Spain eleven councils, of which the oldest and most important was the *Consejo Real y Supremo de Castilla*. This had a president and sixteen counsellors, and dealt with all domestic politics. Diego Saavedra Fajardo, a very active writer and polemicist of the early seventeenth century, who would represent Spain at the Treaty of Westphalia in

1648, would talk of the Castilian Council as being the *ojos de poder* (eyes of power).[19]

We first hear of this Council in 1385 after the Castilian defeat by Portugal at Aljubarrota. In Philip's time, it would meet several days a week, but the king would only attend on Fridays. An offshoot of this body, the Council of the Secretariat of Castile, concerned itself with grants and pardons (*gracia y merced*).

Almost as important was the Council of State (*Consejo de Estado*), created in 1526, which was responsible for foreign affairs.[20] For many years its secretary, and its ears and eyes, was the multi-competent and painstaking Francisco de Cobos. His successors were first Gonzalo Pérez and then his son Antonio. After a while, the latter handed over responsibility for relations with western and central Europe to Gabriel de Zayas, while he, Antonio, dealt with his Mediterranean matters, including the all-important Italian activities. Later still, Juan de Idíaquez, the first of a large cohort of Basque bureaucrats who worked for the Castilian monarchy, looked after both undertakings. The king attended all the meetings of this body, and was by far the most experienced and best-informed member. Although foreign affairs were its principal responsibility, it had other roles: for example, the will of the Emperor Charles V was opened in this Council.[21]

The Council of State also controlled the network of embassies which reported to the king: three in Italy – Rome, Venice, and Genoa; one in Vienna, headquarters of the Holy Roman Empire; and three in the monarchies of Europe, France, England, and Portugal. Most ambassadors had to pay for their expenses out of their own pockets.[22]

The Council of Orders and the Council of the Treasury were also critical. The former controlled much of the economy, while the Council of the Treasury dealt with money voted for the Crown by the Cortes (both the Cortes of Castile and that of Aragon),[23] including sales taxes, rents from royal properties, and, increasingly, the treasure brought from the Indies. There were also taxes on silk from Granada, salt, customs, mines, licences to go to the Indies and also licences to take slaves there.[24]

The Council of the Inquisition and that of the *Cruzada* were the next in importance among the domestic bureaucracies. The first of these two, a reminder that the Spanish monarchy was a confessional undertaking, presided over an institution which was used by successive Spanish monarchs to ensure religious orthodoxy. The Grand Inquisitor was named by this Council, though in practice the king would propose a name which was then approved by the Pope. The Cruzada was concerned with the effective raising of a sales tax which meant much to the working of the monarchy.

Two further councils were created later, those of Portugal and Flanders, in 1582 and 1588 respectively. Alongside the secretaries of these bodies, we find also active within them from the 1560s the personal secretaries who served the king.

This type of government by council had really been invented by Philip's great-grandparents, the Catholic monarchs Ferdinand and Isabella. In the sixteenth century, most members of these councils were *letrados*, that is, middle-class learned men, products of the universities of Salamanca or of Valladolid, rather than noblemen. There were, it is true, a hundred or so noblemen, grandees, and titled men (the first were the great dukes, the second were the marquises and counts) who controlled large tracts of land, which they governed as if they were minor monarchs, but who (with the exceptions mentioned earlier) did not rival the *letrados* in the organization or manipulation of state power. They lived apart from the court, not in it.[25] Sometimes heads of family found that with the principle of primogeniture so firmly established, the second son (the *segundón*) might turn out a *letrado*. But the most remarkable aspect of these arrangements in Spain in the sixteenth century was the large number of clergymen who played a decisive part, often as presidents or chairmen. Such men as the Inquisitor-General, Cardinal Valdés from Asturias, and Cardinal Figueroa, were the dominant statesmen of Spain in the second half of the century.

Philip II of Spain was not a great man, but he was a good one and a serious king. He has suffered in the Anglo-Saxon world because of the failure of his English policy in respect of the Armada in 1588. The fact that he and his advisers were often a voice of tolerance in England in comparison with his severe wife Queen Mary is usually forgotten. He is also remembered as the brutal father in Verdi's opera *Don Carlo* and Schiller's play *Don Carlos*. Both opera and play are magnificent works of art, but not of history.

# 3

# King Philip and his Empire

*Men are not the judges of the thoughts and motives of sover-
eigns. They cannot know just how deeply a King may be
distressed by a rebellion or an act of insolence. They cannot
know the reasons of state or of the heart that may compel him
to take the most rigorous vengeance on his subjects even after
the original rebellion has died down and there is little further
danger and to all seeming a milder policy would have been
politically wiser. No, they cannot understand how it may seem
to a King in his majesty that nothing must come between him
and his vengeance.*

> Diego Hurtado de Mendoza,
> *The War in Granada,* 1570

By 1559, King Philip's empire in the New World – in the Indies, as it
was still known – was controlled by an interesting bureaucracy with
three heads: first, the authority in Spain itself, the Council of the
Indies, a committee of about ten members who remained in semi-
permanent session in Valladolid or wherever the Spanish court was.
Second, the political administration of the empire in the New World
itself, through viceroys, governors, and other public servants who had
been named by the king and the Council of the Indies. Third, the legal
masters of the region who governed via supreme courts (*audiencias*),
of which there were seven by the time of the accession of Philip in
1556: those of Santo Domingo, set up in 1511; the city of Mexico,
established in 1527; Panama, in 1538; Lima, Peru, in 1543; Los Confines, Guatemala, in 1543; Guadalajara in New Spain (present-day

Mexico), 1548; and Santa Fe de Bogotá, Colombia, in 1548. Three more supreme courts soon followed, La Plata de Charcas (Peru) in 1562, Quito (Ecuador) in 1563, and Concepción (Chile) also in 1563. On all these courts there sat about six judges known as *oidores*.

The supreme institution in this improbable confederation of controls was, as it had been since the 1520s, the Council of the Indies. It had begun as a gathering of those members of the Council of Castile who interested themselves in the Indies, but soon (certainly by 1524) became more formal.

For example, the nomination of the viceroys and the captains-general, as well as the judges of the *audiencias*, the bishops and archbishops of the Americas – all those appointments were the Council's responsibility. The Council constituted the final court of appeal in all matters relating to the Indies – civil or criminal and also administrative. Its president in 1559 was Luis Hurtado de Mendoza, a seventy-year-old nobleman who had held many grand positions such as viceroy and captain-general of Navarre and even president of the Council of Castile, to which office he returned at the end of 1559, living until 1568.[1] Characteristically, for a man of his achievements, Hurtado de Mendoza had begun his official life as a royal page, as early as 1502. He was soon serving the king in the battles for Navarre and went to substitute for his father, the wonderfully cultivated Iñigo López de Mendoza, in Granada and, indeed, succeeded him there as governor on his death in 1515. Since then, Luis Hurtado de Mendoza had always enjoyed an important office under the Crown. He was among those who as young men solemnly carried the coffin of Fernando the Catholic from Extremadura to its grave in the cathedral in Granada. Later, he planned a palace for Charles V in the Alhambra which the emperor had used for his honeymoon with his Portuguese queen, Isabel.[2] In 1534, Don Luis had been the chief planner of the emperor's famous expedition to Tunis, in which he participated personally. Next, he concerned himself with trying to reach a peaceful settlement with the Moriscos of Granada and, in 1543, became viceroy of that province. Then in April 1546 the backing of Francisco de los Cobos secured for him the presidency of the Council of the Indies. He had not been to the New World and therefore relied on travellers to tell him what it was like. No doubt Don Luis received letters from his younger brother Antonio, the viceroy of New Spain, which have not survived.

Hurtado de Mendoza's first task was to guarantee the arrangements for a naval escort for the fleets heading to and from the New World, under Spain's best admiral, Álvaro de Bazán.[3] In the meantime his brother was showing himself a most successful viceroy for New Spain, a mission which he might have carried on also in Peru had it not been for his sudden death in 1552. It was Don Luis who pressed his brother to accept the nomination to go to Peru when he was already at, what was for the time, an advanced age.[4]

Don Luis was probably disconcerted to find in 1562 that the new president of the Council of Castile, in succession to Antonio de Fonseca, was Juan de Vega, a protégé of the Portuguese Prince of Eboli. Vega had been viceroy of both Sicily and Navarre, as well as an ambassador in Rome. He was in fact pious and mild while his wife, Leonor Osorio Sarmiento, daughter of the Marquis of Astorga, was one of the earliest female supporters of the Jesuit, Saint Ignatius.[5] All the same, Don Luis withdrew to his estates till the return of King Philip in 1559, a practice which powerful noblemen used often (the Duke of Alba had the technique refined to a fine art).

Don Luis's last significant role was the important one of escorting Elisabeth of Valois, 'the Queen of Peace', to Spain from Paris to become Philip II's third bride. The relevance of this match to his responsibilities in the Indies was not obvious. Even the court of King Philip did not conceive France to be part of the Indies.

Don Luis was succeeded as president of the Council of the Indies by Juan de Sarmiento, who had previously been a judge (*oidor*) as president of the chancellery in Granada. He was a native of Burgos and the son of the Countess of Ulloa. Sarmiento, however, had owed his rise in status to finding favour with the Empress Isabel, who named him a judge at Granada. He joined the Council of the Indies in 1552. By that time, Sarmiento had become an 'Ébolista', that is, a partisan of the Prince of Éboli. Yet Sarmiento was a broad-minded man, for not only was he charged in the 1550s to investigate, once again, the regulations in the Casa de la Contratación, but he was a friend of the soon-to-be-disgraced Archbishop Carranza, in whose interest he acted.[6] Éboli for his part was not a consequential figure but he had his devoted followers all the same.

Sarmiento died in 1565, and was succeeded in the presidency of the Council of the Indies by Francisco Tello de Sandoval, a *sevillano* who was the son of Juan Gutiérrez, a well-known citizen of the capital of the south. Tello could be reproached for his many bureaucratic ways and for his coldness, but he had the great, rare, advantage for a Spanish functionary, in respect of the Americas, of having had real experience of the Indies.[7] Both his father and grandfather had been councillors (*veinticuatros*, or twenty-fours, as they were called) of Seville. He knew the nature of the long voyage across the Atlantic and back, the prison-like confinement on the ship for weeks; he had experienced the risks of being wrecked, and seasickness. Tello had visited the Canary Islands on his outward journey and the Azores on his return, and he would have known of the traditional arrival in New Spain at the now thriving port of Veracruz on the Caribbean coast, as well as the long inland trek from the coastal tropics to the temperate territory of the capital, Mexico City, once Tenochtitlan, past Perote and Puebla and then up along the famous road between the volcanoes. He had, in addition, once been inquisitor in Toledo, and president of the Supreme Court, the chancellery, of Valladolid. Originally a protégé of the discreet Cardinal Tavera, he began his successful career as a canon in Seville, a characteristic beginning to a successful life as a civil servant in those times. Tello was named Grand Inquisitor of New Spain in 1543. In fact he went in 1544 as a 'Visitor' (colonial inspector) to New Spain to explain and put into effect the humane but controversial 'New Laws'.[8] Tello was said to have been an 'excellent' *letrado* with 'an unstained character' but, like all Visitors, he believed that he had an obligation to do something extraordinary. He thereby exceeded his powers, thus making it easy enough for the viceroy, Antonio de Mendoza, to defend himself successfully against all the pernickety charges which the Visitor had made. But the fact that there were any charges at all caused much bitterness all round, since Mendoza had been an admirable proconsul.

Tello returned to Spain in 1547, and in 1550, as a counsellor of the Indies, he naturally formed part of the group of fourteen wise men who were asked to judge the famous argument between Las Casas and Sepúlveda.[9] Tello became president of the Council of the Indies in April 1565, but remained in that position only until August 1567 when he became Bishop of Osma, then a rich diocese.

Most members of the Council of the Indies at the time of Philip II's accession were naturally protégés of the former president Hurtado de Mendoza. To one degree or another all courts resemble life at Versailles, as described by the immortal French historian Saint-Simon, and that of Philip was no exception.[10] Emissaries from various countries intrigued, the monarch hesitated in the centre of his advisers, strong men resigned and went to their estates.

Another councillor of the Indies, Villagómez, had been a judge under Tello before being sent to New Granada (Venezuela and Colombia). He became chief magistrate in Seville (*asistente*) and was then named a commissar or chief adviser on the matter of perpetuity of *encomiendas* (*comisario de la perpetuidad*). (An *encomienda* in the New World, we recall, was a grant of population living in the country. The people concerned were to be at the disposal of the *encomendero*, almost always though not inevitably a Spaniard. In return, the *encomendero* would be responsible for keeping the subject population at work and in the Christian faith. The urgent debate was whether the *encomiendas* were to be permanent assignments of inhabitants and territory to settlers, or were to last only one generation.) But in fact Villagómez avoided going to Peru, by accepting a nomination to the Court of Castile.

Juan Vázquez de Arce, another councillor of the Indies, came from Segovia. His father, Martín, like so many public servants of that time, had been for years in the royal chancellery, indicating the kind of hereditary succession which occurred frequently in the bureaucratic circles of Philip's day. Vázquez had studied at the famous College of Santa Cruz in Valladolid and become rector there. Later, he matured to the Supreme Court in Granada and carried out an investigation of the Casa de la Contratación before joining the Council of the Indies in 1556.[11]

Finally, among these bureaucrats in the Council of the Indies, there was Licenciado Graciano Briviesca who had also received an education in Valladolid, where he had been for a time a magistrate (*alcalde*) in the chancery. His early life was spent as a royal chaplain and he was for a time responsible for the establishment of the royal archive created in 1542 in the castle of Simancas. He helped to frame the enlightened New Laws and was a friend of Luis Hurtado de Mendoza. Briviesca was named to be president of the supreme court of Santa Fe in Colombia. But like Villagómez, he managed by procrastination to avoid going out to assume his imperial assignment. He became concerned in an investigation of the mission of the Marquis of Cañete in Peru. He left the Council of the Indies in 1560 for that of Castile.[12]

Almost all the officials who served the king on councils, including the Council of the Indies, were secular clergymen who became bishops at the end of their lives. With the exception of the Duke of Alba, who seemed an immortal reminder of an older type of rule, the noblemen who previously had dominated the administration of Castile had mostly resigned or given up by 1570.

In the New World, aristocrats held on much longer to the most prestigious postings than they did at home. Thus in 1556, when Philip came to the throne, the viceroy in New Spain was Luis Velasco, then aged forty-five. He was the second viceroy of that magnificent kingdom – it was never itself thought of as a colony – having succeeded the equally noble Antonio de Mendoza in 1550. Velasco had previously been viceroy of Navarre. His grandfather, Pedro, had been a younger brother of the then Constable of Castile – the constabulary had become vested in the Velasco family. Philip thought that, in a year or two, Velasco might leave Mexico (New Spain) for Peru, and Mendoza might return to Spain. But Velasco was soon happy in Mexico. Suárez de Peralta, a historian of those days, the articulate nephew by marriage of Hernán Cortés, recalls that 'every day during his time in office his [Velasco's] table was set for anyone who wished to dine. Almost always he had thirty or forty guests, all served a delicious dinner of over twelve courses.'[13]

Velasco conducted himself as the nobleman that he was. He rode well, loved hunting, and paid his master of the horse in Mexico the princely sum of 2,000 ducats a year. They shot falcon, geese, and crane. Velasco's stables were worthy of a monarch – and a rich monarch at that, in that his fine horses were well turned out and well trained. He had a special bullring made for his own Sunday fights.

There were often race meetings in which the viceroy would himself take part in the most demanding contests. The historian Fernando Benítez says of Velasco that he was an aristocrat who at the same time loved the Indians but, as the royal representative, he did not allow the least insubordination. For him the 'criollos' seemed a crowd of rebellious youths, and he treated them disdainfully.[14]

Velasco's equivalent in the richer kingdom of Peru, and the successor to the great Pedro de la Gasca, was another aristocrat and indeed another Mendoza. This was Andrés Hurtado de Mendoza, Marquis of Cañete, a grandson of one of the illegitimate sons of the famous Cardinal González de Mendoza and thus a first cousin of Ana, Princess of Éboli, wife of the secretary Ruy Gómez. The marquis had married a daughter of that Count of Osorio who had been president of the Council of the Indies in the 1530s, and he took with him to Peru many sprigs of the high Castilian nobility. He was the first viceroy in Peru able to rule the place calmly, from 1556 to 1560, as if it were indeed a Spanish province. The marquis built hospitals and bridges, established a court with pages and guards, and brought several different councils under central control.[15] He generously allocated encomiendas to some aged followers of Almagro,[16] merely because they seemed by then very senior individuals.

It also fell to the Marquis of Cañete to make a successful peace with the heir of the Incas, the so-called Sayri-Tapac, who was received both warmly and nobly in Lima, and whose daughter eventually married Martín García de Loyola, a great-nephew of the founder of the Jesuits, so forging an improbable connection between old Peru and the new religion.

Sayri-Tapac arrived in Lima on 5 January 1558 and was greeted by Cañete in great style. A banquet followed at Archbishop Loaisa's palace where a decree granting an estate to Sayri-Tupac was presented. Banquets were assumed in the sixteenth century to be able to solve all political problems. Sayri-Tupac plucked a thread from the silk tassel of the tablecloth and held it up in order to compare it to the whole cloth, which stood for his grandfather Atahualpa's empire.[17] But soon it transpired that this heir of the Incas had properties in Oropesa, Jaquijahuana, and Pucaría worth over 17,000 pesos. In addition, he had a sister queen in the person of Cusi Huaracay.

Juan de Vivero, an Augustinian friar, undertook the religious instruction of the Inca with some success. Later in the year that he reached Lima, Sayri-Tupac and his wife were baptized.

Despite his political successes the Marquis of Cañete was unhappy in Lima. He spent a great deal and complained of the cost of everything. The captain of the crossbowmen attached to him, Martín de Avendaño, explained that he could not live on his salary of 3,000 pesos, together with 4,000 more in tributes from the Indies.[18]

Cañete himself eventually wrote to King Philip saying that he had sent eleven letters home from Lima to the Council of the Indies without receiving an answer. That must have seemed a complaint, so it was scarcely surprising that the viceroy was recalled. He was replaced by another nobleman, for the age of the professional lay official (*letrado*) had not yet arrived in Peru. This successor was Diego López de Zúñiga y Velasco, Count of Nieva, related to the Dukes of Béjar, Cortés's backers, and who had once been governor in Galicia and had fought for the emperor in Tunis, Italy, and France. Born in Burgos in 1500, Nieva was the son of Antonio de Velasco and Francisca López de Zúñiga, Countess of Nieva. He married a sister of the next viceroy of New Spain.

Nieva was named viceroy in December 1558, at a time when Peru was experiencing alarming epidemics of influenza and smallpox.[19] Neither malady had been known in the viceroyalty before the Spaniards' arrival, so none of the Incas had immunity. Thousands – perhaps tens of thousands – died.

Nieva was eccentric in that he wanted to have himself styled 'his lordship', not 'his excellency'. He lived wildly and dishonestly, leaving a trail of debts. There is, however, no evidence that he was murdered by a jealous husband, Rodrigo Manrique de Lara – whose wife had once been pursued by the viceroy – as was whispered to be the case. For several years after Nieva's death in 1560, the Visitor, Lope García de Castro, ruled Peru, and remained in rough control until the arrival of the most powerful of the early viceroys, Francisco de Toledo.[20]

Both Nieva and García de Castro had trouble with the surviving Pizarros, the family of the original conquerors. Despite their withdrawal from any connection with the administration, that family still constituted a great economic power. In 1556 the income of the still-imprisoned Hernando Pizarro and his new wife Francisca, from their *encomiendas* in Peru (especially from those in the valley of Yucay and in the coca fields of Avisca), was between 100,000 and 150,000 pesos a year.[21] They still had maize and coca fields as well as the silver mines at Porco, which had been the most important mine until the discovery of Potosí.

Yucay lay on the great river Urubamba, an important tributary of the river Amazon on which the Inca Huayna Capac had made his home. It was believed in 1560 that the output of coca had increased fifty times since the Conquest. It was far and away the largest product liable to tithe in the district of Cuzco.

The Pizarros were also rich in Spain, having built the 'palace of the Conquest' in their home city of Trujillo in Extremadura with Peruvian silver; a *criado* of the family, Hernando Chacón, was in control. The Pizarros had properties too in the *pueblo* of Zarza, about twenty miles to the south of Trujillo. The family also retained their old interests in Nicaragua and Panama, where they maintained an *encomienda* on the island of Taboga. They still had a military type of 'Compañía', the Levante Company which had explored, opened up, and settled Peru. It had many investors, though Pizarro and Almagro had originally been the most powerful shareholders alongside Pascual de Andagoya, and Gaspar de Espinosa and his sons.[22]

An important part of the imperial mission in the New World continued to be the *residencias* carried out as inquiries into the services of departing governors or other officials. The origin of the practice can be found in the Code of Zeno which was applied in the eastern empire in the fifth century. The practice was referred to explicitly in the law in Spain known as the *Siete Partidas*: officials were required to remain in their posts for fifty days after their term of office had ended, so that they could administer justice to all who thought that they had been wronged by them. Hence the term *residencia*.[23]

The judge of the *residencia*, a specially designated lawyer, would prepare a questionnaire of a fairly straightforward kind, with questions such as 'Did the retiring official fulfil his instructions as requested?' The judges would then reject biased witnesses. In the sixteenth century there would be about 200 *residencias* relating to the

New World, deriving from Mexico, Guatemala, Panama, Lima, and Santo Domingo. The persons examined in this way included most of the outstanding conquistadors of the century. They included Cortés, Pedro de Alvarado, Nuño de Guzmán, and Francisco de Montejo in New Spain; Hernando de Soto in Peru and Florida; Pedrarias Ávila in Panama; Diego Velázquez in Cuba; Jiménez de Quesada in Venezuela; and Pedro de Heredia in Cartagena de Indias. The investigation into Cortés was by far the longest and ran to nearly 6,000 pages. None of the Pizarro family, however, and few Peruvian conquistadors had to suffer an investigation of this kind.[24]

The regular *residencias* gave birth to many important collections of documents which enable historians to know the activities of all the public servants better than anything. We see a gathering of viceroys intent on carrying out what they interpreted as the king's desires, if often failing to articulate them adequately. The viceroys in the sixteenth century in both New Spain and Peru were usually noblemen determined to live up to royal standards as well as fulfil royal commands. Many succeeded. They inspired palaces, monasteries, convents, churches, roads, and commercial enterprises on a scale never seen in Spanish dominions before.

# 4

# An Imperial Theocracy

*'Knights were created to uphold Christianity,' said the hermit.*
*'They should not return evil for evil but rather humbly forgive*
*their enemies. A knight's first duty is to defend the church*
*which would be lost without him.'*

Joanot Martorell, *Tirant lo Blanch*, 1490
(chapter 33, page 43 of the English translation)

The early days of the Spanish empire in the New World – that is, the
sixteenth century – seem in some ways a chapter in the history of the
Catholic Church – even a chapter in the history of the Franciscan
order. The Dominicans and the Augustinians then played an increasing part and, after 1570, the new order, the Society of Jesus, the Jesuits,
began to dominate.

New Spain was in Viceroy Velasco's day a profoundly religious
place, almost a theocracy. Religion exercised a strong political role.
Thus there were in 1560 eighty Franciscan monasteries, housing
380 friars; forty Dominican monasteries, with 210 friars; the Augustinians too had forty monasteries, and about the same number of
friars as the Dominicans. These figures included lay brothers, novices,
students, administrators, and some very old men. Many of these monasteries were immense buildings which dominated the towns where
they were placed. The Jesuits had not yet arrived.[1] The monks and
friars were the outriders of Spanish, or European, civilization. Many
of the first generation of churchmen were great men, with considerable abilities and strong convictions. The Franciscans seem to stand
out, but we should not forget their brilliant colleagues.

39

The sixteenth-century monasteries of Mexico which survive into our darker times are magnificent reminders of the persuasiveness of religion and the self-confidence of the age. They include Huejotzingo, built between 1550 and 1571; Tlalmanalco, completed in 1531; Cholula, which was begun in 1549 and completed in 1601. Acolman, the best example of plateresque architecture in Mexico, was finished in 1560 with a high open altar; Actopan, an Augustinian foundation with the air of a fortress, was begun in 1546; Yurirapúndaro, also Augustinian, was built between 1548 and 1559. Then there were the Dominican monasteries of Oaxaca and Puebla, begun in 1570 and 1533 respectively.

The architects of these great Franciscan foundations were men from Old Spain. Thus the designer of Huejotzingo was Fray Juan de Alameda, who came to New Spain with the great bishop Zumarraga; the designer of Cholula was Fray Toribio de Alcaraz, who hailed from a small town in Albacete; Actopan was the work of Fray Andrés de Mata, an Augustinian who had lived and worked in Italy; Yurirapúndaro was designed by Fray Diego de Chavez, a nephew of the conquistador Pedro de Alvarado, with the architect Pedro del Toro. The great golden monastery of Oaxaca was the work of Hernando Cavaros. Puebla was planned by Francisco Becerra from Trujillo in Cáceres, who later worked in both Lima and Quito (he was the grandson of Hernán González de Lara, the master designer of the great cathedral of Toledo).[2] Among his works was the cathedral of Lima.

The surviving conquistadors were still taking a great deal of trouble to ensure that their religion was understood by their new subjects. In 1559 Fray Maturino Ghiberti,[3] a Franciscan, published a catechism in Tarascan, the language of central New Spain. But the new – the second – archbishop, Alonso de Montúfar, disliked the language of the book and in 1571, to the author's astonishment, it was brought to the attention of the Inquisition.

The great orders stood for different things. The Franciscans, founded in 1209 by Saint Francis of Assisi, stood for an approach based on poverty not only for the individual friars but for the order corporately. The groups of Franciscans known as the Spirituals and the Observants[4] insisted on a strict adhesion to Saint Francis's Rule. The Dominicans, founded in 1216 by Saint Dominic, a native of Burgos, began by practising strict poverty and living by begging but, after

1475, the order was allowed to possess property. They became devoted especially to preaching but also to study.

The Augustinians, founded in 1244 by Pope Innocent IV, echoed the Dominicans but followed more directly the strict rules of conduct laid down by Saint Augustine of Hippo. The Mercedarians, founded in 1218 by Saint Peter Nolasco, sought to rescue and tend to Christians who had been captured by Moors and Muslims. All these orders responded to the discovery of the Americas and the subsequent conquests with urgency and optimism.

In 1556 the Dominican friars of Chiapas, that Mayan territory in New Spain where Bartolomé de Las Casas had been bishop, wrote to the Council of the Indies. They wanted to be certain that the king knew what had been happening to the orders in Mexico/Tenochtitlan and Central America. For years, they argued, they, the Dominicans, like the Franciscans and the Augustinians, had worked strenuously, despite the shocking heat and the aridity of the land. They had won souls, destroyed idols, and built churches. Sometimes one order or another had created a positive enthusiasm for baptism, several thousand converts occasionally being made in a single day.[5] But 'the devil was always vigilant', stirring up pagan priests who were known to call in infidels to stage a revolt. Once in the 1550s, the Dominican friars and their followers in Chiapas were burned out of their homes and about thirty Christians were killed. Two friars, one of them Fray Domingo de Vico, an immensely learned missionary who was able to preach in seven indigenous languages, were murdered in their church; another friar was sacrificed before a pagan idol. The Spaniards in Santiago de Guatemala refused to assist, helplessly pointing out bureaucratic royal orders forbidding them from entering the territory of Verapaz.[6]

To make matters worse, there were controversies between the Church and the orders and also between the orders themselves over what seemed to be essential matters. In September 1558, Fray Francisco de Bustamante, *provincial* (that is, leader) of the Franciscans in New Spain, denounced the cult of the Virgin of Guadalupe whose effigy had been mysteriously unveiled in 1530.[7] He blamed Archbishop Montúfar for his support of it (he had preached two days before in favour of the cult). Fray Francisco insisted that the picture had been painted by a mere Indian, not by God. Montúfar, a

Dominican who had been brought up in the indulgent world of Granada, and afterwards had worked at the monastery of Santo Tomás in
Seville, organized a special inquiry. Other Franciscans were critical
because the cult of the Virgin of Guadelupe seemed to constitute a
worship of idols. This incident was characteristic of the (bad) relations between the Franciscans and the archbishop.[8]

Meantime, Archbishop Montúfar wrote a statement in which he
described the difficulties posed by having monasteries which possessed
no more than two monks but were supposed to serve 100,000 souls.
He had heard of villages which had not been visited by any churchman
for ten years and even then only hastily, with only time to say mass,
carry out a few baptisms, and bless a few marriages. In their attempt
to avoid being left with insalubrious and inclement regions, the missions quarrelled over access to healthy and rich places. Montúfar also
described how the Prior of the Augustinians brought twenty-four Indians to be ordained as deacons or priests, but few of them could speak
Latin, and many could not even read it. (Though a Dr Anguis alleged
that even some priests ordained by Archbishop Montúfar himself,
being men of no intelligence, were unsuited to the role.)[9]

The Emperor Charles instructed the viceroy, in one of his last official acts, to settle the disputes between the missions in New Spain on
the basis that no order might penetrate a city served by another one
unless that other order gave permission. Montúfar was outraged:
'could there be a more diabolical order than this? There is nothing
Christian in it, for none of the orders are capable of teaching the catechism or administering the sacraments in a fifth, tenth, or even a
twentieth part of their territory? What kind of Christian rule is this
which does not allow one order to go to the help of another . . . ? They
act as if they are disposing of their vassals . . . !'[10]

Not surprisingly, there was prejudice in relation to the religion of
the Indians in New Spain. Secular Catholics disliked the very idea of
indigenous priests if that meant that good Spaniards could receive the
sacrament from a native Indian. The usually open-minded Viceroy
Mendoza gave some support for this prejudiced view when he declared
that it would be wrong to introduce Indians into the priesthood until
they had reached the same level of civilization as priests in Old Spain.
But the more broad-minded Archbishop Montúfar disagreed and

ordained both Indians and *mestizos*, as well, of course, as Spaniards. There had, after all, been indigenous friars as early as 1527 – so the saintly Motolinía said.[11] There had also been a Tarascan priest as early as 1540, when Pablo, the grandson of the last king of the Tarascans, Sintzichu Tanguxan, was ordained. But Montúfar was eventually required to cease such actions by his superiors in Castile.

All the same, the Franciscans gave support to Montúfar. Thus Fray Jacobo Daciano, a friar of Danish origin (he was said to have been a brother of King Christian II) and a well-known theologian, proclaimed that the Mexican Church had been founded in the wrong way precisely because it did not encourage indigenous priests. He spoke as a benign man who had fled the world of religious argument in Denmark in 1513. He was challenged by a Spanish Franciscan, Fray Juan de Gaona. Other early religious men were the Franciscan, Juan de Tovar, a *mestizo* who was the son of a conquistador of the same name as himself and a princess of the royal family of Texcoco, one of the three original royal cities of the Mexica. Tovar learned several indigenous languages through his Mexican mother and became secretary of the cathedral in Mexico/Tenochtitlan. He entered the Society of Jesus in the 1570s, and the depth of his learning earned him the sobriquet the 'Mexican Cicero'. Another holy individual was a native of Tlaxcala, Diego de Valadés, a protégé of the royal bastard, Fray Pedro de Gande. Valadés went to Spain in 1574, where he was celebrated as the first Mexican to publish a book of his own, the *Rhetorica Christiana ad Concionandi et Orandi*, which in 1579 appeared in Latin in Perugia.

Meanwhile, the controversy in Spain between Las Casas and Sepúlveda over the just treatment of Indians remained unresolved.[12] The Council of the Indies doggedly tried to persuade the wise men who were judging that extraordinary affair to deliver their opinions in writing. In 1557 a letter was sent to the clever Dominican Fray Melchor Cano, telling him that, since all the other judges had given their views, his should also be given immediately. In fact, no opinions seem to have survived, except for those of a Fray Anaya, who said that the conquests were justifiable as a way of stopping the Indians' sins against natural law. But, he thought, new expeditions ought to be financed by the Crown and led by captains 'zealous in the service of God and the King which would act as a good example to the Indians, and which would explore, for the good of the Indians and not for the gold which they might find'.[13] The curious *requerimiento* (Requirement) should, however, continue to be used before there was any resort to force.[14]

Fray Bartolomé de la Vega – who had not only been the first to show the justice of the Indians' cause, but had for a long time argued over the matter with numerous doctors of law who had attempted with all their energy to defend the opposite of every truth – tried to persuade the Council of the Indies that Las Casas's defence had to be published. 'What is at stake,' insisted La Vega, 'is nothing less than the salvation or loss of both the bodies and souls of all the inhabitants of that recently discovered new world ... this work is as supremely important, for it is vitally necessary for the whole world. On it, the author has spent so much labour; he has grown old from many anxieties and innumerable sleepless nights.'[15] The *cabildo* (town council) in Mexico/Tenochtitlan, however, wrote (to the king) that Las Casas's writings had caused such discontent in their city that they had arranged for two theologians and the town attorneys to prepare a statement to be sent to the Council of the Indies which pronounced against that 'audacious friar and his odious doctrine'. So the defence was not for the moment to be published.

Sepúlveda wrote to Francisco de Argote, a member of a well-known family in Córdoba, who was the judge of how to dispose of the goods confiscated by the Inquisition in his native city.[16] 'I do not maintain that the barbarians should be reduced to slavery,' Sepúlveda insisted:

> but only that they should be submitted to our rule. I do not maintain that we should deprive them of their property, but only conquer them, without committing unjust acts against them. I do not maintain that we should abuse our power over them, only that our dominion should be noble, courteous and useful for them. Thus we should root out their pagan customs and influence them by kindness to follow natural law and, with that magnificent preparation ... attract them, with apostolic kindness, to the Christian religion.[17]

That was rather a different way of putting matters than the unbending Sepúlveda had customarily used. Perhaps he was mellowing.

There was also at the time a different kind of religious crisis in Spain. In September 1557 a new long list of heretical books to be burned had been prepared by the Roman Inquisition. Two cardinals were to ensure that booksellers did not lose too much all at once. All the books of Erasmus were, however, to be burned immediately, along with the works of Machiavelli and Gian Francesco Poggio's mocking *Facetiae*, a collection of humorous tales with attacks on the clergy and the monastic orders. All permissions to read banned books were revoked, the only exceptions now being Grand Inquisitors and cardinals, to whom special permits were allowed. After the law of censorship of 1502 was strengthened in 1561, all books needed a censor's approval printed among the preliminaries, while the import of any foreign book without a royal licence became a capital offence.

Following the Roman list of September 1557, a new Index of Prohibited Books was then prepared for the Spanish government by a conservative bookseller in Seville named Antonius Bladus, which modified the severity of the first list. Bladus's document was 'a list of authors and books against which the Roman and universal inquisition orders all Christians to be on their guard'. There were authors whose whole works were to be banned, even where they said nothing critical about the faith: the once much-loved Erasmus was an example of that. A second category was that of authors, one or more of whose books were to be banned. The third class was of individual books specifically named as dangerous. All books which did not declare the name of the author, the printer, and the place of publication were also automatically condemned. Latin or other translations of the Bible were not to be read or even owned without permission of the Inquisition. Sixty-one printers were also forbidden.[18] A great many books were in consequence burned: apparently as many as 10,000 in Venice on the Saturday before Palm Sunday in 1558. But both the Sorbonne in Paris and the Spanish Inquisition ignored this list. Archbishop Valdés,[19] the Grand Inquisitor in Spain, issued his own list in 1559.

All the same, heresy seemed to be still growing. Consider, for example, the journey in 1556 of an educated monk named 'El Julianillo' (Julián Hernández) to Seville from Geneva with numerous Calvinist books. He had been in Scotland and Paris seeking liberation from strict Catholic doctrine. He aimed to go to the free-thinking monastery of San Isidoro del Campo, just to the north of Seville. But by mistake, his copy of *La Imágen del Anticristo* (*The Image of Antichrist*) reached the hands of an orthodox Catholic, who informed the Inquisition. Thereafter twelve monks fled from San Isidoro and most were burned in effigy after a few years. El Julianillo himself was captured in Sierra Morena. He was burned to death in an *auto-de-fe* in the square of San Francisco in Seville, but not before he had insulted his executioners on the scaffold.

At the same time, questions were being asked about the orthodoxy of Dr Constantino de la Puente, who had been a chaplain to the Emperor Charles.[20] On 2 June 1558, Grand Inquisitor Valdés wrote to the emperor in retirement suggesting that the Holy Office should be extended to Galicia, Asturias (whence he himself came), and the Basque country; that confession as well as communion should be obligatory for all His Majesty's subjects; that no schoolmaster should be allowed to practise till licensed by examiners; and that no books at all should be published without the approval of the Holy Office. Foreigners were forbidden from selling books; booksellers were to be obliged to have available a list of all books which they were offering for sale; and all informers were to be rewarded with a quarter or even a third of the property of the individual against whom they informed.[21] The Emperor Charles was not himself able to act in any of these matters, but his influence was still thought to be determining.

The news that Archbishop Carranza, at much the same time, had published a dubious work on the catechism caused horror in Rome. Partly in reaction to this, the brilliant but cruel Pope Paul IV (Gian Pietro Caraffa) bestowed on the Grand Inquisitor, Valdés, special powers.[22] On 7 January 1559 an increased income was allocated to the Inquisition by the Crown. The Grand Inquisitor was given the power to hold investigations into the activities of all senior churchmen and arrest them, if necessary by his own decision. Twenty-one people were burned as Protestants in Seville, including Juan Ponce de Léon, a noble youth who was brother of the Count of Bailén.[23] In November 1559 a tide of prejudice swept through all Spanish universities: Castilians studying abroad at unapproved foreign universities were ordered to go home. This step was regarded by many as a catastrophe, even though as yet it only applied to Castilians, not for the moment to Aragonese or Basques.[24]

The Index of the Inquisition of 1559 banned five hundred plays. Exactly why the plays were especially condemned is unclear, but thenceforth all playwrights had to write with closer attention to decorum.[25] The novel *La vida de Lazarillo de Tormes* was banned too, in both its first and second parts (the second part, published in Antwerp in 1554, presents Lazarus as a fish). It was not reprinted in Spain in full until the nineteenth century.

There was a counterpoint: the Inquisition did not seem to mind the publication and distribution of chivalrous novels, a remarkable toleration. Not a single book of the profane type ever figured on the List of Prohibited Books, though sometimes high authorities, even the Empress Regent, even Prince Philip in his youth, would condemn 'many books of fiction in the vernacular such as *Amadís* . . .'[26] Perhaps that was because these extraordinary novels had too many friends at court (the emperor himself, Saint Ignatius, and Saint Teresa of Ávila).[27] What seems to have perturbed the court most was not that the Spanish themselves in the New World would continue to read these books, but that the habit might spread to the Indians, who seemed so easily influenced.

In 1561 a conference on all these vexed matters was held in the Dominican monastery at Atocha in Madrid: Las Casas appeared before King Philip just as he had so often appeared before the Emperor Charles V. The Franciscan Juan Salmerón defended the just wars against the Indians because of 'their bestial sins and human sacrifices'.[28] Las Casas had earlier beseeched the Pope to excommunicate anyone who held the view that Indian idolatry justified war. Philip tried to avoid a difficult debate on that matter by focusing his attention on the matter of regulating the position of monasteries in his new dominions. He ordered that monasteries in New Spain should be at least six leagues (say, eighteen miles) apart: 'We have been informed that monasteries are built close together because the religious people prefer to establish themselves in the green lands near the city of Mexico, leaving stretches of twenty to thirty leagues untended, because the religious seek to avoid the rough, poor, and hot regions.'[29]

Also in 1561, Archbishop Montúfar and Bishop Quiroga, the enlightened utopian who directed the affairs of central New Spain at Pátzcuaro, brought a suit against all the three main orders in New Spain for their abuse of Indians. Quiroga commented: 'When the Indians do not obey, the friars insult and strike them, they tear out their hair, they have them stripped and cruelly flogged, and then they throw them into prison in chains and irons . . .' The Franciscans Fray Francisco de Ribera and

Fray Juan Quijano, both attached to the monastery of Tlaxcala, indeed once had an Indian arrested merely because his words had irritated them and had had him tied to a post and whipped.[30]

The *provinciales* of all the orders working in New Spain then wrote to King Philip begging him to seek to avoid the ruin which seemed to them to be threatening the Church there as a result of all this controversy.[31] They drew attention to the revival of old religions: on 11 October 1565, Archbishop Montúfar and the other bishops of New Spain denounced this phenomenon in a memorial to the Supreme Court (*audiencia*). They described 'the great readiness with which these newly converted Indians return to their old idolatries, rites, sacrifices and superstitions'. For example, the people in Chalma, a cultivated town in the valley of Mexico/Tenochtitlan, known for the work of its people as builders, would gather in remote caves difficult of access; sometimes, as at Cholula, they would skilfully hide effigies of their old gods beneath Christian crosses. These practices were led by *caciques* (chiefs) as well as by old priests and sorcerers.[32] This open letter to the king had little effect. In 1563, Licenciado Alfonso de Oseguera wrote that Franciscans could not be found for New Galicia (where he was a judge), because of the sterility of the country and the barbarity of the people.[33]

Despite these difficulties, the first stones were laid of a cathedral at Mérida in Yucatan, in 1563, and the building was finished in 1599. It was an aisled church, like a hall, comparable to the new cathedral in Santo Domingo.[34] In 1569 an aisled cathedral was begun also in the growing city of Guadalajara in New Spain. There were other positive achievements: on 21 March 1569, for example, the Bishop of Michoacán wrote that the leading Indians there had in general embraced the faith and some of them were already preaching to their colleagues in their native tongue.[35] Ten days later, the tireless Archbishop Montúfar wrote to the Pope that he had personally baptized 5,000 Indians.[36] He had come to realize that only the friars – especially the Franciscans – were really able to interpret the sentiments of the Indians. Years of isolation in the country, combined with at least some knowledge of the indigenous languages and habits, gave them a clearer understanding than anyone else of the Indians' character. The orders came to expect their members to learn minor languages (Otomí, Totonac, Zapotec, Tarascan, Mixtec) as well as the master tongue Nahuatl.

Also in 1569 the Dominican Luis Bertrán, later beatified, began to preach to the Indians with great success in New Granada (Venezuela, Colombia, Ecuador, parts of Peru and Brazil), the exceptional austerity of his life being his warmest recommendation. He made long missionary journeys through apparently impassable forests or under a burning sun, often fasting and always armed with only a breviary. He usually travelled barefoot. He must have won for the Church at least 20,000 Christians.[37] Shortly thereafter, Bertrán left New Spain so as not to be responsible for the iniquities which he knew were being practised by the colonists. But his companion, Fray Luis Vero, continued in his place till 1588.[38] The Dominicans sought to justify themselves to Rome before the Council of Indies in all kinds of ways: 'One of the things of which we are accused,' they declared:

> is the sumptuousness and excess of the buildings which we have erected to serve as our monasteries. It is easy to verify these things exactly because walls cannot be hidden, and Your Highness [the letter was to the Pope] can have them visited and inspected, and take such measures as are fitting for your royal will and service. But one thing of which we can assure Your Highness is that, of forty-eight monasteries and houses which we have established in New Spain, not three have yet been finished, for we see to it that the Indians work on them with their full consent and with their pleasure, without abuse or vexation ... Besides, though there are a few houses of reasonable size, the others, that is most of them, are very humble and simple, with no pretensions, elegance or excess and, in their construction, we have done no violence to the Indians who indeed wish to honour their villages because they have no churches in them other than monasteries ...[39]

Before this, in 1564, Las Casas had written his last work, *A Solution to Twelve Doubts*, which showed if anything that his views had hardened against the Spanish colonists. In May 1565 he sent King Philip a copy summarizing his views in this volume. Alas, it was not published till the nineteenth century.

Las Casas wrote his will too, on 17 March 1564, in which he preached that 'surely God will wreak his fury and anger' against Spain some day for 'the unjust wars waged against the American Indians'.[40] His representative in Rome wrote saying he would deliver any new message to the stern new Pope Pius V (Antonio Michele Ghislieri, the last Pope to be canonized) when Las Casas sent it to him. Las Casas thereupon prepared a new letter. In this he demanded the excommunication of anyone who declared war against infidels merely because of their idolatry or as a means of preaching the faith. He also sent a publication which seems to have been his first pamphlet. It was entitled *The Only Way* and was aimed at attracting all people to the true faith. Pope Pius, presumably on the demand of Las Casas, urged King Philip to make 'the yoke of Christ easy for the Indians'. In November 1568, Pius sent his nuncio in Madrid new instructions concerning the treatment of the Indians in America. He recalled that the kings of Spain had been granted the right to conquer the lands beyond the seas only provided that they plant the Christian faith there. It was, therefore, the duty of the king to see that there were good preachers and priests in those countries, and that the civil authorities supported them through taxes. Baptism should only be conferred on the natives when they had received sufficient instruction. For those already baptized, teachers had to be found to turn them into good Christians. The centres of instruction should be more widespread for the convenience of the natives. Where the Indians lived scattered far and wide, they should be concentrated in villages. Pagan sanctuaries should all be destroyed, and, naturally, all Spaniards in the New World should set a good example.[41]

Of course, Pope Pius knew that the Church in the Indies had theoretically been placed (for the purpose of appointments and translations) in the hands of the monarch by a Bull of Pope Julius II of 1508. The king therefore had the right of nomination to all abbacies as well as prelacies, and all papal bulls which affected the New World had to be approved by the Council of the Indies. But papal permission still had formally to be gained before a church could be built.

Changes in the religious structure of the Americas occurred in the late 1560s. To start with, the first generation of missionaries were dying: Motolinía in 1569; Pedro de Gande in 1572; Fray Andrés de Olmos, who could preach in twelve indigenous languages, and Bishop Toral of Yucatan, both in 1571. Pedro de Gande, probably the emperor's half-brother, was perhaps the most remarkable of all these great men. 'He taught the Indians all the arts,' wrote Fray Diego de Valadés, 'for he is the master of all of them.'[42] 'I am not the archbishop of Mexico,'

Archbishop Montúfar once said, 'that part is played by Fray Pedro de Gande.'

Secondly, among the changes during the 1560s, the missions were becoming towns, and the Holy Office was deciding that the careful recording of the one-time customs of the Indies (as in Sahagún's *Florentine Codex*)[43] had been a mistake because it showed excessive interest in ancient rites. Nor was Sahagún's collection, the *Psalmodía*, of the colloquies of the Indians published, while the printing of Fray Arnaldo de Basaccio's *Evangelios and Epistolas* ceased. Even Fray Alonso de Molina's dictionary of Spanish–Nahuatl was questioned, though the offence turned out to derive from a typographical error.

Not only in New Spain were there controversial difficulties. For example, in Peru, the second of Spain's great viceroyalties – already the first in terms of wealth – Archbishop Loaisa called a meeting of theologians to draw up instructions for confessors to guide them in deciding to what extent *encomenderos* and others who benefited from unjust wars against Indians should be required to make restitution of their riches. Regulations were approved which in certain cases made restitution necessary before absolution could be given. These discussions determined the absorbing handbook for missionaries being prepared by Alonso de la Peña Montenegro, which was used throughout the next two centuries.[44] Fray Luis López, one of the first Jesuits in Peru, wrote of the Spaniards whom he encountered there that 'they are very cruel to the Indians, who seem to them to be not men but beasts because they treat them thus to achieve their end, which is silver . . .'[45] (López was admittedly later condemned by the Inquisition since he showed excessive sympathy for the Indians.)

The controversy and notoriety surrounding Las Casas spread to Peru: his position was passionately denounced in an open letter published in the 1570s, entitled *A Defence of the Legitimacy of the Rule of the Kings of Spain in the Indies, in opposition to Fray Bartolomé de las Casas*,[46] written by a local friar who was a friend of Viceroy Toledo. He pointed out that Las Casas had never been in Peru and so could know nothing of conditions there. The Indies, the author believed, were Spain's deserved reward for eight centuries of war against the Muslims. The Incas had been tyrants. Yet Las Casas, the *Defence* argued, had almost persuaded the emperor to abandon Peru to them until Francisco de Vitoria pointed out the truth about them. Las Casas wielded such power that few questioned him. Harm would come if the question of the king's title to the Indies was not clearly established. Some Spaniards, this author continued, had married Indian princesses in order to be in line should the Incas return to power.

The friar condemned those who 'under the guise of zeal, try to give the Indians titles ... inappropriate for them ... for they are minors who must be governed ... It has been a most delicate subtlety of the Devil to choose as his instrument a churchman and apparently a person of zeal [that is, Las Casas] but a deceived person, ill-speaking and of little discretion, as may be seen from his published books and by the troubles which he created in Peru when [Viceroy] Blasco Núñez came.'

Back in Europe, the Council of Trent, the Church of Rome's great contemporary attempt at radical revision and reasonable repair, was coming to an end. Among the conclusions announced on 3 December 1563 was one whereby all priests were placed under the control of bishops. That presented a problem in the New World, for many parishes were directed by friars, not secular priests. The archbishop of Mexico/Tenochtitlan had to beg the Pope not to insist on the enforcement of that new rule in his territories.[47]

Meanwhile the Pope formally issued the decrees of the Council of Trent and, on 12 July 1564, King Philip accepted them as law in Spain – and in the Spanish domains. The Council of Trent, which expressed the Roman Catholic Church's counter-reformatory philosophy, had taken over twenty years to reach its conclusions, but now that they were announced they were far-reaching. Pius V sent the decrees of Trent to the Bishop of Santo Domingo, and similar letters were despatched to other bishops of the New World, as well as to 'golden' Goa.[48] In January 1565, Philip convened the Royal Council to seek ways of putting all the decrees of the Council of Trent into effect: a reform of all religious orders; the disciplining of parish priests; the revision of religious practice; the abolition of several ancient rites; the adoption of a new mass; a new prayer book; a new calendar with changes to some saints' days of celebration; the training of missionaries; and the establishment of good religious schools. The Catholic Church was thus supposedly ready for all new challenges. To assist it and even to lead it in some respects, a great new missionary order had even been established: the Society of Jesus.[49]

# 5

# The Jesuit Challenge

*Overcome thyself.*
Saint Ignatius Loyola's favourite injunction

After 1570, fathers of the Society of Jesus began to arrive in the New World and they swiftly started to give a lead to the pre-existing orders – even the Franciscans who had been so important to the first fifty years of the Spanish imperial adventure in New Spain.

The Society of Jesus was the nerve of the Counter-Reformation, particularly in respect of education. It had been established on 27 September 1540 in Paris, where ten unknown young men, mostly Spaniards, who were mocked because of their broken Italian, received papal approval for their new endeavours. Their leader was Ignatius Loyola, a Basque. By 1556, when Ignatius died, there were 1,500 Jesuits and sixty-five missions. The Spanish element in the undertaking remained dominant throughout these years, for the main counsellors of Ignatius had been Castilians: Juan Alfonso de Polanco, a native of Burgos who had studied in Paris; Jerónimo Nadal, from Palma de Mallorca; Diego Láinez, from Almazán in Soria; and a Valencian, Juan Jerónimo Domenech. The last named soon became the Jesuit representative in Sicily. Francis Javier from Javier was in Navarre, and Cosme de Torres from Valencia remained in India and Japan. There were by 1556 several Jesuit colleges in Spain.[1] Francis Borgia, former viceroy of Catalonia and Duke of Gandia, became the 'superior', as his title was called, for Spain in 1554. There were similar foundations in Italy, especially in Apulia, where the ignorance of religion seemed so great that the Jesuits teasingly thought of the territory as 'the Italian Indies' (much the same was said in Spain about Asturias).

The essential study at all these colleges was the *Ratio Studiorum*, a scheme of learning issued in 1599. It was written by Fray Claudio Aquaviva from a Neapolitan aristocratic family, and it prescribed an education almost entirely in the classics. Hitherto, no religious order had ever involved itself in education. But from now on, the Jesuits, with a bell in their hands, took children to school in processions all over the world. Even the celebrated if intemperate playwright Lope de Vega went to a Jesuit school.

Ignatius Loyola,[2] the inspiration for this new order, had been born in 1491 in a small castle belonging to his family, in Guipúzcoa, on the road from Azpeitia to Azcotia about twenty miles from San Sebastián, in the Basque country. His father was often away on military campaigns, but he had two elder brothers, one of whom was a priest, Pedro López de Loyola. The other, Martín García de Loyola, was a soldier. Ignatius went to study with Juan Velázquez, the *alcaide* (commander) of the fortress at Arévalo in Castile, a cousin of Diego Velázquez, the first governor of Cuba. Ignatius seemed a child of chivalry until 1521, enjoying several amours and some gambling; he even had an illegitimate child. Then, at the siege of Pamplona (in 1521), he was wounded, his leg was broken and had to be set twice. He was for a long time an invalid in his father's house, being looked after by his sister-in-law, Magdalena. He asked for books of chivalry to read but, instead of popular chivalrous novels such as *Amadís de Gaula* or *Tirant lo Blanch*, he received by mistake the *Vita Christi* of Ludolph of Saxony, a popular book written in the late fourteenth century with many editions in the fifteenth and sixteenth centuries.

Ignatius determined to equal the deeds of the saints whose lives he had read; he thought of entering the famous Carthusian house at Seville, but that desire cooled, for the Carthusian monks whom he knew were too lax. He went instead to Cataluña, first to the Benedictine monastery of Montserrat, then a few miles north to Manresa, where he lived an austere life in a cave for a year. There he wrote his *Spiritual Exercises* in 1522.

At the beginning of 1523, Ignatius made his way to Rome where, in March, he received the blessing of the austere Flemish Pope, Adrian

VI. Ignatius's immense personal magnetism began to influence the Church. Returning to Spain a beggar – his desire to go to the Holy Land had been refused – he studied Latin in Barcelona and then went to study at Alcalá de Henares and Salamanca. He was wrongly arrested in the second of these cities as a Reformer. In 1528 he went to the Sorbonne in Paris where he met a Savoyard, Pierre le Fèvre; a Navarro, Francisco Xavier from the town of that name in Asturias; and three Castilians. These were Diego Láinez, of whom we have spoken; Alfonso Salmerón, from Toledo; and Nicolás Bobadilla, in fact Nicolas Alonso Pérez from Boadilla del Camino, Palencia, son of a *converso*, who had studied in Valladolid. Ignatius also met a Portuguese named Simón Rodríguez. Other early 'Iñiguistas' (as they were known at the time) were Claude le Jay, also from Savoy, and two Frenchmen, Pascasio Bröet and Jean Codure. Ignatius's first real follower, however, was Juan Alfonso de Polanco, who became his secretary. His first German recruit was Peter Canisius, who had completed a doctoral thesis in Cologne. Most of these men were doctors of philosophy.[3] By now, Ignatius had the Pope's permission to seek and to enrol followers.

To these were soon added Pietro Contarini and Gaspar de Dioctis, both from Venice. All went on foot to that city in the winter of 1536 and then on to Rome, Ignatius staying behind (in Venice). In Rome, the followers of Ignatius were welcomed by Pedro Ortiz, the imperial plenipotentiary, and also by the turbulent genius, Cardinal Carafa, who was soon to become an intolerant Pope.

They returned to Venice, where Ignatius, Xavier, and five of the others were ordained. The group then spread out through Italy and, by 1537, these Iñiguistas had come to be called the 'Society of Jesus'. Ignatius set off again for Rome with Le Fèvre and Láinez, and they had a vision of Christ at La Storta, just outside of Rome. Christ said to Ignatius, 'I will be gracious to you.' Cardinals Ortiz and Contarini (a Venetian who saw the Jesuits as the 'special spiritual sons in Christ') gave them much support, Ortiz spending forty days with Ignatius in the monastery of Monte Cassino halfway between Naples and Rome. They then established themselves in a building on the Capitoline hill in Rome and there the members assembled in May 1538. Cardinal Carafa gave them the authority to preach and to dispense sacraments.[4]

They formed an order, the 'Society of Jesus', which gained papal approval in 1540, and Ignatius was named 'general' in April 1541. Pietro Codacio provided a house in Rome for them. Soon Carafa, now Pope Paul III, began building for them the elegant and now legendary church known as the Gesù, the architect being Giacomo Vignola (whose work continued till 1575). But the facade was the creation of Giovanni de Rosis and G. B. Tristani.

Ignatius finished the first draft of his 'Constitutions', the new rules of his new order, in early 1550, living on in Rome where he died on 31 July 1556. In his *Spiritual Exercises*, he hoped that he might obtain 'a thorough knowledge of my sins and a feeling of abhorrence for them'. 'At least,' he thought, 'the fear of punishment will help me avoid falling into sin.'

The fifth *Exercise* was a meditation on hell. The first point, Ignatius considered, 'was to see, with the eye of the imagination, the great fires and the souls enveloped . . . in bodies of fire. The second point was to hear the wailing, the screaming, the cries, and the blasphemies . . . to smell the smoke, the brimstone, the corruption and rottenness . . . to taste bitter things, such as tears, sadness and remorse . . . to feel personally how flames surround and burn souls . . .'5

Souls in hell could be divided into three groups: first, those who had gone to hell before the birth of Christ; second, those who were damned during His lifetime; and, third, the majority, those condemned after His life in the world. It seemed more fitting, thought Ignatius, to scourge oneself with light cords which cause exterior pain than in a way which might cause internal and serious infirmity.

In the second week of study, the first thing to do was to place before Ignatius 'a human king chosen by God . . . to whom all princes and Christians pay reverence and obey'. Ignatius would consider how this king speaks to all his people, saying, 'It is my will to conquer all infidel lands . . .' One had 'to seek honour rather than dishonour . . .' and establish . . . a time of tranquillity during which the soul was not agitated by diverse spirits . . .' Lucifer was the mortal enemy of humankind.

In the third week, one should begin by considering the room of the

Last Supper; whether it was large or small, and of what shape. One had to try and visualize the persons at the Supper, imagine oneself listening to what they were saying and draw profit from one's view of it. One should consider the road from Mount Zion to the Valley of Jehoshaphat, what it was like; and likewise the garden of Gethsemane, its width, its length, of this shape or another. While eating, one should imagine that one was with Christ at His table with the Apostles, how He ate and drank, how He looked and spoke. Other matters to be considered included the fact that the Apostles were uneducated men, most of them from a low station in life.

The ninth rule of Ignatius in the *Exercises* was that 'there were several reasons why human beings were in desolation; the first and most important was because they were torpid, lazy, and negligent in their spiritual exercises, and so, through their own fault, consolation was withdrawn from them'. Ignatius wanted every Jesuit to have all the books which he might need for private studies and therefore to have access to a good library.

\* \* \*

Fortified by these *Exercises*, Jesuits embarked for Peru in 1568. They set off from Seville and Sanlúcar de Barrameda, whither they had been led by Fray Jerónimo Ruiz de Portillo, who came originally from Rioja and had entered the Society of Jesus in Salamanca. He had been confessor to the president of the chancellery of Valladolid. Ruiz de Portillo and his colleagues carried with them a large library of books as well as several Peruvian grammars. On the journey the boat had become a floating school, as the passengers and sailors were divided into groups of four to listen to 'useful and pious books'. They reached Callao, the port of Lima, in March 1568,[6] and Lima itself on 1 April. Fray Diego de Bracamonte, who became the first rector of the new community, exulted that the city 'was another Seville'. The Jesuits were soon granted a suitable site for a college, to be known as San Pablo in the street called *Enfermeros* (nurses). The college became the centre for teaching humanities, for Fray Ruiz de Portillo's multifarious activities, and the enlightened classes given by Fray Luis López for the benefit of the city's slaves.

Four years later, in September 1572, the first Jesuit mission of twelve fathers arrived in New Spain, led by Fray Pedro Sánchez. They preached successfully at Puebla, then in the capital. Jesuit schools were soon established at the central cities of New Spain such as Pátzcuaro, Oaxaca, Puebla, and Tepozotlán, and also at Veracruz on the Caribbean coast. The fathers soon learned several native languages. By 1583 there were eight Jesuit houses and 150 fathers in New Spain. The Indians loved them, for they seemed genuinely interested in them and their lives.[7]

Ignatius's successors were less creative than he had been, though all were highly competent. Diego Láinez, for example, who as already noted was a native of Almazán in Soria, went to the monastery of Alcalá where he met Alonso Salmerón, with whom he went to Paris in order to meet Ignatius in 1534. At the Council of Trent, Láinez opposed the offering of the chalice to laymen and seems to have believed in the divine right not of kings but of bishops. His successor as general of the Jesuit order, Francesco Borja, was one of the most unusual men of his age. Being the son of María Enríquez, he was a cousin of the Emperor Charles V, to whose mother, Juana, he administered the last rites in 1555. Borja was also the great-grandson of Pope Alexander VI. After some years as an administrator, a viceroy in Cataluña, and a courtier, he became a Jesuit in 1548 and founded a Jesuit university in Rome where one could study Hebrew, as well as Greek, Latin, rhetoric, and philosophy. Every day there would be a lecture in mathematics, another in morals, and two more in scholastic theology. Borja became general of the Jesuit order in 1565 and ruled with imagination and energy during a time of extraordinary expansion.

Borja was succeeded as general of the order by Everard Mercurian, a Dutchman who took a strong and positive line about Jesuit activity in the East, naming the Italian, Alessandro Valignano, to be the chief there. Mercurian's successor as general in 1580 was Claudio Aquaviva. He came from a great Neapolitan family who provided the Dukes of Altri and gave several cardinals to the Church. Aquaviva was in many ways the second founder of the order.

On 17 November 1579, Fray Rodolfo Aquaviva, the general's cousin, and Fray Antonio Montserrat, both Jesuits, set off for the court of the Mogul emperor, the great Akbar, in Agra, accompanied by a converted Muslim, Fray Francisco Mohammedan.[8] These fathers were received by the Great Mogul, who was busy devising a new religion of his own, a mixture of Hinduism and Islam, which also borrowed some activities from other creeds. Fray Aquaviva denounced Islam, and also Mahomet, as a false prophet and an irreligious man, a declaration which, of course, infuriated the followers of Islam. The Great Mogul was undecided about what to do, though he wanted to protect the Jesuits. Their order was also supported by the Mogul's chief adviser, Abdul Fazil, who talked of what he called 'the absurdities of the Koran'.[9]

In the Far East, the Jesuits had an astonishing history. The Portuguese were permitted a settlement in 1557 at Macao near what later became Hong Kong. It was the beginning of a colony which would last four hundred years.

In 1559, Cosme de Torres sent the Portuguese missionary Gaspar Vilela and a Japanese (who took the name of Lawrence) to establish Christianity in Japan. Torres was a Valencian who had taught grammar in Mallorca. He then went in 1538 to the West Indies and New Spain, where he was a collaborator with Bishop Zumarraga. Thence he sailed in 1542 as chaplain on the Pacific voyage of López de Villalobos (see chapter 27). Torres became a Jesuit in Goa in 1551, thanks to Saint Francis Javier whom he had accompanied to Japan in 1548. Torres stayed for two and a half years. He then went to India as a missionary. His life was a quite extraordinary one.

The Shogun, the effective prime minister of Japan, gave the Jesuits a safe conduct in 1559. Though they converted several *bonzes* (Buddhist clergymen of Japan), Vilela had to flee to the outskirts of the cities. A father named Fries, who succeeded Vilela, wrote 'Despised, hated, stoned, persecuted in every way, treated as unworthy, Vilela never ceased to do all he could for the spread of the faith.'[10]

In Japan, the Portuguese had landed on Tagoshima, off the southern coast of the island of Kyushu, in 1543, bringing with them the precious musket which transformed Japanese warfare. Saint Francis Xavier, who had become one of Ignatius Loyola's closest colleagues, introduced Christianity to Japan in 1551, preaching in Kyoto and in the feudal lands of the West. He was well received and some lords encouraged conversions in the hope of attracting Portuguese trade.

But the dogmatic intolerance of many Jesuit missionaries also brought with it the enmity of the usually tolerant Buddhist clergy.

The Italian Jesuit, Valignano, left Lisbon in March 1574. He went to Goa, and waited for ten months, in the Jesuit house which had been established there, for a boat to take him onwards from Macao. Valignano informed himself of what was going on in China. He was aware of the various efforts made in the past by Christian missionaries in China: a Jesuit, Núñez Barreto, in 1555; the Dominican, Gaspar de la Cruz, in 1556; the Jesuits Francisco Pérez and Giambattista Ribera in 1560 and 1568. He realized that future efforts to convert the Chinese would have to be carried through by Christians who had taken the trouble to learn the language. He appointed the Italian Michele Ruggieri to go to Peking on the condition he had first learned Chinese.

But great events were soon to unfold. In Japan in 1568, Oda Nobunaga, a wild nobleman, had seized Kyoto and set up a puppet Shogun consisting of three Yoshiaki, lords of the provinces of east of Kyoto, acting in response to a secret appeal from the Japanese emperor. Nobunaga became the despot of central Japan, and the so-called period of National Unification began. His lieutenant, Toyotomi Hideyoshi, conquered most of western Japan, while the death of their chief enemies in the east of the country enabled Nobunaga to preserve his territory without much effort. But the challenge of Christianity was at its height. The conversion to Christianity in 1578 of Otomi Yoshishige, one of the greatest lords on the island of Kyushu, was a special triumph for the Jesuits. Also on Kyushu, Nagasaki was opened by Omura Sumitaba, the local lord, as a foreign port in 1567.

Nobunaga was killed in 1582, but Hideyoshi inherited his place. He asserted his own authority in central Japan in the next couple of years, his victory symbolized by the building of a large castle at Osaka.

By then there were 1,500 Christians in Kyoto, and many more in the surrounding areas. They were headed by the secretary of the first minister of the city of Kyoto who, when the bonzes demanded the expulsion of the Portuguese missionary Vilela in 1586, said that his views had to be examined. The secretary was in fact enchanted with Christianity, which for him was like a breath of fresh air to Japan. There were other concessions too, and despite the power of Nobunaga, who had maintained his control over the centre of the country, he had been tolerant of the Christians.

New products and mechanisms, such as clocks and compasses, introduced from Europe, were now beginning to affect the Japanese economy. The old private customs barriers which had hampered trade were abolished, as were the trading practices of many semi-monopolistic guilds. The artistic and intellectual exuberance of late sixteenth-century Japan made this a golden age. Castles rather than monasteries were the typical structures of the time, the Azuchi castle on Lake Biwa being Nobunaga's greatest architectural triumph. In July 1579, Valignano arrived in Japan as *provincial*, prudent but passionate. He found 150,000 Christians served by about sixty missionaries, of whom most were friars. He established seminaries to train more.

Japan would go through a dramatic reversal of policies under the ageing Hideyoshi in 1587, and afterwards even Portuguese missionaries were banned. But the Jesuits had left an indelible record.

\* \* \*

Saint Ignatius's great-nephew, Fray Martín Ignatius de Loyola, a Franciscan, was the third man, after El Cano (1522) and the English captain, Francis Drake (1580), to circumnavigate the globe. Fray Martín accomplished this feat in 1581–4. From Old Spain he went first to New Spain and then left Acapulco for Manila with seventeen Franciscans in March 1582. He sailed across the Pacific and on 24 May reached Manila. He made for Macao, then Malacca, stopped in India, and was back in Lisbon by August 1584. His 'Itinerario' was published in Rome in 1585 as an appendix to the *History of the Kingdom of China* by the Augustinian Juan González de Mendoza. That book was a best-seller for fifty years, with editions in all the major European languages. In both its sections the work embraces the globe.

Loyola was named Bishop of Asunción and the River Plate in 1601, but died on his way to that see, at Buenos Aires in 1606. González de Mendoza never actually went to China, but he deserves commemoration all the same. He went as a friar to New Spain in 1562, and served in Michoacan as well as Mexico/Tenochtitlan. He left for the Philippines in 1575. Later Mendoza became confessor to Antonio de

Padilla, the president of the Council of the Indies, and was chosen by King Philip to lead a delegation to China, a mission which he did not carry out. But he also became a bishop in three contrasting places: Lipari (Sicily); Chiapas, the old diocese of Las Casas in New Spain; and finally Popayán, in what is now Colombia. Such an achievement is unlikely to be matched in the twenty-first century.

By 1600 the Jesuits had established themselves in the public mind in three continents as spiritual noblemen of distinction and wisdom. Their example was an inspiration. Often accused of arrogance, they were generally high-minded men of intelligence capable of sacrifice, endurance, and patience. Their achievements in the first century after their foundation were astounding. When Claudio Aquaviva, the fifth general of the Jesuit order, died in 1615, there were 13,000 members in 550 houses. No doubt a purist would insist that many of the places which became Jesuit centres were not formally part of Philip II's empire. But informally the Jesuit order was a Spanish inspiration.

# BOOK TWO

# Spain Imperial

# 6

## Trouble in Mexico

*No one could talk of anything but fiestas and galas.*
Jesús Suárez de Peralta in Mexico, 1562

The rulers in Spanish America were given the grand titles of viceroy, governor, captain-general or, especially early in the sixteenth century, *adelantado*, a title previously used among those who had won land from the Moors in Spain. An *adelantado* was a proconsul who, by agreement with the Crown, undertook a conquest at his own cost and, in return, became the happy recipient not only of governmental authority but hereditary rights. The name in practice rarely lasted beyond one generation.

The viceroys were the effective successors to *adelantados* in Mexico/Tenochtitlan and Lima. They were the representatives of the king of Castile and they had both civil and military authority. They behaved and lived as if they were monarchs.

The viceroys in New Spain in the sixteenth century were usually noblemen: Antonio de Mendoza from 1535 to 1550; Luis de Velasco from 1550 to 1564; Gaston de Peralta, Marquis of Falces, from 1566 to 1567; Martín Enríquez de Almansa from 1568 to 1580; Lorenzo Súarez de Mendoza, Count of Coruña (not La Coruña), from 1580 to 1583; Pedro Moya de Contreras, Archbishop of Mexico City, who stood in during what was in effect an interregnum between 1584 and 1585; Álvaro Manrique de Zúñiga from 1585 to 1590; Luis de Velasco, the younger, from 1590 to 1595; and Gaspar de Zúñiga y Acevedo, Count of Monterrey, from 1595 to 1603. All except for Archbishop Moya de Contreras were aristocrats.[1]

The viceroys in Peru were similar in origin, being equally distinguished in blood. The first was Blasco Núñez, who ruled from 1544 to 1546. Antonio de Mendoza, who had been in New Spain, ruled briefly from 1551 to 1552. Mendoza was followed by Andrés Hurtado de Mendoza, Marquis of Cañete, who lasted from 1556 to 1560; Diego de Acevedo y Zúñiga, Count of Nieva, from 1560 to 1564; Licenciado Lope García de Castro ruled as governor from 1564 to 1567 and was a *letrado*, or educated university man, not an aristocrat; Francisco de Toledo, the greatest of Spanish proconsuls, ruled from 1568 to 1580; Martín Enríquez de Almansa, who had been in New Spain, ruled from 1580 to 1583 and would found the college of San Martín in Lima; Fernando Torres y Portugal, Count of Villardompardo, a village in Jaén from which he took his title (he also had royal Portuguese blood), ruled in 1586; García Hurtado de Mendoza, a second Marquis of Cañete, was viceroy from 1588 to 1595; and Luis de Velasco the younger, who had also been in New Spain, ruled from 1596 to 1604. The last named in particular did much to improve the conditions in which most Indians were living. But the majority of these men had a benign independence of mind.

In accord with Castilian procedure, all municipalities within the empire enjoyed a measure of self-government under town councils (*cabildos*) which, on strictly Castilian models, were composed of councillors (*regidores*), elected by local residents, and magistrates (*alcaldes*) named by the councillors. Before the end of the sixteenth century, the councillors were often named by the Crown, but something close to hereditary tenure was also common. There were, however, sometimes *cabildos abiertos*, or meetings of all male property-holders in the towns concerned. Though increasingly under the control of appointed royal officials, all municipal governments had executive, judicial, and even legislative authority within their districts. Protectors of the Indians were created and were sometimes effective. Fiscal authority was from the beginning directed from Seville by the great commercial entity the Casa de la Contratación through its accountants, supervisors, treasurers, and factors (*contadores*, *veedores*, *tesoreros*, and *factores*). The pattern was more or less the same everywhere in the Spanish New World.

Councillors were in theory supposed to be elected by the property-holders. The second president of the Supreme Court (*audiencia*) in

New Spain, Dr Sebastián Ramírez de Fuenleal, recounted his astonishment at the orderly procedure in indigenous electoral processes. He
even commented additionally that 'to introduce Indians into the *cabildos* of Spaniards would be to acquaint them with all the evils that are
to be found among the latter'.[2] The benign Bishop Vasco de Quiroga
had a similar view about an Indian election in the provincial city of
Otumba, the site of one of Cortés's victories, an election which he said
was accomplished with such efficiency and deliberation that one
could hardly believe it.

The characteristic institution of the early days of the Spanish empire
was the *encomienda*, which still meant the allocation of a place and
of its inhabitants to a specific conquistador. This semi-feudal system
did not work very well, and fixed quotas of tribute and labour were
soon preferred. By the end of the sixteenth century, the meaning of
*encomienda* had often been reduced to the right of the settler to
receive revenues from specific places. The Crown also assumed direct
control of many *encomiendas* after the first *encomendero* had died.

The organization of fiestas was another obligation for *criollo* officials. The modern historian Charles Gibson wisely commented that, if
the rulers had ceased to provide fiestas, they would have ceased to be
obeyed. How similar to the official behaviour in old Rome![3]

In the second half of the sixteenth century, the chief institution of
both Indian and Spanish towns was the *cabildo*, or town council. It
was a word often used in Spain, especially in Andalusia, as a substitute for *ayuntamiento*. Most *cabildos* had two magistrates (*alcaldes*)
and about ten councillors (*regidores*).

The main official revenues which were expected to pay for all the
institutions of the empire in the Americas were, first, the *quinta*, a
word meaning a fifth of the produce of the place concerned (gold,
silver, diamonds, and other precious stones); second, the *almojarifazgo* (a customs duty); third, the tributes of the *naturales* (natives);
fourth, other taxes such as the *media anata* on ecclesiastical and civil
offices, and the *cruzada*, a tax which was supposed to be in anticipation of the good life in the next world.

Apart from the collection of taxes, the economic policy of the Spanish empire was based on what came to be regarded as 'mercantilist'
theory. This meant that trade remained a monopoly of the home

country and was reserved to Seville; any economic activity which competed with that of Spain was restricted. Intercolonial trade was bureaucratically prohibited,[4] and trade with the mother country was confined to the ports of Portobelo and Nombre de Dios, the port of Cartagena in what became Colombia, and Veracruz in New Spain.

A new functionary was named in December 1556 for Cadiz, to register the ships sailing from there to the Indies, because by then the sandbar at Sanlúcar was giving such trouble to ocean-bound boats from Seville that the usual route had to be rearranged. This new official was Juan de Ávila, who was at first paid 112,000 *maravedís* (see Glossary) annually, a sum which, after 1557, was increased to 130,000. From then on, all outgoing boats would be loaded at Cadiz and would leave from there. Registration of passengers continued to be a matter for Seville, and all returning ships had to go direct to Seville, even if they had started their journeys at Cadiz.[5] (The return journey up the Guadalquivir was easier via the sandbank than the outward one.)

Despite the restrictions, there were many positive elements to be considered in establishing cultural connections to the New World. Thus learning was very definitely not overlooked. Universities were founded both in Mexico/Tenochtitlan and Lima (that of San Marcos) in 1551, and in Santo Domingo (that of Saint Thomas Aquinas) seven years later. All these institutions echoed procedures in Salamanca University. The first colonial printing press was established in Mexico/Tenochtitlan by Viceroy Mendoza in 1535. Its director was Juan Cromberger, a son of the famous Jacob Cromberger of Seville. Juan's success can be gauged from what he left behind when he died in 1540. His stock included 446 copies of *Amadís de Gaula*, over 1,000 copies of the *Espejo de Caballerías* (a translation in prose of Mateo María Boyardo's romantic epic, *Orlando Innamorato*), and 325 copies of the tragicomedy *Celestina* by Fernando de Rojas – a larger collection of printed books than his father Jacob had left in Seville when he died in 1529.[6]

Mexican painter-scribes found rewarding employment in the Spanish empire painting Christian murals, and codices, which could be rendered as accounts of tribute as much as of legal evidence in courts. Many Mexican religious objects were readapted for Christian purposes. Thus one large basin of curved basalt stone was reused as a baptismal font in the capital's cathedral, even though the carvings on the outside showed that it had once been used for human sacrifice.[7] Several indigenous painters produced wonderful compositions of Christian imagery based on European prints. Manuscript painting played a part not only as religious propaganda but as evidence in support of claims of inheritance and property, status, and labour. These designs could have other purposes too: the famous though now lost *lienzo de Tlaxcala* – 'the canvas of Tlaxcala' – of about 1550 made a political rather than a historical point by showing the adhesion of Xicotencatl, the prince of Tlaxcala, to the Spaniards in 1520, conveniently forgetting that that leader had fought fiercely against Spain.[8]

In both New Spain (the city of Mexico) and Peru (Lima) there were extraordinary developments in the 1560s. Consider New Spain first. On the one hand, an understanding was reached between Spanish conquistadors and conquered Indians. By controlling the old society from the top, and using the local elders, the *tlatoques* as they were once known, Cortés and his comrades and successors easily managed to control thousands of Indian workers. The saintly Franciscan monk Motolinía testified thus in his denunciations of what he argued to be the wild exaggerations of Las Casas.[9] The majority of Indians were by then directly subject to the Crown. The effect of the conquest had been to weaken the stronger tribal units, such as the Mexica, and strengthen the less assertive ones, such as the Chalca.[10] In 1564 the Visitor, Jerónimo de Valderrama, a citizen of Talavera de la Reina and a graduate of Salamanca University, was found reporting to the king that the friars seemed to be hoping that soon there would be no Indians paying tribute. (They were being listed for substantial payments in the heartlands.) In 1561 the town council of Mexico/Tenochtitlan had recommended that six of the twenty-four councillors in the city should henceforth be Indians. The council should undertake 'to fasten the union and conformity of the two races'. A modern historian, Felix Hinz, is confident enough to assert that the old Indian cultures had 'in no way been completely, but rather only partially suppressed and that a lot of [indigenous] cultures managed to outlive the conquest'.[11]

Many reforms insisted on by the conquerors had been inevitable – the abolition of human sacrifice, for example, the end of the Mexican priesthood, the insistence on monogamy, an end to the old Mexican schools and the old system of tribute. Other reforms were less obvious, such as the need to humanize the condition of indigenous slaves in line with ordinary workers and, indeed, to end native slave-holding altogether. Quite soon, too, the Spanish Crown permitted Indian *principales* – ex-noblemen of the old regime, members of the old royal families, even mere elders – to carry swords and even firearms, and to ride horses with saddles and bridles. Some indigenous title-holders retained their ancient places and had indigenous successors.[12]

Great supply routes were by then linking the city of Mexico with Caribbean ports in an ever easier and more effective manner. As early as 1540 one hundred mule trains might be on their way at any one time between Veracruz and Mexico/Tenochtitlan, whilst a little later Tacuba just outside the capital to the west had a regular supply of 3,000 horses. By 1600, 3,000 mules were entering Mexico daily.

Privately owned Spanish *haciendas* (farms), free of any kind of feudal bond or obligation to service, were by 1560 outranking *encomiendas*. Three of Montezuma's children moved quite easily into the Spanish colonial nobility. A few years later, the indigenous councillors of the town of Huejotzingo, on the eastern slope of the volcano Iztaccíhuatl (the 'White Lady'), expressed their gratitude at one aspect of Spanish policy: 'Your Majesty should know that the good that has been done to us all, in soul and body, by congregating us [in a new town] is beyond description. In fact, since our congregation, if anyone falls sick, he can confess and receive the sacraments and his neighbour can help him and, if he wants it, he can be buried in church . . . and we can come and hear the sermon and the mass and live together like men . . . All these things were impossible while we lived scattered among the mountains.'[13] Such a statement is an unusual testimony to the benign effects of empire, even if only a minority of *naturales* would have endorsed it. This town had once been an *encomienda* of the conquistador from old Castile, Diego de Ordaz (a follower of Cortés).

An institution which helped the idea of racial collaboration was the *cofradía*, the secular brotherhood of celebrants in honour of a specific deity or Virgin. This offered both spiritual serenity and a sense of collective identity, and originated in Old Spain. In Seville alone, there were a dozen such bodies dating back to the fifteenth century. (Some still survive in the twenty-first century.) Several of these were refounded in dependent form in sixteenth-century Mexico, and even more would be inspired in the seventeenth century. From the 1520s onwards, the imaginative Franciscan missionary Pedro de Gante tried to foster the fusion of Christian ceremonials with indigenous culture. These celebrations might mark the cult of a local patron saint or a relic of one of the early missionaries. Often these events would constitute a 'syncretic compromise' between Christianity and paganism.[14]

New Spain remained after the conquest much as it had been before, namely what Jacques Soustelle, in his great book *Daily Life in Ancient Mexico*, called 'a mosaic of towns'.[15] The *cabeza*, or head town, was the seat of the old nobility, the centre for the collection of tribute as well as the concentration point for the recruitment of labour. But after the first generation following the conquest, the old Indian nobility lost their authority, and both the arrangements for tribute and its policy of labour recruitment changed. The privately owned *hacienda* soon became the supreme community of New Spain.[16] This was so even though all *corregidores* (co-councillors) had a Christian mission, including obligations to deal justly with Indians and their possessions, for example by ensuring that Spaniards avoided damage to farmlands when grazing their herds of cattle there. Yet by the 1560s, of thirty-six *encomiendas* in the valley of Mexico alone, eleven had returned to royal control, representing three-quarters of the income of those undertakings at that time.[17] They were seized when the first grantee died, which meant that new allocations could then be made.

The second viceroy, Luis de Velasco, like the first, Antonio de Mendoza, was a great gentleman. He had been born about 1511 in the historic town of Carrión de los Condes near Palencia in Castile. We have already noted his capacity as a host, a horseman, and a racing man.[18] Thanks to his own assiduity, he was paid a quarter more than Mendoza had been.[19] Velasco also presided over a grand ecological change. The Spaniards had, after all, conquered a new world to which they instinctively offered their old methods of farming as well as their much-loved livestock. 'Pastoralism' and the chickens, pigs, donkeys, goats, sheep, cattle, mules, and horses which came with it, were as much 'conquistadors' as the men who brought them. The

Spaniards also had their special preoccupations. For example, the first generation of conquistadors cut quantities of timber both to provide building material and fuel. Spanish ploughs cut much more deeply than the digging sticks of the natives, and cattle and sheep cropped the land bare (the consequences included the erosion of land). By the end of the sixteenth century, herds of sheep of 12,000 or 15,000 were recorded, for, given the right conditions, a herd could double in size in the course of a year.[20]

Some changes were remarkable. Thus the cultivation of the maguey cactus had intensified because of the reliance of the new generation of Indians on pulque, which was used to alleviate the anxieties caused by epidemics and the collapse of the old society. By 1570, the main maize farms were in Spanish hands. All the same, the conquerors continued to use old pre-conquest techniques such as arranging their plants on little hillocks in regular rows, providing five to six kernels per hillock, at 4,000 kernels per acre.

By then the golden valley of Mexico was dominated by the huge *encomienda* in Xilotepec which at first had been assigned to Juan Jaramillo, originally an extremeño from Salvatierra de Barcarrota, near Jerez de los Caballeros. Jaramillo had once been married to Marina, Cortés's famous interpreter – hence the size of his *encomienda*. The region was threatened in the 1560s by Chichimec raids against the docile Otomí Indians (whose apogee seems to have been in the twelfth century) as well as the Spanish settlers.[21] These raids occurred when the plough was generally replacing the indigenous people's digging stick, when pastoralism was everywhere on the increase, and when one crop – usually maize or wheat – was being cultivated at the expense of the diversity of other crops used in the past.

Despite these changing practices in agriculture, there does not seem to have been any comparable revolution in eating among the indigenous people. The Indians continued to have their primarily maize diet flavoured with salt from Lake Texcoco, as well as aquatic products such as frogs, shrimps, salamanders, larvae of dragonflies, watersnakes, grubs, duck, and geese, and also other birds, coyotes, dogs, deer, armadillos, and weasels. Maize continued to be eaten in tortillas made fresh for each meal for, unlike bread, these became dry and inedible after a few hours.[22] Dogs were eaten at fiestas. There were many drinks, most of them alcoholic, such as mezcal, *chinguito*, *sangre de conejo* (rabbit blood), and, above all chocolate, using beans from Colima or Socunusco.

By the end of the sixteenth century, the use of all pastureland, wasteland, woodland, and water in New Spain was open to all. Indeed it could be said that animals grazed wherever grass grew. There were no indigenous grazing animals, so that there were no old rules governing the use of grass – a contrast with Spain where the conduct of farmers was affected by many ancient and complicated laws and customs. Very frequently in Old Spain, cattle farmers were also agriculturalists – that is, ploughmen as well as cattlemen. In the New World the 'pastoralists' were the white Europeans, whilst the agriculturalists were the conquered *naturales*. The cattle masters were always the Europeans, but those whose rights were neglected were the indigenous agriculturalists. In order to maintain their control over pastureland, Spaniards often used the force of African slaves, who could be strong, insensitive, and ruthless, and were often the effective sub-agents of Spanish landlords. Indeed most shepherds in the early days of Spanish rule were black, slave or no.

Transport across the lakes for people and products would, as before 1520, be in large canoes, cut and hollowed out from single tree trunks. These canoes had powerful shallow drafts and square bows, and they could be made in a week or so by a good carpenter. Indians retained their skills in these respects, whilst Spaniards mostly used animals or wheeled vehicles for transport.

Naturally there were rivalries between *encomenderos* and pastoralists, even though both were Spanish in origin. The former would treat their *encomiendas* as great estates in embryo, on which they decided the crops they wanted to be grown. They would use their allocated Indians for a variety of entrepreneurial activities.

In the Valley of Mexico in the late sixteenth century there were probably twenty-six farms each planting fewer than twenty *fanegas* of wheat,[23] which could produce 5 per cent of the total grain of the region. There were about eighty moderately sized farms which produced about 70 per cent of the grain, planting an average of twenty to ninety *fanegas* each; and about seven large farms responsible for 22 per cent of the grain. Most wheat farms were, by about 1570, about 150 acres in size, though the largest was 600 acres.[24] The land planted with wheat perhaps increased fourfold between 1560 and 1600, and grain perhaps increased production by twelvefold.[25]

Viceroy Velasco did much to clear Indian villages of animals, in order to prevent land being used for grazing by irresponsible pastoralists. Even the customary right to communal pasture was banned within a league (three miles) of these villages, and grazing on stubble was officially limited to two months (the 'aftermath'). But by 1600, because of the decline of the indigenous population, the pastoralists were presiding over what has been described by a great Californian historian, Lesley Byrd Simpson, as an 'ecological revolution of vast proportions'.[26] This revolution, if such it was, was enacted by the coming of *latifundia* (large properties), sometimes developed by *encomenderos* or sometimes being the work of religious orders such as the Jesuits. The Jesuit *hacienda*, Santa Lucia, in the valley of Mezquital, was a great achievement.[27]

In principle, while allocating the carefully delineated *encomiendas*, the Spanish administration did what they could to respect the legitimacy of many private Indian properties. Montezuma, for example, had an exceptionally large private patrimonial inheritance, gained via his father. But the disruption caused by the conquest and Spanish greed interrupted most arrangements, Cortés handing out direct grants of private land as well as *encomiendas*. There were probably about 850 private estates in Spanish hands in the Valley of Mexico in the first hundred years after the conquest.[28]

Private native holdings were accepted as such if they could be shown to have been inherited from private persons in the old days before the conquest. But depopulation as a result of deaths on a large scale happened so fast that much land was left unoccupied for months.

The Spaniards were concerned to destroy everything that remained of importance in old Mexico. Thus they prohibited the old ball games of the Mexica, because they supposed that these were governed by magic or witchcraft. Also banned was the ceremony of the *volador*, in which an Indian would spin around on a vertiginous cord attached to a high pole, gradually descending until he reached the ground. But both activities survived all the same. What indigenous people wore had changed also. Textiles were now usually made from maguey fibre, cotton or even wool. Maguey cloth (henequen or sisal) was generally displaced by cotton, the making of which was largely but not exclusively a woman's occupation.

All in all, both the Spaniards of the New World, the future *criollos*, and the native Indians made astonishing adjustments to meet each others' interests. Setting aside understandable prejudices for a moment, such a capacity for change reflects much credit to both peoples and their cultures.

# 7

# The Sons of the Conquistadors
# Ask Too Much

*Madrastra nos ha sido rigurosa*
*Y dulce madre pía a los extraños*
*[To us she has been a stepmother harsh*
*And a gentle mother to foreigners]*

Francisco de Terrazas, New Spain

The flamboyant pretensions and ambitions of the sons of the conquistadors were to inspire real difficulties in New Spain in the 1560s. These began with the return from Old Spain of Hernando Cortés's eldest son, Martín, the second Marquis of the Valley (del Valle). Martín was accompanied by his legitimatized brothers, Luis and Martín II, sons of the great conquistador by Antonia de Hermosilla and the interpreter Marina respectively.

The second marquis, born in 1533, was the son of Cortés by his second wife, Juana Ramírez de Arellano, niece of the rich and powerful Duke of Béjar, and he had grown up at the court of the emperor in Spain. Martín Cortés had accompanied King Philip to Flanders in 1548, and even formed part of the committee of aristocrats which went to London in 1554 to celebrate Philip's marriage to Queen Mary Tudor. Martín had been in the tragic royal expedition to Algiers with his father in 1541, and at the successful battle of Saint Quentin with Count Egmont in 1558. All his father's possessions, including his 23,000 vassals, had been confirmed to the second marquis, so he was very rich. King Philip arranged for his return to New Spain in 1563.[1]

The estates of Martín Cortés in New Spain then totalled 50,000 square miles of land, which produced 80,000 pesos every year. This

1. The Treaty of Cateau-Cambrésis and the Embrace of Henry II (1519–59) of France and Philip II (1527–98) of Spain, 2–3 April 1559.

2. The tournament in the Rue Saint-Antoine, Paris, on 30 June 1559 between King Henry of France and the protestant knight Gabriel de Montgomery. Henry was fatally wounded, dying ten days later.

3. King Philip II in his mid thirties, painted in 1565 by
Sofonisba Anguissola, an Italian painter from Cremona,
employed by the Spanish court from 1560 onwards.

**4–7.** Philip was a good European: his wives were (*top to bottom, left to right*)
Portuguese (María Manuela, here painted by Anthonis Mor *c.* 1550), English (Mary
Tudor, painted by Anthonis Mor in 1554), French (Elisabeth de Valois, painted by
Alonso Sánchez Coello in 1570) and Austrian (Anne of Austria, painted
by Sofonisba Anguissola in 1573).

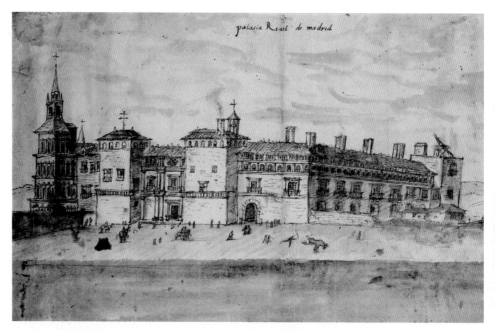

8. The old Royal castle (or Alcázar) in Madrid, built by the Moors and often enlarged before it was burned down in 1734. It is here painted in 1569 by Anton van den Wyngaerde.

9. The Escorial, half palace, half monastery, became after 1573 the centre for Philip II's administration of his empire. It is depicted here, still under construction, by Juan de Herrera c. 1575.

10. Don John of Austria, the illegitimate half brother of Philip II and victor of the battle of Lepanto in 1571.

11. The Duke of Alba, Philip's general and military confidant, painted by Titian.

12. Francisco de Toledo, the most
powerful Peruvian viceroy,
in the 1570s.

13. Gaspar de Zúñiga y Acevedo,
count of Monterrey, viceroy in
New Spain 1595–1603.

14. Don Martín Enríquez de Almansa,
an intelligent moderate of royal
blood who served as viceroy in both
New Spain (1568–80) and
Peru (1581–3).

15. Luis de Velasco II, son of a
viceroy and a viceroy himself of both
New Spain (1589–95 and 1607–11) and
Peru (1596–1604), and President of
the Council of the Indies (1611).

**16.** Viceroy Luis de Velasco I and Archbishop Montúfar,
the supreme authorities in the city of Mexico, caught informally
by an anonymous artist at the laying of the first stone of
the first cathedral in 1562.

**17.** The existing cathedral of Mexico, begun in 1573 and inaugurated in 1667.

18. Chichen Itza in Yucatan. Temples and pyramids played an essential part in the religion of the ancient Maya and Mexica.

19. The Franciscan Monastery in Quito. Built by a Franciscan architect from Brabant, Jodoco Ricke de Marseler, it was the first Christian church in South America. It was begun in 1535 and completed seventy years later.

represented a large fortune and made him perhaps the richest private person in the world. The property included the towns of Tacubaya and Coyoacán in the valley of Mexico, and land in Oaxaca.

In New Spain, the second marquis had conducted himself in a manner which was both arrogant and ostentatious. He wanted to have himself recognized permanently as the second man after the viceroy in the new kingdom. He commissioned a large silver seal, with his coat of arms and a crown on it, which declared MARTINUS CORTESUS PRIMUS HUIUS NOMINIS DUX MARCHIO SECUNDUS.[2] On the first occasion that this seal was used to pay the *quinto real*, the official accountant Ortuño de Ibarra, a new grandee of New Spain, said that it was wrong to use a seal similar to the royal one. The viceroy confiscated it and had it sent to Spain.

In August 1563, Martín Cortés refused to meet the Visitor, Jerónimo de Valderrama, in company with the viceroy, Luis de Velasco. Instead the second marquis arranged his own private welcome, which was carried through with a pomp that infuriated Velasco, as it was intended to. The distinction between the power of the viceroy and the Visitor was unclear anyway, and Martín Cortés only exacerbated the problem. At the beginning of his visit, Valderrama even stayed with the second marquis. There were bitter arguments over these and other matters of protocol, which (as usual in human affairs) caused widespread anger. The descendants of old enemies of Hernando Cortés, such as the offspring of friends of Governor Velázquez, were all hostile to the new marquis. The enmities of the 1520s lived on.

The most serious difficulties in New Spain were, however, still those relating to the treatment of *encomenderos* and of *encomiendas*. Isabel Montezuma, daughter of the former emperor and *encomendera* of Tacuba, gave money away so freely that her Augustinian beneficiaries asked her to desist. The New Laws of 1542 – designed to protect the indigenous population by limiting the power of *encomenderos* – had not been fully introduced nor even understood, but many settlers had begun to think that the Crown was planning to abandon the entire structure of *encomiendas*. The possession of Indians in *encomiendas* – by the viceroy, officials, the clergy, and monasteries – was suddenly prohibited. It was also announced that no new *encomiendas* were to be granted. On the death of an *encomendero*, his *encomienda* would be forfeited to the Crown rather than be passed on to his heirs. Indians in an *encomienda* which had lapsed would be subject to a *corregidor*, that all-purpose official whom the Crown found so useful. An Indian still working in an *encomienda* would henceforth be obliged to pay his tribute in cash or kind to the *encomendero*. There were to be no more personal services allowable in lieu of tribute.

Despite the legacy of goodwill left by the first viceroy to New Spain, Antonio de Mendoza, there was resentment among the most powerful settlers in the 1560s and this provided a groundswell of discontent. The death of so many Indians because of diseases such as typhus (*matlazhuatl*) was an additional reason for distress. The decline in population meant that the question of the supply of labour became an urgent matter.[3]

Another anxiety for settlers was that the Indians discovered fairly quickly that redress in all kinds of disputes could be obtained by them through litigation. Velasco, the viceroy from 1550 to 1564, was partly the cause of this, because he sent out inspectors to tour the country districts and define abuses. This was quite an innovation so far as the indigenous people were concerned and perhaps did something to compensate for the terrifying spread of new diseases, for smallpox, typhus, measles, and even influenza were causing an unprecedented collapse in population numbers. The two worst epidemics were in 1545–8 and in 1576–81 (in which half the population seem to have died), but lesser or more local attacks often caused much damage in smaller areas.[4]

The settlers had recourse to many illegalities in order to cope with the problems caused by epidemics and disease. One recourse was the employment of Indians in small workshops (*obrajes*) for the manufacture of woollen cloth, workplaces which were a natural corollary to the new sheep farms. These workshops were originally the workplaces of criminals or slaves, but then free Indians began to be employed in them on contracts. Labourers were being hired for wages to work in wheatfields as early as the 1530s,[5] though there were many *obrajes* whose owners locked their essentially private workers into buildings patrolled by Indian guards that became little more than prisons. In Texcoco there were eight *obrajes*, in Xochimilco and Atzcapotzalco four and two respectively. By 1595, the new city of Puebla de los

Angeles had forty *obrajes*, averaging forty-five workers each (though the biggest one had 120).[6] In 1573 these new workshops were producing 50,000 pieces of wool cloth a year.[7]

Another source of social difficulty was that the sons of the first conquistadors often resented the Franciscans' good treatment of Indians. What were they, rough men of the world, to make of Antonio Valeriano, the cultivated Indian governor of the city of Mexico for twenty years, who knew Latin so well and could translate Virgil? He was one of the best scholars in New Spain and married to a niece of Montezuma. Or, what would they think of Fray Bautista de Contreras, who, like Valeriano, was a product of the Franciscan school of Santa Cruz de Tlatelolco, and who translated Thomas à Kempis into Nahuatl? Furthermore, for Christmas in 1553 an Indian from Azcapotzalco, Francisco Plácido, had composed a hymn in which angels celebrating the birth of Jesus appeared as Quecholli, birds of Tlaloc. The three kings from the East were made to greet Jesus as 'a jewel, a quetzal', and King Herod's child victims were compared to the pieces of a broken necklace of jade.

This was dangerous territory. A clerk in the 1550s named Jerónimo López repeatedly predicted that a knowledge of Latin and 'the sciences' by indigenous people would lead to heresy and sedition: 'Hence, of what use was it for the Indians to learn Latin except to see if the Spanish priests were talking nonsense or not?'[8] He was not alone in speaking thus. A Church council in 1555 ordered that all hymns and songs by Indian authors should be censored.

The decline in population, the shortage of labour, and threatening signs of changes in Indian culture all therefore contributed to the difficulties of the sons of the conquistadors in the 1560s. The eventual outburst came in a typically temperamental and flamboyant fashion. There were many fiestas at the house of the second Marquis del Valle in the 1560s. Jesús Suárez de Peralta, the marquis's first cousin (the son of the brother of Cortes's first wife), who was an excellent writer, said, 'No one could talk of any thing but fiestas and galas, and there were more of them than ever before.'[9] Vast sums were gambled away. On one occasion, Martín Cortés introduced a toast with a challenge as to who could drink the most, and a penalty that anyone who refused to accept a challenge to drink his opponent under the table risked having his cap cut to pieces. There were masquerades in which a hundred drunken men in fancy dress would ride out after dinner looking for Indian girls. The second marquis seemed to have an ungovernable fondness for pleasure.

He had also embarked on a lawsuit against a rich cousin, Hernando Gutiérrez de Altamirano, who had unwisely given a great dinner for him and who, Martín thought, owed him money. (Gutiérrez de Altamirano was a cousin of Hernando Cortés, being a son of the judge of the *residencia* of Diego Velázquez, the first governor of Cuba.)[10] Martín Cortés's return from Spain in 1563 gave the *criollos* in New Spain (as the Spanish population now thought of themselves) a confidence hitherto unknown.[11] By birth, young Martín seemed superior to the Spanish officials with whom he came into contact. There was wild talk of making him king.[12] The viceroy of New Spain remained Luis de Velasco, a model of good manners, tolerant, charitable, humane, very fond of horses, but disinclined to allow Indians to work more than their regular commitments.

On 31 July 1564, Velasco died of a heart attack; his son later alleged that that death had been hastened by the bad behaviour of the Marquis del Valle.[13]

Fernando Benítez described Velasco's funeral as being almost as grand as that of the Emperor Charles V. The procession moved from the house of Ortuño de Ibarra, the official accountant, to the church of San Francisco. It was attended by six bishops, the judges of the Supreme Court, with the Visitor, Jerónimo de Valderrama, leading the mourners, of whom thirty poor Indians and thirty poor Spaniards were in the lead. (Legazpi, the future conqueror of the Philippines, also attended, marching at the head of 600 soldiers who had already been assigned him for the conquest in the East.)[14] Velasco was the first viceroy to die in office in New Spain. The elaborate ceremony of his official funeral marked the first of many such baroque occasions which came to characterize the colonial style in old Mexico.

The death of Velasco in 1564 left behind a lacuna in New Spain. The only supreme authorities left were the judges Pedro de Villalobos and Jerónimo de Orozco, along with Francisco Ceinos, the elderly dean of the Supreme Court. No new viceroy was named for months, though Velasco's son Luis was anticipating a call to office: it would come eventually, but not for many years.

During this long interregnum, there was much dissatisfaction among the colonists of New Spain. For example, the *cabildo* of the city of Mexico had been infuriated by the recent royal decision in Spain that *encomiendas* should not extend beyond the life of the current holder. Some prominent counsellors even asked the Crown not to name any more viceroys. If that high office were to survive, they thought, it should be vested in a son of the conquistadors. This dangerous proposal was formally put in a resolution of the town council in the city of Mexico on 21 August 1564.[15] The council members then suggested that the second marquis, Martín Cortés, should be appointed captain-general. Two other conquistadors' sons, Alonso de Ávila and Gil González de Ávila, nephews of an old companion of Hernando Cortés (an earlier Alonso de Ávila who had been with Montejo in Yucatan), threatened to cause a storm, but received no real support from Martín Cortés.[16]

The discontent grew. The Supreme Court decided to detain Martín Cortés pre-emptively and hold him and the Ávila brothers in the common jail. They also arrested two other sons of Cortés and some other 'activists', including Baltasar de Sotelo, brother of Diego Arias Sotelo, who had married Leonor, a granddaughter of Montezuma.[17]

The main families implicated in this alleged conspiracy were the Pacheco Bocanegra, the González Dávila, the Villanueva Cervantes, and the Suárez de Peralta.[18] All these claimed a right to rule the viceroyalty.

In April 1565 matters in the city of Mexico went from bad to worse. There was outright rioting in Martín Aberraza Street in the capital, between Bernardo de Bocanegra and his brother Hernando de Córdoba on the one hand, and Juan Suárez de Peralta, Alonso de Peralta (*encomendero* of Tezuatlán), Alonso de Cervantes, and a certain Nájera on the other. Alonso de Cervantes was wounded before the guard arrived. Martín Cortés took the side of the Bocanegra brothers, being apparently romantically attached to Marina Vázquez de Coronado, wife of Núño de Chávez Bocanegra, who was the *encomendero* of Acámbaro in Celaya near Guanajuato.[19] By this time, Martín Cortés 'had come to expect anyone whom he greeted in the street would automatically join his suite', encouraged if necessary by the heavy-handed pressure of his bastard brother, Luis Cortés, who acted as his steward. But Martín's burgeoning fraternity was refused by Juan de Sámano, the chief magistrate (*alguacil mayor*), and by Juan de Valdivieso, a councillor who was one of the earliest graduates of the university of Mexico, whose sister Guiomar Vázquez de Escobar had married Luis Cortés. Further brawls followed. Two prominent *criollos*, Luis Cifuentes and Hernando Pacheco, were held prisoner in the town hall, while Valdivieso was held in the public prison.

In the summer of 1565 the enraged *encomenderos*, headed by Licenciado Espinosa de Ayala, repaired to the house of Alonso de Ávila, the aforementioned son of the famous conquistador of the same name, with what sounded like a proposal for a rebellion against the viceroyalty – in effect the Crown – which they saw as determined to disinherit their grandsons. This group included Pedro de Aguilar as well as the brothers Baltasar and Pedro de Quesada, who were *encomenderos* of the valuable Xilotepec property, and Cristóbal de Oñate (nephew of that Oñate who had begun the new life of Guadalajara and was *encomendero* of Cadereyta). These were the most powerful and wealthy men in the region.

Similar meetings were held in the autumn of 1565, above all in order to maintain the *encomiendas*. Alonso de Ávila and Martín Cortés declared fatuously that 'the King wanted to take the bread from their mouths'. They talked of killing the judges of the Supreme Court and other officials, not to speak of Luis and Francisco de Velasco, the son and the brother of the late viceroy, and of rousing the country to rebellion. Alonso de Ávila led a masquerade to the Zócalo, the great square in the centre of the capital in front of the cathedral, dressed as Montezuma and wearing a crown, and he and his friends paraded ostentatiously in front of Martín Cortés's palace. A ball was held at De Ávila's house, at which all the china sported a device with an 'R' placed under a crown, suggesting 'Thou Must Reign' to the second marquis. Then Alonso held a meeting at which he sketched out a plot to some of his close friends and apparent co-conspirators.

One plan seems to have been to kill the judges and the Visitor, while another group of assassins would murder other royal officials. A third group of plotters would burn all the papers in the official archive. Martín Cortés would then address the people in the Zócalo. Luis Cortés would take over the port of San Juan de Ulloa, while the second marquis's bastard brother, also called Martín, would seize the rich city of Zacatecas, including all its silver. Francisco de Reinoso, another conquistador's son, would establish himself at Puebla. Then Martín Cortés, the second marquis himself, would indeed be proclaimed king. New dukes and marquises would be created, and all the land reapportioned. Alonso Chico de Molina would journey to the Pope and present him with a substantial gift of treasure, securing as a result papal recognition of what would be in effect a *coup d'état*. Licenciado Espinosa de Ayala would bring back from Seville Martín Cortés's son and heir. But that courtier, now vacillating between vaunting ambition and craven fear, suddenly became less enthusiastic. Alonso de Ávila, meanwhile, wanted to pin down all the plotters by getting them to sign a document backing rebellion.[20]

The plot of the *encomenderos* was then interrupted by an illness which affected Alonso de Ávila. As a result a simmering, speculative calm reigned for a time, though everyone continued to talk about what was really being planned by the Council of the Indies for New Spain.[21] In the spring of 1566 another Spanish aristocrat, Gastón de Peralta, Marquis of Falces, an experienced administrator originally from Navarre, was named the next viceroy of New Spain. His instructions from the Council ran to fifty-seven turgid paragraphs which repeated the orders given to his predecessor.[22]

On 5 April 1566 the 'Cortés conspiracy', as it came to be known, suddenly collapsed when Baltasar de Aguilar treacherously revealed details of the plot to Luis de Velasco *hijo* (the younger). Alonso and Agustín de Villanueva testified as witnesses, and Pedro de Aguilar told all he knew to the Dominicans, who informed the Supreme Court. The Quesada brothers and Licenciado Espinosa de Ayala also betrayed their friends. The idea of rebellion was kept alive by the circulation of fresh rumours about the Crown's hope of securing an end to the existence of *encomiendas*. Throughout June, however, the Cortés family and their friends were preoccupied with celebrations for the christening of the second marquis's newborn twins. Fireworks, the music of violins, flageolets, and lutes, merged with mock battles and artillery salutes in a ceremony at the cathedral in Mexico/Tenochtitlan, which included large deliveries of hogsheads of wine.

On 16 July 1566, Martín Cortés was accused by the judges of the Supreme Court of leading a conspiracy to divide New Spain from the Spanish Crown. Cortés was astonished: he was supported by many discontented *encomenderos*, headed by Alonso and Gil González de Ávila. It had never occurred to him that he might be officially challenged. Some kind of conspiracy certainly existed, but it is unclear just how far Martín Cortés and his brothers Luis and Martín *el bastardo*, who were also arrested, were actively embroiled.

The Ávilas, who were probably the deepest embroiled, were charged, tried, and swiftly executed in the Zócalo, their elegant heads being exposed for several months on spikes.[23] Luis Cortés was also charged and condemned to death, but the sentence was not carried out. Several high-ranking *criollos* were placed under house arrest.[24] Anxiety and alarm reigned everywhere, and the richest *encomienda* in the valley of Mexico, that of Cuauhitlan, which had belonged to the Ávilas, was taken over by the Crown.[25]

The charges against the *criollos* awaited the arrival of the new viceroy, Gastón de Peralta, and a new prosecutor, Céspedes de Cárdenas, who came from Santo Domingo. Peralta was, however, benign, tolerant, relaxed, and intelligent. He arrived at Veracruz with his wife, Leonor, in July 1566 – the first viceroy to New Spain to be accompanied by his wife – and soon started for the city of Mexico, reading innumerable contradictory statements about the state of New Spain as he travelled.[26] He took office formally in the capital in December. Once there, he suspended all trials against the conspirators and read all the trial papers as well as personally examining several of the accused. He was tolerant towards Martín Cortés, the second marquis, and allowed him out of prison, even inviting him to attend a tournament in his company. That angered the judges, who had become accustomed to wielding power themselves, and so they invented compromising stories about Peralta's connections with alleged French conspiracies – always a convenient diversion in the Spanish world. They also managed to ensure that Peralta's forgiving report was destroyed on the way to Veracruz, whereas their own much harsher despatch, with accusations against the viceroy, quickly reached the Council of the Indies.

In June 1567, Philip II named a commission of deputy judges[27] to investigate the whole affair of the alleged plot. Viceroy Peralta was ordered to return to Spain, leaving Judge Alonso de Muñoz in his place without the title of viceroy (one judge, Gaspard de Jarava, had died at sea). Peralta prepared a valuable memorial in March 1567 about the problems which he had encountered during his investigations.[28]

Muñoz was the reverse of Peralta. He was intolerant and enthusiastically commissioned the construction of new prisons; 'Muñoz's dungeons' were being built even before the judge reached New Spain. Sixty-four people were then charged with conspiracy, eight of whom were condemned to death (seven were actually executed), the rest being subjected to fines or exile from the capital. Six *criollos* were condemned to serve on the galleys in Oran in North Africa. The brothers Baltasar and Pedro de Quesada, Cristóbal de Oñate the younger, and Baltasar de Sotelo were all hanged, drawn, and quartered, without any guilt having been proved against them. Alonso de Ávila's servants were also so executed. The Bocanegra brothers (Bernardino, Fernando, Francisco) were racked and submitted to a form of water torture. None confessed, for they had nothing to confess. Bernardino de Bocanegra was reprieved because of the appeals of his mother and wife, but he was nevertheless condemned to serve twenty years on the king's galleys and forfeit his properties. Other *criollos* received lesser punishments. Martín Cortés, the second marquis, and his brother Luis were sent back to Spain with orders, on their honour, to report to the Council of the Indies as political prisoners.[29] Luis was condemned to serve ten years in Oran. Marquis Martín was released but required to stay in Spain. His bastard brother Martín was apparently tortured but was then released in New Spain since, as the viceroy admitted, 'he was guilty of little'.[30]

There were so many complaints about the judges that King Philip concluded Alonso de Muñoz had lost his reason. He also lost his position. He was replaced by licenciados Dr Luis de Villanueva and Dr Vasco de Puga, two junior judges who had earlier been dismissed by the Visitor, Valderrama. They returned once again to New Spain. In the monastery of Santo Domingo in the city of Mexico, Villanueva told Muñoz that he and his colleague Luis Carrillo had been relieved. They were to set off for Spain immediately – within three hours of the notice being served. Instead, Muñoz and Carrillo fled to Veracruz – where they embarked on the ship carrying Viceroy Peralta and several others home to Spain. Carrillo died of apoplexy after a few days at sea.[31] Peralta was well received by King Philip. Muñoz went into retirement and died soon thereafter.

In this affair, rumour was piled on rumour, so that it is now hard to know exactly what occurred. A plot of some kind was surely conceived but it conspicuously failed to get far in practice. It was clearly a struggle for power between the Spanish Crown and the local aristocrats. The conflict had initially been generated by the distrust caused by the New Laws of 1542. It was tragic that New Spain, a glittering jewel in the Spanish imperial crown, should have experienced such a disturbance as this 'rebellion', for relations between the two main races in the country had improved significantly.[32] The absorption of so many old aristocrats of the Mexica into the upper sections of society was also remarkable. Many now saw themselves as conquistadors, not as a conquered people, and they lived as such, with all the equipment of horses, swords, and even armour.

# 8

# New Spain in Peace

*For the majority of Mexicans, independence was a restoration,*
*that is an event which closed the interregnum begun by the*
*Conquest. Conversely the attitude towards the 'viceroyalty' of*
*New Spain was barely a parenthesis.*

Octavio Paz, *El peregrino en su patria*, 157

In May 1568, Martín Enríquez de Almansa was named the fourth
viceroy of New Spain,[1] and his rule there was inaugurated on
11 November. He remained in office for many years, until 1580, and
gave the new kingdom – for such it really was – a stability which it
had lacked under his amiable predecessor, Gaston de Peralta. Enríquez
was, however, inflexible. He explained that his philosophy of government was 'to avoid all innovations and when occasionally they may
be necessary, to proceed very cautiously'.[2] To King Philip and his
court Enríquez seemed the perfect bureaucrat. He was interested in
history and in the safekeeping of documents, which he rightly recognized as one of the best guarantees of good government. He conducted
himself as a responsible official during all his time in New Spain and
afterwards in Peru, where he was also the viceroy. Enríquez certainly
did not tolerate fractious dissension between the *criollos* and the *pen-*
*insulares*. Nor did he tolerate rivalry between the secular clergy and
the Franciscans. He was certainly prudent – and determined.

Enríquez was the third son of the Marquis of Alcañices, who was a
direct descendant in the male line of King Alfonso XI of Castile and
distantly related to Juana Enríquez, the mother of King Ferdinand of
Aragon. The marquisate of Enríquez's father had been granted in

recognition of his loyalty to the Spanish Crown during the rebellion of the *Comuneros*. Martín seems to have been born in Valladolid and to have enjoyed a youth at court. He married María Manrique de Castilla, daughter of the Marquis of Aguilar y Campóo. Of Martín Enríquez's many sons, all but one (also named Martín) became friars. One of his sisters married the Conde de Nieva, who had been viceroy in Peru. Enríquez was thus part of the great cousinage of public servants in Spain who played such an important role in the early years of the empire. He seems to have been sixty years old when he was sent to New Spain in 1568, but it is not evident that he had any experience of administration before then. It appears to have been accepted that any nobleman could command men and deal with Indians, rather as the Duke of Wellington later assumed that any gentleman could be a captain of men.

Enríquez accepted Dr Pedro Moya, a clergyman from a noble family in Córdoba, as Archbishop of Mexico in recognition of that prelate's desire to establish the Inquisition there. There were splendid ceremonies to mark this event – in particular, a light-hearted play by Juan Pérez Ramírez was performed, entitled *The Spiritual Betrothal of Pastor Pedro and the Mexican Church*. Ramírez, who soon became a priest, was the first Mexican-born playwright. The play was followed by a dramatized conversation about the consecration of Moya by the playwright Fernán González de Eslava, a well-known sevillano who had come to the New World about 1560. The protagonist, a mulatto, delivered his lines in a way which both made the inquisitors laugh and infuriated the viceroy.[3] Characters such as Faith, Hope, Charity, and 'The Mexican Church' made allegorical and – to the strait-laced viceroy – intolerably satirical allusions. A joke about excise taxes, not customarily a subject for wit, caused Enríquez to stop the production: 'It did not sit well in my stomach,' Enríquez wrote to the Council of the Indies, rather severely, 'indeed, no one could approve of it, for a consecration and the assumption of the pallium are surely not subjects for farce.'[4]

A lampoon mocking both the viceroy and the excise tax soon appeared nailed to the door of the cathedral. A furious Enríquez promptly gaoled the alleged wits, González de Eslava and Francisco de Terrazas. Archbishop Moya, meantime, excused himself from the controversy on the grounds that the censor of the Inquisition, the clever and tireless Fray Domingo de Salazar, a priest from Labastida in Álava in the Basque country, had approved the presentations. (Moya had once been Inquisitor of Murcia in Castile.) González de Eslava did not seem to suffer in the long run from his brief imprisonment, for he continued to write witty dialogues.

Enríquez's viceregal instructions of 7 June 1568, signed by King Philip in Aranjuez, had run as usual to fifty-seven paragraphs. The new viceroy was to pay especial attention to the establishment of new monasteries and also to colleges for the education of both *mestiza* and indigenous girls. New hospitals too were required. The viceroy was to continue the concentration of Indians in towns and not allow them to live higgledy-piggledy in the countryside. Monasteries were not to be built too close to one another. Indians working in silver mines were to be especially well treated. If some Indians were treated as slaves when their official status was as free men, the matter should be sorted out. Sugar mills were to be worked by black Africans, not by Indians. Inspections should be carried out to ensure that none of the volumes so laboriously and carefully shipped from Spain were on the Inquisition's Index of Prohibited Books.

Enríquez was tested by fire even before he began to take up his duties. He arrived in New Spain in September 1568 with the *Flota* (the fleet used to transport treasure and goods from New Spain back to the mother country), accompanied by an escort from Spain. But before the new viceroy reached the port of Veracruz, the audacious English sailor John Hawkins had put into the harbour of San Juan de Ulúa with a cargo of slaves. Hawkins was surprised by the size of Enríquez's escort. In the battle which ensued the little English flotilla was destroyed, and only one ship, that of Hawkins and the gifted young Francis Drake, his cousin, was able to limp home to England in poor shape. Hawkins devoted himself thereafter to the creation of a hardened and serious English battle-fleet, while Drake spent the rest of his life doing what he could to revenge himself on Spanish shipping.[5]

In 1580, the year when Enríquez left New Spain for Peru, Fray Antonio Ponce described New Spain lyrically in his diary for the *comisario general* of the Franciscan order. The place still retained its watery beauty, for it seemed to him as if the great lakes embraced the now-Spanish city. Vegetables and fruit were still grown on the *chinampas* – known as 'floating gardens' – as well as hay for horses. Charcoal and firewood, cereals, blankets, and pottery arrived daily in canoes propelled by Mexicans with long poles. There were, as Enríquez put the matter as he left for his new post, 'two republics to be governed' in New Spain, the Indians and the Spaniards. Alas, 'the Indians were such a miserable people', he said, 'that it behoved all good Christians to sympathise with them'.[6]

But there were two anxieties: first, many canals were beginning to choke because of the rubbish left in them; and, second, the buildings of the old city were sinking little by little every year. In order to correct this, builders resorted to the construction of new piers beneath the great edifices. But there was a constant risk of floods and a 'pestilent' odour in summer from the lagoon.

The poems of Bishop Bernardo de Balbuena, a Spanish priest from Valdepeñas in Castile, summed up the scene admirably. In 1600 he was still a parish priest but was on the point of coming to the capital. There he would write *La Grandeza Mexicana* (1604) and the immense *El Bernardo o Victoria de Roncesvalles* (1624). He later became Abbot of Jamaica and then Bishop of Puerto Rico. He was a fine lyric poet and his sonnets are deservedly famous. For example:

> Perdido ando senõra, entre la gente
> Sin vos, sin mí, sin Dios, sin vida,
> Sin vos porque de mí no sois servida,
> Sin mí porque sin vos no estoy presente . . .
> O vos por quien perdí alegría y calma
> Miradme amable y volveréisme al punto
> A vos, a mi, a mi ser, mi Dios, mi vida.

> (Lost I wander, lady, among people
> Without you, without me, without God, without life,
> Without you because you are not always served by me,
> Without me because without you I am not present . . .
> O you for whom I lost happiness and tranquillity
> Look at me amiably and return to me
> To you, to me, to my being, my God, my life.)

There were at that time in the city of Mexico perhaps 4,000 white residents, supported by the labour of innumerable Indians.[7] There were also probably as many black Africans as Spaniards, mostly slaves but also some free Africans who by sheer determination and the threat of physical strength in numbers exercised control over many of the city's supplies. The Indians would enter the capital by the old causeways with their goods, only to be obliged to sell to Africans at nominal prices. The prices of goods then sold in the city would be high in comparison with what the Indians could raise for them.[8]

A new cathedral had been rising in the capital since 1573, thanks to the efforts of the architect Francisco Becerra. Like the Pizarro family, he was a native of Trujillo in Extremadura. Becerra had come with Viceroy Enríquez from Spain,[9] and his work on the cathedral was continued by the Burgos-born Claudio de Arcienaga.[10] There were five naves, as was often the case with cathedrals of the Spanish Renaissance. It appeared as if the roofs were Gothic, but the lower storeys were Renaissance. Gothic domes could be seen in the side chapels. The gates (*portadas*) were Doric. These changes were largely due to Juan Miguel de Agüero, a Cantabrian who was the architect of the cathedral at Mérida and who later worked in the capital on the convent of Carmen. There was a sacristy and a chapter house to the cathedral. From its early days it boasted a fine picture of the Virgin Mary by Simón Pereyns.[11]

There were six hospitals in the city of Mexico at this time, of which four were for Spaniards, one was for Indians, and one was for Africans and *mestizos*. There were seven monasteries: one of Dominicans (Santo Domingo); two of Augustinians, one of which was unusually designed as a secondary school; two of Franciscans (barefoot monks of Saint Cosmas and Saint Damian, also observants of Saint Francis); and one of Jesuits, who established themselves in a residence in 1572 when their first twelve fathers arrived.[12] There were also the Carmelites, who built the Indian district of St Sebastián. Seven convents existed for women: Reginists, Santa Claras, Conceptionists, Marianists, and Jeronymite nuns, also penitents and recluses. The nuns included brilliant cooks. They made pretty dresses for the ever-present images of the Virgin. They chanted charming cradle songs and were, from time to time, allowed to swoon in amorous ecstasy. The Jesuits paid special attention to the cultivation of maize and were, therefore, able to devote much care to the production of pulque, the white syrupy alcohol made from the maguey cactus. Their remarkable *hacienda* of San Xavier in the valley of Mexico would produce 3,000–3,500 tons of pulque a year in the eighteenth century.[13]

The different orders operated in different zones. Thus the resourceful Franciscans now dominated the missions in Tenochtitlan, Tlateloco, Texcoco, Tlamanalco, and Xochimilco. The Dominicans were to be found in Chalco, Tacubaya, and Coyoacán. The Augustinians were concentrated in Acolman but were also in Culhuacan and Mixquic.[14]

In the 1570s most convent orchards contained European fruit trees. Oranges, lemons, apples, peaches, pomegranates, and grapes were cultivated. Willows and white poplars also grew there. European wild flowers were common by this time.

The Indians continued to live their mysterious lives, frustratingly hard for European historians to imagine. Indian men usually went barefoot and barelegged, although sometimes they had sandals and long trousers. They often wore a shirt and a cotton mantle knotted over their shoulders. Sometimes they now wore hats. The women still had their *huipiles* (embroidered dresses) and skirts. Few Spaniards knew what they were thinking and every year, on account of diseases, there were fewer of them.

Indians still slept as they had always done, on *petates* (mats), not in hammocks, much less in beds. They ate sitting on the floor of their simple houses, without chairs or tables. They would certainly now have a few Christian images, and they might have baskets for storage and *metates*, or grinding stones, on which to make tortillas. The introduction of candles from Spain was a success, and to the indigenous people they provided a real improvement in their lives.

Viceroy Enríquez must take much of the credit for this period of tranquillity. A serious outbreak of smallpox in 1576 had been endured, and Enríquez even gallantly tried to tend some sick Indians himself. The viceroy also exempted many natives from the tribute which they formally owed to the Crown. Despite that, he managed to ship home to Spain in 1569, his first year of residence, silver worth 1,111,211 pesos, a larger annual figure than ever before.[15] He also embarked on an attempted system of drainage of the lake of Texcoco, the so-called *desague* (draining) of Huehuetoca, an Otomí-speaking town in the north-west of the valley of Mexico.

This was a prodigious operation which in some respects took over three centuries to complete. An army of 2,000 Indians was at work in 1600 and, by 1608, water had begun to flow from the valley to the sea through a new tunnel from the lake of Texcoco to the lower lands. The tunnel was 13 feet high and 213 feet wide, and at its deepest 175 feet deep. It was four miles long.

Martín Enríquez was a devoted advocate of the 'amalgam', the radical method of using quicksilver, that is, liquid mercury with silver.[16] He also advocated the export of Brazilwood and other red wood. The viceroy supported King Philip's *'protomedico'*, Dr Francisco Hernández, who in the 1570s was at work assembling all the data he could find on herbs, trees, and plants of medicinal value in New Spain. By 1576 he had filled sixteen volumes with analysis and illustrations.[17]

Despite his loss of temper over the dialogues of the playwrights Ramírez and González de Eslava, Enríquez was a patron of the arts and of learning. Thus he supported the publication of evangelical books in indigenous languages: the *Doctrina cristiana en lengua México* (*Christian Doctrine in the Mexican Language*), prepared in the late 1560s by Fray Benítcz Fernández, a Dominican; the *Vocabulario en lengua castellana* by the remarkable Franciscan Fray Alonso de Molina, completed in 1571; and *Arte en lengua Zapoteca* by Fray Juan de Córdoba, from 1578. Some scientific works were also published, for example, the *Summa y recopilación de cirugía* (*Treatise on Surgery*) by Alonso López (1578) and the *Tratado breve de anatomía y cirugía* by Fray Agustín Fajardo, as well as the *Opera medicinalia* by Dr Francisco Bravo.[18] Bravo was a *sevillano* who went to New Spain in the 1560s and became a friend of the cultivated Francisco Cervantes de Salazar, a Latinist and official historian of the capital. Bravo became known for a series of Latin dialogues. He published three of them, which were excellent introductions to the university and its purposes.[19] Bravo also became an expert on American diseases, especially *el tabardillo*, a fever which, like measles, brought out those affected in spots.

In Enríquez's day New Spain was the recipient of large imports of the best contemporary Spanish books, ranging from *La Celestina*,

Fernando de Rojas's brilliant dialogue,[20] to *Lazarillo de Tormes*, the anonymous satire of 1554, from *Amadís de Gaula* to *Tirant lo Blanc*, and the poems of Garcilaso de la Vega and Juan Boscán Almogáver. Volumes by Latin poets such as Virgil, Seneca, and Ovid were also to be found in the big book parcels being carried up from Veracruz. They were of course brought by mule led by an experienced muleteer (*arriero*). By the 1570s these last had come to be accepted as part of the landscape in New Spain, as indeed they were in the mother country.[21]

Martín Enríquez wanted to retire in 1580, but the king then asked him to go to Peru as viceroy. He accepted out of loyalty but, like the first viceroy Antonio de Mendoza, knew that it was a death sentence since he was already seventy-two. Enríquez went first to a Spanish villa in the village of Otumba (site of one of Cortes's victories), where he awaited his successor Lorenzo Suárez de Mendoza, Count of Coruña,[22] whom he briefed intelligently about the problems and possibilities then latent in the viceroyalty. Uniquely there was no demand for a *residencia* in relation to the mandate of Enríquez, just as there had not been in his time a Visitor.[23] Enríquez left Acapulco on 9 February 1581, making for Callao in Peru, a journey by boat which took him three months.

The subsequent viceroys in New Spain were of the same social standing as Enríquez but were less high-minded. Lorenzo Suárez de Mendoza, who was inaugurated on 4 October 1580, lasted till early 1583. He was incapable of dealing with the many municipal problems that he met with and he died in office, as Velasco had done. His successor was Álvaro Manrique de Zúñiga, who ruled until 1590.[24] Before his arrival, however, there was an interregnum in which Archbishop Pedro Moya de Contreras stood in for him. Moya's position was unique since, in addition to being archbishop and interim viceroy, he was also Grand Inquisitor and Visitor. He was simple, austere, and honest. Manrique de Zúñiga, Marquis of Villamanrique, a son of the Duke of Béjar who eventually succeeded, had a lively and rather dissipated court; his wife Blanca de Velasco, daughter of the Count of Nieva who had been viceroy in Peru, was a great-niece of Viceroy Enríquez. But Villamanrique did denounce the ill-treatment of Indians in *obrajes*, which he often visited, and he even condemned the very establishment of such workshops, insisting that wages should be paid in the presence of his officials, while all lists of free Indians henceforth had to be checked by a *corregidor*, that is, a royal-appointed municipal councillor, an important official until the nineteenth century.

Villamanrique was viceroy from 1585 to 1590, and he imposed what he conceived as the royal will in all particulars – that is, he made no concessions whatever to the remote circumstances of the viceroyalty. That distressed many landowners and others well established in New Spain. Villamanrique maintained a strict control of the valuable quicksilver market,[25] regulated the sale of wine, and sought to supervise the Church in a way that guaranteed the interests of the king. He tried to preserve the declining Indian population, though his approach alienated the Church as well as the landowners, since both in the long run depended on Indian labour. He intensified his predecessors' efforts to concentrate the Indian population in organized towns.

Villamanrique came to grief over the desire of one of the judges on the Supreme Court in New Galicia to marry a citizen of Guadalajara. Though the lady was a *criolla*, that association was forbidden to a colonial judge, but the local population supported the idea so strongly that the viceroy had to organize something like an army to impose his will and carry out what he supposed to be the royal law. But his position seemed preposterous and he was relieved of his post, even spending some time in confinement.[26]

Villamanrique was succeeded in 1590 by a second Luis de Velasco, son of the second viceroy of that same name. Luis de Velasco the younger married María, a niece of the first viceroy, Antonio de Mendoza. She was the daughter of a prominent conquistador, Martín de Ircio, one of the few emigrants from Logroño in northern Spain, who had come to New Spain with Cortés's enemy, Pánfilo de Narváez. Luis de Velasco the younger received a most thorough briefing from Villamanrique on New Spain, where he had spent so much of his youth during his father's time there.

Luis de Velasco the younger was the last viceroy of New Spain in the sixteenth century. (He served there as viceroy again from 1607 to 1611.) He was also viceroy in Lima between 1596 and 1604, eight years which left him wearied and craving for Castile. He was the only viceroy of New Spain to serve in that post twice (except for a Bishop

Ortega, who would serve very ephemeral periods in 1696 and 1701). Luis de Velasco the younger was also president of the Council of the Indies afterwards, from 1611 to 1617 – again the only time a viceroy went on to higher things in the Council. He was a super-viceroy, it would seem, having held that title for an unprecedented seventeen years. After a while, however, viceroys were forbidden to take their families, including their wives and sons, to the New World. That was an insurance against the establishment of a new aristocracy.

All these high officials brought with them from the mother country a gathering of relations, favourites, and friends whose status as Europeans gave them an advantage in relation to the *criollos* born in the New World. By 1600 the gap between these two classes of Spaniards seemed to be turning into an unbridgeable gulf. Another gulf was opening between secular officials and clerical ones. The latter as a body were now rich and probably controlled about half the land of New Spain.

Any account of the character of New Spain in the late sixteenth century should not forget the large numbers of Indian craftsmen, tailors, artists, and jewellers who had been trained by the conquerors. Saddlery, leather goods including gloves, woollen cloth, shoes, and hats were all being produced effectively. A large class of indigenous workmen were earning a good living from their new skills. In the countryside, peasants had learned to plough with oxen and to grow crops which were new to the Americas, such as wheat.

All the same, by the time of King Philip's death in 1598, the Indians of New Spain seemed to be losing much of their spirit, just as the conquistadors had lost much of their energy about the time of his father's abdication in 1555–6. Many Indians learned Spanish but few abandoned the use of Nahuatl. As a result the *criollos* were suspicious of Indian culture, which seemed to them little more than folklore. Fray Pedro de Gante's college in Tenochtitlan barely outlived its remarkable founder. The Franciscan school at Tlatelolco was also in decline by 1580.[27] That was partly because the subsidies provided by the first viceroys were no longer forthcoming. There were some extraordinary architectural achievements, such as Mexico City's cathedral and its Hospital Real, the Dominican monastery, and the Augustinian monasteries, but they were essentially creations of the first generation of colonists. New Spain in the seventeenth century would be full of learned men, but they were *criollos* or Spaniards rather than *mestizos* or Indians. The Jesuits had their wonderful schools, but they educated Europeans. The Mexica learned to paint, but they did so in a European manner and ceased to use indigenous Mexican styles.

The Mexica had had some practices such as marriage, baptism in water, fasting, a form of confession (constant, not just annual), and holy offerings. But similarity is not equivalence and nowhere was it possible for ancient rites to be converted directly into new ones. The Indians accepted the idea of a soul but extended it to animals and inanimate objects – which, of course, was not a Christian belief.

At the very end of the century, the traveller Fray Martín Ignacio de Loyola, great-nephew of Saint Ignatius, wrote of New Spain that it was so large that one could never reach the end of it. Every day new peoples were being found who were easy to conquer and 'subject (*reducir*) to our saintly catholic faith because they were a docile people and with good intelligence and understanding'.[28] Many Indians by 1600 were addicted to the ceremonies of the Church and were really given over to the divine cult, thought Fray Martín. In some respects, the indigenous people seemed to exceed many Spaniards in their zeal, decorating and adorning churches with much skill and devotion. He also thought that the Mexica were ingenious and there seemed to be nothing which they could not imitate. Thus they were admirable singers and players of musical instruments, though 'their voices do not help them'.

Motolinía, the enlightened Franciscan monk who had come to New Spain in the 1520s, thought that these and other such practices meant that the Indian population of New Spain had abandoned witchcraft and idolatry. Fray Bernardino de Sahagún, another equally great Franciscan, disagreed. The contrast, he thought, between old Indian and orthodox Christian ways was more marked than it had at first seemed to him.[29] Thus Jerónimo de Mendieta, the Basque historian whose *Historia Eclesiástica Indiana* was written in the 1580s, with the help of a knowledge of Nahuatl reported that, before the coming of Christianity, the Indians thought that 'no one did other than that which they were ordered to: now we (the Indians), that is, have great freedom. But it is bad for us since we are not now obliged to hold anyone in fear.'[30]

The books that were shipped most frequently to New Spain were less ambitious than Mendieta's *Historia*. The new dominions had a large reading public, who wanted first and foremost works of an ecclesiastical character. There were, too, collections of high-minded thoughts, such as those included in the *Golden Book of Marcus Aurelius*, the collection of sayings which had been the brilliant idea of Bishop Antonio de Guevara. After these, there were, as ever, the popular romances of chivalry such as Garci Rodríguez de Montalvo's *Amadís de Gaula* or *Las Sergas de Esplandián*. Even more popular for a time was *Don Florisel of Niquea* by Feliciano de Silva, which offered 'incentives to further heroic action, vicarious adventure in the intervals between his own prodigious experiences, and a consoling balm to his frustrated aspirations'.[31] Every year or two, like modern best-sellers, a new novel of this type would make its triumphant appearance.[32] Another immensely popular work was Alonso de Ercilla's admirable *La Araucana*, about the Spanish conquest of Chile, an epic poem apparently inspired by Ariosto (author of *Orlando Furioso*) and Tasso (author of *Gerusalemme Liberata*).[33] Strange Gothic tales also flooded into the city of Mexico and Lima alike in the 1570s; for example, Pierre Bouaisteau's *Historias Prodigiosas*, translated from the French,[34] was full of ghosts and earthquakes, souls in torment, and monsters. Many flourishing booksellers were able to make money out of these sales. One such was Juan de Timoneda of Valencia. He was also the editor of *La Sobremesa*, published in Valencia in 1564, a collection of anecdotes which included 'The After-Dinner Conversation'.

# 9

# Viceroy Toledo at Work in Peru

*Your Majesty is the legitimate ruler of this kingdom.*

Viceroy Toledo to King Philip II

In 1568 a long period of instability in Peru, caused by rivalry among the heirs of the first conquistadors, came to an end. The reign of Philip II since 1558 had been relatively stable, but that of the Emperor Charles V before him had been unpredictable. The viceroyalty of Peru had experienced civil war and a chronic crisis. That lamentable and surprisingly violent era concluded with the nomination, on 20 May 1568, of the able and intelligent Francisco de Toledo as viceroy.

Francisco de Toledo was a son of the Count of Oropesa and a cousin of the Duke of Alba. He was a serious Christian who received the sacrament every week, at that time a rare thing to do. He was also a member of the military order of Alcántara and he had attended the ailing Charles V at the monastery of Yuste. He was a close friend of San Francisco de Borja, the new general of the Society of Jesus.[1]

The modern Peruvian historian Guillermo Lohmann considered Toledo the best viceroy among the forty who ruled Peru during 250 years of Spanish rule.[2] His instructions were drawn up in Madrid and Valladolid by a committee chaired by the overweening Cardinal de Espinosa. Also concerned in preparing the brief were Luis Méndez de Quijada, the then president of the Council of the Indies, Juan Vázquez de Arce, and Licenciado Gómez Zapata, both also of the council; Dr Juan de Muñatones of the Council of Castile, as well as the ever available Ruy Gómez, the king's chief secretary. Gómez Suárez de Figueroa (the Duke of Feria), a great courtier, profligate, and ex-ambassador, was also on the committee. He was a devoted friend of the king, though an enemy of the Duke of Alba. Toledo himself also attended the committee.

The only original section of Toledo's instructions was a paragraph warning the new proconsul against free-speaking friars. King Philip said that he understood how 'churchmen who have resided ... in those parts on the pretext of protecting the Indians have wished to busy themselves concerning the justice and the lordship of the Indies ... which leads them into much scandal'.[3] Toledo toyed with the idea of asking the Inquisition to quieten these friars, who he thought were exceeding their authority.

The new viceroy, it must be said, found the legacy of Las Casas unacceptable: 'the books of the fanatical and virulent Bishop of Chiapas,' he complained, 'seem to be used as a spearhead of the attack against Spanish rule in America'. The friars, Viceroy Toledo noticed, were quick to condemn many things which he himself did, or thought of doing, as 'tyrannical and unjust'. They even tried to protect Indians from tax collectors.

The instructions drawn up in Spain also required Toledo to stop the circulation of romantic chivalrous novels, or *libros profanos*, which were now seen as morally corrupting for quite different reasons. These novels were, however, relentlessly popular in the New World. Even a viceroy as powerful as Toledo could not much affect the export from Spain of these kinds of publication.[4]

Toledo had spent a considerable time before he left for the New World familiarizing himself with the conditions in Peru. He talked to everyone whom he could find who had served there. He then left Sanlúcar de Barrameda for the New World on 19 March 1569 and reached Lima just over eight months later, on 30 November – a typical length of time for a high official on his way to that post.[5] There was ample opportunity for reading on the ship, and little distraction at the ports of the Canary Islands, at Cartagena and at Panama. On arriving at last in Peru, Toledo's first official act was to visit the Franciscan monastery in Lima, and then the Jesuit college of San Pablo. He needed to know what those holy but active men who were there were thinking. Next, the new viceroy did all he could to collect as many copies of Las Casas's works as possible and had them destroyed. He even asked the king to ban the export of any further editions. He returned to the Jesuits at San Pablo on 1 January 1570 and dined with them.

Toledo chose a cabinet of seven to assist him. This was unusual, for viceroys preferred as a rule to be their own ministers of all work, and to rely on the advice of friends, but it was a wise decision. The cabinet consisted first and foremost of the viceroy's cousin, the Dominican *provincial*, Fray García de Toledo, a distinguished and elegant writer, author of a famous *Memorial de Yucay* (he had been in New Spain with the first viceroy, Antonio de Mendoza, and later became a great friend of Saint Teresa of Ávila); the Jesuit José de Acosta, who had arrived in 1570 from Medina del Campo, the home of his very spiritual family which consisted of five Jesuits and two nuns;[6] the Supreme Court judge of Lima, Dr Gregorio González de Cuenca, who had already been in Peru for about fifteen years and had worked with the two preceding viceroys, the Marquis of Cañete and the Count of Nieva; the judge's colleague in La Plata, Juan de Matienzo; the clever observer, Licenciado Polo de Ondegardo;[7] and the implacable secretary in the domestic section of government Alonso Ruiz de Navamuel, who left a famous account of the viceroy's endeavours, the *Testimonio en relación de lo que hizo el Virrey Toledo*. Finally, there was another judge, Licenciado Pedro Sánchez de Paredes. These men were the '*éminences grises*' of the regime of Viceroy Toledo.[8]

Toledo encountered several working institutions of quality. For example, the first Bishop of Lima, Jerónimo de Loaisa, had opened an admirable school in the shadow of the cathedral, under the direction of the learned Gonzalo de Trejo. There were other such academies run by Dominicans, whose monastery was the progenitor of the university of San Marcos. Alonso Martínez began to teach Quechua using the first grammar in that language, which had been published by Fray Domingo de Santo Tomás the year before Toledo had arrived. (Martínez had also taught philosophy and theology.) Santo Tomás had arrived in Peru about 1540 and had been prior of the *convento* in Lima. Quechua was the most important indigenous language of the region and was spoken everywhere that the Incas had ruled. We should note the high level of education insisted upon by most people who lived in Peru, Spanish as well as Indian. Many rich families, Indians as well as Spaniards, employed private tutors, Indian as well as

Spanish, to educate their children. The Jesuits, as we have seen, had reached Lima in 1568 and had begun to teach and proselytize both races with dedication.

The viceroy's first problem had nothing to do with education but once more concerned the *encomiendas*. *Encomiendas* in Peru in 1570 were generally held by the families of the same conquistadors who had been granted them in 1538. There was, as elsewhere in the New World, a prolonged discussion about the question of perpetuity. In Spain itself (as we have seen), the disciplinarian Cardinal Espinosa convoked a committee in 1571, though its discussions never reached a conclusion. It was increasingly accepted that in Peru a third of the *encomiendas* should be reserved in perpetuity. Espinosa's committee thought that all holders of *encomiendas* should be given titles such as count or baron. Only heresy, sin, or treason would be a reason to confiscate a *feudo*. After all, some *encomenderos* had been great benefactors to the fledgling colony. Had not Isabel Muñoz, the dynamic sister-in-law of Francisco Pizarro, organized the cultivation of wheat for the first time in Peru?[9]

In 1555, Antonio de Ribera, on behalf of the settlers, told the Council of the Indies in Spain that there would be considerable disquiet if the *encomiendas* in Peru were not reserved in perpetuity. In 1556, King Philip told the Council of the Indies, no doubt for financial reasons, that he had decided to concede the permanence of the *encomiendas*. (He had been promised five million ducats by the settlers.)

The Council of the Indies were, however, bleakly opposed. King Philip's father, the Emperor Charles, was still alive in Yuste and still free with advice. 'I have never been easy in respect of this question,' he said, 'and have always wanted to keep clear of it.' While he was on the throne, he had not agreed to any new policy. It would in fact be best if Philip delayed any decision until he became king, and then, Charles said, 'you will be able to act according to your wishes and do something of your own'.[10] But Philip, when he became king, did not find a decision on this matter any easier to make than his father had done.

As late as 1584, Gaspar de Ribera, a prominent landowner, who had been in Spain since 1563, raised the matter of *encomiendas*. All kinds of ingenious proposals were made to solve this problem, but all were ignored. The subject was once more neglected.

During Viceroy Toledo's first year in Peru, he was faced with a remarkable upheaval among the Jesuits, which reverberated as far as Rome and which went to the heart of the scope and purpose of this magnificent, thriving new order in the New World. The Jesuits were led into the controversy by Fray Juan de Acosta and Father Miguel de Fuentes from the college of San Pablo in Lima on the one hand, and on the other by Fray Juan de Zúñiga, who became the first rector of the first Jesuit college at Cuzco.

The Jesuits concentrated their attentions on the Indian population, with great success. Viceroy Toledo wanted to increase the number of Jesuit colleges, but the Jesuits were instructed by their able general in Rome, Cardinal Borja, not to think for the moment of any such expansion.[11] He did not want any uncontrolled development of the order. Toledo sent Father Bracamonte to the Vatican to try and persuade Borja, who had once been his own close friend.

But Borja died in September 1572, so ending an astonishing career. His successor as general of the order, the Flemish Everard Mercurian, sent an emissary of his own to Peru on a *visita* in the shape of Juan de la Plaza, an experienced but unimaginative bureaucrat, who was, however, accompanied by some creative and gifted men. These included Juan de Montoya, who had taught philosophy at the Jesuit college in Rome; Baltasar Piñas, who had been rector of a Jesuit college in Spain; an Italian painter, Bernardo Bitti;[12] and a musician, Melchor Cano. Plaza, bureaucratic though he might be, thought that it would be desirable to have a theological seminary in Spain to train all men destined to work in the Indies – an idea rejected by Father Acosta, who soon became *provincial* of all the Jesuits in Peru, and who argued that the training of new missionaries was best done at the college of San Pablo in Lima, not in Seville.

Acosta was by then presiding over a most successful enterprise at San Pablo, in Lima. Both he and Baltasar Piñas from their rooms could hear the voices of 250 indigenous children solemnly reading aloud Cicero and Homer. What a triumph! Several hundred mature students would be waiting for Acosta's own seminars on moral problems. Francisco de Toledo proceeded to found chairs in Indian languages, Aymara as well as Quechua.

The Jesuits of Lima wrote hexameters in the manner of Virgil as well as Horatian and Pindaric odes, and allowed the reading and writing of poetry to fill innumerable hours. Drama also had an important role.

Acosta failed to persuade the viceroy, however, that the main purpose of the Jesuits in Peru should be to help the Indians. In the 1580s there was controversy over whether *mestizos* as well as *criollos* could become Jesuits. This matter was resolved in favour of tolerance of the idea, and the *mestizos* in particular thereafter had played a most important role in the order. But the new general of the order, the able Neapolitan aristocrat Claudio Aquaviva, was always hostile to this conclusion. The Jesuits of Peru lived on tenterhooks lest their legal status might be further undermined; however, that did not happen.[13]

In 1596, Father Aquaviva, contradicting his previous views, pronounced that no Jesuit in Peru should be promoted to the priesthood unless he knew Quechua well. He was nothing if not serious in his desire for an understanding with the indigenous people. Other Jesuits were ordered to study the 'language of Angola', which was supposedly spoken by African slaves.

Alonso de Barzana was the outstanding linguist in Peru in the 1580s. He had been a protégé of Francisco de Toledo and a native of the village of Belinchón near Tarancón, Cuenca, in Spain, where his father had been a doctor. As well as instructing his compatriots in Quechua and other indigenous languages, Barzana visited numerous Indian villages in the valley of Lima, stressing the need for instruction rather than conversion. The rector of the college of San Pablo, Bartolomé Hernández, made the same point in a letter to the president of the Council of the Indies in Spain, Juan de Ovando, in April 1572. Before trying to convert the Indians, Hernández thought, they should be helped to lead a civilized life within a well-organized political system.

From the beginning, the Jesuits in Peru owned many good books, held in a small library in the convent of San Pablo. This was eventually expanded, with allocations made for special budgets, the situation being transformed at the end of the century when two enlightened entrepreneurs, the brothers Perlín, provided the rent of a house in Madrid to finance books in Lima. There were at that time other bequests of books or even libraries in Spain, which were despatched to Lima. A Peruvian printing press was set up in San Pablo, having been brought from New Spain by Antonio Ricardo, and there the first book printed in Peru, a bilingual catechism, appeared in 1584.

A further promising moment came in the 1590s when Fray Hernando de Mendoza, who built a new infirmary, became rector of the college of San Pablo at the same time as his brother, García Hurtado de Mendoza, was viceroy. They were responsible for launching several, later famous, brotherhoods (*cofradías*), such as were already inspiring the lay Catholics in Spain. (With their annual processions through the streets, their music, and their imaginative floats, *cofradías* continue to inspire the faithful to this day.) Within ten years a brilliant Italian pharmacist, Augustino Salumbrino, had also transformed the pharmacopoeia of the college, with febrifugal bark making its famous contribution to the history of quinine.[14]

In the 1580s the college of San Pablo was becoming one of the largest landowners in the New World. Extensive rural properties were the firm economic foundation for the Jesuit order over the next two hundred years. The first *haciendas* owned by them in Peru, near Chancay and Surco, were given by two Christian philanthropists, Juan Martínez Rengifo and Diego de Porrás Sagredo. The farm at Chancay produced wheat, vines, and olives. Surco had 800 head of cattle and 250 goats, and there was also a sugar mill as well as fields of cane. Later, the college of San Pablo also bought a *hacienda* about a hundred miles from Lima, which became home to about 8,500 sheep, providing the college with meat as well as wool.[15]

Fray José de Acosta was an outstanding Jesuit missionary. To serve his order as well as Viceroy Toledo, he went to Cuzco to see what was being done in the Jesuit foundations there and he diverted on the way to look at the mercury deposits at Huancavelica. Acosta inspected the layout of the *socavones* (mining pits), in particular the labour and housing conditions there, and enquired into the financial reward which the miners received and even the climate of the place. He knew that the mercury mines of Huancavelica were an essential support for the extraction of silver at the more remote mining town of Potosí, which he also visited. His complaints were twofold: first, the low income paid to the miners, and second, the spiritual and human isolation of the Indians, two elements which would surely trouble any Christian conscience.

Acosta, it is reasonable to add, thought that with no element of forced labour (the so-called *mita*), it would be impossible to establish a viable society in Spanish Peru. But he wanted a humane approach to the problem. The tributes which Viceroy Toledo sought to impose were, in his view, worse than anything, and he said so. Acosta's journey in Peru was followed by others, for example to Panama (1585), Quito (1586), Chile (1593), and the Peruvian province of Jauja (1596).

In 1578 there had seemed to be a growing danger of the Jesuits' great institution at San Pablo clashing with Viceroy Toledo's own creation in Lima, the royal university of San Marcos. In April most of the serious students had registered for San Pablo whereas the lecture halls at San Marcos had been deserted. The rector of the university, Dr López Guarnido, complained to the viceroy that all intelligent students wanted to go to a learned institution run by religious orders. Toledo thought that the Jesuits at San Pablo were refusing to be an integral part of his educational plan and, backed by the Church and ultimately the Papacy, were set on an independent course which could ruin his undertaking. In short, the Jesuits, after only ten years in Peru, were beginning to exercise more influence than suited the interests of the Crown. On 11 October 1578 a town crier read a decree of the viceroy which forbade the attendance of lay students at any private college and imposed the obligation that students must attend classes at the university. The decree was read out first to the Dominican fathers at the university, and then to the Jesuits at San Pablo.

Acosta made the brave decision that the viceroy's decree had to be resisted. He appealed to Rome and Madrid for support. In the Escorial, King Philip studied the papers and then, in a decree of 22 February 1580, proposed, as was his wont, a compromise between the viceroy and the Jesuits. Viceroy Toledo would be asked to reopen San Pablo, and the Jesuits would be permitted to teach languages and the humanities. Philosophy and theology could also be taught at San Pablo, though not at the same time that the university offered its regular courses on those subjects. San Pablo could not offer any degree. Students could attend the Jesuit college as they desired but if they wanted an official degree, they would have to register at the university and go there. The royal university of San Marcos would be the only institution capable of granting degrees in the categories of doctor, master, and bachelor.

In subsequent years, San Pablo's department of humanities turned into the official preparatory school for the university of San Marcos. Moreover, the Jesuits had an exclusive right to teach classics, that is Latin and Greek, in Lima, but without salaries.

Despite these limitations, by 1600 the college of San Pablo had recovered its sense of well-being, its seminars were well attended, and persons from every walk of life were accustomed to knock at the gate of the college in order to seek advice and guidance as Christians. Even Luis de Velasco the younger, the viceroy at the end of the century, asked the Jesuit fathers – regardless of what had already been done by his predecessors – whether he could oblige Indians to work in mines which had been newly discovered. The answer, thought Fathers Esteban Ávila and Juan Pérez de Menacho, was that they were not going to say anything about forced labour, but the response to the specific question asked by the viceroy would clearly be negative. He would not be permitted to force men to work in the newly discovered mines.[16]

Thereafter the fame of Lima's Jesuit professors spread, and all kinds of moral and legal problems were constantly referred to San Pablo, from Paraguay as from Chile, with some immensely learned fathers replying in subtle ways.[17] Meanwhile, San Pablo continued to be maintained by benefactions from individuals: in the 1580s rich *encomenderos* and agriculturalists endowed the college with a vineyard, a sugar mill (*ingenio*), and other lands, together with slaves to work these properties.[18]

Against this background, Viceroy Toledo inaugurated a series of administrative reforms which marked Peru for ever. His legislative activity was immense.[19] Codes were promulgated, mining was stimulated and regulated, and *corregimientos* (government-appointed municipal councillors) were established for both Indian and Spanish towns. The tribute of the indigenous population was regularized as ducats. The *mita*, the system of forced labour in mines and public works, was underpinned. The natives were concentrated in towns, as in New Spain, to assist both administration and Christian indoctrination. Many public works, such as new roads and bridges, were undertaken there. Most such towns had their elections. Thus in

November 1575, Viceroy Toledo planned for such contests in all the larger towns of the viceroyalty.[20] In theory, all men over twenty-one could vote.

It is true that Sir Francis Drake, in one stage of his journey around the world, raided the Pacific coast of Peru, but that was no more than a pinprick in the majestic onward movement of empire.

Viceroy Toledo was already in his sixties, but he had considerable energy, a remarkable perspicacity, and he knew a great deal about human nature. Thus he was aware of how far he could press his Jesuit advisers in their knowledge. Being an aristocrat, he also felt able to write directly to King Philip about the weaknesses of the colonial administration. He had no hesitation in criticizing the judges of the Supreme Court with whom he came into contact, even at the risk of damaging his own good name with the Council of the Indies.[21] Toledo, it seems, had such grand ways that the censor, Licenciado Cristóbal Ramírez de Cartagena, a frequent critic, denounced him to the president of the Council of the Indies, Juan de Ovando, saying that in Peru there was a deity in the viceregal palace, not a public servant. A satirical song was composed which was an appeal for the recognition of Viceroy Toledo as a divinity.[22]

When the king ordered Toledo to pacify the brave, ingenious, but cruel tribe known as the Chiriuguanes, a sub-group of the Guarani, those people sent thirty leaders to negotiate with the viceroy at Chuquisaca in the highlands (now in Bolivia). In 1576 they wisely insisted that Saint James had just appeared to them in person. They assured the viceroy that they would never again fight the Spaniards, nor eat flesh on Fridays, nor marry their own sisters. They wished to serve God and the king of Spain, they hoped that some friars might be sent to them, and they even presented some crosses to the viceroy.[23]

Viceroy Toledo earlier in the same year was faced with much local cruelty by settlers towards the Indians and set himself to humanize the way in which the Indians were treated. There was, he found, a great shortage of priests. In the whole diocese of Quito, for example, there was only one priest (the land which became Ecuador was at that time part of the viceroyalty of Peru, as it had been part of the realm of the Incas). Many Indians said that they could not understand the way in which their new masters often behaved to them. Even those who had been baptized fell back into the secret practice of old worship. That explains why Toledo in consequence began a general inspection of the viceroyalty and sought to extirpate pre-Colombian religious survivals, also helping the Chilean settlers against the Araucanian natives who lived, and fought, in the south.

The viceroy soon embarked on an elaborate tour of his entire large domain, accompanied in part by the Jesuit Acosta, the judge Juan de Matienzo, and by that serious observer Licenciado Polo de Ondegardo. When he eventually returned to Lima, Toledo divided his viceroyalty into fifty sections, each of which had its own *corregidor* and governor. Every town was obliged to have a town hall (*cabildo*), headed by a mayor or a judge who would normally have various magistrates as subordinates. The *naturales* would be governed by their own *caciques*, or chiefs. This division into two types of government characterized the Spanish approach from that time onwards. Those *caciques* who had over 100 subjects were called *pichacas*, those with over 500 were to be known as *picho-pichacas*. These arrangements reflected the governance of the provinces of Peru in the old days under the Incas.

No Indians were to possess any European weapons and no blacks or mulattoes were to be allowed to live among Indians, to avoid the latter becoming contaminated by radical views. The *caciques* had usually retained hereditary authority, and were themselves free from the need to pay tribute, but they had a responsibility to collect tribute from the adult males in their towns (those between the ages of eighteen and fifty).

Viceroy Toledo sponsored an inquiry into the history of the Incas and their customs, gathering views from the evidence of 200 Indians in eleven different places between January 1570 and March 1572. This was the sort of general inspection which the Incas themselves had been accustomed to carry out.[24] The kinds of questions asked were as follows: Was it true that the first Inca, Manco Capac, had tyrannically subjugated the Indians of Cuzco by force of arms, and deprived them of their lands? And was it correct to suppose that the succeeding Incas did the same until the fourth Inca, Maita Capac, completed the conquest? Was it true that the Indians never recognized voluntarily the Incas as their lords and only obeyed them through fear of the cruelties which would be inflicted on them if they opposed the indigenous people? Further, was it 'true that neither you nor your ancestors elected the Incas as your lords but that they won their tyrannical posture by force of arms and by the inculcation of fear?'

Other answers to questions conveniently established that the Incas sacrificed the most beautiful children, that many were lazy, and that some were cannibals. The overall drift was that the entire history of Peru under the Incas had been one of brutality. So the viceroy and the Spaniards could argue that their arrival was a liberation; and Toledo could conclude in his summary of his findings to King Philip, 'Your Majesty is the legitimate ruler of this kingdom, while the Incas are rightly to be seen as tyrannical usurpers . . . Your Majesty rightly exercises jurisdiction over the Indians and, given their weak reason and rude understanding, Your Majesty must devise laws for their conservation and require them to obey.' Toledo hoped that the variety of opinion on such matters of importance would bring an end to any controversy and that 'the King, his advisers and the people of Peru' would no longer have their consciences disturbed and confused, as in the past, 'whenever some ignorant person [for example, Las Casas] dares to open his mouth and cry out to high heaven'.[25]

Toledo was wise to obtain the support of the judge Juan de Matienzo, a grandson of the first prosecutor in the Casa de la Contratación in 1505. Judge Matienzo wrote *El gobierno del Perú*, describing the tyranny of the Incas in the past, how they had often murdered and sacrificed children, and indeed had thousands killed. He added: 'The Indies were justly won by the concession of the Pope, either because these kingdoms were found empty by the Spaniards, or because of the *naturales'* abominable crimes against nature, or because of their infidelity. Although the least reason would be adequate in itself, the tyranny of the Incas was enough to establish the fact that the kingdom of Peru was justly gained.' The conquest had led to the Indians learning to trade and therefore make profits, not to speak of beginning to use European mechanical and agricultural instruments – a supreme benefit.[26]

By increasing taxes, Viceroy Toledo enlarged the Crown's revenues in Peru from 100,000 to a million ducats, the total treasure reaching Seville in 1580 being 64 million ducats. That was an increase from the

1560s when the figure had been a mere 30 million. By then Peru was providing Spain with two-thirds of the total precious metals of the Americas.

Toledo always wanted to make peace with the last of the Incas. That meant inviting the heir of the Incas, Tupac Amaru, down from the mountains. But Tupac at first refused. The viceroy then sent Fray Martín García de Loyola to see the Inca, who said that he would indeed surrender to a kinsman of Saint Ignatius, a saintly individual of whom he had heard. The Inca set off with an expedition of 250 men, assuming that they were going to Chile. He was, however, diverted to Cuzco where he was swiftly tried and, most remarkably, eventually executed for the improbable charge of treason. Women in Cuzco demanded, 'Inca, what crimes have you committed to deserve this fate? Beg your killer to slay us all. We shall be happier to have died with you than to remain as serfs and slaves of your murderers.'[27] Toledo was eventually rebuked by King Philip, who, echoing his father's reproach to Pizarro for the death of Atahualpa, said that the viceroy had been sent to Peru not to kill kings, but to serve them.[28]

Finally, Toledo asked Pedro Sarmiento de Gamboa to write a history which would counter the false account by Diego Fernández (known as 'el Palentino' since he had been born in Palencia), published in 1571 in Seville and called *La Historia del Peru y la historia del alzamiento y tiranía de Gonzalo Pizarro*; this had argued that, contrary to what had been said by Matienzo, the Incas were justly established in Peru because they had been elected. The Council of the Indies forbade the circulation of Fernández's book among the general public, an act which Spaniards in Peru applauded. The *cabildo* de Cuzco declared, on 24 October 1572, 'when we read the histories written about us [the conquistadors], we think they must be describing another type of people'.[29]

Sarmiento, one of Viceroy Toledo's ablest officials, travelled all round Peru recording the memories of its oldest inhabitants. Relying to some extent on the formal declarations (*informaciones*) by the conquistadors of what they themselves had done, but also on his own informants, Sarmiento presented his history to Toledo for examination on 29 February 1572. Toledo had it read aloud to the most distinguished native Peruvians and they made corrections. They generally declared that, except for some small errors, the history had been well done, and so said also the few surviving conquistadors who had first arrived with Pizarro. A corrected version of the book was then sent to the king.

Naturally not everyone agreed. The brilliant Acosta denounced 'those false titles of dominion which some persons are trying to propagate, unnecessary defenders of royal authority in my opinion, not to say deceivers, who would prove their assertions by insisting on the tyranny of the Incas . . . which we do not understand and admit, for it is not lawful to rob a thief, nor does the crime committed by someone else add to our own justice.' Perhaps characteristically, King Philip never had Sarmiento's book published. It only became available three centuries later, when it was published in 1906 by Richard Pietschmann in Göttingen, Germany.

In April 1577 the new building of the university of San Marcos had been inaugurated in Lima in what had been the Augustinian monastery of San Marcelo, but the inauguration day was that of Saint Mark, so that saint's name prevailed.[30] The Supreme Court (*audiencia*) was persuaded by Viceroy Toledo to allow a free election to the rectorship, and a lay judge, Pedro Fernández de Valenzuela, who had been born in Córdoba, was chosen as the first rector.[31] Fernández had studied at Salamanca University, and his election enabled the European university tradition to be carried into creative fulfilment thousands of miles away in the New World.

# 10

# Convents and Blessed Ones

*O Jesus of my soul*
*How handsome you look*
*Among roses and flowers*
*And green olive branches.*

*It is already midnight.*
*My Jesus has not arrived.*
*Who could be the lucky one*
*Who is keeping Him?*

Santa Rosa of Lima, c. 1598

On 26 May 1580, Martín Enríquez de Almansa, the successful if undemonstrative viceroy in New Spain for many years, succeeded the great Francisco de Toledo in Peru. Enríquez's new instructions were contained in a memorandum dated 3 June 1580. Although as usual long, the requirements made of the new viceroy were precise and clear. His first priority was to resolve the fractious politics surrounding religion and education in Lima.[1] Enríquez was of a gentle disposition, which inclined him to try and establish an equilibrium between the proud Jesuits at the college of San Pablo and the royal university of San Marcos.[2] So in February 1581 he was able to tell King Philip that the Jesuits, under the sage direction of Fray Juan de Atienza, sometime rector of the Jesuit college in Valladolid (and a son of Bartolomé de Atienza, a counsellor of Castile), were now ready to take care of all the teaching of the humanities in Lima as a full part of the university.[3] San Pablo was reopened without restriction in July 1581.

That Enríquez, a tolerant man, was sent to Lima to succeed Toledo, suggests that the king wanted a change of approach from Toledo's ruthlessness – not least in respect of his treatment of the Inca as related in the last chapter.

In the 1580s another brilliant inspiration was Fray Pablo José de Arriaga, an accomplished humanist, born about 1563 in the Basque town of Vergara, who enabled the college of San Pablo to complete the curriculum of five classes which made up their much-vaunted *Ratio Studiorum*.[4] (Arriaga wrote an admirable textbook for San Pablo, the *Rhetoris Christiani, Partes Septem*, printed in Lyons in 1619.[5] One aim was to teach the advanced students of humanities at San Pablo how to become effective public speakers.) That Lima was by now a remarkable centre of culture was shown by the fact that Cervantes, in his pastoral novel *La Galatea*, included a poem which he called the 'Canto de Calíope'. Here he listed the names of eleven poets in Peru of whom he had heard in Lima.[6] That city had a printing press which had been established in 1583, and the first book published in the viceroyalty was *La doctrina Cristiana del catequismo* (*Christian Doctrine and the Catechism*), which was approved by the Inquisition in 1584.[7] The first part of Cervantes's famous work *Don Quixote* reached the viceregal city in 1605, in the year of its first publication.[8]

As in New Spain, and throughout the Spanish world, romances of chivalry continued to figure in the lists of books imported to Peru. But so did law codes, and works by mystics such as Fray Luis de León and Fray Luis de Granada. Equally there then appeared the works of philosophers such as Domingo de Soto and Saint Thomas Aquinas. The sciences also figured in the reading material circulating in Lima, as is demonstrated by the sales of the *Libro de Medicina* by Bernardus de Gordiono or of Pedro de Medina's *Regimiento de Navegación* – an important handbook of marine lore.[9]

The beginning of Viceroy Enríquez's mandate in Lima included his reception of a new archbishop, later canonized, Toribio de Mogroviejo. He was a learned man from Villaquejida in León, who had much impressed King Philip when they had met in Seville. Toribio was an exceptional individual. He was a lay professor of law at Salamanca University and had not yet taken orders when the king appointed him archbishop. Toribio did not want to accept such a commission but was ordered to do so, and he reached Lima in 1581. His vast diocese, he discovered, comprised many thousands of acres of forest, extraordinary mountains, and amazing coastlines, and his visits to the people for whose spiritual life he was responsible took him seven years. There were innumerable baptized Indians,[10] he learned, who knew nothing whatever of Christianity. To assist the process of real conversion, Toribio commissioned the building of churches, hospitals, religious houses, and seminaries (the first such in Lima was in 1591). He learned Quechua and some other indigenous languages, and became a second apostle of the Indies of whom Las Casas would have been proud. The archbishop's championship of Indians' rights infuriated many colonists, but he was revered by the indigenous people for his great persistence. He visited every part of his archbishopric, despite the dangers and the often unpassable roads.

Restless would-be conquistadors, meantime, clamoured for the viceroy's backing. For example, Enríquez received a letter in 1582 from Agustín de Ahumada, one of the brothers of Saint Teresa of Ávila, asking permission to organize an expedition to a nearby *El Dorado* which he described as 'the richest in gold and people ever seen'.[11] This turned out to be the Peruvian province of Tucumán. The letter testifies to the power of viceroys to open – or at least allow others to open – untapped veins of wealth in South America. (Enríquez approved Ahumada's adventure.)

Subsequent viceroys in Peru were of the same aristocratic origins as Toledo and Enríquez de Almansa. The latter left Acapulco in New Spain on 9 February 1581, arrived in Lima apparently on 23 September 1581, and died in office on 12 March 1583. He was followed by Fernando de Torres y Portugal, Count of Villardompardo, who was named viceroy on 31 March 1584, reaching Lima on 21 November 1585. Before that, he had built a palace in his home province of Jaén above the Arab baths, and he became *alferez mayor* (chief magistrate). Then from 1579 to 1583 he was *asistente*, or mayor, of Seville. That experience helped Villardompardo as a viceroy in Lima, a post he held during most of the later 1580s; but by 1590 he seemed too tired and was dismissed (he died back in Spain in October 1592). He was succeeded by García Hurtado de Mendoza, who was viceroy from

1588 to 1595 and was yet one further member of that great clan of public servants. Hurtado de Mendoza was the son of the Marquis of Cañete, viceroy from 1556 to 1560, and he had previously been governor of Chile in fierce wars against the Araucanian Indians. He was the first viceroy in Lima to take his wife with him.

The last viceroy of the century in Peru was Luis de Velasco, son of the second viceroy in New Spain. Velasco the younger passed his childhood and youth in New Spain, where he too went on to serve as viceroy, twice, between 1590 and 1595 and from 1607 to 1611. He was viceroy in Lima between 1596 and 1604, eight years which left him wearied and craving for Castile. Velasco the younger was the only viceroy to serve in that capacity twice (except for Bishop Ortega, who served very ephemeral periods in 1696 and 1701). He was also president of the Council of the Indies afterwards, from 1611 to 1617.

That Council much preferred aristocrats as their viceroys in both Peru and New Spain, rather than educated middle-class individuals, *letrados*. Between 1603 and 1695, following the precedent left by Enríquez, seven of the thirteen viceroys of Peru had previously held that same position in New Spain.

During his distinguished viceroyalty, Francisco de Toledo had found himself in constant argument with the abbesses of convents whose unpredictable conduct posed an unrelenting challenge to his and the Crown's authority.[12] The best historian of those institutions, Fray Luis Martín, refers to these nunneries as being 'unruly, independent kingdoms of women which flaunted their freedom and self-sufficiency in the face of a male-controlled society'.[13] One viceroy would write to the king, 'if husbands cannot control their wives, how could he be expected to control thousands of women living behind cloister walls in semi-autonomous kingdoms?'[14] Viceroy Toledo complained to the king that the Augustinian nuns of Lima were rebelling against their friars.

During Toledo's time there were thirteen nunneries in Lima alone, as well as six *beaterios* (houses for pious women).[15] The land occupied by these institutions took up a fifth of Lima and contained more than that proportion of the female population of the city. The six so-called *conventos grandes* in Lima had each a population of several hundred women. Nearly all were *criollas*, Peruvian-born but not

Indian. By 1600, the major institutions of this kind were La Concepción, established in 1561 by Leonor de Portocarrero, widow of a royal treasurer; La Encarnación, set up in 1573 by Inés Muñoz de Rivera, sister-in-law of Francisco Pizarro (she was also a rich woman in her own right, being *encomendera* of Anahuanacas); La Santísima Trinidad, founded by Lucrecia Sansoles in 1584; Las Descalzas, which was founded in 1602 by Inés de Rivera, sister of the Marquis of Mortara; Santa Clara, which was established two years later in 1602; and Santa Catalina, founded in 1624 by two formidable sisters, Lucia and Clara de la Daga, who were for years the abbesses of the convent. Then in Cuzco there were three *conventos grandes*: Santa Clara, a female branch of the order of Saint Francis, whose nuns wore a Franciscan robe; Santa Catalina, a convent of Dominican nuns but who were directed by the Bishop of Cuzco; and the Carmelites, whose nuns followed the rule of Saint Teresa of Ávila. There were also about a dozen minor *beaterios* and small nunneries. There were *conventos* too in Arequipa, Potosí, La Plata, Córdoba, Santa Fe and Tunja, a small town in the north, as well as in Huamanga, where the convent of Santa Clara was ruled by Luisa Díaz de Oré and her five powerful daughters. An *encomendera* there was controlled by another powerful mother superior, Isabel del Estete.

All these institutions left an indelible mark on the geography of the province, and their long stone walls often extended far more than a single block. On entering the *conventos*, the visitor might be overwhelmed by the long, beautiful cloisters, the well-maintained gardens, the elegant little courtyards with fountains in their centre, and the array of workshops, classrooms, dining rooms, dormitories, and common rooms. Probably there would be an infirmary and a pharmacy. The cells would, however, be the central point of most large nunneries and sometimes these would have rooms upstairs as well as downstairs. Many cells were large, adequate for several tenants. Here there might be musical evenings, concerts, and even theatrical productions. There were parlours where nuns could receive outsiders, friends as well as relations, officials, and even merchants. There was a hierarchy within these nunneries, the women being of several classes within their institution, with the black-veiled nuns constituting a special aristocracy. There would also be a number of novices who were preparing themselves for a religious life, so-called *donadas* who, though they wore the habits of nuns, were not yet formally so; they were essentially superior ladies who were able to live as imitators of nuns. Many servants and a number of African slaves lived here too – sometimes Peruvian-born slaves. There were sometimes Japanese and even Muslim slaves. Often grand ladies who had become nuns would have slaves entirely dependent on themselves, living in their cells, serving only them and taking their names. One should not forget also the professional messengers known as *recaderos*, who would be the specially chosen links between the nuns and the outside world. Sometimes these *recaderos* would act on behalf of an entire family, for there were occasions when a whole extended family would go into a *convento* and maintain themselves as a cohesive unit comprising mothers and daughters, cousins and sisters, aunts and nieces, distant relations and close friends. Such families might organize concerts, firework displays, dramatic performances, parades, and processions. Viceroys and bishops were sometimes dazzled by the luxury and glamour of life in the *conventos grandes*, where many nuns abandoned their religious habits and dressed in splendid finery. A good singer or a good practitioner on the lute or the guitar could put those talents forward as a substitute for a traditional dowry. The musical entertainment in Peruvian nunneries became famous, and different *conventos* would compete to offer the most elaborate musical programmes, which might include a *juguete musical* – almost an 'opera bouffe'. There might too be *canciones de negro* – songs of the African slaves.

Contact between nunneries and the outside world was easily maintained by discreet conversations over low fences or street-level balconies. Confessors and chaplains came into the *conventos grandes* daily, since the former had their business with confessions of nuns and the latter went to celebrate mass. Bishops came less often, perhaps no more than once annually. But they made their visitations in grand style, being greeted by a choir of nuns singing 'Ecco Sacerdos et Pontifex' ('Behold the High Priest') and accompanied by an organ, violins, lutes, and harps. The bishop would be served a fine breakfast and he would then inspect the convent carefully, conferring with the abbess but talking at random with a few nuns, novices, and even a *donada* or two. Eventually a report would be prepared and read out by the abbess to the nuns in the chapel. Comments were often made about excessive luxury in the cells, that there were too many unruly maids and slaves, and that some entertainments which had been presented were illegal; there was too frequent a use of fashionable clothes instead of veils and robes; there were too many secret contacts, there were even special bullfights, and excessive expenditure on music. Meantime a question might be asked: who is that elegant, well-dressed young man standing near the fountain by the *donadas'* library? The nephew of the abbess? The lover of the prioress? The secretary to the bishop? Or, could it be Christ himself? In a *convento grande*, who knew?

Frequent visitors to these nunneries were *beatas* and *tapadas*, the former being usually women who wore the habit of a consecrated virgin, practised many acts of charity and devotion, and spent much time in churches and chapels, but who were not complete nuns. A *beata* was seemingly a person endowed with special powers to whom ordinary people could turn for religious help. A *tapada* was a worldly lady often dressed, fashionably, with silks from China, lace from the Netherlands, and perfumes from the East. Her most frequent garment was a long shawl worn in a flirtatious style to conceal her identity. *Tapadas* were a scandalous element in Lima's population by 1600, and remained so. We should perhaps allow ourselves to think that when they went to nunneries, they were visiting relations.

The queen of *beatas* in late sixteenth-century Peru was undoubtedly Flores de Oliva, better known as Santa Rosa of Lima. She was born in 1586 and the Indian maid who looked after her in her cot as a baby saw that she had two beautifully formed roses on her cheeks. That allowed for her early beatification. The baby was considered a new 'rose without thorns'. Rosa was a most popular *beata* and from 1606 she wore the white robe of the Dominicans. Saint Catherine of Siena was her inspiration. Rosa visited daily the chapels of Our Lady of the Rosary, Our Lady of Loreto, and Our Lady of Remedios, the first in the Dominican church and the other two in the Jesuit church of Lima, and she became the *camarera*, that is, the faithful dresser and attendant, in all three. She lived in a shed in her family's garden and enjoyed a life of intense prayer and penance, but also of sewing and embroidering. Rosa also sang well. She was witty and she composed beautiful poems which turned into songs of divine love. It was believed that her music attracted all kinds of birds. She was said to be able to grow wonderful flowers overnight, and she could quickly dispose of the mosquitoes which infested her garden. Distinguished ladies of all ages thronged Sister Rosa's dwelling, as did grand figures in the Jesuit and Dominican orders. Just before she died, a portrait of Christ by Angelino Medoro, of Rome, in a chapel frequented by Rosa, was said to have begun to sweat. This was held to be a miracle. The subsequent death of Rosa in her early thirties was an occasion for a religious upheaval, and heroic dedication. Holy ladies passed whole weeks in prayer, while strong men offered themselves for heroic sacrifices.

The convents of Lima were not the only centres of cultural life in that city, however. The monasteries, though less impressive than the nunneries, had their artists too. Thus in a Dominican monastery, Fray Diego de Hojeda, the Seville-born prior of the Convent of Rosario, would write *La Cristada*, a life of Christ in popular language and probably the best sacred epic in Spanish in the last years of the sixteenth century.[16]

Lima, with its fashionable shops, its *calle de mercaderes* (street of merchants), its craftsmen, its busy candlemakers, its street of silversmiths, its fine private houses with heavy studded doors beneath elaborate coats of arms, and its extraordinary convents, was a worthy capital of a rich territory in a great new empire. Frequent jousting competitions (for example, the game of hoops) also showed that Peru had nothing to learn from Europe in the way of unusual entertainments.

Cuzco, a thousand miles inland, should not be forgotten for, unlike Lima, it lay in a fertile valley, full of fruit trees, and it now boasted two great squares in the Spanish style, linked by a lively street full of shops and stalls. Magnificent religious buildings such as the cathedral, the Jesuit college, and the Franciscan, Mercedarian, and Dominican monasteries, together with the frequent fountains, made Cuzco a jewel all of its own.

# 11

# Chile and its Conquerors

*The country which was the stage to these actions is the remotest of the new world, and the furthest trodden by Spaniards beyond the borders of Peru, so that it is hard to have news of it ...*

Alonso de Ercilla's preface to his poem *La Araucana*

The second half of the sixteenth century in Chile was marked by continual warfare between Spanish colonists and the indigenous Indians. The latter had learned how to use Spanish weapons and knew how to handle horses in war. The consequence was that the cities founded earlier in the century by the brilliant conquistador Pedro de Valdivia were often isolated, though Santiago remained the capital. Francisco de Villagrán, a long-time collaborator of Valdivia, had been appointed governor by the viceroy in Lima in 1558 and was named *adelantado* in 1563.[1] But that did not guarantee effective rule.

Villagrán, a native of Santervas de Campos in León, and a veteran of the war in Tunis against the Turks, did, however, withstand the conqueror of Valdivia, Lautaro, the Indian Mapuche commander who was killed whilst advancing on Santiago in 1557, having already captured Concepción. By 1558, Villagrán's successor as governor, García Hurtado de Mendoza, had recovered all the lost cities, but that did not lead to a secure triumph. One of his more intelligent successors, Martín García de Loyola, was killed in action at the battle of Cuvalva in 1598.

The loose tribal organization of the Indians in Chile meant that it was especially difficult to inflict a decisive defeat on them. (The

Spaniards gave them the name of Araucanians if they lived south of the river Bío-Bío.) The mountainous and wooded countryside made it easy for the Indians to carry out guerrilla wars of ambushes and surprises. Expedition after expedition was mounted from Lima against those Indians in Chile, and the campaigns were conducted with savagery, but a complete conquest remained elusive. Spanish settlements were decimated but they recovered with regularity. If one Indian chief was killed, another swiftly took his place. In 1600 it was quite unclear what future Chile would have – whether it would be part of the great Spanish empire or not.

These endless military engagements were, however, marked by the participation of a remarkable poet, Alonso de Ercilla y Zúñiga, a conquistador of aristocratic Basque origin. In his epic poem *La Araucana* he illuminated the Spanish fighting against Indians in the sixteenth century as no one else did, and his marvellous lines elevate the conflicts which he described into legend.

Ercilla was born in 1533, six years after King Philip, to whom he eventually dedicated his work. His parents were Fortún García de Ercilla and Leonor de Zúñiga from Bermeo, a fishing port on the Basque coast between Bilbao and San Sebastián, in Vizcaya (Guernica lies a few miles inland from it). The early death of Fortún placed the Ercillas in a difficult financial position, but they were helped by the royal family. Ercilla's mother Leonora became a maid of honour to the Empress Isabel and Alonso himself became a page to Prince Philip – in which capacity he travelled extensively in Italy, Germany, and the Low Countries. In 1551 he went to live in Valladolid, the informal capital of Spain at that time, and was present at part of the famous debate between Bishop Las Casas and Juan Ginés de Sepúlveda.[2] He then accompanied Princess María to Vienna to be married to Maximilian II, later the Holy Roman Emperor. Alonso also accompanied Prince Philip to England to marry Mary Tudor in 1554, and thus was able to see for himself the lovely water meadows in the Thames valley on which *Amadís de Gaula* dwells so lovingly.

In 1552, Philip named Andrés Hurtado de Mendoza, Marquis of Cañete, to be viceroy in Peru; and at the same time Jerónimo de Alderete, of the well-known family of Tordesillas which we encountered while considering the conquest of New Spain, was named governor of Chile.[3] Alderete took Ercilla with him as part of his colonial court. Cañete's first task in Peru was to deal with a recent *criollo* revolt led by a disgruntled settler, Francisco Hernández Girón. Then, like all viceroys, he had to consider what to do about Chile.

Hernández Girón, who came originally from Cáceres in Extremadura, had taken part in most of the scandalous civil tumults in Peru since his arrival in the New World in 1535. He hated the New Laws and launched an uprising against their introduction, but he was swiftly outmanoeuvred by Cañete's forces. He was hanged, drawn, and quartered in the main square of Lima in 1554. His wife, Mencía de Almariz, with his mother, founded the convent of the Incarnation in that city and became its first prioress.

In Chile there were by the 1570s several convents, of which the most important were Las Agustinas and Santa Clara. The former was established in 1575 in Santiago by a group of widows of captains who had accompanied Valdivia. Santa Clara was founded by Isabel de Plasencia in Osorno, south-central Chile, a little later, and eventually it merged with Las Agustinas in Santiago.

When Alderete died in 1556, before he could take up his post, Cañete appointed his own sharp-minded son, García Hurtado de Mendoza, as governor in Chile. Hurtado de Mendoza promptly left Lima with Ercilla and others to take up his new post. Ercilla was sent to direct Spanish defences at Concepción, and lived there several years fighting his way to survival through the deaths of a large number of Araucanian Indians, perhaps as many as 50,000. He seems to have been especially impressed by the role of the delightful *conquistadora* Mencía de Nidos, a woman as beautiful as she was brave, in the heroic defence of Concepción. At this time, Ercilla began his famous poem *La Araucana*, which concentrates on the conquest by Spain of a relatively small valley between Peru and Chile. But his small valley symbolizes a continent.

A few stanzas from Canto I are worthy of quotation:

> Chile my scene: a fertile crescent remote,
> Hard by the border of antarctic seas.
> Home of a stiff-necked people, bred to arms,
> Renowned in war, by neighbour nations feared;

Whose not distempered blood alike rebels
At rule domestic and at stranger yoke,
No king among themselves they own, nor e'er
Have bowed the knee to foreign conqueror.

Far to the North and South its shores extend
Along the borders of the uncharted main
We call the Southern Sea; from East to West
Scarcely a hundred miles this narrow land
Measures at broadest; and from where the Pole
Stands in the altitude of twenty-seven
Runs southward to a strait, where Ocean Sea
And Chilean waters blend their meeting tides.

Those mighty seas that on opposing sides,
Beat on the scarpments of the Southern land
Shaking the Terra Firma with the roll
Of their tempestuous surges, rage in vain,
Eager to meet and mingle till at length
They fend the land asunder there and rush
Together through the cleft Magellan first
Of Ocean-pilots found and gave his name.[4]

While in Concepción, Ercilla was implicated in a brawl with a youthful friend Juan de Pineda and others, who were celebrating with excessive enthusiasm the proclamation in 1558 of Philip as king of Spain. Ercilla was imprisoned, condemned to death by the new governor, Hurtado de Mendoza, and only narrowly escaped to liberty. He went to the city of La Imperial to seek food but was ambushed by the Indians, whose leaders he eventually captured and executed. Among those who suffered were the Indian leaders Tucupal, Caupilican, Rengo, Galvariño, and Lincoya, all of whom figure in *La Araucana*. Galvariño had his hands cut off, while Caupilican became a Christian just before he was beheaded.

Ercilla then went to Lima, was pardoned, and took part briefly in several expeditions such as the organization of the royal forces against the dangerous and rebellious Lope de Aguirre.[5] He then left for

Panama, crossed to the city of Nombre de Dios on the Atlantic coast, and sailed home to Spain in 1562 after about eight dramatic years in the New World.

Not long after arriving back in Castile, Ercilla set off for central Europe in 1562 to seek out his sister, María Magdalena, who was now working for the Empress María as well as his mother. Back in Madrid in 1565 he published the first part of his famous poem. Parts II and III followed in 1570 and 1590. Part I made him famous and probably rich.

Ercilla married, in 1565, María Bazán, a daughter of Gil Sánchez Bazán and Margarita de Ugarte. Margarita was a maid of honour to the Queen of Spain; she was also a cousin of the famous Marquis of Santa Cruz, who had been the victor of the battle of Lepanto in 1571. Ercilla was present at several of the famous battles which Spain fought in the 1580s, such as that of the Azores against Don Antonio de Crato. One of Ercilla's illegitimate sons was in the expedition of the Armada against England in 1588 and died when the galleon *San Marcos* was sunk.

Ercilla's famous work is a rare example from this period of an auto-biographical poem. An American literary historian has written: 'The intensity of the emotions expressed, the sweep of the story, and the vivid pictures of the opposing peoples, make it not only America's best epic but the greatest epic in Spanish in the sixteenth century.'[6] Ercilla's descriptions of local customs are masterpieces, as, for example, the fiesta in Canto X. Voltaire, in an essay on epic poetry, compared the speech of Colocob to the Araucanians with that of Homer's Nestor to his son Antilochus and other Greek leaders in the *Iliad*.

*La Araucana* dwells vividly on the many events both in the Americas and Europe in which the author was engaged. Ercilla also writes about the battle of Saint Quentin in 1557, about which he only heard.

The most interesting section of the poem treats of the fighting against the Araucanian Indians after the death of the conquistador Valdivia in 1553. The poem devotes a great deal of space to the personal combats between the leaders of the two opposing forces. Ercilla, with his Genoese companion, Andrea, presents himself as an architect of victory, which naturally made him the enemy of the governor of Chile, García Hurtado de Mendoza, who resented being cast in an inferior role. The governor therefore commissioned Pedro de Oña, a Chilean-born poet, to write a rival poem which would be called *Primera Parte de el Arauco dominado* and was finished in 1596. It has some splendid descriptions of nature and would have been much admired were it not for the infinite superiority of *La Araucana*.

Ercilla's praise of the courage of the Araucanian leaders stands in conspicuous contrast with most writing of this kind, but his poem became very popular and went into ten editions in the author's lifetime alone.[7] Considering the generosity of his approach to the character of the Araucanians, the success of the poem was an astonishing event for its time. Cervantes, who was probably a friend of Ercilla, greatly admired his work, and readers of *Don Quixote* will remember *La Araucana* as one of the three books which were saved from the fire organized by the readers in Don Quixote's house. (The other two were *La Austriada* by Juan Rufo of Córdoba, an epic about Don John of Austria and Lepanto, and *El Monserrato* by Cristóbal de Virués of Valencia,[8] about the origins of the monastery of Montserrat.)

Ercilla died in Madrid in 1594. By then, Chile had become a quiescent captaincy-general dependent on Peru, whose viceroys were instrumental in securing it.

Wild rumours of what existed to the south of the country persisted, however. Thus in the 1540s, Agustín de Zárate (historian, civil servant, and tax collector, originally from Valladolid) had made extensive journeys down the west coast of Chile, to the south of which there was, he reported, a 'large province inhabited entirely by women who permitted men among them only at a time suitable for procreation . . . their queen was Gaboimilla which in their language means "heaven of gold" because it was said they raise a great deal of gold'.[9] But neither Zárate nor any other conquistador made the journey which was needed to reach the Amazons. The tale of Amazons was, of course, the stuff of legend. Everyone fell back an apparently very short distance from that incomparable unknown. That did not prevent Zárate from proving himself a successful historian, whose history of the conquest of Peru would be translated into French, English, German, and Italian.

# 12

# The Conquest of Yucatan

*. . . they turned back to the island of Yucatan on the north side. We went along the coast where we found a beautiful tower on a point which is said to be inhabited by women who live without men. It is believed that they are a race of Amazons. Other towers were seen seemingly in towns but the Captain [Grijalva] did not allow us to go ashore.*

Fray Juan Díaz, May 1518

*Oh how simple were our ancestors who knew no other means of killing each other except with bows and arrows, sticks and stones, and no other poisons except those which they could distil from herbs.*

Hurtado de Mendoza,
*The War in Granada*, 1627

By the time of the accession of King Philip to the throne in Spain in 1556, Yucatan had been effectively won for him by an able group of Castilian conquistadors, led by the Montejo family. The Montejos were originally natives of Salamanca. Not for the first time in the New World, members of one family spearheaded a number of conquests (other such families were the Pizarros, the Alvarados, and Cortés and his cousins).

At this time New Spain consisted of territory from California in the north down to the isthmus of Panama in the south, an enormous stretch of land later divided into several smaller countries. California, christened thus by Cortés in memory of a mythical country of Amazons in

Garci Rodríguez de Montalvo's magical novel *Sergas de Esplandián,* was the northernmost province of this new empire. The Maya Indians inhabited parts of the provinces of Chiapas, of Yucatan, and Guatemala. The whole territory had been skilfully divided into provinces roughly equal in size and population, insofar as the latter was known.

A Franciscan, Fray Jacobo de Testera, and four other friars went to Yucatan either in late 1535 or early 1536 in search of souls who might become Christians.[1] Both the viceroy, Antonio de Mendoza, and the Supreme Court backed them. Testera became commissary, or leader, in 1541, went back briefly to Castile and, on his return to the New World next year sent the famous friar Motolinía and twelve other friars to Guatemala, with orders to carry missionary activity into the adjacent province of Yucatan. These included four men who later became well known in the province (Luis de Villalpando, Lorenzo de Bienvenida,[2] Melchor de Benavente, and Juan de Herrera). Motolinía told the conquistador Francisco de Montejo, then in Gracias a Dios (on the extreme eastern cape of central America), that he supported the spreading of missionary teaching in Yucatan, and he inspired Bienvenida to enter the province by the south, via the so-called Golfo Dulce. Such was Motolinía's reputation that his wishes were seen as orders. Villalpando, Benavente, and Herrera went to Yucatan in 1545 from Chiapas and Palenque in New Spain. Their aim was conversion. Four further Franciscans arrived in Yucatan direct from Spain:[3] Fray Villalpando learned Maya and often preached in it, carrying out the conversion of what he claimed to have been 28,000 Indians.

Testera is a good example of a man for whom the New World offered a great opportunity. He was a brother of the chamberlain to the brilliant, if unreliable, Renaissance French king, Francis I. Testera first went to the Indies in 1529, when he was already about fifty years old. Custodian (titular leader) of the Franciscan mission in New Spain in 1533, he was later commissar-general for the Indies. He had preached in Spain before he arrived in New Spain, where he communicated by means of pictures, since he had not learned any indigenous language (his pictures became known as the 'Testerian hieroglyphs'). He and four other friars then went to Yucatan, as mentioned, probably late in 1535 or early in 1536.

Testera then returned briefly to Spain itself and, on his return, despatched Motolinía and the twelve other well-known Franciscans to Guatemala, with orders to carry missionary activity into the adjacent provinces. Testera had written to the Emperor Charles V in May 1533 denouncing those devils who were seeking to persuade the colonists that the Indians were not capable of living a normal life. He criticized 'those who were too fastidious and lazy' (including, he admitted, people like himself) to undertake the labour of learning their languages, 'and who lacked the zeal to break through the wall of language in order to enter their hearts'. He added wisely:

> How can anyone say that these people are not capable, when they can construct such impressive buildings, can make such subtle creations, are silversmiths, painters, merchants, able when presiding at meetings, in speaking, in the exercise of courtesy, in sponsoring fiestas, marriages, solemn occasions . . . able to express sorrow and appreciation, when the occasion requires it? They can even sing plainsong and also perform contrapuntally to organ accompaniment. They can compose music and teach others how to enjoy religious music. They even preach to the people the sermons which we teach them.[4]

In July 1543, in the wake of the promulgation of the controversial New Laws, Fray Testera was received in Mexico/Tenochtitlan, the capital, by a great crowd of *naturales*:

> These Indians bestowed gifts on him, erecting triumphal arches, sweeping clear the street along which he was to pass and strewing upon him cypress branches and roses and bearing him in a litter [much as they had greeted old Mexican monarchs such as Montezuma], and all this because he and other Franciscans had informed the Indians that they had come to restore them to the state in which they were before they were placed under the rule of the King of Spain. These statements had excited them and they went out to receive Friar Testera as if he had been a Viceroy.[5]

Francisco de Montejo el *Mozo* (son of the conquistador and *adelantado* Francisco de Montejo) also greeted the new Franciscans in Yucatan warmly.[6] He took 'them into his house and displayed all respect and veneration, so that the Indians would do the same',[7] and he did everything he could to help them. He built a church for the

Franciscans in Campeche, and told the local *caciques* that the friars had arrived to instruct them in the true faith and guide them to a better life. The *caciques* were of course the Maya.

Montejo *padre*, the *adelantado*, old companion of Cortés, had been named governor of Honduras/Higueras in 1535, but he wanted to exchange that province for Chiapas, which was then ruled by the great conquistador Pedro de Alvarado. Viceroy Mendoza and Alvarado, usually easy to deal with on such matters, agreed. Alvarado went to Honduras/Higueras, saved it from destruction as a colony, and then returned temporarily to Spain. The Council of the Indies insisted in 1540 that he should return to Honduras/Higueras to suppress a serious revolt of Indians. Having re-established Spanish control, Alvarado returned to Guatemala furious because the Council now insisted on a forced exchange of provinces – something which Montejo no longer wanted, because he had become positively interested in his new territories. Nevertheless, in 1540, Alvarado assumed the governorship of Chiapas. Alvarado offered Montejo his rich *encomienda* of Xochimilco in the valley of Mexico, with its abundant fruit and flowers, as additional compensation.[8]

Then, early in 1542, Montejo received an appeal for help from the town halls of Honduras/Higueras which fell into confusion after Alvarado's sudden death in 1541.[9] There was further conflict when the viceroy and the *audiencia* of New Spain named the Supreme Court judge Alonso Maldonado to be acting governor of Guatemala, including Honduras/Higueras. Later in May 1544, Maldonado became president of a new court, 'de los Confines', which was first set up at Gracias a Dios.

The *adelantado* Montejo was at that time pressing his claim for an extended Yucatan which would have stretched from the Copilco river in Tabasco province to the Ulua river in Guatemala. He succeeded. In 1535, Yucatan and Honduras/Higueras were merged into one large territory, of which Montejo was named governor. In 1539 he incorporated Chiapas into it. He was, however, still without full responsibility in Yucatan until in 1540 the new court, 'de los Confines', replaced the governors in central America. An entrepreneur, Juan de Lerma, from the city of that name near Burgos, who had made money selling indigenous slaves from central America to the

Caribbean islands, was named treasurer of Yucatan and inspector (*veedor*) – that is, controller of finance – in Honduras/Higueras.

Soon Montejo *padre* began to send more troops to Yucatan, including his nephew (*el Sobrino*), yet another Francisco de Montejo, then aged only eighteen. Soon, too, the *adelantado*'s son Francisco *el Mozo* was ready to move, strengthened by a new instruction from his father: 'You must strive to see that the people who go with you live and act as true Christians, keeping them from evil and public sins, and not allowing them to blaspheme . . . Third, you shall . . . go to the town of Campeche . . . and you shall establish nearby, at T-ho, a town and carry out a *repartimiento* . . .'[10] Montejo *padre* was now beginning to show himself the model of an enlightened despot.

*El Mozo*, who was more intelligent, but less resilient, than his experienced father, knew that, though there was no gold to be had in Yucatan, there were good exports such as embroidered cotton cloth, honey, wax, indigo, cacao, and slaves.[11] The first Montejo, the *adelantado*, retained control of Yucatan but, at this stage, he seemed to have confined his activity to finding good captains, soldiers, and colonists.

*El Mozo* set off by canoe and joined his cousin (*el Sobrino*) at Champoton. Then with about forty men they went to Campeche, which they re-established under the name of San Francisco, with thirty men choosing to become citizens there.[12]

Before they were fully under way, they were now reinforced by 250 to 300 well-equipped Spanish soldiers from New Spain and many Indian auxiliaries. The latter included some Nahuatl-speaking Mexicans recruited from the senior Montejo's large *encomienda* at Atzcapotzalco. *El Mozo* left behind Beltrán de Cetina as his lieutenant in Campeche. Montejo *padre* was technically in breach of all the rules of the *encomiendas* when he sent 'his' Indians to work so far away from their base. But he was not a man easy to defy.

*El Mozo*'s plan for conquest in Yucatan was to mount a slow movement into villages, each of which would be rendered self-sufficient in terms of its citizenry and provided with a well-ordered system of supply. Subjugation of the next district would not happen until sufficient forces had been mustered, and every column of soldiers would include a communications unit to avoid isolation.

This 'admirably conceived' system has been described as 'Roman in its efficiency'.[13] Both *el Mozo* and the *adelantado* Montejo worked on it. The plan required the development of new tactics, including a provision of ditches beside roads, and mounted troops in the centre of any column for use in any engagement, as well as two wings of foot soldiers. In pitched battles, the impact of horsemen was in those days as decisive as ever, for the indigenous people were never able to find any real defence against the horse. The *Relación de Mérida*, an official account, comments that 'at the beginning, they [the Indians] really thought that the mount and man were all one animal'.[14] But in addition firearms, lances, daggers, crossbows, and, above all, swords gave Spain as great a superiority as ever. Though they often stood their ground, the *naturales* never overcame their fear of arquebuses and the terrifying noise that those weapons made.[15]

The conquistadors left Campeche in the autumn of 1541, sending a captain to T-ho, where the Indian *cacique* received the Spaniards well, and there they established a Spanish city. This eventually became the city of Mérida. Relations turned sour when the Indians there began to show 'haughtiness and stubbornness in their souls', as reported by a conquistador named Diego Sánchez.[16] So did the Spaniards.

This country, which the Spaniards had already in the 1530s known so well, was now barely recognizable: it had been laid to waste when the lords of Manu had waged fierce wars with the Cocum of Sotuta and after the treacherous killing of important Xiu leaders. Moreover the inhabitants of the whole peninsula had used up their stores of food, including maize. A famine followed in 1542 which was so serious that the natives were reduced to eating the bark of trees, especially that of the soft and tender *kumche*. The Xiu offered sacrifices to their gods to escape starvation, throwing slaves into the deep well of Chichen Itza in the hope of salvation, while the Cocum set fire to a building where the Xiu lords were lodged.

The hostility of the Maya of Chakan to Spaniards was resolute. They were encouraged by H-Kin-Chuy, a priest from the small *pueblo* of Peba, who preached a war of extermination against the invaders. Still, the Spaniards had their native friends, and they were warned of an attack (by 'more Indians than the pelt of a deer has hairs') said to be threatening them at Tuchican. Montejo *el Sobrino* seized H-Kin-Chuy under the cover of darkness.

Mérida was eventually founded on the site of T-ho in January 1542, after bitter fighting in which pitched battles were replaced by guerrilla warfare. The name 'Mérida' was chosen because 'on its site, the conquistadors found buildings of lime and worked stone with many mouldings which reminded some of them of the Roman city of Mérida in Spain'.[17] Seventy soldiers were named citizens, and a municipal council (*cabildo*) was formed. Fray Juan de Sosa from Puebla, an experienced planner, was commissioned to lay out a new town, while Fray Francisco Hernández was asked to design a church. Mérida, now a delightful city, has remained the capital of Yucatan ever since.

# 13

# Conclusion in Yucatan

*Of the moral effect of the monuments themselves, standing as*
*they do in the depths of a tropical forest, silent and solemn,*
*strange in design, excellent in sculpture, rich in ornament . . . I*
*shall not pretend to convey any idea.*

John Lloyd Stephens, 1839

But the conquistadors could not rest. Fray Diego López de Cogulludo recalled in his *Historia de Yucatán* that 60,000 Maya, led by a certain Nachi Cocom, were subjected in 1543 to the next aggression: 'Only through sword thrusts could the Spaniards defeat their enemies.'[1] He went on to say that the natives who remained alive fled away forever and never again offered pitched open battle.[2]

Francisco de Montejo *el Mozo* now sent armed companies to carry the war into outlying districts of Yucatan. The Indians responded by seeking to destroy everything which might be useful to the Spaniards. But the battle of Mérida had broken the back of Indian resistance. The local chieftainships were under Spanish control. Montejo's secretary, Rodrigo Álvarez, divided up seventy Mayan *pueblos* 'in a very Christian manner', as he himself reported in a later inquiry.[3]

*El Mozo* told his father that he should stay where he was in Mérida for the time being, so the *adelantado* sent his nephew, *el Sobrino*, to occupy the general area of Conil. The two cousins, *el Mozo* and *el Sobrino*, drew up plans for moving against the tribes of the Chikinchel and Ecab. Loyal Spaniards all hoped that Conil would become a centre of commerce. *El Mozo* moved against the interior chieftains, such as Sotuta, to all of whom he proclaimed the *requerimiento*, but which, of course, they rejected; meanwhile, although defeated, the proud Nachi Cocom agreed all the same to accept the overlordship of the Spaniards. *El Mozo* allowed him to retain his authority, but as a vassal of the king of Castile. He then sent his uncle, Alonso López, to Calotmul and the south and south-east. These areas consisted of Xiu territories which had not followed their Maní kinsmen into an alliance with Spain.

*El Mozo* next led a well-equipped expedition in 1543 into Cochuah, while *El Sobrino* concerned himself with the north-east. The Montejo cousins met at Tecoh east of Mérida, and they continued together to Chauaca where, on 24 May 1543, they established the town of Valladolid. Forty or fifty of their soldiers were named as citizens. The *caciques* of nearby Sací started a new revolt with the support of many *pueblos*, but Sací itself was seized on behalf of *el Sobrino* by Francisco de Cieza with only twenty men. Meanwhile an incipient rebellion at Mérida was forestalled by Rodrigo Álvarez. *El Sobrino* continued through Ecab, then on to Cozumel, an island in the Caribbean discovered by Cortés, which was conquered with no opposition.

The journey to and from Cozumel was difficult not because of threats from the Indians but because of the storms at sea encountered both ways. *El Sobrino* asked Cieza to continue the battle with a handful of men against the Maya of Cochuá, in which they were successful. Afterwards Valladolid was transferred there with thirty-nine *encomiendas*, because 'this location is in the midst of all the land and ... because the region is healthier and drier than Chauaca ... it is the best town that there is in the entire Indies ... This town was founded in ... meadows surrounded by a large, rough, stony, bushy-covered region ... between two great wells (*cenotes*) of sweet water ... At their bottom, there is a great water table over 1,790 feet in diameter of extraordinary depth ... Captain Montejo laid out this town north–east and east–west and ... gave it its broad streets.'[4]

Next, the *adelantado* Montejo and then his son abandoned the command in the south-east, the area of Uaymil-Chetumal, first to a new conquistador named Jorge de Villagómez and then to Gaspar Pacheco and his family, his son Melchor and nephew Alonso. Early in 1544, Alonso moved into Cochuah, but the Indians resisted, leading to the most cruel of Spanish campaigns, in which the Pachecos resorted to wanton acts of brutality. But they were successful in their aim of destroying the enemy. The Montejos, who were Renaissance gentlemen, did not approve of the Pachecos but were unable to control them.

The Franciscan Fray Lorenzo de Bienvenida denounced the Pachecos in February 1548: 'Nero was not more cruel than this man [Alonso Pacheco],' he reported:

> Even though the natives did not make war, he robbed the province, and consumed the foodstuffs of the natives, who fled into the bush in fear ... since, as soon as this captain captured any of them, he sets his dogs on them. And the Indians fled and did not sow their crops so they all died of hunger ... there used to be *pueblos* of 500 and 1,000 persons and now one of 100 is considered large ... This captain with his own hands ... killed many with the garrotte, saying, 'This is a good rod with which to finish off these people'. And after he had killed them, he is supposed to have said, 'Oh, how well I finished them off' ...[5]

In 1544 eight Franciscans, four from Guatemala and four from New Spain, were named to initiate the conversions of the Maya Indians in Yucatan. The campaign was to be a Franciscan monopoly and the friars concerned included the aforementioned Lorenzo de Bienvenida, who came specially from Guatemala. He walked all the way to Campeche, preaching as he went. Another colleague, Fray Luis de Villalpando, was the first Spaniard to get to grips with the Mayan language, of which he even prepared a grammar and dictionary. What determination, what persistence! Within a short time, 2,000 Indian boys were in a Franciscan school in Mérida, being taught to read and write their own language. Fray Villalpando even prepared a Mayan to read European script as well as to learn the elements of Christianity in Spanish and sing Latin in choirs. A Franciscan house was set up in Oxkutzcab in the land of the Xiu, where there was also a school by 1547. An alleged plot to burn down the monastery was betrayed. Twenty-six Maya nobles were about to be burned alive in the square when Fray Villalpando interceded successfully on their behalf. Ah Kukum, lord of Maní, was baptized as Francisco de Montejo Xiu.

The Spaniards won their battles in those days thanks to their 'superb discipline under pressure'. Also important, however, was their tight formation, their awareness of the value of every Spanish life, and a remarkable capacity to move through the land with no scruple as to the human cost of their actions to the Indians. Once again, crossbows, muskets, arquebuses, and mastiffs, and above all Toledo steel, played a decisive part in these engagements; horses had their usual success where the terrain was good, though the narrow stony paths of Yucatan often did not suit them. The Maya were tough and strong ('bellicose, valiant and experienced in war', commented the colonial *cabildo* in Mérida), and they were innovative: for example, their use of pits to trip and injure their enemies' horses. They were, however, parochial, being anxious only to see the foreigners leave their land. They thought of the Spaniards as birds of passage. According to traditional Maya warfare, the seizure of loot and of captives for sacrifice was, as with the Mexica, the prime aim. The Maya found the Spaniards much more difficult to deal with than they anticipated. They brought new diseases as well as new weapons with them, which led to large declines in populations. The population on the peninsula of Yucatan may have fallen in these years from 800,000 to 250,000.

The four towns of Yucatan were now Mérida, with about seventy Spanish families in 1550; Valladolid, with forty-five; Campeche, with about forty; and Salamanca de Bacalar, with a mere fifteen to twenty. Between them, these places divided up the administration of the peninsula. Nearly ten years later, at the time of Philip's proclamation as king in 1558, there were perhaps 400 Spanish families in Yucatan. Their houses were naturally Spanish in design but, being built by the Maya, they had what Inga Clendinnen calls 'an ineradicable Indian flavour'. Spaniards slept in hammocks for coolness and, like Indians, became used to waking at the sound of women grinding maize on stone slabs. Only the lowest class of Spaniard would take an Indian woman for a wife – others maintained them as mistresses.[6]

The great Bartolomé de Las Casas, Bishop of Chiapas in what was then the province of Vera Paz, set about preaching the faith without the use of force, in support of his brother Dominicans. As we have repeatedly seen, he infuriated many colonists because of what they considered his excessively tolerant attitudes towards the Indians. A pastoral letter of his of 20 March 1545 on this subject deserves to be recalled. In that document, Las Casas refused to receive confession from Spaniards unless they handed back land taken from the Indians, and he advocated the full enactment of the New Laws of 1542 for the protection of Indians, admonishing the colonists in unmeasured terms if they seemed to hesitate. The colonists, refusing to recognize Las Casas's spiritual jurisdiction over Yucatan, tried to cut him and his fellow Dominicans off from food, and they even refused to pay tithes. In this the colonists were supported by the Franciscans, who had come to think of Yucatan as their domain. Las Casas had to content himself with preaching to, not receiving confession from, the colonists.

Unsurprisingly, a new Maya revolt was about to occur which would be coordinated throughout the peninsula. The chiefs of various cities such as Cupul (the heart of the rebellion), Cochuá, Sotuta, and Uaymil-Chetumal had accepted Spanish masters, but many, especially the priests, lived for revenge. The system of *encomiendas*, with its precarious labour regulations, seemed intolerable to most of them. Long before, the Maya had disliked Toltec overlords as much as they now did the Europeans.

At the full moon on 8 November 1546 the Maya in the east of Yucatan rose with violent fury. Their greatest concentration of force was against the new town of Valladolid. There the *encomenderos* and their wives and children were mostly slaughtered. Some were crucified, some were roasted over copal, a resin used for the making of varnish, some were set up as targets for arrows, while some had their hearts torn out. Among the latter was Bernardino de Villagómez, who was dragged through the town by a rope, before his head was cut off as well as his vital parts. The rebels sent such trophies by swift couriers throughout the land to incite their fellows to greater fury.[7] The Spaniards in Valladolid and Salamanca de Bacalar were almost overrun.

The Indians killed not only Spaniards but also any indigenous people who had worked for them and indeed any who would not join in their uprising. Many Indian labourers, perhaps as many as 600, were thus killed. The natives also killed animals owned by Spaniards, their horses and cattle, other livestock, chickens, dogs, and cats. They uprooted European trees and plants. It was a wholesale slaughter.

The Spaniards soon rallied, giving permission to friendly tribes to enslave any rebels whom they caught and who could thus be sold to the planters on Caribbean islands.[8] The council of Mérida, headed by

Rodrigo Álvarez, busied themselves mobilizing as many fighters as they could to defend Valladolid. Álvarez seized some local *caciques* to prevent them from joining the rebellion, while a colleague, Francisco Tamayo, took forty Spaniards and some 500 Indians to relieve Valladolid. They were blocked on the way, especially at Izamal, but broke through to relieve the beleaguered garrison. *El Sobrino* set off for Valladolid with thirty horse while Montejo the *adelantado* remained at Campeche. Tamayo Pacheco, now commander in Valladolid, sought to break out of the siege and eventually did so, while Juana de Azamor, widow of the prominent *encomendero* Blas González, acted as a nurse (her brother and his family having been killed on their *encomienda*): 'I, being of but slight age, was with my husband, for we were living in our home and we would not abandon it. I gathered into our house many wounded and sick soldiers and, with great care, I healed them and cared for them till they were cured . . . for there were then no doctors in this town. I likewise encouraged them not to leave this land but to remain for the service of His Majesty.'[9]

*El Mozo* soon assumed the general direction of the military response, while *el Sobrino* concerned himself with the reconquest of the Cupul territory, the heart of the revolt. By March 1547 it had been quelled.

Hundreds of Maya were burned at the stake, and there were many arrests. The *caciques* and priests most responsible were executed, among them Chilam Anbal who had claimed to be 'the youngest son of God', a consanguinity rarely emphasized in religion. Chikinchel was the last area to be conquered.

The campaigns to suppress this revolt were carried out with much more harshness than previous ones by the Montejos. Even *el Sobrino*, who was relatively pacific compared to his fellow conquistadors, committed some acts of startling cruelty. For example, he set dogs against certain male warriors and had some women killed. But after the revolt, Montejo the *adelantado* took legal action against captains who were guilty of flagrant cruelty (or so he reported in a letter to the Emperor Charles in February 1547).[10] Following the uprising, the Spaniards enslaved about 2,000 Indians, mostly Cupul, but Montejo the *adelantado* soon declared that the taking of slaves was now against the law. He directed that all slaves should be brought before him so that they could be freed. *El Sobrino* also summoned the principal *caciques* of the province and told them that it was his aim to govern with justice and equity, for their benefit. When he asked them through interpreters why they had risen in rebellion, they explained that it was because of the exhortations of their priests.[11]

The Montejos then shrewdly sought out the Maya chiefs, lodged them in their houses, and strove to gain their goodwill. Fray Villalpando preached extensively in Maya and explained the essence of Christianity, inviting the *caciques* to send their sons to a new school which the Franciscans were preparing in their monastery at Mérida, to instruct youths in religious doctrine, writing, and contrapuntal singing. The school was a success and as a consequence some important *caciques* became Christians. Fray Villalpando and Fray Benavente went to Maní, where the *adelantado* still dreamed of forging a Christian country, and there they established another school. But they also encountered many difficulties, partly because the institution of slavery was well established among the Maya, especially among the Spaniards' allies, the Xiu.

There was considerable support now for the idea of a separate bishopric of Yucatan which would be independent of Chiapas. Las Casas lent his magisterial support to the idea. Eventually, in 1562, Fray Francisco de Toral was named the first bishop.[12] Las Casas made an arrangement with Alonso Maldonado, acting governor of Guatemala, whereby the Indians became direct vassals of the Crown and were overseen exclusively by his order, the Dominicans. There would be no *encomiendas* in the name of individual conquistadors.

The Dominicans met with success. From the beginning, the Indians accepted them much more than they did the Franciscans, and they willingly gave them obedience. Las Casas returned to Chiapas as bishop, and secured confirmation of the exclusive jurisdiction of his order.

But Montejo the *adelantado* thought that these friars were going too far in their desire to assist the Indians. Montejo's view was bolstered by that of the president of the Supreme Court *de los Confines*, his (eventual) son-in-law Alonso Maldonado, who would marry his daughter the *conquistadora* Catalina de Montejo.[13] The *adelantado* received the support of Maldonado for his idea of colonizing the

Golfo Dulce. But Diego de Herrera, a Supreme Court judge (*oidor*) in New Spain, assumed the place of advocate on behalf of the friars, and against Maldonado. The *audiencia* began to restrict Montejo and to tell him that no further expeditions of conquest would be allowed. Montejo paid no heed: he believed that the Golfo Dulce was his. The two younger Montejos followed him there, and *el Mozo* founded a town which he named Nueva Sevilla in 1564.

Thus it was that the well-watered, fertile, and historically significant territory of Yucatan passed into the hands of the colonists of New Spain. Criss-crossed by violence for two generations, and soon forgetful of its famous Maya past, it had made the fortunes of a powerful family from Salamanca in old Castile, the Montejos. But its troubles were not yet over.

# 14

# A Great Conquistador
# from Asturias

*They have many wars and no chief among them is recognized
as all powerful.*[1]

Menéndez de Avilés in Florida, 1565

In March 1565, Pedro Menéndez de Avilés, an Asturian conquistador
of experience and majestic appearance, was requested by King Philip
to mount an expedition to the south-east of North America. This was
a region which an earlier adventurer, Juan Ponce de León, the hero of
Puerto Rico, had named 'Florida' in 1513, since there had seemed to
be so many flowers there.[2] Menéndez, a native of Avilés, the second
most important port of Asturias (the first being Gijón), was to undertake two tasks: first, to declare the territory to be Spanish and,
therefore, subject to the king of Spain; and second, to drive out the
French Protestant intruders who were believed to be there. Since the
reign of Francis I, the French had argued that they had a right to settle
in the Indies wherever Spain was not in actual occupation.

The Spaniards had made several earlier attempts at the conquest of
Florida – one by Ponce de León himself, and another in 1512 by two
judges of the Supreme Court in Santo Domingo, Juan Ortiz de Matienzo and Lucas Vázquez de Ayllón. They had been followed by
Pánfilo de Narváez, the rival of Cortés in New Spain, accompanied by
the great walker Núñez Cabeza de Vaca. But though the last named
survived this ordeal,[3] none of those attempts had been successful.
None of the explorers or conquerors seemed to have had any idea
about the size of the North American continent, nor its varied riches.

The French activities in Florida were a direct challenge to the peace concluded so happily in 1559 at Cateau-Cambrésis when France recognized the control of Spain over the Indies. The French fleet which left Dieppe in February 1562 under Jean Ribault, an experienced sailor of great courage, infuriated the king of Spain and persuaded the Duke of Alba to criticize the Council of the Indies for having failed to prevent the religious wars of Europe being taken to the New World.

In naming Menéndez de Avilés, King Philip had chosen a personal friend who had already carried out several important and delicate missions for him. Menéndez had, for example, brought decisive naval help to Spain during the campaign of Saint Quentin and, as a result, had been asked to escort the king home from Flanders to Spain in 1559. That was a great honour as well as a great responsibility. Philip thereafter specially favoured Menéndez de Avilés. It was as if he had realized that the conquistador was a superior personage whom he might need in later, as yet unforeseen, circumstances.

Now, in March 1565, Philip asked Menéndez to make a report on the position in Florida. Once his expedition was under way, his protégé would reply by describing how not only French but English and Portuguese 'pirates' had made an unwelcome intrusion into the region.[4]

Menéndez left Cadiz for Florida in July 1565 with 995 soldiers and 117 *labradores*, that is settlers and their families. He picked up more volunteers in the Canary Islands so that, in the end, he had over 2,600 persons under his direction, on twenty-six ships. He had been to the Indies several times before so knew perfectly well what he was taking on.

Menéndez de Avilés was fanatical in matters of religion. Thus he thought that Protestant heretics and American natives in Florida shared the same 'satanic' beliefs. He believed too that there was undoubtedly a north-west passage from the Atlantic into the Pacific ('the Southern Sea' as it was still generally known). He thought that if, as seemed likely, the French had settled in Florida, he should himself mount a punitive expedition of four galleys to drive them away, which would be serviced by 1,000 men, including some soldiers, some sailors, and four Jesuits. The cost might be 50,000 ducats in all.

The Caribbean, after all, seemed to be under a constant threat of invasion, especially by the French. The number of times when either Santiago de Cuba or Havana had been sacked by them in the 1540s was scandalous. In 1550 a French fleet had even burned Finisterre in Galicia in Spain, kidnapping twenty-six citizens and killing four people: the French captain had confessed that he was on his way to the Indies. In one of his reports, Menéndez de Avilés explained to King Philip how the French, with just four ships, had, only one year before, robbed even Santo Domingo of such wealth as it still possessed, and had ravaged the pearl island of Margarita. Then in 1555, another French 'pirate', Jacques de Sorès, who was saddled with the added inconvenience of being an ardent Lutheran, had seized El Morro, the headland which dominates the harbour of Havana. Juan de Lobera, the captain of the fortress, was captured, and Gonzalo Pérez de Angulo, the governor of Cuba, was obliged to take refuge outside the town.

Cuba had always been a peculiar colony.[5] Its Indian population had plummeted, but so had its small number of Spanish settlers. The island had been allowed to defer the application of the New Laws of 1542. The city of Havana had been moved from the south to the north coast of the island to make each rendez-vous easier for the treasure fleets from Portobelo and from Veracruz. These great undertakings would plan to join up there and pick up a naval escort to guard them on their way home to Spain through the Bahama Channel and the benign Gulf Stream. Havana had a splendid harbour, large enough to accommodate hundreds of ships, and the mouth opening to the sea was so narrow as to make the harbour easy to protect.

The defences of Havana had been reconstructed after the departure of Sorès, with African slaves brought in as usual to do the hard work.[6] There would soon be three forts to protect the capital (as it was becoming) and about 400 men. The building of a new cathedral was also begun, and there were soon three monasteries in Havana – that of San Francisco remaining even today one of the triumphant architectural achievements in the Caribbean. There would shortly be a population of some 600 persons of Spanish origin as well as several thousand black slaves.[7] Over 1,000 vessels berthed in Havana between 1571 and 1600.[8] In the course of the century its harbour had become a great starting point for the journey to the Indies (*la carrera de Indias*), because of the role of the treasure fleets.[9]

Menéndez de Avilés knew that there were dangers in the Caribbean other than simply attacks by corsairs. For instance, in or near the city of Santo Domingo there were 50,000 black slaves and a mere 4,000 Spaniards. The risk of a slave revolt was thus always considerable. Menéndez also pointed out in his reports that all the *pueblos* 'in the Indies are without fortifications and without artillery'. There seemed to be another problem: 'If there is anywhere with two hundred residents, only about fifty of them turn out to be vassals of Your Majesty. The rest are Portuguese, Lebanese, Greek, Marseillaise, Flemings, Germans – indeed, people of all nations ... And as they have no zeal to serve your Majesty, they have allowed every corsair under the sun to disembark, and allowed them to do much damage.' Menéndez further argued that in none of the towns in the Spanish Indies was there anything in the way of real fortification. Even a modest wall was usually lacking. In the face of the new dangers, he suggested some counter-measures, including arming the Spanish ships and establishing a real battle fleet.[10]

Havana, in the meantime, was growing fast. Its importance as a harbour for the treasure fleets was well established and it was becoming a bustling and exuberant city. One Cuban historian dwelt on the large number of notaries there: a sure sign of prosperity, he shrewdly commented.[11] Others noted the prodigal quantity of Chinese porcelain which seemed so abundant in Havana, as well as the extravagance of its theatrical performances, balls, and other entertainments. The great adventurer, Francis Drake, threatened Havana in 1586, but it was by then too well defended for him to make anything in the way of a landing, much less a sacking.

With regard to the planning of the expedition to Florida, King Philip agreed with Menéndez's recommendation about the need for extra fortifications, and he authorized him, as the *adelantado*, to begin their construction upon his arrival in North America. The preaching of the Catholic Church would also be an essential part of the scheme. In addition to the four Jesuits mentioned earlier, the Spanish fleet might also include ten or twelve religious persons of other orders. It was supposed that the proconsul would have at his disposal the support of the aristocracy of his native Asturias. Menéndez himself agreed to finance four *zabras* (small coastal vessels), six shallops (sloops), and 500 men. Of these, a hundred would be farmers and another hundred sailors, and there would also be a stonemason, some carpenters, farriers, blacksmiths, barbers, and surgeons. All would be armed with arquebuses, crossbows, and shields. Two hundred would be married men – an indication that Spain planned to establish a permanent colony. Five hundred African slaves would be available for the really dirty hard work.

To permit these considerable shipments of people, Menéndez de Avilés would set sail on his 900-ton *galliass*, the *San Pelayo*,[12] which could carry easily 300 men and most of the necessary supplies. It was a fast ship, it had a good gun deck, and was easily manoeuvred. After delivering the supplies for Florida, the *San Pelayo* could go on to New Spain. Menéndez would be paid 15,000 ducats, assuming that he set off before the end of May 1565. His *adelantamiento* would be granted for the span of two generations – his own and that of his son or son-in-law. He would receive another 2,000 ducats a year to compensate for having himself to finance the posts of governor and captain-general. He could name a lieutenant if he wanted and he could authorize him to have powers inferior only to his own. Menéndez could also distribute land in Florida for plantations, farms, and stock-breeding, but he was not to interfere with the rights of the Indians where they were clearly settled. He himself could have twenty-five square miles of land which he could farm and so maintain a marquisate. All underground mineral rights were reserved as usual for the Crown. Menéndez would himself be allowed two fisheries, one for fish, the other for pearls, and two galleons of up to 600 tons burden each as well as two pinnaces and six sloops. All these vessels would be permitted to sail direct to the Canary Islands and not have to submit to inspection at Seville or Sanlucar. Every foreign ship captured by Menéndez would be his to dispose of, accepting that one-third of its contents would go to the Crown. On the other hand, Menéndez was expected to pay for the entire expedition, whose profits should accrue to him too.

The whole document which allocated these rights and duties seemed to be written with a desire to please the Asturian, and permit him to engage in the West Indian trade with as little regulation as possible. Menéndez made clear that he wanted an expedition of men from Asturias and Vizcaya (Biscay), who, he thought, 'are the people best fitted to rule in Florida, some because of their nature and some because of kinship and friendship'.[13] In return, the Crown would get a bulwark against France – something which the Duke of Alba (as King Philip's chief military adviser) strongly desired for overall strategic reasons. But, as it happened, there were indeed two French expeditions at that time to Florida, one under way led by the experienced Norman Jean Ribault, and another which had already arrived under René de Laudonnière. Taken together, these were similar in size and power to Menéndez's force.

Menéndez finally set off at the end of June 1565, not quite as originally planned. There were now three caravels to carry the supplies. There was the flagship, the enormous *galliass*, *San Pelayo*, as well as four one-deck shallops. There was a galley (a galiot to be precise)[14] with eighteen banks of oars as well as a brigantine, the *Esperanza*. The *San Pelayo* carried 300 soldiers, artillery, ammunition, and marine supplies including wine, ship's biscuit, olive oil, rice, and beans – supplies supposed to be enough for a year. Menéndez also took with him about 250 arquebuses, 100 helmets, thirty crossbows, 600 other firearms, many pikes, harness for fifty horse, eight church bells and some altar furnishings – these last for the new churches expected to be built soon. There was cloth for trade with the Indians.

The 300 soldiers included 138 men who possessed the skills of artisans or craftsmen.[15] These men came from all over the Spanish peninsula but especially from Castile, Extremadura, and Andalusia. The chief pilot was Gonzalo Gayón, an Asturian. He would be paid 400 ducats.

This large fleet was delayed by a storm, but it reached Las Palmas in the Canary Islands on 4 July. The crossing of the Atlantic was also turbulent, and so the fleet was slightly diminished in size when it re-assembled in San Juan, Puerto Rico (some vessels were in bad shape). There Menéndez de Avilés reorganized his forces in about twelve companies (*tercios*) of fifty men each, under a captain. Each *tercio* was also served by an ensign, a chaplain, sergeant, piper, and drummer. A *maestro de campo* was also named to be overall commander of the *tercios*. This task fell to Menéndez's son-in-law, Pedro de Valdés, who, though only twenty-five years old, was experienced (he had already fought in Italy), and he was paid 300 ducats a year.

The French settlements now included a command post at Fort Caroline on Saint John's River which, named after the French King Charles IX, was intended to be the local headquarters. The place had been founded by twenty-eight men under the leadership of a Captain Aubert. But that officer was himself soon murdered and, as Ribault was back in Europe, the command was taken over by Laudonnière, a responsible sailor who, however, seemed too affable a character for the determined Huguenots under his command.[16] He also offended them by living with a prostitute.

Menéndez's regrouped fleet left Puerto Rico for Florida on 15 August 1565. They lingered at Cape Canaveral just as the French under Ribault were about to arrive to stave off the ruin of Fort Caroline, Laudonnière's colony. Menéndez landed near San Agustín, a city which he founded, and formally declared Florida to be part of King Philip's dominions. He knew a great deal about where he was going and whom he was going to meet: not the French so much as Indians, with whom he made careful diplomatic contact. He described the ceremonies of the Florida Indians thoughtfully in a letter to a Jesuit friend:

> . . . for the most part they worship the sun and moon. They have dead stags and other animals for idols. Each year they celebrate three or four feasts for their devotions when they worship the sun. They are three days without food, drink or sleep; these are their fasts. He who is weak and cannot put up with this is regarded as a bad Indian. He then goes about scorned by his colleagues. He who passes best through these troubles is named a principal and is shown the utmost courtesy thereafter. These Indians are a people of great strength, swift of foot and excellent swimmers.

'They have many wars,' Menéndez de Avilés added, 'and no chief among them is recognized as all powerful.'[17]

Meanwhile the French conferred in Fort Caroline. They resolved to attack the Spaniards who were, however, more imaginatively led. Menéndez realized that, if there were a major attack against him at San Agustín, Ribault could have left only a small garrison in Fort Caroline. Menéndez therefore stationed 300 men at Saint Agustín under his brother Bartolomé and, with the rest of his force, made for the French fort whose main gate he broke open. The Spaniards swarmed in and killed whomever they could of the French garrison – probably about 130 men. Fort Caroline was immediately rechristened as Saint Matthew (San Mateo) because of his day on the new calendar.[18] Many other French commanders offered to give themselves up if Menéndez agreed to save their lives. The latter reported home that he had obtained the surrender of these Frenchmen – mostly Lutherans – with no conditions, so he had proceeded to execute 200 or so, including the commander Ribault. A few were spared because they were Catholic or musicians.

Leaving behind strong garrisons on the Florida coast, Menéndez then made his way to Cuba and accepted the support of reinforcement which had been sent from Spain under the command of his nephew, Pedro Menéndez Márquez. Menéndez de Avilés wrote to the king on 5 December 1565, describing what he had achieved in Florida. In return, he asked for and was granted the title of Captain-General of the Indies, Tierra Firme (that is, the mainland of South America, specifically Venezuela-Colombia), and the Ocean Sea. Menéndez undertook to provide a small fleet of fast frigates, which he would use to secure the entire North American coast from the Caribbean to Newfoundland. The Catholic religion, he said, would be guaranteed by the arrival of three intelligent Jesuit brothers. The new capital of Florida would be in the far north of the region at Santa Elena, where the French had established a base which they knew as Port Royal (near what is now Savannah in Georgia).

In return, the *adelantado* wanted a licence to sell 1,000 slaves. He obtained it. Four Asturians of high birth became his lieutenants.[19] A substantial reinforcement was guaranteed by a Basque, Sancho de Arcienaga, who arrived in Cuba with seventeen ships and 1,500 men. These compensated to some extent for the loss of many of Menéndez's men due to a mutiny on the *San Pelayo*, which was later discovered to have foundered – off northern Europe!

Leaving his appointees in control of the new territory which he had conquered, Menéndez de Avilés returned to Madrid to be thanked by the king in July 1567 and to receive new assignments in the Windward Islands, which Spain was planning to subjugate.[20] Menéndez was now recognized in Spain as an exceptional commander who always won his battles. No wonder he was soon being spoken of for a European command.

On 1 April 1566 it became clear just how much Menéndez de Avilés had done to safeguard the Spanish Indies.[21] First of all, he had founded in Florida the city of San Agustín. He had also destroyed the French settlements made a year or two before by Jean Ribault and René de Laudonnière. All the executions which he carried out were, he insisted, 'not of Frenchmen but of Lutherans'. The French ambassador in Madrid, Raymond de Fourquevaux, in audience with King Philip protested at the 'massacres'. The king airily replied that the people concerned had been heretics and had gone to Florida without the permission even of the French government. 'To preserve kingdoms and states,' Philip added, 'it is sometimes necessary to depart from the rules in order to repel violence.'[22]

Dominique de Gourgues, a French Catholic, replied by mounting yet another aggressive expedition in Florida. When he captured Fort San Mateo in the spring of 1568, he hanged all his Spanish prisoners, inscribing a retaliatory tablet: 'I do this not as unto Spaniards but as to traitors, robbers and murderers.'

Among the difficulties encountered both by the government in Spain and by the *adelantado* in Florida were the quarrels which the latter had with the governor of Cuba, the self-important Francisco García Osorio. Osorio was a native of Ocaña, a favourite place of Queen Isabel the Catholic, just south of Madrid, and a veteran of the light vessels which, years before, had carried Hernando de Soto to Florida. Osorio had been named to the governorship in Cuba in 1565, the same year that Menéndez set sail for Florida. Osorio was so certain of his dignity that he did everything possible to impede Menéndez de Avilés. Two of Menéndez's men, captains Godoy and Córdoba, were somewhat frivolously executed in Santiago de Cuba for alleged insolence to Martín de Mendoza, Osorio's deputy.[23] Menéndez then nominated Baltasar de Barredas to command the fort overlooking the entry to the harbour of Havana (which had been christened La Fuerza). But there was a dispute over competence. Osorio seized and imprisoned Barredas, and replaced him with a creature of his own, Pedro de Redobrán. Then Menéndez himself arrived unexpectedly and arrested Osorio, re-replacing him with his protégé, Banderas. For a time Cuba, like Peru and New Spain before it, seemed to be heading for a conflict among Spaniards. But Menéndez de Avilés was too powerful a personality and too admired at the Spanish court for Osorio to be able to stand a chance in an outright clash. So, on 24 October 1567, Menéndez de Avilés, fresh from his triumphs in Florida, was himself named as governor of Cuba in effective succession to Osorio. He would, however, remain at his military command in Florida and govern Cuba through a deputy, Licenciado Francisco Zayas, who would carry through a *residencia* (judicial inquiry) of Osorio.

It was therefore Zayas who had to face the threat of yet another French attack, by Pierre Franc (also known as 'Pedro el Vasco'). He led a piratical expedition to Havana from Tortuga in 1579. (Tortuga in the west of Hispaniola was increasingly used as an unofficial French base, an anticipation of their colonization of 'Saint-Domingue', which eventually became the French-speaking Haiti.) Baracoa near the eastern tip of Cuba was sacked and a Spanish slave ship, with fifty-nine slaves on board, was captured by the French off Cape Maisi. At the same time an English sailor and companion of Francis Drake, John Oxenham – a pirate to the Spaniards but a hero in Devon – preyed on Cuba from Jamaica.[24] He was, however, eventually seized by the Spaniards and hanged at Lima in 1575.[25]

The arrangement whereby Menéndez de Avilés in Florida governed Cuba through his deputy Zayas lasted until March 1571, when the Council of the Indies advised a different order of things, because 'Havana needed a Governor who would be neither an *adelantado* nor his creature'. But the removal of the governorship marked no demotion for the Asturian. On the contrary, Menéndez was named captain-general of a fleet to clear the coasts of both Spain and Flanders of corsairs – the 'sea beggars' who had done so much harm to the Spanish cause off the Netherlands. Dr Alonso de Cáceres Ovando sailed to the Spanish Indies to carry out a *visita* into Menéndez's time in office (named on 3 January 1573, he arrived on 14 November in Havana), but Menéndez was not one to answer any criticisms. On 13 December of that year, Gabriel de Montalvo, from the famous family of Medina del Campo of that name, was named his successor as governor of Cuba.[26]

Menéndez de Avilés did not have time to make a serious contribution in the Netherlands as was expected of him, for he died shortly of the plague in Santander on 17 September 1574. He nevertheless left a vivid account of his experiences in the New World.[27] His loss was a serious setback to Spain, since he was one of the few commanders who could be counted upon for victories in the Old World as well as in the New.

A small colony of Spaniards remained in Florida and there were no further French inroads for the time being. The rumour then spread that the English were about to start a settlement in Virginia (led by the Tennysonian hero Sir Richard Grenville and Sir Ralph Lane, the first governor of that rich colony) near Santa María Bay, which the Spaniards thought of as Florida. The rumour was false, but it was an indication of the shape of things to come in the Americas. For the moment the English were a shadow, not a substance.

Menéndez de Avilés's achievement in Florida remained for the time being undisputed, but for geographical reasons the region never played a large part in Spanish thought or strategic considerations, nor did it loom large in Spain's imperial identity. That same geography would make the history of Florida turbulent and vulnerable to international ambitions until its final enclosure by purchase within the United States in 1845.

# 15

# Franciscans in Yucatan

*Yucatan is not an island.*
Fray Diego de Landa, *Relación de
las cosas de Yucatán*, 1566

By 1560 the Spanish conquest of Yucatan seemed complete. The following year Yucatan became a Franciscan province of its own and the Franciscans then secured the exclusive right to carry on the conversion of the Indians there. They divided the province into districts, and established powerful monasteries at Campeche, Maní, Izamal, Conkal near Mérida, and one at Ah Kin Chel, as well as another at Mérida itself. Religious instruction was performed at serious schools in all these places. Yucatan began to seem a model colony, directed by friars.

Fray Molina Solís has left a description of life in Mérida at this time. Every day after sunrise, the older members of the congregation left the church carrying a cross raised like a standard:

Passing house by house, they called the children . . . chanting prayers, they repaired to the church . . . a Friar talked of Christian doctrine until the hour of Mass. The Friar would then question the children to determine their knowledge. After some years of daily attendance, the pupils would be permitted to leave the school. The boys could then help their fathers in the fields, and the girls could help their mothers in their 'feminine tasks'. The parents might then be asked to repeat the tenets of Christian doctrine by praying with the children at night . . . In the school, adult Indians were taught singing and music. The Friars also

organised choirs, using flutes, an organ, violins, even the flageolet.[1] The
Indians learned to play all these instruments with singular perfection.[2]

Some *encomenderos* were against these Franciscan programmes
because they thought that they impeded work on their estates. But
others, such as Marcos de Ayala, warmly supported the Christianiza-
tion. (He had served in Italy against the Turks, in Hungary, and before
in Vienna, as well as having been the chief magistrate of Montejo *el
Mozo* during much of the conquest.) Ayala became an *encomendero*
outside Valladolid in Yucatan and he gave considerable support to the
Indian school there, himself preaching to the *caciques*. He also enter-
prisingly introduced the mulberry to Yucatan.[3]

In 1549, after some opposition by conquistadors such as Hernan
Sánchez del Castillo and Francisco López, certain Franciscans such as
friars Lorenzo de Bienvenida and Luis de Villalpando thought that the
town councils – consisting of Spaniards only – should have a voice in
local matters. Even the original conquerors, the Montejos, who had
estates but were not townsmen, were in danger as a consequence. A
certain Francisco Velázquez seized their *encomiendas* in Tabasco.
Montejo the *adelantado* hastened there from Mérida, while an old
supporter, Íñigo Nieto, captured Velázquez and imprisoned him at
Campeche along with another councillor, Alonso Vayón. Montejo
demanded the keys of the royal coffers, but Velázquez refused to give
them up. So Montejo broke the coffers open, took back his *encomiendas*, and returned to Mérida.

Velázquez continued to protest, and he was supported by the
Supreme Court, whose members were determined to force Montejo's
surrender of his Tabasco *encomiendas*. Judges did not generally like
conquistadors, and they now named Francisco de Ugalde as judge to
enact the seizure of all the Montejos' *encomiendas*. Faced with documents whose implications seemed inescapable, the Montejos gave up
the struggle. The *adelantado* even had to give up his *encomienda* at
Maní, which he had hoped to make into a hereditary estate. Dr Blas
Cota, a Portuguese doctor of canon law, was asked in February
1549 to carry out a *residencia* of the elder Montejo.

Cota had earlier been lieutenant to Alonso Maldonado when he
had been acting governor of Guatemala after Pedro de Alvarado's

death, and he took over authority in Yucatan from the moment the *residencia* began on 13 May in Mérida. Cota suspended the *adelantado* as well as his son and nephew (*el Mozo* and *el Sobrino*, as we know them),[4] and his report was made public in late June 1549. That was sent back to Spain, but though the sentences took time to implement, the legal authority of the Montejos in the colony was removed – even though Fray Nicolás de Abalate returned from Spain with the news that the entire territory of Yucatan had been transferred to the ownership of the Supreme Court of New Spain.

Finding that the *residencias* were complete, Viceroy Mendoza of New Spain then appointed Gaspar Suárez de Ávila (an old 'Montejista') as *alcalde mayor* of Yucatan and Alonso de Manrique as the same in Tabasco. Suárez was in effect to act as governor of the colony with full powers. He was to carry out a *visita* of the province, and to prohibit forced labour, though he was able to arrange for Indians to work on churches and monasteries. Enslavement was prohibited. Those Indians who worked were theoretically to be paid a wage. Further expeditions of conquest (*entradas*) were forbidden. The conversion of Indians was to be given priority. Suárez de Ávila arrived in Yucatan in April 1551, and Manrique took office in Tabasco at about the same time.[5] By then the Supreme Court of Guatemala (with López de Cerrato at its head) had again taken over full responsibility for Yucatan and Tabasco. But soon they were returned to New Spain.

In March 1551 the *adelantado* Montejo went home to Spain to seek compensation for his surprising dismissal, Viceroy Mendoza having appointed him temporary captain-general of the flotilla which would carry home a large instalment of Mexican silver and gold. Such temporary appointments were quite normal. At Havana, Montejo met the returning Peruvian fleet under Sancho de Biedma, who would have overall command of the two groups of ships.[6]

Tomás López Medel then became *juez de residencia* (judge of the *residencia*). He seemed yet one more new broom, being sympathetic to the friars in their reliance on detailed prescriptions to regulate life. He wanted to restrain the Indian *caciques* from calling their people together to sing at old pagan sites. He also wanted the Indians to be gathered together to live in villages, not scattered. López Medel insisted on the new Spanish subjects submitting to a curfew and on sitting at tables for meals (something which Spaniards have always considered important). He also demanded that Indian chiefs should have only one wife – something quite radical for a Maya, but which Spaniards considered essential despite their tolerance of mistresses.

By June 1551, *adelantado* Montejo was back in Seville. He went to Madrid, then to Valladolid, and finally to the Council of the Indies, in the latter city at the time, to present his case. Thanks to the help of his son-in-law, Judge Maldonado, he received a careful hearing. He was absolved from most of the charges of self-aggrandizement brought against him. But in the autumn of 1553, before he was completely exonerated, Montejo died in his native Salamanca, the city he had left forty years earlier to join the fleet of Pedrarias and begin his remarkable career in the Indies.

Montejo had been an enlightened conquistador. When he left Yucatan in 1550 it was full of the products of the Old World, such as figs, dates, and pomegranates. He had also cultivated vegetables and fruit which were new to the Americas: cabbages, lettuces, turnips, onions, beans, and sugar cane, as well as vines, oranges, and lemons, while he had also attempted to grow wheat. Montejo had introduced coconuts, plantains, and mammee trees from the West Indies to the new continent, while native crops such as maize, American beans, and peppers continued to be grown, as did cotton. Spanish farmers had tried to develop the breeding of livestock. They also shipped hard black wood (*palo de tinto*) from Yucatan to both old and new Castile. Fernando de Bracamonte introduced indigo into Europe, while the *adelantado* himself had set up a small sugar plantation at Champoton, based (as most sugar mills were) on the labour of black slaves from Africa (mostly Mozambique). The Indians continued their weaving with Yucatec cotton, salt still came from the coast of Catoche, and, as in the past, other natives still produced wax and pottery. Cotton continued to be used as currency, as did cacao beans. The Spaniards used the Yucatec Indians as servants, ploughmen, and weavers. An ethnic mixture of populations developed as soon as the Spaniards arrived, the proportion of *mestizos* being significant in Yucatan from at least 1545.

The religious structure in Yucatan in those days was characterized by the fact that, as Tomás López Medel noted, Maya lords continued to call their people together regularly for the worship of idols and the celebration of their histories.[7] At the same time, there were now twelve monasteries in the province, six built of stone, and all Franciscan. Two hundred villages in Yucatan had their own church, school, and mission-trained schoolmaster. All the important chiefs had accepted baptism, though no one quite knew what that meant to them. A web of control had been established by the Franciscans, the days governed by church bells summoning children to school and adults to prayer. The months were marked by obligatory Christian feasts comparable in frequency to old Maya celebrations. Indians had access to the sacraments of baptism and marriage but only rarely to extreme unction, for there were too few priests for regular attendance on the dying to be possible. Indians also seldom confessed, because of the shortage of friars who knew Maya. Few Indians took communion: they would watch the mass but did not often participate. Of course, the friars knew that vestigial idolatry continued, but such offences were punished with nothing more serious than the occasional whipping. In 1560 a Franciscan discovered what he called 'very great knaveries and idolatries', but he was for a time content merely to summon the chiefs and lords together and give a solemn lecture before granting a pardon. Similar lapses had been reported in Zapotec territory.

But then, in May 1562, something like a revolution occurred – the most serious protest in imperial Spain during its first fifty years. Two Indian boys who were out hunting found a cave full of idols and skulls. They told Fray Pedro de Ciudad Rodrigo, the guardian of the Franciscan monastery of nearby Maní, who had with him six other friars who were studying Maya. The friars were 'learning to read and write in the language of the Indians which had been so successfully reduced to a grammatical form that it could be studied like Latin'.[8]

About forty Indians from nearby were rounded up and questioned. They admitted that they owned the idols and had occasionally worshipped them. Such worship, they said, took place everywhere in the vicinity. Quite arbitrarily (justice being the preserve of the secular), Fray Pedro had the Indians submitted to the torture known as the *garrucha*, or 'hoist': they were whipped and large stones were attached to their feet until they confessed to the whereabouts of other idols. Another torture was the *burro*, alas a still well-known form of water torture which gives the victim the impression that he is drowning. Later, the Indians were made to take part in an *auto-de-fe*.

A new Franciscan commissary, Fray Diego de Landa, then arrived in Yucatan with a notary, Francisco de Orozco, to undertake a formal investigation.[9] Landa was very intelligent, but also very serious, hard-working, and harsh. He and his staff carried out mass arrests and the indiscriminate torture of over 4,500 Indians, of whom 158 died and about thirty killed themselves. This contrasted with a comparable inquiry by the great Bishop Juan de Zumárraga into the idolatries in the capital, Mexico, an inquiry in which all torture was prohibited. The penalties in 1562 of floggings, fines, and forced labour for ten years in Yucatan were also far in excess of the limits laid down by the archbishop in the capital.

There was also on 12 July 1562 an *auto-de-fe* orchestrated by Fray Landa, who addressed a large crowd in excellent Maya. He was followed by the governor of Yucatan, Dr Diego Quijada, who spoke in Spanish on behalf of the secular authorities. Sentences were immediately handed down, men were tied to whipping posts, and 200 lashes laid anew on already lacerated flesh. These punishments extended to those whose only 'crime' was that they did not betray their relations' ownerships of idols. A large pile of idols and jewelled skulls of ancestors were put on the fire. Quijada acquiesced in these moves, so that the government could be seen to have supported the friars absolutely.

This was a really brutal event, one of the worst in the history of the conquest, the dread of torture causing estimates of hidden idols to increase at every moment. There were many suicides, for example that of Lorenzo Cocom, lord of the province in Sotuta. Fray Landa extended his inquiry to all nearby provinces, where he sent friars to investigate, and his denunciations were severe: the Indians of Maní, he said, had returned to their ancient and evil customs, worshipping idols and sacrificing to them both publicly and in secrecy, so that many pagan rituals had been performed in churches, before altars, and in front of crosses along the roads. Indians had been heard saying that 'our true Lord is not God but the devil, the enemy of their souls . . .'[10]

But the real enemies of the Franciscans were the settlers, many of whom were shocked by the friars' casualness about establishing the truth. One colonist spent many days defending Diego Uz, the chief of Tekax in Maní, being persuaded of his innocence. Uz, a heavy man, had found the agony of being 'hoisted' unbearable. Secular priests such as Lorenzo Monterosso, curate of Sotuta, had been persuaded by hearing the friars' terrible interrogations.[11] The council of Mérida sent two senior officials, Joaquín de Leguízamo and Francisco de Bracamonte, to beg Landa to change the style of his inquisition.

In the capital, Mérida, there now arrived a new bishop, Francisco Toral, a wise, humane, and cultivated man. Toral was a native of Úbeda, the home city in eastern Andalucia of the famous imperial secretary Francisco de los Cobos. Toral had been a missionary in Poland before becoming *provincial* of the Franciscans in New Spain in 1557. There he had helped Fray Bernardino de Sahagún with his *Florentine Codex*, allowing him to be relieved from routine duties while he worked on revisions of it.[12] (Sahagún had by then realized that many conversions of indigenous people in the first years of the conquest had been only skin-deep.) Toral himself could preach in Nahuatl as well as Spanish. He also not only mastered Popoloca, the language of Puebla, but wrote a grammar and a vocabulary of it. He returned to Spain in 1552 to attend a general meeting of the Franciscan order as custodian of the Mexican friars and brought back with him to New Spain thirty-six new members from Castile. In 1555 he tried unsuccessfully to have the Indians exempted from the tithe.

Bishop Toral's welcome to Campeche was a sad occasion, for he was met by Fray Leguízamo with a grim account of recent events. By a serious breach of etiquette, it was only when he was three leagues from Mérida that Toral was formally greeted by two friars, though he was technically their superior. Landa had been urged to place the whole issue of idolatry in his hands, but he had refused to do so and, instead, remained in Sotuta, insisting that Toral should not be received in the Franciscan monastery of Mérida.

On 14 August 1555, Toral first took over the monastery then sought lodgings elsewhere, being obliged by his feud with the friars to stay in the palace of the Montejos. This had a coat of arms over the door of armoured Spaniards trampling on wailing Indians. But it was airy and ample. Toral immediately allowed several imprisoned chiefs more comfortable quarters.

On 20 August he was joined by Landa, who was now convinced that some Indians of Sotuta had recently offered human sacrifices as in the old days, and he alleged that some nominally Christian schoolmasters had not only been present but had been among the organizers. Landa had been convinced that the central expression of the conspiracy had been the ritual killing of children in the parish church. Those deaths had, he thought, included both crucifixions and extractions of hearts, the chief criminal having apparently been the now dead Lorenzo Cocom, though Landa's own old comrade, Juan Nachi Cocom, had played a part. After the ceremonies, the bodies had been thrown into *cenotes* (wells).[13] Where did the children come from? Sometimes, it was supposed, they had been kidnapped from neighbouring villages, and sometimes they had been bought outright.

At their meeting on 20 August, Toral confirmed Landa and his friars in their inquisitorial authority, but he absolutely forbade the further use of torture. That infuriated Landa, who refused to participate in any further investigation, and the two communicated thereafter only through notaries. Toral concentrated on the legal inadequacies of his colleague, the excessive punishments, and the shortage of records. Landa for his part denounced the seriousness of the crimes.

Toral decided to interrogate the imprisoned chiefs personally, using Gaspar Antonio Chi as his interpreter, though Chi had been all along an intimate of the friars, especially of Landa. Every *cacique* offered much the same explanation:

> They had been speaking honestly before the fathers began their enquiries and, because the latter did not believe them, they ordered them hoisted, for the torture. The chiefs had agreed among themselves that all should speak of deaths and sacrifices lyingly as soon as they were asked about it, counselling each other and understanding that, by this method, they might escape both the said torments and prison . . .[14]

Toral asked Landa to allow two Franciscans, Fray Felipe Bruselas and Fray Juan de la Puebla, to take formal written statements from the Indians whom they had interrogated. These were to be voluntary and the prohibition of torture was to stand. So between 3 and 9 September 1555 the two friars took down fifteen written statements. The Indians were said to have performed thirty-five human sacrifices over the previous ten years in which children had died. These had never taken place in churches, they said, but in old, secret shrines. There were variations. Thus, at Chichen Itza, a dead body was thrown into the great well, but a living child had also been thrown into the water 'to consult the oracles'. It seemed that most of the chiefs had been present at one or other of these rituals.

Toral received a report from the *encomendero* of Sotuta, Julio de Mangaña, whose task had been to seek the whereabouts of children said to have been sacrificed and to search for corpses in specific places. He was, however, not able to find out much, partly because he was defeated by the repetitive similarity of the Indian names.

Toral came to the conclusion that, in the long run, very few Indians had been guilty of more than trivial idolatries, themselves the direct consequence of inadequacies in the friars' teaching. He decided that the friars were guilty, above all Landa, the *provincial*, of excessive behaviour. Landa, meantime, worked furiously to find evidence which might be damaging to the bishop. There was an angry scene on 16 September between Fray Juan Pizarro and Fray Francisco de Miranda.[15] Pizarro took Landa's side, Miranda took Toral's. The governor or chief magistrate of Yucatan, Dr Diego Quijada, tried unsuccessfully to remain neutral. (He had after all already supported Landa's actions.) On 17 September the friars said they could not administer the sacrament of baptism to any Indian on the grounds of their 'pertinacious idolatry'. They said, too, that they could not man more than five monasteries until the idolatries were remedied.

Of course, no Spaniard could tolerate human sacrifice, but its regular occurrence had not been proven. Idolatry was a different matter. The friars claimed that mass idolatry was an affront. The settlers were more relaxed. They wanted the Maya to be their labourers, pagan or no, whatever happened. They also needed some end to the uncertainty. In particular, they wanted to know who was going to win the dispute, Landa or Toral.[16]

When Fray Lorenzo de Bienvenida, commissary general of the order in New Spain, returned to Yucatan in 1562 and supported Toral, the balance of power began to shift in the bishop's direction. In January, Toral began to deliver his judgments about the Indian chiefs in custody and gave them light punishments, usually returning them to their villages. Most settlers accepted this denouement. Toral found that the friars had killed about 160 people whilst collecting evidence of their idolatry,[17] and condemned the *provincial*. The bishop was supported by many settlers who thought that Landa was consumed by a lust for power. They hated his impatience of restriction as well as his arrogance. In January 1563, Landa declared that 'hoisting' was no more than a minor vexation, while the floggings had been a matter of only a few strokes, which had usually been laid on with moderation.[18]

Landa took his case to Spain in 1563. Toral meantime celebrated mass in the Franciscan monastery at Mérida. Fray Juan Pizarro, who was related to that great family of this name from Trujillo, was to preach the sermon. Speaking of Jesus going from Galilee to Judea, Pizarro prayed that 'it would please God that Spanish Christians could hate so much these heretical idolatrous dogs who were the enemies of God and of our Holy faith'. He lamented that 'those who were to punish them . . . are defending them and, instead of harassing them, are giving them comfort'. Outside, Toral denounced Fray Pizarro in Nahuatl and ordered the Indians never to give the friar so much as a glass of water. Pizarro believed that he had humiliated the bishop.[19]

Several friars wrote to the Crown in support of Toral, some drafting letters purporting to be from Indian *caciques*. One Maya, Francisco de Montejo Xiu, and three other chiefs are said to have written:

> The Franciscan friars of the province have written certain letters to Your Majesty and to the head of the order, in praise of Fray Diego de Landa and his other companions who tortured, killed and put us to scandal. And they gave certain letters written in Castilian to certain Indians by their familiars. They signed them and sent them to Your Majesty. May Your Majesty please understand that these are not our views, we who are the chiefs of this land did not have to write lies and falsehoods and contradictions. As for Landa, may he and his companions do penance for the evil they have done us.[20]

The Council of the Indies in Seville at first accepted Bishop Toral's version of events. But Landa had taken with him to Spain new material about secret idolatries which had not been discussed there before.

A committee named by the Franciscans in Spain made an investigation. It decided that the conduct of Landa had been justified, given the heinous nature of the Indian offences. It was the bishop who had made a mistake. So Landa was exonerated and went triumphantly to San Juan de los Reyes, the great Franciscan monastery in Toledo where he had first studied. In Yucatan, meantime, a notary named Sebastián Vázquez was asked to inquire into the behaviour of officials in the province and spent three months there investigating.[21] Luis Céspedes de Oviedo was named governor of Yucatan and ordered to act as *juez de residencia* in respect of Governor Quijada.[22] Céspedes arrived in November 1565. He found that Quijada had improved roads and encouraged the use of mules to save the Indians their burdens, but the governor had been rather frivolous and had not seemed to have the character to lead well in tumultuous times. He had also allowed himself to be under the control of the more powerful Landa. Céspedes imprisoned Quijada for debt and the (former) governor was then returned to Spain, where the Council of the Indies promptly reduced his punishment. He died there in 1571.

The Council of the Indies had, meantime, turned against Bishop Toral because of continuing disputes over the demarcation of authority between him, the town council, and the friars. Toral made an extensive episcopal visit throughout the province, even travelling to the island of Cozumel, where few Spaniards had been since Cortés's visit in 1519. The bishop found the friars there so embittered that he was unable to act.[23] Toral wanted to resign, being increasingly obsessed with the terrible events of 1562, judging that the friars had then behaved as culpably as Landa. The bishop was beginning now to think of the Indians as saintly, and that the land was 'a lake of pure stone'. The Crown refused his request to return to live in Mexico but, all the same, he did return to live in the Franciscan monastery there in 1571.

Toral was a man of fine character who was destroyed by the brutality of the times and by the remorseless enmity of Landa. Meantime a regulation by Viceroy Enríquez de Almansa in 1570 forbade the imprisonment and flogging of Indians by ecclesiastics. The Indians were henceforth excluded from the investigations of the Inquisition because they were held to be too simple, and many had not been well instructed.[24]

By this time, the Franciscan mission in Yucatan was in a desperate state, necessitating Landa's return; and return he did, being improbably named Bishop of Yucatan after Toral's death in 1571. Landa had already written his remarkable *Relación de las cosas de Yucatán*, in which his prejudices were balanced by an unexpected sophistication and breadth of knowledge.[25] He arrived in Campeche in October 1573 with thirty new friars whom he had recruited in Spain, and he ordered all secular priests out of the province save a few needed in the cathedral and three who were already fluent in Maya. Landa set his other friars to learn Maya.

Yucatan had changed a great deal in the eleven years since 1562. Bishop Landa now delegated Fray Gregorio de Fuenteovejuna to investigate alleged backsliding towards idolatry in Campeche, and he began to punish the guilty. A new local governor, Francisco Mai, supported by leading Indians, denounced both the friar and the bishop before the Supreme Court of Mexico. Landa was ordered to abide by a new regulation which insisted on more humanity towards all the Indians.

Landa sent a message to the governor of the province, now Francisco Velázquez de Gijón, requesting permission to continue the punishments, but he was refused. He then set off for Mexico to plead before the *audiencia*, which heard him out but did not give him their support: Governor Velázquez stood his ground. Landa continued to wrestle fruitlessly with these restrictions until his death in 1579.

What was the truth behind this brutal controversy? The admirable modern historian of the Maya, Inga Clendinnen, assumes that some human sacrifices did survive into the time of commissary Landa.[26] She is probably correct.

But all the same, when the Franciscan commissary toured Yucatan a few years after the controversy, he was pleased by the enthusiastic welcome which he received in village after village, by the showers of fruit, turkeys, and flowers, and by the dances presented for his pleasure. The Spanish empire even in Yucatan had begun to conduct itself as a civilizing mission. In one place, the *naturales* brought out a kind of pulpit on which a well-dressed Indian addressed the commissary with rattles and another by his side performed on a *teponaztli*, or log drum.[27] Ceremony was needed for all such concessions, and ceremony was procured.

# 16

# The Rivers Plate and Paraguay

*And when he [the Chief] came to speak of the Amazons and gave us to understand their great riches, we were very glad to learn of it, and our commander presently asked whether we could reach them by water and how far it was ...*

Voyage of Ulrich Schmidl to the rivers Plate and Paraguay from the German original of 1567 (in *The Conquest of the River Plate*, Hakluyt Society 81, London 1891)

Legends of old Paraguay tell of the neighbouring country of what is now Brazil being conquered by two brothers who came from the Atlantic Ocean. Their names were Guarán and Tupí. The wives of these two heroes quarrelled and the families agreed to separate. The Tupí remained in Brazil, the Guaraní went to Paraguay and eventually dominated a vast swathe of territory including the low-lying so-called Chaco country, on the western bank of the river Paraguay.

These Guaraní were until the sixteenth century often nomadic and lived principally on the fish with which the great rivers of the region were amply stocked. They also killed some game. The stationary Guaraní had a primitive system of agriculture but no central government and no apparent need of one. They obeyed a local chief who managed his subjects through sheer force of character. There were, however, tribal councils and the chiefs were subservient to them. The Guaraní, a tough people – stoical in the face of pain, for example – were normally peaceable. Their instincts were to make friends with newcomers even if they were conquerors.

The Chaco tribes on the western or left bank of the river Paraguay were less conciliatory. Their usual attitude towards new people, whether travellers or conquerors, was to fear, hate, despise, and frighten them. But these tribes experienced eras – for example, in the fifteenth century – when they were ruled, indirectly at least, by the Inca in Peru, far away though they were.[1]

The Spanish intrusion into the world of the Guaraní and Tupí derived from several voyages. First, there was that of Juan Díaz de Solís in 1516, which, as we have seen, led to his death and the massacre of his comrades by the Churrúa Indians. The second expedition was that of Magellan, who sailed into the estuary of the river Plate (*el río de la Plata*) in 1521 and, after many changes of direction, reached the Southern Sea.[2]

Then there was the expedition in 1526 of the Venetian explorer Sebastian Cabot, which left Sanlúcar in April in three ships, theoretically en route for the Moluccas. Cabot sent Juan Álvarez Ramón to sail up the river Uruguay. But Ramón met with catastrophe and was killed by a tribe known as the Yaros.

Cabot himself, forgetting that his real mission was to go to the Moluccas via the straits of Magellan, sailed up the great estuary of the Plate as far as its confluence with the river Carcaraña, where he founded a fort, Sancti-Spiritus, some thirty miles north of the modern city of Rosario. Leaving there a small garrison of 120 men, under the command of an Andalusian named Nuño de Lara, Cabot continued north up the river Paraná as far as he could. But he turned round when the waters became too swift for him and, instead, sailed further up the river Paraguay as far as its confluence with the Bermejo. Then he turned back south to meet Diego García de Moguer,[3] whose help he spurned and whom he sent back to Spain. After three years or so seeking silver and gold without much success, Cabot returned to Spain.[4]

The garrison at Sancti Spiritus then underwent its own tragedies. Lucia Miranda, the lovely wife of Sebastian Hurtado, one of Lara's captains, had attracted the admiration of a local *cacique*, Mangoré. Carefully choosing a time when half the garrison was away hunting or prospecting, Mangoré attacked the Spanish camp and, though he was killed, his brother Siropo escaped with Lucia. Further fighting followed. Most of the Spaniards, including Lucia, were killed, and the few survivors fled east to join the Portuguese in Brazil, whose settlements they reached after extraordinary hardships. By 1530 therefore, there was no longer a Spanish presence on the river Plate or its tributaries. Cabot himself was in disgrace in Oran in north Africa for failing to carry out his instructions.

There was, it was true, the myth of a silver city in the far interior, known optimistically as 'the city of the Caesars'. García Moguer was, however, still biding his time in Seville, and there were no other serious attempts for a time at further exploration up the river Plate.

As it reaches the Atlantic Ocean, the Plate looks like the sea itself, since there is no shoreline visible northwards from the south bank or from the now great city of Buenos Aires. Like the sea, the river is tidal and 'differed from the sea only in its colour which was a muddy red instead of a blue or green'.[5] The river Plate is a magnificent sight, unforgettable in the minds of all who see it at whatever the angle they come upon it. But it was not easy to cross in the late sixteenth century.

The great estuary was, of course, known and, as we have seen earlier,[6] was the destination of a grand expedition of eleven ships and 1,300 colonists under Pedro de Mendoza in 1534. This led to the first settlement of a colony which would eventually become Buenos Aires (*el puerto de nuestra señora de Buenos Aires*).

There were renewed combats with the Guaraní, and a severe shortage of food due to the lack of any local agricultural tradition. Juan de Ayolas,[7] a citizen of Burgos (born in Briviesca, about twenty miles to the north-east), second-in-command to Mendoza and formerly one of the great merchants of his native city, founded a new colony at Sancti Spiritus, which he christened Buena Esperanza in 1535. There Ayolas remained, with Francisco Ruiz Galán as his own deputy, while Gonzalo de Mendoza sought food in Brazil and Jorge Lichtenstein sailed up northwards on the Paraná river. Ayolas soon founded another settlement, Corpus Cristi, on 15 June 1536, this time at Carcaraña. Here a hundred Spaniards under the royal treasurer, Gonzalo de Alvarado, a nephew of Pedro de Mendoza, held out in a building which seemed half-inn, half-fortress.

Ayolas began a second expedition up the Paraná in berganting.

Another citizen from Espinosa de los Monteros in what is now the province of Burgos, a royal official named Juan de Salazar de Espinoza, followed him with a hundred men on some newly built bergantings.[8] He was in turn followed by Gonzalo de Salazar. On the journey, Ayolas had time to marry the daughter of a local *cacique*, Tamatía – an association which would have inspired less scandal than if the girl concerned had not been from a locally respected great family.

Meantime, far to the south, Pedro de Mendoza, who was suffering from a permanent fever, limped home to Spain with half his men, dying en route. He had named Ayolas as his successor, but the new settlement of Buenos Aires, whose last governor was Francisco Ruiz Galán, was soon abandoned – less from the threats of Indians than because of the fever contracted by the weakened colonists who lacked food, a shortage leading scandalously to cannibalism.

Ayolas was still sailing up the river Paraná, excited by the occasional signs of wealth which he thought he detected in the form of manufactured silver objects. A fine account was given by one of Pedro de Mendoza's companions, an articulate German conquistador named Ulrich Schmidl, who came from Straubing in Bavaria and was originally under the auspices of the Welser banking family.[9] He provided eloquent testimony of how astounded they were by the exotic tropical birds, the wonderful blossoms, the magnificent alligators, as well as the terrifying snakes.

Schmidl's account goes on to describe a tribe of Amazons whom he claims to have encountered, each with just one breast and all demonstrating great skill with bows and arrows. He reported that these Amazons had neither gold nor silver, but they did have great riches on the mainland where their menfolk apparently lived.[10] The most dangerous challenge to this expedition came from the Mepene Indians, who mustered what the Spaniards recalled as 500 canoes in order to oppose their progress. But Spanish arms, particularly the swords with their Toledo blades, won the day as usual. A Guaraní army led by the *cacique* Lambaré also made an effort to halt the Spaniards in a bend of the river Paraguay which eventually became the site of Asunción, the capital city of the colony. It was a healthy spot surrounded by fruit and flowers growing on good soil. Here Ayolas embarked on a programme of urban building. A city, after all, was the premier construction of Spaniards in the New World as in the Old. Asunción was, however, 1,000 miles from the sea and, after the eclipse of Buenos Aires, there was no settlement between it and the ocean. The colonists of Paraguay thus felt themselves to be isolated.

Juan de Ayolas, the citizen of Burgos, was the real founder of what became the colony known as Paraguay. He was greatly assisted by the tolerant docility of the Guaraní. On the west bank of the Paraguay river, it is true, some Chaco peoples such as the Agazes and the Guaycurús were hostile to Spaniards, but the Guaraní mostly accepted them.

Ayolas could now have settled happily in Asunción and concentrated on extending its wealth and prosperity – a plaza, a governor's house, a prison, a Franciscan monastery, and a cathedral had all been established. But in 1537 he embarked on a new expedition of discovery, probably inspired by the hope of finding the magic 'city of the Caesars', that city of silver supposedly somewhere in the interior: indeed the great river whose estuary had once been colonized by Pedro de Mendoza was now called the river of silver (*río de la Plata*), because of the rumour that there were vast quantities of that metal near its headwaters. Ayolas reached the river port which he himself had established and christened 'La Candelaria' on an earlier expedition. Then he struck west overland with 127 men to try and discover where his vast colonial domain adjoined Peru. He got close in 1538 to what seemed to be that place, but unhappily he fell into the hands of Indians who killed him and everyone on his expedition.

Ayolas had left behind at La Candelaria a resolute Basque named Domingo Martínez de Irala. He had been born in Mondragón,[11] a well-known town in the province of Guipúzcoa between Vitoria and Durango, and had sailed to Buenos Aires with Pedro de Mendoza in 1534. Martínez had commanded a brigantine in the first expedition of Ayolas in 1536. He had been accompanied by Rodrigo de Cepeda, a brother of Saint Teresa of Ávila and a *converso* of the second generation. It was Martínez who had conveyed most of the inhabitants of Buenos Aires up to Asunción by boat in 1536, where he acted as leader of the 250 settlers there. Some said that he had wanted to destroy the first Buenos Aires so as to be able to present himself as the only Spanish commander in the region. Cabeza de Vaca alleged that he had acted thus so as to make possible the killing of Ayolas, but there is no evidence at all for that harsh accusation. Ulrich Schmidl, the German conquistador, tells us that Martínez was a man of great qualities, and he must certainly have had great powers of endurance as well as of persuasion.

Martínez de Irala at first seems to have considered setting himself up at La Candelaria, but he returned to Asunción in search of provisions. On the way, he was surprised to find himself greeting Juan de Salazar de Espinoza, who had sailed up the river from old Buenos Aires with a view to helping Martínez's new settlement. Later, both leaders went to Asunción where they devoted themselves to city-building. These two captains were soon joined by a third commander in the shape of Ruiz Galán, the last governor of Buenos Aires, who had lingered on the lower part of the river Plate. Martínez de Irala now had with him about 600 men, mostly survivors from Mendoza's original mission. Several were experienced conquistadors. They had become accustomed to the extraordinary circumstances of Paraguay itself, helping to establish real agriculture. They also became used to sending Guaraní home to Spain – as slaves.

Martínez de Irala, a typical conquistador in many ways, was not slow to allocate *encomiendas* to his followers. He devised two types of tenure: first, *yanconas*, which were properties where conquered Indians were gathered and treated in effect as slaves, with all the duties, but also some rights, attached to that often ambiguous status; and second, *mitayos*, settlements where the Indians concerned had surrendered voluntarily, and so enjoyed various privileges, such as the right to select any site which they desired for settlement.

The arrangement on the *mitayos* was that all males between the ages of eighteen and fifty were called on to work two months of the year for the *encomendero*. A priest was in theory attached to every settlement.

Asunción was now developing all the characteristics of a city. Magistrates had been named and courthouses set up. A coat of arms depicting Saint Blaise and the Virgin of the Assumption, as well as a castle and a coconut palm, were granted by the Crown of Spain.[12] (The coconut palm was soon supplanted by the effigy of a lion sitting under a deciduous tree.) Other towns were soon founded, usually with churches, prisons, plazas, and government houses arranged in the customary symmetrical plan.

Martínez de Irala had thus laid the foundation for a new colony before the unexpected and not wholly welcome arrival in the spring of 1542 of the famous walker, Alvar Núñez Cabeza de Vaca, newly named *adelantado* of what one historian refers to as 'the great river country' in the heart of South America. He had walked to Asunción from Santa Catalina on the Atlantic coast of what is now Brazil in six months. Cabeza de Vaca insisted that Santa Catalina was well to the west of the boundary line of the Portuguese empire in Brazil, arguing that the river Santos marked the boundary.

Cabeza de Vaca had made history with his five-year-long walk in the 1530s from Florida to Sonora in New Spain. This new, more tropical journey, in which he was accompanied by a good gathering of followers, was somewhat easier. He began to walk from Santa Catalina in October 1541 and arrived, by way of the Iguazu falls, in March 1542. A full account was given by Pedro Hernández, who, having accompanied Pedro de Mendoza, had become secretary to this later expedition.[13] Cabeza de Vaca had many critics because of his lack of courtesy to his fellow Spaniards, but Hernández does not mention any action on his part which adversely affected the Guaraní Indians.[14] Cabeza and his men crossed country which they reported to be of great beauty and variety.

On their arrival at Asunción, Cabeza and his friends were at first welcomed warmly, the more so since the citizens of that new capital had had no news of Spain for several years. But bad relations between the newcomers and their experienced hosts soon became noticeable. Accusations about ill-treatment of Indians were of the first importance. Thus Martínez de Irala accused Cabeza de Vaca of treating Indians cruelly, while Cabeza, who had actually been so benign in his relations with North American Indians in Florida, found plenty of evidence that Martínez had been brutal to the Guaraní. But it was not the Guaraní who were the cause of the real trouble; it was the unpredictable Guaycaró tribe who were responsible for the bad relations that existed between Europeans and natives.

Martínez de Irala had not ceased to be an explorer. Shortly after

Cabeza's arrival, he set off with four brigantines to sail further up the river Paraguay, perhaps wanting to carve out a fiefdom for himself. He was attacked by the *cacique* Aracané, who, when captured, was executed, a punishment which led to further protests by other *caciques*, namely Tabaré and Conaramblané. Martínez made further ventures into the Chaco territory on the upper reaches of the Paraguay. Another journey of exploration was undertaken by Cabeza de Vaca in 1542 from Asunción. He sailed upstream with several hundred horse, 400 arquebusiers, and 1,200 Guaraní bowmen.[16] But this expedition was unproductive and Cabeza, intrepid as he certainly was, returned to Asunción, where, unexpectedly, he found himself challenged by several people: one, Francisco de Mendoza, an illegitimate son of Pedro de Mendoza; another, Felipe de Cáceres, an intriguer who had made himself an official;[17] a new royal treasurer, García Venegas; and finally Juan de Salazar de Espinoza. The latter was a cultivated member of the order of Santiago, moderate, brave, and sharp-minded. Some skirmishes followed, in the course of which Cabeza de Vaca, *adelantado* though he might be, was seized and imprisoned. Martínez de Irala was elected *adelantado* by the citizens of Asunción, though no elective process had ever been formally decided upon. Cabeza was placed on a brigantine which then set off for the river Plate, the Atlantic, and Spain. His chief allies, Juan de Salazar and Pedro de Estropiñán, were also seized and sent off down the river to the sea.

Skirmishing between the friends of Cabeza de Vaca and those of Martínez de Irala went on for some years, until finally the Guaraní and the Agaze Indians planned a rebellion to recover all their lost lands. But Martínez de Irala faced them in the jungles of Arequía and the Spaniards registered an easy victory. The victor then ruled in Asunción as de facto *adelantado*.

Haunted by dreams of the kind of wealth that had been so easily discovered in Peru, Martínez de Irala now put a searching question to his colleagues: would they prefer to go on a dangerous expedition to Peru, an immensely long journey across the river Paraguay and the risky Chaco territory, or would they prefer to remain in Asunción, in relative comfort? About half of Martínez's friends chose the Peruvian alternative. Martínez himself agreed to lead them and he named

Francisco de Mendoza, Pedro de Mendoza's illegitimate son, as a temporary governor in Asunción.

Martínez de Irala sailed further up and along the river Paraguay, as far as San Fernando, where he left his brigantines, asking their captains to remain at their moorings there for the extraordinarily long time of two years. Martínez and his expedition then started westwards across completely unexplored territory. They forced their way across raging rivers, toiled across waterless deserts, fought fever and heat as well as hostile Indians. The men struggled against clinging mud and waded through stagnant waters, wary of the spikes of poisonous jungle plants, alarming reptiles, and monkeys. They eventually found themselves at what their leader believed to be the border of Peru. Waiting there for some weeks, they then received a message from Lima requiring Martínez de Irala to remain where he was. It was later rumoured that the acting Peruvian viceroy Pedro de la Gasca had even sent a bribe to Martínez to induce him not to move west.

Martínez de Irala had, of course, only been informally named *adelantado* in Asunción, so his status was insecure. He therefore sent to Lima his most resourceful follower, Nuflo de Chaves, an *extremeño* from Santa Cruz de la Sierra, a town near Cáceres which had once belonged to the Pizarros. Chaves was to try and negotiate the formal nomination of Martínez de Irala as *adelantado*. He was unsuccessful. But La Gasca's messenger to Martínez de Irala, explaining this unwelcome news, was waylaid by Indians who had been suborned by Martínez. In fact, when the letter finally arrived, it turned out to be vague and non-committal, but it was enough to persuade Martínez that his wisest move would be to return to Asunción.

The decision was greeted with derision by the conquistadors with him, for they had envisaged that the end of their journey would be crowned with both glory and gold in Peru. Martínez de Irala pacified them and led them back to La Candelaria, where they met the ships which they had left behind and which remarkably had remained in that desolate bay far up the river Paraguay for eighteen months. When they returned to Asunción in 1549, Martínez and his men discovered that that city had been suffering what was little short of a civil war. Francisco de Mendoza, the acting governor, had given out that Martínez de Irala and his expedition had all died. Mendoza had substituted himself as *adelantado* in Martínez's house in the Plaza de Armas, although he was now swiftly challenged. Diego de Abreu, a disgruntled captain from Seville who, like so many conquistadors, had first come to the Indies with Pedro de Mendoza, took action, captured Mendoza, and had him executed and himself proclaimed in his stead. But Abreu soon heard the alarming news that Martínez de Irala was in fact alive and, worse, was approaching Asunción. Shortly thereafter, Martínez was to be found camping just outside the city, where a majority of its Spanish inhabitants gradually joined him. Abreu was in the end left with a mere fifty men, mostly his close friends and relations. They all eventually fled to the nearby forest, giving Martínez de Irala a victory without bloodshed, and he was able to return peacefully to his old house in the Plaza de Armas.

Soon Nuflo de Chaves also returned, bringing with him from Peru the first sheep and goats to be seen in Paraguay. He was also accompanied by some conquistadors from Lima, whose primary purpose was to act as his bodyguards but who had also been given a secret instruction by La Gasca: to organize a rebellion against Martínez de Irala. The plan was skilfully foiled by that *adelantado*, who seized the leading plotters and had two of them, Camargo and Miguel Urrutia, executed. Nuflo de Chaves seemed to be innocent of any involvement, and shortly thereafter married a daughter of Francisco de Mendoza.

Martínez de Irala undertook the pursuit of Diego de Abreu. He was eventually caught and killed in the nearby forest. Thereafter, Martínez devoted his time exclusively to the organization of his large but as yet borderless colony. In 1553 he established a fort at San Juan where the river Paraná runs into the river Uruguay, but consistent Indian attacks obliged him to abandon it in 1555. Sometimes even the normally peaceful Guaraní conducted themselves threateningly, as indicated by reports of the eating of a Spanish soldier. On the other hand, at other times Indian leaders would make an appeal to Martínez; for example, in 1555 several Guaraní *caciques* begged him to help them against the Tupís in Brazil, who were continually molesting them in the interest, as the Guaraní supposed, of the Portuguese. Martínez de Irala, therefore, led what was virtually a crusade against the Tupí, killing many of them before they accepted vassalage to the Emperor Charles in a fine yet improbable ceremony held near the dramatic Iguazu falls.

On their return after this enterprise the Spaniards were misled by a *mestizo* interpreter, Hernando Díaz, who falsely assured them that a certain cataract on the Paraguay could be easily mastered by canoes. Instead, the cataract mastered the canoes and many Indians and some Spaniards were drowned. Moreover, several of those who had set out with Martínez de Irala became ill and a special ambulance expedition by boat had to be mounted by Alonso Encinas, a *hidalgo* from Extremadura, along with a group of strong and healthy indigenous fighters. These boats escaped the torrent of the perilous river, as did the ill men on them, but the banks of the river were steep, forested, and inhospitable.

The treacherous Hernando Díaz was, of course, condemned to death. But the night before he was due to be hanged, he escaped and fled to Brazil. Díaz was condemned there too for other crimes, this time to be marooned on a desert island, but from this too he eventually escaped. His motives are impossible to detect.

Having failed to establish a new port at the entry of the river Plate, Martínez de Irala determined to build a similar establishment on the way north to Brazil on the river Paraná. Here he came up against the ambitions of the Portuguese. All the same his deputy, García Rodríguez de Veragua, skilfully established a new settlement at Villa de Ontiveros. There the small Spanish contingent was soon reinforced by Martínez's son-in-law, Pedro de Segura, as well as some one-time supporters of the rebellious Diego de Abreu. At that point, to everyone's surprise, an Englishman, Nicolas Colman, made a great impression as 'the most resolute and daring of all those there, as he always showed in such a way that seeing captain Pedro de Segura had the measure of these people determined to spend a night secretly on a makeshift raft'. When this raft was about to leave, over a hundred large canoes full of Indians made their appearance. The Spaniards repelled them by shooting their arquebuses, to which the Indians replied with bows and arrows, killing one soldier as well as some Indian allies of the Spaniards. Meanwhile, Martínez de Irala busied himself with the foundation of a church which eventually became the cathedral of Paraguay.

One personal setback for the Basque *adelantado* was the nomination in Spain by the Council of the Indies of, first, Jaime Resquín and then Juan de Sanabría as *adelantados*. But the first died on his voyage out, and the latter lost his nerve and delayed leaving Castile. All the same, Sanabría appointed a deputy in the shape of Juan de Salazar de Espinoza, who already knew Paraguay well and who set out from Sanlúcar in 1552. He reached San Vicente near Santo. There he remained till 1555, when he began the last stage of his journey to Asunción, taking with him a small herd of cattle, including a bull and several cows. Horses were sent along from the plains of what is now Argentina, where they had greatly multiplied since the time of Pedro de Mendoza. Martínez de Irala welcomed Salazar, and the surprisingly friendly encounter was sealed by the arrival of Pedro Fernández de la Torre, a citizen of Baena who had arrived in Asunción in 1556. Torre became the second Bishop of Paraguay and he had brought a letter from Spain which at last formally named the resolute Basque as *adelantado*.

But Martínez had little time to enjoy his new position. He died in early 1557, aged seventy, a great age for any conquistador, especially one who was so relentless in his endeavours and who had faced many dangers. He had been a diligent and tireless commander who left behind an imperial colony built along a great river, a colony almost of the significance of Peru, or of New Spain.

# 17

# The Mad Adventure of Lope de Aguirre

*No one has ever seen me saddened by reverses or cheered by triumphs.*

Joannot Martorell, *Tirant lo Blanc*, 1490

When the royal ban on new expeditions was surprisingly lifted in 1558 (the prohibition had been the achievement of Bartolomé de Las Casas), the viceroy of Peru, Andrés Hurtado de Mendoza, the Marquis of Cañete, planned to carry through the conquest of 'the province of Omauga and El Dorado' – the supposedly golden region to the north of Quito. The expedition was not to be led, as at first planned, by Gómez de Alvarado, a brother of the great Pedro, 'son of the sun', a survivor of the conquest of Mexico, even though Gómez had wished for the command.[1] Instead it was led by Pedro de Ursúa, a Navarrese adventurer from a *pueblo* near Pamplona who in 1545 had accompanied his uncle Miguel Díaz de Armendáriz, the new judge and governor of New Granada (Colombia),[2] to Cartagena. Ursúa had successfully suppressed rebellions by the Tayrona Indians in New Granada's isolated mountain range, the Sierra Nevada de Santa Marta. He had afterwards become chief magistrate of Santa Marta.

Ursúa was most successful in this enterprise and had won golden opinions as a military commander. He combined a good education with a sweet nature, as well as uncommon bravery and dexterity in martial exercises. Garcilaso de la Vega described him as a perfect gentleman who was generally admired.

The viceroy gave Ursúa the title of governor of the provinces which he might discover and conquer, with the added power to appoint officers. Ursúa was also 'to have a care for the conquered Indians, to form settlements of such Spaniards as he thought proper and to do all for the good of the church and the crown of Spain'.[3] The cost of the expedition would be paid by the viceroy, an idea which was most unpopular in Lima since the viceregal expenses came from local taxation.

Despite that, there was all the same much enthusiasm for this new expedition. All Peru had heard of the legend of 'the golden man' believed to live in New Granada, and there were many unemployed conquistadors available and anxious for new adventures. Some 370 Spaniards, survivors of innumerable Peruvian rebellions and scandals, joined Ursúa, and thousands of Indians also signed up.

One cannot avoid thinking that one purpose of the expedition was indeed to give these adventurers a new livelihood. Many would have been glad, too, to accompany Ursúa's beautiful *mestiza* mistress, Inés de Atienza. She was renowned in the 1550s as 'the most beautiful woman in Peru', the daughter of Blas de Atienza, originally from Guadalajara in Castile, and an Indian girl from Jaujá. Disturbed by Inés's charms, even the elderly Viceroy Antonio de Mendoza had asked her to join his court, though she had already married the *encomendero* of Piura, Pedro de Arcos. When he died in 1559, Inés was then swept up by, and apparently fell in love with, the then famous Ursúa. He persuaded her and twelve other women, mostly *mestizas* but also some black women (slaves presumably), to accompany him to 'El Dorado' as part of a veritable court.

The expedition which now began, on 26 September 1560, was in many ways the most extraordinary of all the journeys of Spaniards in the sixteenth century. Ursúa and his followers set off north from Lima and soon came upon the river Huallaga, a tributary of the Marañón, a great river which itself flowed into the Amazon. But the persistent rain of the forest soon destroyed morale and the presence of Inés and her ladies, who were treated as if in a royal court, came to be resented. All the same, the Spaniards built a town, Machufaro, on a river bank, with many edible turtles nearby.[4] The explorers had by now almost reached the river Marañón, and these expeditionaries became known henceforth for a time as the *Marañones*.

Ursúa maintained his control for a time. But he was soon faced by a conspiracy headed by Lope de Aguirre, a bitter Basque conquistador who hated the Spanish administration, and who wanted to promote Fernando (Hernando) de Guzmán as the figurehead leader of the expedition, 'lord and prince of Peru, of the Main and of Chile'.[5]

Aguirre, a remarkable monster, came originally from Oñate in Guipúzcoa in the Basque country, a town near Mondragón, the place of origin of Martínez de Irala, the conquistador of Paraguay. Aguirre is a common Basque name. He was probably the illegitimate son of a *hidalgo*. He seems to have gone out to the Indies in 1539 and to have taken part without distinction in all the civil upheavals in Peru in the tragic 1540s, eventually siding with the viceregal forces of La Gasca against Gonzalo Pizarro, and for a time earning his living by breaking in young horses. Father Pedro Simón, in his account of Ursúa's expedition, which he accompanied, described Aguirre as being:

> of short stature, and sparsely made, ill-featured, the face small and lean, beard black, with eyes like a hawk's and, when he looked, he fixed them sternly, particularly when angry; he was a great and noisy talker; when well supported in conversation, he seemed most determined but if without support, he behaved as a coward; he was very hardy and could bear much fatigue. On foot as well as on horseback, he always went armed and well-protected and was never without one or two coats of mail, a breast plate of steel, a sword and a dagger, arquebus and lance.

Aguirre had been lame since he was wounded at the battle of Chuquinga in Peru in 1554. Fray Simón went on to say that he:

> was the enemy of good men and good actions, particularly of praying. And he would allow no one to pray in his presence. So when he saw any of his soldiers with rosaries in their hands, he took them away, breaking them, and saying that he did not want Christian soldiers, nor praying ones ... but that, if necessary, his men should play with the devil at dice for their souls. He told his followers ... that the earth was a territory reserved for the strongest, and that he knew for certain that there was no salvation and that being alive was to be in hell; and that, as he could not be blacker than the crow, he would commit every species of wickedness and cruelty so that his name might ring throughout the earth and even in the ninth heaven ... and that he would show the

King of Castile the will of Adam to see if he had left him as his heir in the Indies . . .'[6]

Ursúa had been warned against Aguirre before he left Peru, but he took no notice and trusted to his own great reputation and legend to preserve him from danger. He was also urged to leave Inés and the other women behind, but he refused. He took few precautions, and indeed spent most of his time with the lovely Inés, whom he liked to say took all the serious decisions.

On the night of 1 January 1561, Ursúa was, however, alone with a page named Lorca. The conquistador had probably become ill because of the unhealthy climate of the damp forest. Aguirre went to his lodging with some men in the middle of the night. 'What seek you here, gentlemen, at this hour?' Ursúa asked, a question which led to his being stabbed to death there and then. The friends of Ursúa were also killed in quick succession, though, for the moment, Inés was spared.

Aguirre persuaded the expedition to support Fernando de Guzmán as their new leader, and 186 out of the remaining 270 Spaniards signed a document saying that they supported Guzmán as their prince and lord, starting to call him 'Excellency'. Aguirre, who soon showed himself to be an extraordinary orator, also insisted that the expedition formally renounce all loyalty to King Philip. Guzmán became, says Fray Simón:

> proud and haughty, with the hope of seeing himself crowned as King. He also became grave and severe, for such appeared to him necessary for one who in a short time was to be invested with royal honours. He ordered that his dwelling, service and servants should correspond to that of other princes; he appointed a *majordomo*, a carver, pages and gentlemen, to whom he assigned large salaries . . . to be paid eventually out of the royal treasury in the kingdoms of Peru.

Guzmán always dined alone and he was served at table with ceremony. What an irony to have such a monarch high up on a remote and unknown tributary of the Amazon in a 'kingdom', where the food supply was inadequate, the security unreliable, and the climate intolerable. Meanwhile, Aguirre persuaded the expedition to give up the idea of seeking El Dorado and instead to return to Peru by sea in order to mount an attack on the viceroy and his administration. Aguirre had built two large brigantines, and began the journey downstream.

Fernando de Guzmán, Aguirre, and their companions soon found themselves on the Amazon, but many jealousies, suspicions, and hatreds remained. Aguirre ordered his followers to murder both Guzmán and Inés de Atienza, as well as her new lover Lorenzo de Salduendo, whom Inés had dominated as much as she had Ursúa. In fact she dominated 'all other persons of quality'. Her strength of character was remarkable. She was apparently killed with a spade by two creatures of Aguirre named Antón Llanosa and Francisco Carrión. Aguirre then addressed the expedition in one of his most brutal denunciations, not only admitting, but boasting, of crimes and treacheries. He apparently said:

> Caballeros, what madness and gross ignorance is this into which some of us have fallen which, certes, looks more like a pastime than an affair of such importance. You have killed the king's governor, one who represented his royal person, one who was clothed with royal powers; and do you pretend that with documents concocted by ourselves we shall be held blameless? Think you that the King and his judges will not understand how such papers were got up? This is madness; and well is it known to all that if those who sign it be asked questions against themselves, it will go against them if they have said so much in their own favour. Yes we have all killed the governor and the whole of us have rejoiced at the act; and if not let each man lay his hand on his heart and say what he thinks. We have all been traitors, we have all been party to this mutiny and have agreed that the country (in search of which we are) shall be sought for, found and settled.[7]

They then sailed as fast as they could downstream. To lighten the boats, Aguirre left behind 170 loyal Christian Peruvian Indians on a bank of the Amazon. Anyone who intervened on their behalf was garrotted.

Aguirre's expedition reached the Atlantic in early July 1561, and they then sailed fast up to the island of Margarita off the coast of Venezuela, which they reached on 21 July. Aguirre landed, seized the island, and murdered the governor, Juan de Villandrando. He then disembarked at Borburata on the Venezuelan coast, by then an important port. Aguirre set about killing with great cruelty suspected traitors, such as his *maestro de campo*, Martín Pérez. The account of these terrible murders, which included friars and women, beggars description. One Portuguese named Antonio Farias was killed for asking whether he were on an island or the mainland. A well-known local lady was garrotted because a soldier who had lodged in her house had fled. Another member of the expedition was killed because he was ill, and a placard was placed on his corpse saying that he had been executed for being useless and backward. In relation to another murdered man, Aguirre passed by and shouted at his severed head, 'Ah, are you still there, friend Alarcón? How is it that the King of Castile does not come to bring thee back to life?'[8]

Aguirre and his men, who now numbered only about 140, moved inland, and assailed the Andes in bad weather: 'Does God think that, because it is raining, I am not going to reach Peru and destroy the world?' the increasingly deranged Aguirre demanded. 'Then He does not know me!'[9]

They reached the Spanish city of Barquisimeto, on the east side of Lake Maracaibo, a settlement which had been founded in 1552 by Juan de Villegas, and from which most of the citizenry had fled out of prudence, or fear. They had taken with them all the provisions in the place, leaving behind only letters of pardon to all who wanted to avail themselves of such a thing. But by now royal forces were moving north towards Aguirre's men, led by the local governor, Pedro Bravo, from Mérida, with the clever *extremeño* Diego García de Paredes, and numbering about 200 well-armed and mounted men. The Chilean poet Alonso de Ercilla, author of the epic poem *La Araucana*, was among them.[10]

Another defence against Aguirre's force was organized in Bogotá, New Granada (Colombia), by the governor and adventurer Jiménez de Quesada, who had been named an *adelantado*. Then in October 1561, Aguirre wrote a mad letter to King Philip:

> Consider, Lord and King, that you cannot, with any just royal title, take any income from these lands where you personally risked nothing, until those who did labour and sweat for them have first had their reward . . .

I take it for certain that few kings go to hell because there are so few of them but, even if there were many, none would go to heaven. For I believe that you are all worse than Lucifer, and that you hunger and thirst for human blood . . . I think little of you and I despise you all, nor do I look upon your government as more than an air bubble . . . Alas, alas, what a misfortune it is that the Emperor thy father conquered Germany at such a price and has spent on that conquest the money we procured for him in these very Indies . . . because of thy ingratitude, I am a rebel against thee till death. Signed Lope de Aguirre, the Wanderer.[11]

Aguirre soon became engaged in a real battle against the well-established settlers. But though he still had many arquebusiers, that helped him little. He prepared to return to the coast. Finding that more of his men had deserted, he killed his own *mestiza* daughter, Elvira, and her serving woman, with a dagger, in order to save them from rape by the royalist soldiers. Aguirre's own men at last then killed him with their arquebuses on 27 October 1561. His body was quartered, and four sections were hung outside four towns, his head being kept in an iron cage at the city of Tocuyo, which had been founded on the coast at the end of a beautiful valley. His hands were thrown to the dogs and then into a river. It was the end to a story as tragic as it was extraordinary. Aguirre was one of those characters not unfortunately as infrequent as one would like to suppose, a man of pure evil with superior talents. The twentieth century provided many examples. Werner Herzog rendered this expedition vividly in his film of 1972, *Aguirre, Wrath of God*.

# 18

# Guiana and El Dorado

*... yet unspoiled/Guiana whose great city Geryon's sons/Call
El Dorado ...*

John Milton, *Paradise Lost*, 1667

By 1560 the south of South America had been colonized and conquered. Numerous cities had been founded. Heroic journeys had been accomplished.

Matters were different in the north of the continent, which was still haunted by myths, particularly that of El Dorado, the magical kingdom of gold which had been sought by three generations of adventurers without success. There were other legends: for example, that 200 conquistadors had been left behind from Diego de Ordaz's expedition of the 1530s and lived on in a palisaded building under the control of an indigenous monarch named Carivan, near the source of the river Orinoco.[1] An inquiry was held into this rumour in early 1560 in Bogotá.[2] A certain Juan Rodríguez said that in this region he had seen golden lizards, frogs, and other animals – whether of metal or of skin was not immediately evident – and alleged that it was a place of vast wealth.

Before that, Juan de Avellana de Temiño, who came originally from Quintanapalla north-east of Burgos on the road to Miranda del Ebro, founded a town at San Juan de los Llanos (Saint John of the Plains), on the banks of the river Ariare, about 150 miles south of where Aguirre had met his well-deserved end. This was on the edge of the great plain to the south of the colony of Venezuela. Avellana had been in that territory since 1532, during which he travelled 600 miles.

Originally, he had gone up to Bogotá with the brilliant German Nicolas Federman, and he became the mayor there in 1555. Avellana then received an instruction from the conquistador of Venezuela, Jiménez de Quesada, to seek gold in the province of Guayupes, near Bogotá, where he had an *encomienda*. After founding San Juan de los Llanos, Avellana embarked on another journey of discovery. He divided his followers into two – one section being henceforth led by Francisco de Bastidas and Francisco Barba, the other by Alonso de Ortega and himself. Subsequently, Avellana founded a town which he agreeably named Burgos in a valley known as San Jerónimo.[3]

These successful ventures led to great interest being shown by Gonzalo Jiménez de Quesada, who, though nearly seventy, sought and obtained a patent to explore and then govern what was at the time known as 'the southern *llanos* [plains]'. He received this grant from King Philip in July 1569, when he was named governor of Pauto and Papamene, a large territory which included land as far north as Guiana and extended south to the Amazon. Jiménez, happily considering himself a *victor ludorum*, agreed to go to these places with at least 400 men, including eight priests. He took black slaves with him to assist in the building of houses. He was promised a marquesate like Cortés and Pizarro, if he were successful (both Cortés and Pizarro had become *marqueses*).[4] He organized an immense expedition, consisting of 300 Spaniards, 1,100 horses, 600 cows, 800 pigs, 1,500 Indians, and a large though unknown number of African slaves.

Perhaps Jiménez de Quesada had heard the tale of how Gonzalo Pizarro, before his expedition with Francisco de Orellana, had himself heard of a prince who was covered daily with powdered gold, so that, from head to foot, he resembled a golden figure worked by the hands of a great sculptor. Jiménez and his friends left Bogotá in December 1569 and travelled across the vast plains, enduring fever, hunger, mosquitoes, unexpected deaths, and frequent desertions.[5] He found neither gold nor silver and limped back after several years' absence, his expedition destroyed. Jiménez died soon after, nearly eighty years old.

The lure of El Dorado was such that the Crown was excessively active with its commissions to find it. Diego Fernández de Serpa, a sometime carpenter and yet another citizen of Palos, near Huelva,

Andalusia, to make his mark in the New World, sought this magical place in the mountains south of the river Orinoco. He set out in October 1569 for what he called 'New Andalusia' – an unoriginal usage. He had arranged to have the right to administer the territory there for three generations, and was granted a payment of 4,000 ducats a year. He also asked to be called the *adelantado* of the land concerned and to have thirty square leagues given to him.

Fernández de Serpa had, to begin with, been engaged in pearl-fishing. He went to Quito in 1535, but had had interests in both Santa Marta and Santo Domingo, in Margarita, as well as back in Spain. By 1569, Fernández was sixty years old. He travelled with great herds of cattle and almost a tribe of agricultural labourers. His settlement stretched across the modern provinces of Anzoátegui, Monagas, and Sucre. His main town of departure for his travels became Cumaná in the north of Venezuela. He carried out expeditions in search of salt as well as of gold. One of his biographers described him as 'belonging to a new generation of doradists'.[6] But going south towards the Orinoco, in 1570, he and his comrades were surprised by Indians in an ambush and Fernández was killed by an arrow, along with two other captains and seventy-four of his men.[7]

Another licence to seek El Dorado was given to Pedro Maraver de Silva, who had been part of the first expedition to Bogotá from Chachapoyas. His patent was for a territory about 1,000 miles beyond that allocated to Fernández de Serpa, which Maraver called 'New Extremadura'. But he does not seem ever to have reached it. His force split up, with some of his captains deserting him.[8]

A more serious successor to Jiménez de Quesada was his nephew by marriage, Antonio de Berrio, a Segoviano who had married Jiménez's niece María and who was bequeathed the 'governorship of [El Dorado]' in Jiménez's will.[9]

Berrio was an old soldier who had survived many campaigns in Europe. Born about 1520, he was from his teens a squire attached to numerous knights at court. He lost three brothers in the Emperor's service. He was himself in Flanders, Germany, and later in the Alpujarra campaign against the Moriscoes,[10] and he was present at the capture of Siena in 1555. He and his wife, the heiress, with their many children, made their way to Bogotá in 1580, hopeful of great gains.

They settled in Chita high up in the Andes, and began to accumulate a substantial income from *encomiendas* there. One year later Berrio started off eastwards for El Dorado, as he hoped it would be, with about eighty men. Like so many before him, he expected to establish a new kingdom or at least a marquisate, as the great Cortés had done in the 1520s.

Berrio reached the river Meta by February 1584 and was close to the Orinoco by August, in the rainy season. From his own account, we learn how the thatched *bohios* (huts) of the Achagua Indians were well sealed against mosquitoes, how the same tribe made a strong mescal from pineapples, how they ate fish and *guaja* fruit, how they had a strong poison for use on arrows against enemies or, in one instance, as defence against Amazonian women who attacked men who did not make love adequately.[11] There were stories of a large number of well-populated settlements in the mysterious hills south of the Orinoco with 'great riches of gold', and how there was much of the same on the bed of the mysterious saline lake of Manoa, which was so large that an Indian would take three days to paddle across it in a canoe. Once this lake was crossed, the grand territory of Guiana was expected to stretch as far as the Amazon. Or was it the Orinoco?

The hills beyond the river Orinoco then became the focus for those seeking El Dorado. Juan de Salas, the governor of the pearl island of Margarita, reported 'there is much news that there is gold in the province of Guiana both from Arawak Indians who came to this island and also from the Spaniards who go to trade for slaves . . . Lords who possess riches order that, when they die, all their treasures should be thrown into this lake.'[12] Berrio set off for this range of hills with thirteen companions. They cut their way through to a cliff which overlooked the Orinoco. Thence they canoed down that river towards the Atures rapids. They then returned to Bogotá to seek more men. Berrio thought that he needed 3,000.[13]

He set off again three years later in March 1587, though still with only eighty followers, half of them arquebusiers, 500 horses, and about the same number of cattle. But other explorers, such as Felipe de Cáceres, were now in the field. Berrio, raising 25,000 ducats to finance his journey, canoed first down the river Casanare and then the Meta. Next, he went down the Orinoco, leaving a lieutenant, Álvaro

Jorge, a Portuguese survivor of many expeditions of the past in search of El Dorado, to manage the cattle and horses on land.[14]

Berrio established a small settlement near the Atures rapids. There he was joined by his wife María, but he was obliged to abandon his expedition yet again because of the rebellion of several of his new followers.

He then organized a third expedition in 1589, which he estimated would cost 40,000 ducats. Álvaro Jorge again acted as second-in-command in charge of the horses and cattle. Berrio's thirteen-year-old son came too.[15] But there were further disasters. Seeking to weather the rainy season on the banks of the river Cuchivero, a tributary of the Orinoco, an illness in the form of madness seized hold of most of the expedition, including their dogs and horses. The men also began to die of hunger. Still, when the rains abated, Berrio went on and ascended the river Parucito. Finally, having killed his horses in the tradition of Cortés, 'so that the soldiers would lose any hope of returning home' to Bogotá, he sailed down the river Caroní. He had previously met and talked with the chief Morequito at the river's mouth (it joined the Orinoco), which Berrio believed was certain to lead to El Dorado. Some indigenous people had confirmed that to him, at least in his report: 'They revealed great secrets about the land and confirmed all the information which I had received higher up . . .'[16] 'Those great provinces,' Berrio declared, 'lie between the two very great rivers, the Amazon and the Orinoco . . . from the mouth of the first and that of the Orinoco, the map indicates more than 400 leagues in latitude and 1,500 in longitude.'

Berrio began to find large Indian towns sixty leagues (about 180 miles) inland. In every district during his long journey he had come across gold, which the Indians said came from 'the far side of the mountains and they exaggerated the quantity so much that it is incredible . . . I shall enter into Guiana without delay and, if it is one twentieth of what is believed, it will be richer than Peru.'[17] But he did not explore the Caroní valley because his men were dying, and he had to withdraw to the island of Trinidad in September 1591, and then Margarita island, to find reinforcements.

We learn from a romantic memorandum written by a new conquistador in the region, Domingo de Ibargoien y Vera, a giant of a man and an easy-going one, who proved himself Berrio's best supporter, how 'many captains with many people, horses and cattle were lost seeking the entrance to these new provinces . . . but could not find the way in because of the mountains and high and sharp-shaped ranges and huge rivers which could be called lakes of sweet water which in one way or another surround them'. Ibargoien had already founded San José de Oruña, a new city on the island of Trinidad. He was a skilful talker who could persuade almost anyone to join him, and he did so, men from Caracas, Bogotá, and even from back in Spain.

As a result in 1593, reported Ibargoien, Berrio (and the Lord):

> conceded this adventure to me and I with thirty-five soldiers, found the entrance easily and with no difficulty whatever; so I went into the land which is called Guayana [sic] which is 35 leagues long where I saw many large settlements of well-disposed Indians . . . who went about completely naked with only those parts covered which honestly I cannot name. The territory is healthy, of moderate temperature, peaceful, fertile, with the fruits of the Indies and above all amenable and which appears a perpetual forest. There is much game, much fish and, among all the new lands which I have seen, it is the most appropriate for recreation and pleasure. It is extremely rich in gold and the *naturales* want to show me where it is that they mine it. But in order not to seem covetous, I have insisted that my expedition was not being carried out for seeking gold, but was intended to establish friendship with the local people. I only brought back seventeen pieces of worked gold which I destined for His Majesty, and three hatchets of stone which show that, though these people are sometimes barbarous, they do not lack the skills to stop them being so. They have told me that, at seven days distance in the interior, there is an infinite amount of gold, and that no one goes to the mines except *caciques* and their wives. They take it out with great superstition, fasting first for three days; but in the rivers where there is much gold, they can take what they want, the grains being as large as those of maize. I found the people amiable, good-mannered, and liberal, and they treated us well and arranged everything very well. And from there having few followers, I returned to the island of Trinidad whence I had set out on the orders of our captain-general and governor . . . Antonio del Berrio.[18]

Ibargoien went on to describe how, by offering innumerable gifts, he had befriended all the Indians whom he had encountered. This memorandum is of interest not because of what it reports, but because it was an invention, comparable to an advertising prospectus. Ibargoien goes on to say later that the towns in Guiana – there were at least a hundred of them – included anything from between 1,000 and 10,000 Indians each. He could not avoid fantasy and, indeed, did not want to. But in all the towns where he went, he did leave behind crosses, and he took possession of the land in the name of King Philip. Ibargoien was certain that he had entered the outer ring of the golden land of El Dorado. Some, such as the chronicler of Peru Pedro Cieza de León, thought 'it certain that the land in this part is populated by the descendants of the famous [Peruvian] captain Ancoallo'.[19] Berrio, on the other hand, thought that the Inca had derived from Guiana.

Sir Walter Raleigh, the English adventurer, who was now beginning to take an interest in these geographical conundrums, intervened in 1592 to burn the Spanish township of San José de Oruña on Trinidad, and he captured Berrio and Álvaro Jorge there. Raleigh too, like Berrio, seems to have thought that the mighty, rich, and beautiful empire of Guiana had been the refuge of the last Inca, and at one point he seized a copy of Ibargoien's report of the Caroní valley.

A few years before, Raleigh seems to have inspired the grand chronicler Richard Hakluyt to publish in 1589 his *Principal Navigations, Voiages, Traffiques and Discoveries of the English Nation*, which a modern historian has called 'the prose epic of a modern English Nation'. This chronicle denied Spanish claims to North America, denounced the cruelty with which (so Hakluyt claimed) the Spaniards had treated the Amerindians, and urged colonization as a solution to all the problems at home. Raleigh, realizing that Spain's power was founded on silver and gold from South America, plotted an English empire on the north coast of that continent. A second edition of the first volume of Hakluyt's book appeared in 1598, with the two further volumes following in 1599 and 1600.

Raleigh's own work about Guiana, *The Discovery of the large, rich, Empire of Guiana*, published in 1596, was based on that imaginative text, though Ibargoien did not mention the phenomenon of oysters growing on trees nor the even stranger vision of the Ewaipanoma, an alleged tribe in Guiana who had eyes on their shoulders and mouths on their breasts. Raleigh read Spanish, having learned it in the 1570s. Like Ibargoien, Raleigh thought that Guiana had 'more abundance of gold than any part of Peru'. He reflected the Spanish report about 'Manoa . . . the imperial City which the Spaniards call El Dorado . . . for the riches . . . for the excellent seat . . . [on] a lake of salt water of 200 leagues long . . .'[20]

Berrio and Jorge were eventually set free at Cumaná, a port on the mainland near the island of Margarita, whence Fernández de Serpa had set off on his original expedition. Berrio immediately left for the enticing river Caroní, as he had done so often before. There he founded a small settlement, Santo Tomé de Guiana, a 'ranchería of some twenty or thirty houses', as an English observer, Laurence Keymes, called it, which Berrio planned as the base camp for his next great journey. But this time he was thwarted by his old follower, Ibargoien, who returned to the New World in 1596 with a fleet full of enthusiastic volunteers for new conquests – or rather a new conquest, in Guiana. There were perhaps 3,500 of them. Whatever their numbers, the food was inadequate. Luis de Santander wrote: 'It is a great tragedy to see so many men, women and children dying of hunger.'[21]

They died, too, from Indian attacks and from disease. Ibargoien had to return to Trinidad, whilst Berrio sent up to 400 men to cross into Guiana. They went 100 miles up the Caroní and several Indian tribes provided them with food. Álvaro Jorge died and there was no successor. The survivors quarrelled and became an easy prey to the Indians who attacked them on the hill of Totumos and slaughtered them. Some 350 were killed, while the remainder were led by a Franciscan to Santo Tomé. They were back in Trinidad by August 1596.

Some months later the great adventurer Berrio himself at last died, almost eighty years old. The main advocate of the adventure of El Dorado had thus departed. Nevertheless, his son, Fernando de Berrio, devoted ten years and eighteen expeditions to his father's dream. He seems to have reached the Angel Falls (the Salto del Angel), the world's highest waterfall, on a tributary of the Caroní. He also came to know the river Caroní well and tried, albeit fruitlessly, to cross the *cordillera* separating the Orinoco from the Amazon. Fernando also sailed up the river Cuchivero. Ruined, he was eventually made governor of Guiana in 1619. But when sailing to Spain in search of further support, he was captured by Barbary pirates and died a prisoner in Algiers in 1622.

English and French explorers tried to take Berrio's place, and they carried out some remarkable journeys in the first years of the seventeenth century. But the noble Sir Walter Raleigh, the 'shepherd of the Ocean' as the poet Edmund Spenser called him, discredited himself.[22] His book about Guiana was racy but worthless, since it was full of falsehoods.[23] Condemned for treason, he was executed at Westminster in October 1618.

# BOOK THREE

# The Imperial Backcloth

# 19

# Portugal Joins Spain

*Uniting some realms with others does not follow from having
the same ruler since though Aragón and Castile have a single
ruler, they are not united but as separate as they were when
they had different rulers.*

King Philip to the Duke of Osuna and Cristóbal
de Moura, 30 June 1579 (*Colección de documentos
inéditos para la historia de España*, V, 519–20)

The Portuguese monarchy had been an independent sovereign institution since that country had been freed from the Moors in the thirteenth century. On 4 August 1578 a Portuguese royal army was crushed at the battle of Alcázarquivir, in Morocco, about a dozen miles inland from the Atlantic coast. The charming young King Sebastian[1] – he was barely twenty-four years old – was never seen again after the battle. His brilliant commander-in-chief, Francisco de Aldana, a poet of immense promise, also died: he had once written 'O great, o grand conquests/of the Indies of God, of that great world/so miraculously hidden from mundane view!'[2]

The Duke of Alba described the defeat as being 'the worst possible occurrence'. King Sebastian was, after all, a second cousin of King Philip as well as his nephew by marriage.[3] For several years the idea persisted that Sebastian had not been killed, and various fraudulent impersonators of him were put forward.

Sebastian had been a visionary obsessed with the idea of a crusade against Islam. King Philip had tried to dissuade him from embarking on such a foolhardy campaign. The small Portuguese army was, however, perhaps predictably overwhelmed by a better equipped and much larger Moroccan force, and Sebastian turned out to be incapable of command. A large number of Portuguese noblemen were captured and had to be ransomed for large sums.

The news reached Philip in the Escorial nine days later, on 13 August.[4] By then in Lisbon, Cardinal Enrique, the late Portuguese king's great-uncle, had been proclaimed King Enrique of Portugal. But he was old. He had been born in 1512 and so was already approaching seventy – that seemed a great age in that era – and he had spent all his life in the Church. Though reasonably astute, the cardinal-king was weak in health, suffering from bad gout as well as tuberculosis. He reigned incompetently for as long as two years (1578–80), which in itself seemed something of a miracle. Enrique had summoned the Portuguese Cortes (the parliament) to pronounce on who should be his successor. He himself favoured King Philip of Spain, who indeed had the best claim being, through his mother, a grandson of the late King Manuel.

But the Cortes of Portugal was divided between inviting to take the throne João, the Duke of Braganza, a fourth cousin of the cardinal-king, and Antonio, the Prior of Crato, an illegitimate first cousin of Sebastian. If a septuagenarian cardinal could take the throne, why not a bastard prior?[5] Unfortunately the prior's mother was a beautiful *conversa*, Violante Gomes, a new Christian of Jewish ancestry, a genealogical consideration which did not assist his cause. Another claimant was Catalina, daughter of Cardinal Enrique's younger brother Duarte, who was married to the Duke of Braganza.

When the cardinal-king died in January 1580, seven candidates laid claim to the throne of Portugal. Prior Antonio made a firm bid, though he was soon defeated by a Spanish fleet off São Miguel in the Azores. In February, less than a month after Enrique's death, Spanish troops were poised in Castile ready for a *coup de main* against Lisbon, if King Philip should make such a move. The Duke of Medina Sidonia, the future commander of the *Armada Invencible*, raised 4,000 infantry and 450 cavalry. The king was reluctant to use force, but Cristóbal de Moura, a clever Portuguese nobleman who advised him on many things, assured Philip that eventually the Cortes in Lisbon would offer him the throne. Moura probably gave bribes to several noblemen.[6]

The Jesuits, who were increasingly powerful in Portugal, seem also to have backed the royal Spanish candidate.

On 13 June 1580, having accepted that some military action might be needed if he were going to win the Crown in Lisbon, Philip mobilized an army of 20,000 infantrymen and 1,500 cavalry, under the command of the now aged but ever ready Duke of Alba. In two weeks Alba ordered his army to enter Portugal. He commandeered many carts, apparently the first time such vehicles had been used in a military campaign.[7] Wheeled traffic was then rarely used except in big cities and even there it was considered a 'German fashion'.[8] A 'coach' was considered a mysterious Hungarian object, since the word originated in the Magyar *kocsi*.

Despite his defeat in the Azores, Prior Antonio of Crato had proclaimed himself king of Portugal. Had Philip not intervened, Antonio would no doubt have reigned. The major cities of Setubal, Santarem and even Lisbon had declared for him. An important if minor campaign then ensued in August 1580. The Duke of Alba demanded the surrender of Don Antonio's cities. When their commanders refused, the cities were sacked. A small army led by Antonio was defeated outside Lisbon.[9] The fighting was on a larger scale than had been expected but it was nevertheless successfully concluded by Alba, and all Portugal then passed under Philip's sway. Don Antonio himself escaped, being defeated again at Terceira in the Azores, and he remained a ghostly threat to Spain's control of Portugal until he died in Paris in 1595. King Philip, meantime, undertook to rule the country and its empire through Portuguese subjects, nobles, and civil servants, not Spaniards, and on the whole he fulfilled that promise.

To ensure the symbolic union of the two realms, King Philip then travelled to Portugal in April 1581, freeing all the prisoners taken in the recent fighting in the towns through which he passed. He was proclaimed king of Goa as well as of Ceylon, both being dependencies of Portugal. In Lisbon he and his favourite architect, Juan de Herrera, designer of the Escorial, modified the *Paço da Ribeira*, the great square to the north of the estuary, realigning its windows to overlook the port, and building a domed tower, the *Torreão*. Philip ordered a cross to be made from the timbers of a Spanish galleon, *Las Cinco Llagas*, which had foundered and been abandoned on the beach of Lisbon.

The timber had come originally from the East Indies. This cross was eventually placed on the high altar in the church at El Escorial.[10]

Further confirmations of Spanish rule followed. In March 1581 the Bolognese Pope Gregory XIII, Ugo Buoncompagni, recognized King Philip as the ruler of Portugal, and the former Portuguese ambassador in Rome, Gómez de Silva (a cousin of the Prince of Éboli), paid homage to the Pope in the name of his new sovereign. Pope Gregory had once been nuncio in Spain and so had come to know, and also to appreciate, Philip on his own ground.

Philip was proclaimed king of Portugal outside the door of the Templars' Church in the Convent of Christ in Tomar, a beautiful city on the river Nabão. He wore robes of state and complained at having to do so (they were uncomfortable) in a touching letter to his two daughters.[11] The Cortes in Tomar insisted on the absolute separation of the administration of Castile from that of Portugal and even forbade trade between Spain and Portugal, though the merchants of both countries had become used to their enriching interchanges.

All the same, when news of the identity of the new monarch of Portugal reached Manila in the Philippines, it led to a reconsideration of several plans for further conquests in the Far East. It also stimulated the previously condemned trade in silk and porcelain from Macao in exchange for arms and munitions. The Portuguese in the Far East continued to be alarmed at Spanish ambitions there, but in the Indies news of the union of the crowns was welcome. Philip began to see that he now had something close to a universal monarchy covering Brazil as well as Goa, Malacca and Macao.[12]

The constant procession of ships which Philip could observe from the windows of his palace in Lisbon was described in another of his touching letters to his daughters.[13] Lisbon, as Fernand Braudel commented, was a magnificent observatory from which to scan the ocean.[14] In April 1582 the king, still in Lisbon, witnessed the spectacular sight of the Spanish and Portuguese fleets leaving the majestic harbour together, and later that month he accompanied his fleet out of Lisbon on the first stage of its journey to the New World. He breakfasted on the royal galley at the mouth of the port, and passed the day there. In the course of it, he made the Duke of Braganza, one of the claimants to the Portuguese throne in 1580, a knight of the Golden

Fleece, and the two went to mass together. The event was a good example of Habsburg tolerance.

Nine months later, in February 1583, after a two-year stay in Portugal, the longest that King Philip had been away from Spain anywhere since his return from Flanders in 1559, he went home to Castile. He left behind as Regent in Lisbon his brother-in-law and nephew, the Archduke Albert, the son of his sister María who had married the Emperor Maximilian. Albert, though not formally a priest, was already a cardinal.

It was probably a mistake of Philip not to have made Lisbon his capital city. As Braudel wrote, it could have been transformed into a city comparable to London or Naples and more beautiful than either.[15] But the fact was that the Castilian nobility had begun to move to Madrid, residing to begin with in ugly or uncomfortable houses but soon purchasing grand properties, seduced by the broad and agreeable promenades of the city, not to mention the elegant churches and palaces. So the Spanish court returned slowly via Setúbal, Evora, Badajoz, Guadalupe, Talavera, and finally the Escorial. Then Philip continued to Madrid, arriving there on 29 March. He had brought back from Portugal an Indian elephant and a rhinoceros, both of which made a dramatic appearance at the Escorial.

The attachment of Spain to Portugal seemed the final great act of creative politics by the monarchs of Castile: it marked the re-unification at last of the peninsula for the first time since the overthrow of the Visigothic monarchy in 711. The setbacks at the hands of Islam had thus been finally overcome. Having joined Portugal, Spain had gained the large if untidy gathering of dependencies which the Portuguese had aquired in Brazil and the Far East. World responsibility if not world power seemed to lie in the hands of King Philip II. It was as well that he never succumbed to delusions of grandeur.[16]

# 20

# The Money Behind the Conquests

*There is a tremendous trade in hides and sugar and in a herb*
*which in everyday Spanish and Arabic is known as carmesí. It*
*makes a purple dye which is just as good as purpura and far*
*less expensive.*

Hurtado de Mendoza, *The War in Granada,* 1627

Most of the great expeditions of the sixteenth century had the services of a major entrepreneur behind them. Thus Hernando Cortés was backed early on by the *sevillano* merchants and *conversos* Luis Fernández de Alfaro and Juan de Córdoba, and latterly by the *burgalés* Pedro de Maluenda,[1] who had previously served Pánfilo de Narváez. (Maluenda's contribution to Cortés's expedition was probably the most important of all, since his family rose to be the most powerful providers of finance in the all-important city of Burgos.)[2] The Pizarros were substantially assisted by Gaspar de Espinosa. In New Granada (Colombia) and Venezuela, Jiménez de Quesada had behind him businessmen from Córdoba, while Pedro de Heredia in Cartagena was backed financially by Pedro de Cifuentes of Madrid. Pedro Fernández de Lugo in Santa Marta (present-day Colombia) was financed by the clever Genoese businessmen Alberto Gerardini and Cristóbal Francesquini. Fernández de Lugo took the lion's share of the produce from the pearl merchants of Margarita island, but half of the profits went to his Genoese backers. The Welser family was behind the expedition of Juan García de Loaisa to the Moluccas, while Sebastian Cabot, in his explorations of the river Plate, also had the backing of Genoese bankers.

Other merchants who invested imaginatively in the New World included Cristóbal de Haro of Burgos, latterly a banker in Seville, who was able to sell 480 *quintales* of the cloves brought back on the *Victoria* by Juan Sebastián El Cano in 1522;[3] his first fortune had been made from sugar in Madeira.[4] The most important shipbuilders in Spain in the sixteenth century were Juan Antonio Corzo and Rodrigo Bazo de Andrada, both *sevillanos* and both *conversos*.[5]

We cannot make even a rough guess as to the size of these investments. But it was a great help to every conquistador to know that, in an emergency, money or equipment might be found to ease a local difficulty.

Even more significant, the opportunities opened up by the New World marked a fresh and invigorating stage in the history of capitalism. Many are familiar with the arguments of Max Weber and of his disciple, R. H. Tawney, with Werner Sombart's discussion of the history of Jewry, and with the rise of the bourgeoisie as depicted in the brilliant work of Henri Pirenne. Many theories explaining the rise of capitalism in the sixteenth century have talked of the role of religion and culture. But all new considerations of capitalism should include the New World. Investments in *entradas* (new expeditions) were gambles in a world of wagers. Fernand Braudel reminded us that gambling held an important place not only in the lives of nobles but also in those of merchants; the price of sugar, of quicksilver, or of wine could be gambled upon. But any subject could be a pretext for a wager, such as the number of cardinals to be promoted, the sex of unborn children, even the death or the survival of famous men.[6] The capture of a new province or 'island' could also amount to a real fortune for the merchant or banker who gained control of it.

Merchants now required an efficient and wide-reaching postal service, an innovation that was almost as important as printing. The postal services which evolved in various European countries made possible the development of the letter as a literary form as well as one of convenience.

France under Louis XI, the central figure in the great novel by Sir Walter Scott *Quentin Durward*, had made the first endeavours along these lines. The king had established a system of postal relays each occupying seven leagues (39 kilometres); in succeeding reigns the number of roads in France served by this arrangement increased considerably.[7]

In Spain the control of the post was already in the hands of one celebrated family, the Taxis from Bergamo. In the fifteenth century they had established a reliable service between Venice and the Netherlands. François de Taxis (Tassis), captain and master of posts of Philip the Fair, became in 1505 'postmaster-general of Castile'. This office passed to his sons (Mateo, then Raimundo, then Juan), while Leonardo de Taxis lived at Brussels as chief of posts.[8]

By the end of the sixteenth century there were in Spain six main postal routes, all beginning in Madrid: to the north-east towards Saragossa and Barcelona; to the north towards Irún and Burgos; to the south-west towards Toledo, Cáceres, and then Portugal; to the south towards Córdoba, Seville, and Tarifa; to the east towards Valencia. A sixth route took mail to Valladolid, north-west of Madrid.[9]

A courier left Madrid on horseback every fifteen days for Genoa, Milan, Rome, and Naples, passing through Irún and Lyons. One would expect the journey from Madrid to Rome to take twenty-four days in the summer, twenty-seven in the winter. The post from Burgos to Brussels, however, took just seven or eight days in 106 relays over a distance of 314 leagues, or about 1,700 kilometres. In France, King Francis gave permission for the passage of Spanish couriers across his territories. Burgos was important since it was the centre of maritime insurance for Castile, as Rouen was for France.[10] According to Braudel, the fastest speeds in Europe in the sixteenth century were probably achieved by couriers working for Gabriel de Tassis on the 500 miles of the Italy–Brussels route via the Tyrol. The distance was covered in just five and a half days.[11]

By 1580, communications between Spain and the New World had been well established. It was based on the grant in May 1579 to Martín Olivares, a dependent of the viceroy, of the monopoly of the postal service between New Spain and the rest of the world. A year later, postal offices were set up in Veracruz, Puebla, Oaxaca, Querétaro, and Guanajuato. This service remained in private hands until the Bourbons seized it in the eighteenth century.[12] Similar arrangements were made in Peru in 1580, Viceroy Enríquez playing a part in the organization of the postal service, as he had previously in New Spain.

Genoa was such an important financial connection for Spanish commerce that effective communication with it was essential. It was through exchange (*cambios*), Braudel insists, that the Genoese were able to set up their Sevillian trade with the Americas. They had gained monopolies of salt and wool. When we say 'the Genoese', we mean of course the great families, the *nobili vecchi* – the Grimaldi, the Spinoli, the Centurioni, and the Lomellini.[13]

Genoese dominance in Spanish economic affairs began with the maritime *renversement des alliances* carried through by the great Italian admiral Andrea Doria in 1528; and the end of Genoa's dominance was marked by the Count Duke Olivares's promotion of the Portuguese *marranos* (converted Jews) to be chief moneylenders to Castile in 1627. Still, Genoa's financial empire was the greatest undertaking by any city in the sixteenth century,[14] for that city was the centre for the redistribution of American silver.[15] Merchants in Genoa could probably lay their hands on whatever currency they needed in their very own city, even if they wanted finance to enable them to lend to the Spanish monarch to settle the pay of his armies in Flanders. For the soldiers of both the Duke of Alba and of Alexander Farnese always demanded part of their pay in gold.

The *ordinario* – the regular postal service – from Seville northwards to Medina del Campo, some 300 miles, ran every week. (It was appropriate to measure the distance from Medina, since the most important fair in Spain was held there.)[16] The post arrived at that city on Tuesday night and the service set off back to the south at midday on Wednesday. Sometimes couriers were entrusted with larger parcels, including packages of jewels.

Another type of letter was the so-called *peón* (or *propio*), of which we hear in *Don Quixote*. Sancho Panza sends one to his wife Teresa.[17] Letters from Seville to northern Europe would go to Madrid and thence to Saragossa and Barcelona. The despatch of letters to the New World was given as a monopoly in 1510 to Lorenzo Galíndez de Carvajal, a senior royal counsellor from Extremadura who was Cortés's distant cousin.[18] Carvajal sublet his licence to members of the Casa de la Contratación – the body which administered relations with the New World from emigration to trade. From 1562, the *correo mayor* (postmastership) was in the hands of a cousin of Don

Lorenzo's, Juan de Carvajal y Vargas. He sold his licence for Spain to the *sucursal de correos* (postmaster) of Seville, Juan de Saavedra Marmolejo,[19] and ceded his licence in the Indies to his brother Diego. The *sucursal de correos* of the Indies was soon Rodrigo de Jerez, a *veintecuatro* (counsellor) of Seville, a position bought by the Taxis (Tassis) family in the seventeenth century.

The shortest time that a letter took to reach Lima from Seville in the late sixteenth century was eighty-eight days, whereas from Mexico to the same destination the shortest time was 112 days. The longest time that letters took from these two capitals of viceroyalties to places further afield was respectively 175 and 262 days.[20] It is therefore apparent that the post favoured Lima, which was then richer than Mexico. Postal costs measured in relation to weight and distance were high but they were almost the only costs which did not seem to increase during the reign of Philip II. Thus a letter from Seville to Medina del Campo in the late sixteenth century cost seventeen *maravedís*, while one from Valladolid to Medina would be just ten *maravedís*. The agent for the powerful Burgos businessman Simón Ruiz[21] paid 6,656 *maravedís* for his postal account in 1561, which meant that he sent 350 letters in that year. It is less easy to make comparable estimates in the New World, but a letter of one or two folios to Seville would probably have cost the substantial sum of two *reales* (see Glossary) in Peru or New Spain.

The king's great friend, Luis de Requesens, wrote in 1575 to his colleague Diego de Zúñiga, the Spanish ambassador in Paris, 'I do not know how your lordship fares for letters from Spain. I have received nothing from the King concerning the affairs of the Netherlands since 20th November . . . His Majesty's service has suffered greatly.'[22] King Philip himself once commented that 'it is more important that the letters should travel by a safe route than that four or five days be gained'.[23] But there were fast times too. The Constable of Castile once wrote that a letter had arrived so quickly in Valladolid that 'if it had been a trout it would still have been fresh'.[24]

The participation of foreign merchants in the commerce to the Indies was both irregularly permitted and prohibited. Thus in 1578 a *sevillano* historian of Italian origin (his father came from Lucca), Francisco Moroveli de Puebla, complained that 'All commerce is in

20. Potosí, a city built around a mountain of silver, in what is now Bolivia.

21. The fortress at Portobelo, now in Panama. For several hundred years Portobelo was the most important port of the Caribbean of the Spanish Empire, from which all the commerce of Peru, Potosí included, flowed.

22. Alonso Ercilla, painted here *c.* 1577 by El Greco, wrote a great epic poem about the conquest of Chile in the late 1550s.

23. Virgin and Child by the Jesuit painter Bernando Bitti. Born in Camerino (Ancona), Bitti went out to the New World in 1575 to paint, and became active in Peru, Potosí, La Paz, Lima and Cuzco.

24. This picture shows the extraordinary marriage between a member of
the remarkable Loyola family, of which San Ignacio was a relation, and an
Inca princess, the last of her distinguished Peruvian royal family.

25. Maize, the stuff of Indians' life, depicted here
in a beautiful Aztec-carved basalt stone.

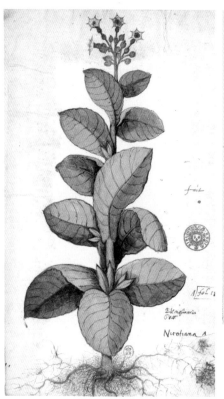

26. Nicotine (tobacco), a product
of the Indies, which gave pleasure
to Europeans for 450 years.

27. The potato, the great vegetable
of the New World whose roots have
transformed our diets.

28. The pursuit of agriculture and weaving of textiles in the New World,
as depicted in a sixteenth-century Spanish and Nahuatl manuscript. The work
is being done by Indians, and supervised by Spaniards.

29. The pursuit of gold was one of the main motivations of the
conquest of the New World. Here is an Indian worker shaping a gold
object of beauty and value. From the *Florentine Codex* by
Bernardino de Sahagún (*c.* 1540–85).

30. Sugar was boiled into syrup by the first generation of Spanish conquistadors, beginning in the Caribbean, but by 1590 Brazil was the greatest manufacturer.

31. One particularly gruesome punishment favoured by the Spaniards was to throw their enemies to the dogs ('*aperrear*' was the word for this).

**32.** Stocks and beatings were the punishments favoured by the Spaniards for their Indian servants or slaves. Both these and more were listed in 1563–65 by the 'Visitor' Jerónimo de Valderrama, as evidence against Viceroy Luis de Velasco I.

the hands of Flemings, the English and the French.'[25] But foreign merchants were not really supposed to participate in the trade with the Indies after 1538. A Spanish shipper had to act as a front. Often Genoese were registered as Spaniards and, indeed, after two or three generations, merchants such as Agustín Spindola, Lucián Centurión, and Pantaleo Negro seemed to be more Spanish than they were Genoese. The richest men in Seville were probably Tomaso Marino (Marín) and Adamo Centurione (Centurión), each being Genoese with a Spanish identity, and each of whom was probably worth a million ducats. Centurione bought the villages of Estepa and Pedrera in 1559 and his eldest son Marcos became Marquis of Estepa. The family became Castilianized.

With the foundation in 1579 of a great exchange fair at Piacenza, halfway between Milan and Bologna, as well as within striking distance of Genoa, Genoese bankers became the unquestioned masters of international payments.[26] There were Florentines too, such as Andrés del Baño, Cortés's friend Jacome Boti, and Leonardo Angelo, as well as the Milanese Juan Bautista Rovelasca, who obtained an *asiento* (contract) to sell 300 slaves a year to whatever point in the Indies he liked (he paid the Crown a third of what he obtained). A list of Venetian merchants active in Seville were of the same families as their countrymen who had dominated trade in Seville in the 1520s, but they were now trading cochineal, sometimes brazilwood, sometimes pearls, mercury, linen, lingerie, alum, sometimes wheat, oil, leather, as well as slaves, and they were much better off. By 1600, the coffers of the Venetian state treasury were overflowing with money, and seven or eight hundred ships went out of her port every year.[27]

French products, such as linen and underclothes (*lencería*) for men as well as women, were furthermore deemed to be essential in the Indies. The most important items – three-quarters of the sales – were *ruanes* (linen from Rouen) and *angeos* (a coarse linen comparable to canvas). In the sixteenth century, Nantes and Rouen were the main exporting ports in France, but Neubourg, Louviers, and Beaumont-le-Roger were also important.[28] Production of cotton goods in the rural hinterland of Rouen grew prodigiously. Referring to the shipment of *angeos*, a seventeenth-century French author would comment, 'They may have the ships but we have their wings.'[29]

The French also supplied white cloth, *coletas* (Nankeen yellow cloth as if from Nanking), *bretañas* (fine linens), paper, scissors, and other haberdashery, teasels, and combs for exchange in the Indies. The demand in the New World for tapestries from Brussels was substantial. So was that for fine Dutch linen (*holandas*), including some from Malines in Brabant.[30]

The consequence was that French merchants, like the Flemings and English, were well established in the smiling ports of Andalusia, even though their trade was later destroyed by the rebellion in the Netherlands. Soap, for which Seville was famous as a producer, was traded on a large scale: black soap from the district of El Salvador, the great church in the old centre, white soap from Triana, the harbour suburb to the west.

An important item in the export trade of Castile was wine. At the end of the sixteenth century, 20,000 pipes (casks), or 300,000 litres of wine, were being shipped annually across the Atlantic.[31] That was partly the consequences of the taste of the indigenous peoples of the New World for it, often to their detriment. Much of the wine came from the Canary Islands (*vino de islas*), but the historian Fernández de Oviedo describes the wine of the Sierra Morena, such as that from Cazalla, as virtually a secret weapon in Spanish hands.[32] Sherries from Jerez de la Frontera were also popular. The settlers in the New World sought to build a new Mediterranean culture in the Americas, based on wheat, wine, and olive oil.[33] The demand for oil and wine in the Indies explains the noticeable increase in the production of both in the sixteenth century.

Mercury became essential in respect of silver mining, after Bartolomé de Medina of Seville introduced a method that became known in the 1550s as the *beneficio de plato*, which depended on mercury. This method remained in use until the twentieth century (when *patio cerrado* was introduced). A German, Maese Lorenzo, had wanted to introduce the *beneficio de plato* to New Spain ever since he had visited the mercury mines of Almadén in south-central Spain, near Ciudad Real, but he was refused permission and Medina had to learn from him.

Several Spanish officials wrote to the Emperor Charles V about the enlightened ideas of Medina.[34] A Valencian, Mosen Antonio Boteller, claimed to have used his method earlier, but Boteller's claim was not recognized.[35] Medina then obtained a licence.

King Philip decided to employ the ubiquitous but ever helpful Fugger family to arrange the despatch of mercury to the New World. They, after all, controlled the mercury mines in Almadén. Though mercury had been known for generations, it was not until the 1550s that its usefulness in producing silver became evident. In 1563, Cristóbal Hernán, however, signed the first agreement to ensure a supply of mercury. The royal works at Almadén would be run henceforth by a series of contractors (*asentistas*).[36] The receivers of the mercury were all *sevillanos*, but their names were often Genoese, such as Centurión or Fiesco.

Mercury was then shipped to the New World in boxes, each of which contained a *quintal*. The cost of transporting them was reckoned at the large sum of 500 *maravedís* per box.

The silver mines of Potosí in Peru received a steady supply of mercury from the accessible sources of cinnabar (a bright red mineral containing mercury sulphide) at Huancavelica, which was relatively near (though still 500 miles from Potosí as the crow flies). Cinnabar was also sought after for the vermilion that it yielded, which was increasingly used by artists when painting the flesh tones of a human face. Enrique Garcés, who had been in New Spain, saw in 1563 how the mines at Tomaca and Huacoya in the state of Parás could also be exploited for mercury. They were at 11,000 feet above sea level, and had been discovered by a conquistador from Extremadura, Amador de Cabrera.[37]

From 1570 onwards, Viceroy Toledo was insisting that Potosí and Huancavelica should become principal pillars of his territory. He sought to incorporate Huancavelica into the royal patrimony, allowing Cabrera, the chief exploiter of the mines, to pay to the Crown a fourth of the proceeds, not the fifth which was normal.

In 1569, Huancavelica in Peru was producing 310 *quintales* of mercury a year, but Almadén, in Spain, was contributing much more – 1,700 *quintales*. These figures increased dramatically thereafter and by 1578 there was usually an adequate supply of mercury from Huancavelica for the silver mines of Potosí. About a fifth of the mercury used in New Spain to assist silver production came to be of

Peruvian origin, being sent up along the Pacific coast to Acapulco. (The largest mine owner in New Spain, judging from his use of mercury in the 1560s, was Gracian de Valcola, who at that time was obtaining 200 quintals of mercury every year.)[38]

Potosí, high up in what is now Bolivia, was the answer to every colonialist's dream. The mountain of silver there reached to nearly 16,000 feet above sea level. Its riches, as we have seen already,[39] had been discovered in 1545. In the first twenty years after the discovery, the ores in Potosí were so rich that only very simple smelting was needed to refine them. Then mercury was introduced to the production process. The Emperor Charles V was already calling Potosí 'The Imperial City' and had allowed its first coat of arms to bear the words: 'I am the rich Potosí, the treasure of the world, and the envy of Kings.'[40]

Viceroy Toledo was himself in Potosí in 1572 and called a convention of miners to consider the construction of ore-grinding mills operated by hydraulic power. He also proclaimed a regulation which provided that miners could never be imprisoned for debt. Soon Potosí would become the largest of all South American cities. Treasure seekers (*peruleros*, as they were called mockingly) flocked there from all over the world, above all from Spain, in search of the silver fortune which they thought that they would be sure to find. When Cervantes wrote *Don Quixote* (published in 1606), the word 'Potosí' (mentioned twice in the text) was a synonym for wealth. A fiesta given there to celebrate the accession of Philip II in January 1556 lasted twenty-four days.

By the time that Philip died in 1598, there were in Potosí thirty-six casinos, a theatre, fourteen dance halls, and eighty churches. Fountains spouting wine and the light beer-like drink known as *chicha* were numerous. There were many brothels and innumerable prostitutes.[41] Large reservoirs were beginning to be built to guarantee a good water supply. The annual fair at Potosí stimulated a cornucopia of vast dimensions: silks and swords, iron and linen, satin and slaves, mules and horses. Contraband trade through Buenos Aires, wrote the Argentine economic historian Raúl Molina in 1956, 'had but one objective: to reach Potosí, the Mecca of Spanish commerce . . . the American Samarkand'.[42]

The Spanish administration would scour the land for hundreds of miles to bring Indians to work in the mines at Potosí. But many died there, for Potosí was for the Dominican Fray Domingo de Santo Tomás the 'mouth of Hell'.[43] All the same, Indians did the hard work there. Viceroy Toledo organized a general division of Indians, the *mita*, a scheme by which a certain number had to serve in the mine for a specific period of time. The system lasted for several generations – indeed until the eighteenth century.

Gold began to be traded from the New World soon after 1492. But by the reign of Philip II, trade in that precious metal had become relatively unimportant. The great treasure fleets brought back to Spain silver instead – and on a large scale. In 1580 the king's personal secretary Juan de Idiáquez wrote to Cardinal Granvelle: 'The King is right to say that the Emperor never amassed as much money as Philip did.'[44] In theory, these precious metals were not supposed to leave Spain. But they did, either illegally in merchants' trains or legally through wheat importers and war expenses of the monarch. Thus between 1580 and 1626 over 11 million kilos of precious metals were imported into Seville; 2.5 million kilos found their way to the Netherlands, and 800,000 went to Italy.

Wealth is hard to estimate. In Lima, anyone who had over 11 million *maravedís* was thought rich, but in New Spain the figure was considerably less – 7 million perhaps. In Seville anyone with over 15 million *maravedís* was considered very rich, though that figure was far exceeded by Simón Ruiz, the merchant of Medina del Campo, who was believed to have a capital of 136 million *maravedís*.[45] Even richer were the Jorges, a family apparently worth 183 million *maravedís*. Their principal contribution to the commerce of the New World was wine from their *viñedo* at Cazalla in the Sierra Morena in the south-west of Spain, though they also had a large olive farm at Alamedilla, between Guadix and Jaén in Granada.[46]

Banks began their operations in the New World in a climate of unencumbered freedom, which lasted until 1576 when the Epinosa and Morga banks, based in Seville, collapsed (liabilities in respect of the first were 750 million ducats, 480 million in respect of the second). The ruin of these banks was the consequence of a suspension of payments by King Philip himself in 1575, after a long period of governmental over-spending. There followed a monopolistic era in which the banking system was dominated by one important figure, or at most two: in the first place, Juan Ortega de la Torre, then Diego de Alburquerque, and then Miguel Lambias in the 1580s. Their successors were Baltasar Gómez de Aguilar and Alonso Pérez de Salazar, then Gonzalo de Salazar and Juan de Carmona, and finally, in the early seventeenth century, Adam Vivaldo. Most merchants kept their money in one or other of these banks, not in their own houses. Fernand Braudel argued that 'the collapse of these private banks was the consequence of their being too ready to place their clients' money in commercial circuits which moved too slowly. If there were an emergency, payments could not be made in a matter of days because the money was still "on the road".'[47] In 1576 the Fleming Peter van Oudegherste tried unsuccessfully to persuade King Philip to create a state bank.

Yet certainly by 1600, the dominant financial influence in the Indies, even overshadowing the Genoese, consisted of the citizens of Burgos. There were the de Isla family, several generations of whom were active in the Indian trade, as well as many Maluendas, Colindres, and Núñezes. Basques were also active, albeit on a smaller scale. The accumulation of wealth in those days was assisted by the introduction of a new coin, the 'piece of eight', *ocho reales*, a small silver coin struck in Castile from American silver. The coin dominated the Mediterranean market in the second half of the sixteenth century.

A discussion of commerce in the Spanish American empire in the sixteenth century must conclude with a word about the traffic in black Africans. From the 1440s, slaves had been brought from west Africa to Portugal by merchants looking for gold.[48] The first arrangements had been proposed in 1510 by Ferdinand the Catholic and then in 1518 by his grandson Charles V.[49] Thereafter a series of contracts were negotiated by the Spanish Crown with different merchants, each of whom had different rights and different styles.

In the beginning, the African slaves derived from depots on the Cape Verde islands, but later they were more likely to be from Guinea or San Tomé. But all those were transit camps. The slaves really originated in the Cameroons or the Congo. Later, Angola would become the centre of slave trading, and in the seventeenth century it was the main one for both the Spanish and Portuguese markets. Small ships of shallow draft would sail up African rivers in great numbers. Slaves would naturally be worse off if they were taken immense distances, such as occurred in respect of slaves intended for Peru who had to be taken across the isthmus of Panama and down the Pacific coast. Those who were shipped to Veracruz on the Caribbean coast of New Spain and then up to the capital were also usually harshly treated. Those sold in Cartagena, Santo Domingo, or Cuba had a shorter voyage to endure and so usually suffered less.

In the 1570s there was much pressure placed on Spanish ports and merchants from representatives of the Portuguese who had dominated the traffic in slaves for a hundred years. Pedro de Loronha, Benito Báez, and Gómez de Acosta asked for licences for 1,650 slaves. After the union of the two crowns in 1580, this Portuguese pressure became even greater. Philip agreed that between 300 and 750 slaves should be despatched every year from Portuguese ports to the Spanish empire. The most important merchant was Pedro Gómez Reinel, a powerful Portuguese. He exported to Portugal or the Americas nearly 40,000 slaves in nine years from 1595, or almost 4,500 a year.[50]

The general rise in prices during the sixteenth century affected all the countries with which Spain had any connection. Everyone was surprised by the rise, but it was never explained. The surge of precious metals from the Americas certainly played a part, as was suspected at the time and as the great American scholar Earl J. Hamilton showed in his famous book of 1934, *American Treasure and the Price Revolution in Spain, 1501–1650*.[51] In 1937 the Italian economic historian Luigi Einaudi made the astonishing calculation that about 300 per cent of the total rise in prices of 627 per cent between 1571 and 1598 could be attributed to the coming of precious metals.[52]

# 21

# Piracy and Buccaneering

*In 20,000 nights he had read with unwearied enthusiasm one single book,* The History of Charlemagne and the Twelve Peers of France.

María Cadilla de Martínez, *La poesía popular en Puerto Rico*, 1933, quoted in Juan Alfonso Carrizo, *Antecedentes hispano-mediaevales de la poesía tradicional argentina*, Buenos Aires 1945, 79

The first twelve years of King Philip's reign were years of illicit trading rather than piracy. But after 1568, piracy was the normal form of maritime encounter between Spain and her neighbours. The English in particular attacked the Biscay *zabras* (small coastal ships) which carried silver from the New World to the Spanish Netherlands. From the 1580s, Spain tried to avoid pirates by sending bullion to be deposited in Lisbon, where it was traded for bills of exchange. Sometimes money was transferred through France. In 1572 a large consignment of 500,000 ducats in silver and gold was despatched from Spain for the Netherlands through France, with the agreement of the French government. There were other similar transactions. Spain needed money in the Netherlands to pay her soldiers. Later the most favoured route became that from Barcelona to Genoa. Sometimes this money was sent on to the Netherlands, sometimes it remained in Italy to pay Spanish debts incurred either in Genoa itself, the principal clearing house for silver, or in Florence or Milan.[1] A typical year would see 10 million ducats arriving in Spain, of which 6 million would then be exported – half by the king and the rest by private persons. The other 4 million would be either smuggled out of Spain or remain there.[2] True, in 1573 one of the English captains who had been humiliated at Veracruz a few years before, Francis Drake, stole the gold and silver from a mule train near Panama. But that was the only one bad Spanish loss in twenty years of such raids.[3]

A fellow Devonian and a half-brother of Drake's, Sir Humphrey Gilbert, persuaded Queen Elizabeth in 1578 to seek 'remote heathen and barbarous lands' in the north of North America. But in 1583 he was lost in a storm, his last words, according to the chronicler Richard Hakluyt, being 'We are as near to heaven, by sea as by land'.[4]

In 1585, Drake sailed from Plymouth for the Spanish Caribbean with twenty-two ships. It was a full-scale military operation which led to the sack of both Santo Domingo and Cartagena de Indias in 1586. Havana was then swiftly and effectively reinforced by the Spaniards. A chain was slung across the entrance to the harbour. Drake was also kept at bay by the tropical diseases which affected the crews of his fleet. The great commander made a brief landing at Cabo de San Antonio, west of Havana, and told his subordinates that he would not go ahead with an attack on that port unless he could do so without risk. The English refrained.

The years between the defeat of the Armada in 1588 and the death of King Philip in 1598 and of Queen Elizabeth in 1603 were marked by a series of acts of piracy by English sailors against Spanish vessels or in Spanish territory. Between 1589 and 1591 alone, English vessels made no fewer than 235 privateering journeys along the coasts of Spain, Portugal, the Azores, and the Caribbean. In the Atlantic the ships mostly sailed and sacked singly or in couples, but in the Caribbean the English pirates – for such they really were – sailed in groups of four or more 'consort ships' or 'fellow-travellers', as they were known at the time.[5]

Most were merchant ships capable of carrying 50 to 100 tons, 'barks', usually with three masts, including a foresail, a foretopsail, a mainsail, and a maintopsail, as well as a lateen mizzen sail.[6] Each ship would as a rule have four guns (a 'minimum', a very small gun, and three falcons, or light cannons, each firing two to four pounds of ammunition) and perhaps a crew of forty in all. The cost of a ship of this kind might be about £300 without armaments. The crews of some vessels carried muskets and pikes. There were also some smaller boats, such as 50-ton pinnaces, usually equipped with oars as well as sails.[7] They might be manned by twenty to twenty-five men, who carried out a lot of coastal raiding.

These pirate ships often came from Bristol, some were from Devon ports, but mostly they originated from the dominant port of London. The ownership of these vessels was sometimes spread between several people. Thus the *Rose Lion* of 1595 had eight owners. Food on board sometimes had to last for many months, sometimes as much as a year.

Some vessels were much bigger, occasionally 350 tons with six sails and six guns, making them scarcely inferior in fighting power to the queen's ships. These privateers might cost £4,000 or even £5,000 to build. Ships of this size played a major part in West Indian privateering and also in West African and Mediterranean ravaging. Sometimes these vessels would be included in naval operations such as Drake's raid on Cartagena de Indias in 1586 or that on Cadiz in 1587. They might be armed with small artillery such as culverins, demi-culverins, or sakers.[8]

These private expeditions of piracy were semi-official in that the Lord Admiral (still Lord Howard of Effingham, who had been in command against the Armada) had a right to a tenth share of all prizes captured. Usually captains who seized Spanish ships agreed to give the admiral a fee of £3,000 per ship.[9]

Some private warships belonged to important individuals. Prominent among these were the commander of the English navy, namely Lord Howard of Effingham himself, the Earl of Cumberland, and Sir Walter Raleigh. Some substantial fortunes were made, while the later famous East India Company gained its first leaders from among privateers in the West Indies: among them John More, Paul Baying, Thomas Cordel, Thomas Myddleton, John Watts, Christopher Newport, and Captain Lancaster. John Watts's prizes made him £40,000.

On most voyages there would be a pilot who might be someone with special knowledge of the Caribbean. A typical privateer might also boast a lieutenant to the captain, a first mate, master gunner, purser, carpenter, surgeon, boatswain, cook, steward, cooper, trumpeter, and quartermaster. Ships were usually overmanned because of a general expectation both of gaining prizes and of losses.

Privateering, like all outdoor activity, had its seasons. Captains aimed to leave England in March or April. The vessels would then head south to the Canary Islands as if they were Spanish merchant ships. Thereafter, they would sail west with the trade winds to Dominica and then on to Puerto Rico and Hispaniola. They would then make for the beautiful Caribbean, with its cattle ranches, sugar mills, and unprotected ports. The first of these prizes was by far the most frequently attacked, for hides constituted the most sought-after loot – even more than precious metals. After cattle hides, sugar, silver, gold, pearls, cochineal, logwood, balsam, and ginger figured on the list of objects sought. Cassava bread was also stolen, as were hogs and turtles, but all these delights were generally eaten by the crew there and then, rather than taken home.

A privateer might then sail through the Windward Passage towards the Spanish colony of Jamaica and then on to Honduras, perhaps stopping off by the Venezuelan pearl coast at the island of Margarita. Here were many possible trophies to be captured. Some Spanish vessels were easy prey on the open sea, but there were also many little ships to be seized near the shores. If a prize seemed worth it, she might be taken over by a small English crew. The Spanish sailors would be put ashore except for one or two men who might be carried off with the prize to testify about the vessel to the English Court of Admiralty. Privateering attacks on farms and ports had a different rhythm to them. Often the inhabitants there would negotiate with their attacker, in order to arrive at an understanding based on payment of a fine or the delivery of a certain number of cattle hides. Often too, anticipating a raid, the townspeople of a *pueblo* would evacuate as much as possible of their moveable goods and money into the hills nearby.

All ships' captains knew that it was desirable to leave the gulf of Florida before the end of August in order to avoid hurricanes. Spanish treasure fleets would converge on Havana during June or July and it was best to avoid them too because they were well armed. The English privateers rarely attacked substantial ports such as Havana or Veracruz. But small-scale corsairs were more than a match for the authorities in the ports of Santiago de Cuba or Azua in Santo Domingo. The local populations never knew what the next target would be nor how many English ships would suddenly appear offshore.

The Spanish authorities often exaggerated the dangers from English corsairs, in order to help them obtain more military support and as much other protection as might be possible from the mother country. The government's aim was to protect the main arteries of their wealth, the routes of the great treasure fleets, which they almost always managed to do.

The Spanish Caribbean had by 1580 built defences around their larger ports such as San Juan in Puerto Rico, Havana in Cuba, and Cartagena de Indias on the north coast of New Granada (present-day Colombia). These defences were the work of Bautista Antonelli, an Italian who had begun his long career as a builder of forts in Spain – at Cartagena, Valencia, and in Navarre – and also at Oran in Algeria. In 1581, Antonelli set off for the Indies, where he worked on new defences for Cartagena de Indias, Panama, Havana (El Morro), then along the Pacific coast of New Spain, San Juan de Ulúa, Portobello, and San Juan de Puerto Rico. The smaller ports of the empire such as Azua in Santo Domingo or Santiago de Cuba remained open to attack, but the larger ones remained largely free of incursions thanks to Antonelli's work.[10]

When a Spanish ship was captured, its cargo would be stacked up on the privateer's deck near the main mast and be divided up among the victorious crew. The captain of the privateer would usually seize the Spanish captain's sea chest, while the rest of the plunder would be divided up according to certain established rules, seniority playing a decisive part. Thus the master gunner would take the Spanish gunner's possessions and the second-best gun. As a rule, no one in the privateering crew would be paid any wages; their expectation was that they would be rewarded through pillage.

These rules would vary in practice and were often disregarded altogether. In the heat of boarding a Spanish ship, a sailor's idea of fighting was often a matter of each man for himself. There were also mutinies, brawls, and riots. The best arrangement was when the crew agreed to sell their share of plunder to the quartermaster or captain. If drink was among what was seized, the privateer's crew might almost waste themselves in a wild bout of intoxication. One governor of Havana, Juan de Texeda, was no doubt correct in 1595 when he dismissed one group of English pirates as drunkards.[11]

The English 'corsairs', as the Spaniards had called the pirates since the 1530s, were an ever-growing menace. Diego de Ybarra, the treasurer of Santo Domingo, wrote in October 1595 that for the previous four years, corsairs had been as numerous and assiduous as if these territories had been part of their own countries.[12]

Coming or going, we have always a corsair in our sight. If this continues, either this island will be depopulated or we shall be compelled to do business with them rather than with Spain ... They make their incursions safely and find persons with whom to barter ... The only way to avoid the damage done by these thieves is to drive the corsairs from the seas and this can only be accomplished by galleys which Your Majesty is entreated to send promptly.

In fact by the end of the sixteenth century, the Spaniards felt that they had to evacuate the north-west of Hispaniola and move the towns of La Yaguana (150 houses), Bayabe, and Puerto Plata to the south of the island. The west and north-west of the island was left to buccaneers and in the next century it would constitute a home for French interlopers – hence eventually their rich colony of Sainte Domingue, known by 1780 in Paris as 'Pérou'.[13] The Venezuelan island of Margarita was also abandoned by the Spanish and the pearl trade forgotten.

The English privateers continued their activities throughout the 1580s and 1590s. The pride of these ships was *The Drake*, owned by John Watts, who also had a part ownership of *The Examiner*. There were also Robert Abraham's *The Black Dog*, and John Chidley's three ships, *The Wilde Man*, *The White Lion*, and *The Delight of Bristol*, in which a cousin of Queen Elizabeth, Lord Hunsdon, had invested. Elizabeth herself backed some of these privateers. In 1591 there were no fewer then eleven English privateers busily creating mayhem in the Caribbean, five being owned by John Watts, three by Hunsdon, and two by another group of London merchants of whom Sir Walter Raleigh was a shareholder. Christopher Newport was found causing no end of trouble with his four ships in 1592. Then there was Sir John Burgh, a brother of the Lord Burgh who was lord deputy in Ireland. Sir John was involved in attacks on Guiana, Trinidad, and Margarita.

One typical account describes how in 1593 two English ships with two pinnaces arrived at the port of Yaguana in Santo Domingo. They landed men who went up to a sugar mill owned by Gregorio de Ayala, a councillor of the city. They burned the wooden church there as well as the sugar-purging house, the slaves' huts and much of their clothing, carrying off what sugar there was and also some hides. They seized the small copper tools used in sugar-making and also took all the chairs and household furnishings. They kidnapped a black slave and through him wrote to Ayala that, within six days, he should bring or send them 6,000 ducats as a ransom for what had not been burned, such as the cane still standing and the sugar mill itself. The mill's inhabitants thereafter wrote a letter of entreaty to King Philip begging him to station two galleys from the royal fleet offshore in Santo Domingo. We do not know how or whether he responded.

A report from the *sevillano* Gerónimo Sánchez de Carranza, Spanish governor of Honduras from 1589 to 1594 – a noted fencing master, many of whose detailed refinements he invented – makes a similar impression:

> Knowing how ill-prepared these ports are to resist even a pinnace, the enemy is no longer afraid. This year a large shallop of sixty tons burden [a clumsy boat propelled by both oars and sails] as well as a big ship of about 250 tons burthen appeared with three pinnaces, all well-armed with artillery and small shot. They opened fire on the flagship which was here commanded by Diego Ramírez. Although they and five other ships defended themselves bravely, because they were short of men and [most of] those whom they had were sick or wounded, the enemy [the English] took them all and carried off the flagship with which they loaded the best of the cargoes of the others. He left them without artillery or sail so that it will be impossible for them to sail anywhere this year. After I wrote this to your lordship [25 April 1594] and as I lay in bed with fever, having been bled not five days before, the look-out made the smoke signal meaning that large ships had been sighted. When they came into view they seemed to be English. I dressed at once and ordered that I be carried to the beach in a chair. I caused many mules to be fetched and in good order with great haste caused the residents and the merchants to take away their money and valuable merchandise from the town. I then ordered the town crier to bid them on penalty of death to come to the defence of the place. Only twenty men ... responded. The five arquebuses which they brought had neither powder nor shot. Nevertheless I divided them into three squadrons ... manoeuvring these, my few men seemed to be many. Though my fever was rising, and though the enemy fired heavily on the town, I did not leave the beach ... About six in the evening the English landed and because, in the first houses, they found no

money and saw that the inhabitants had withdrawn so silently, they suspended their advance and very hastily returned to their ships. Next day the English captain [Christopher Newport] sent a letter to me in which he declared that he had taken the ships and the town in fair fashion and bade me ransom them or he would burn them. He also demanded refreshment. I answered that, a fortnight before, a Captain Langton had attacked my ships and taken them, but had done no damage to the town since it was not legitimate warfare to burn deserted houses and ships. I said that I had now received reinforcements and that the refreshment which they brought consisted of horses and that he might come and burn the town if he liked at his own risk for I would defend it. I assure your lordship that all the reinforcement that I had received was a single man from San Pedro ... with this and other stratagems, I put such fear into the English captain that I drove him out of the port where the greatest damage he did was to burn the ships which he left behind ... He departed without receiving a single *maravedí* from the town.[14]

Another and more serious attack was made on Havana in 1595 by Captain Michael Geare of Limehouse in London. Geare landed some miles to the east of the town, and then marched westwards to try and seize the harbour. The onslaught was held off and Geare had to admit defeat. A great many were killed on both sides.[15]

The eminent historian of the privateers, the able late Professor Kenneth Andrews, commented: 'In spite of the greed, the squalor, and the cruelty of life on the privateers where prisoners were sometimes tortured, there was, it should be said, a certain contempt for cowardice and treachery, and a willingness to stand together against strong odds. Some of the captains at least, and some of their men, were partly inspired by national and religious sentiment.' This buccaneering was after all officially approved and sanctioned. It was driven by a curious mixture of criminal entrepreneurship and anti-Spanish foreign policy.[16]

By the seventeenth century, French adventurers were also well established in the Spanish Main, dedicated like the English to the sacking of towns, the theft of sugar, weapons, meat, and precious metals. The French were especially happy at their possession of the island of Tortuga just off the north coast of Hispaniola, or the Isle of Pines off Cuba. The long war between the French and Spaniards in the Caribbean had begun in 1537, when the guardian of some buildings on top of the fort of El Morro in Havana reported that a French pinnace was manoeuvring in the harbour. A day later in Santiago de Cuba the *sevillano* governor, Gonzalo de Guzmán, who had been on the island since he first went there accompanying Diego Velázquez in 1511 (having previously been one of the first sugar merchants of Santo Domingo), reported that a Spanish ship had been seized by the French at Chagres in New Granada. The French vessel seems to have been the same one as that seen in Havana. The Spaniards pursued it to Mariel and demanded surrender with no combat. The French captain replied 'Die who will die, here we are', and himself made a swift return to Havana where he seized some ships carrying Mexican silver as well as salted meat and papers. The consequence was the building of the fortress of La Fuerza to guard Havana Bay from further attacks.

Other acts of piracy followed, and in 1555 the prominent French corsair Jacques de Sores sacked Havana very thoroughly, remaining in the city for a month. Another French pirate was Guillaume Merriott, who made a point of seeking out wheat, wine, leather, and sugar.

We should not forget in these recollections a famous Spanish *mulatto*, Diego Grillo, who, though a Cuban, sided with the Dutch pirate Cornelius Jol and other international corsairs. But he seems to have learned his brutal trade from Francis Drake, who seized him on a Spanish galleon at Nombre de Dios on the isthmus of Panama in 1572. Grillo later accompanied Drake on his voyage around the world. He subsequently had a successful career as an independent corsair, sometimes in alliance with the English, sometimes with the French and, later, occasionally with the Dutch.

The most dangerous pirate of all was undoubtedly Piet Heyn, a Dutch admiral who in 1628, in command of thirty-one ships, 2,300 sailors, and 1,000 soldiers, seized the Spanish treasure fleet of twenty-two ships, of which only two were men-of-war. Spain lost 4 million ducats of gold. The value of the silver was many million florins. The Spanish fleet was trapped in the harbour of Matanzas on the north coast of Cuba, and its commanders, including Vice Admiral Juan de Benavides, were later executed for neglect of duty. Tragic though this loss was for Spain, it should be recalled that this was the only occasion on which the great treasure fleet was successfully attacked.[17]

# 22

# The Galleon, a Very Narrow Prison

*A ship is a very narrow and stout prison from which no one can escape.*

Report of Fray Tomás de la Torre, *c.* 1544

*After them came a coach and four or five a-horseback accompanying it and two lackeys that ran hard by it. There came therein, as it was afterwards known, a certain Biscaine lady which travelled towards Seville where her husband was going to the Indies with an honourable charge.*

Miguel de Cervantes, *Don Quixote* (1605), I, 62

To begin with, ships sailing from Spain to the New World and back did not really need an escort. Until about 1580, Spain dominated the ocean, which the French historian Pierre Chaunu called 'Seville's Atlantic'.[1] All the same, as early as 1521, Spanish vessels operating off the home peninsula were being guarded by a patrol of five ships known as the *armada de avería*, 'a fleet to repair damage'. This was paid for by a special tax. The range of these defences was extended in 1525 to include the Portuguese islands, the Azores, and later the radius of defence was extended to Tarifa, near Gibraltar, and the Canary Islands as well. The meticulous Spanish historian Guillermo Céspedes del Castillo argued that the unprecedented size of the Spanish empire made naval defence necessary.[2]

These schemes had no Caribbean or New World equivalent, but there, after the French began their damaging raids in the 1530s, the citizenry of ports began to make a point of escaping into the interior of the settlement concerned when threatened. They also often made an arrangement with their attackers, asking them to spare the place in return for payments, a habit leading to a mood of defencelessness.

As we have seen, English ships soon became as big a threat as French ones. The reaction of Spain was slow, however, there being little money available for defence: the matter had never previously been considered on this scale by any state. In 1558 the Emperor Charles V's debts were 7 million ducats, but by 1574, when Philip had already been reigning for eighteen years, the royal debts were over 80 million ducats – an increase due to over-spending by the state, especially on official salaries.

Soon Spanish navigation became *de conserva*, that is, in convoy with other ships.³ Warships were also appointed to register docking in the Caribbean. An *armada de barlovento*, a windward fleet, was named for Santo Domingo – a system finally established only in 1557, due to lack of boats. But from 1554 a regular convoy system had been more or less expected and it became fixed between 1561 and 1564. It used a defensive strategy which had been employed by the Venetians in the Middle Ages when they travelled to the Eastern Mediterranean.

The Spanish fleets on the outward journey to the Indies would stand far higher out of the water (due to the absence of booty and other prizes) than those on the return journey. In order to avoid coming back in ballast, homecoming ships would often contain a substantial amount of tropical goods of little or no value.

These fleets would include not only galleons but also light *caravelas* and frigates, heavy *urcas* (storeships), *pataches* (pinnaces), and brigantines. The placing of cargo on board on the return journey might be slow and difficult to direct. There would be much waiting for favourable winds and for an indication of calm seas. There would be dead times, when boats could not move but when crews needed to be paid all the same.

There had always been far more small ships than big ones in the Mediterranean. Most vessels there were under 100 tons or even below 50 tons. But much of the surviving material about shipping relates to big and even very big boats – about 1,000 or even 2,000 tons.⁴ In the Atlantic the use of small ships was declining. By 1552, ships en route to the Indies had legally to be bigger than 100 tons, with a crew of at least thirty-two men. The minimum tonnage was raised in 1587 to 300 tons.[5] A few ships were bigger than 500 tons, but they met difficulties in crossing the bar at Sanlúcar de Barrameda. Yet the carrack *Madre de Dios*, at over 1,800 tons, could carry 900 tons of goods, 32 guns, and 700 passengers. She was captured by the Earl of Cumberland for the English in 1592.[6] The wood needed to build a ship of this size was colossal. Even the iron required to make the necessary nails weighed 500 tons. The crew on the *Madre de Dios* seems to have been about 900 men.[7]

An important change in the sixteenth century had been the gradual eclipse of the once all-important galley. It was practically eliminated in the Mediterranean, being replaced by the roundship (*nave*). This meant that the large merchant ship of, say, 600 tons replaced the powerful oared galley.[8]

All ships setting out for the Indies had to submit to three inspections, all at Sanlúcar de Barrameda, at the mouth of the river Guadalquivir: first, when the vessel was empty; second after loading; and, third, when the ship was ready to put to sea. The last inspection was the most important since the official responsible would be looking to check any possible overloading of goods, as well as for contraband and stowaways.

The consignments of goods for use in both New Spain and Peru and their dependencies, not forgetting the Caribbean islands, included parcels of books. All packages would be checked in Sanlúcar to ensure that they did not include volumes condemned by the Inquisition. This inspection was carried out by one of its officials.[9] The parcels might include anything from twenty to a hundred books, many of which were substantial volumes. The first edition of *Amadís de Gaula*, which we must suppose was shipped in large quantities, is for example, a large book.

The size of the naval escorts varied. There were sometimes as few as two naval vessels as an escort, one of them named the *capitana*, on which would travel the captain or the general. The other vessel would be known as the *almirante* (the admiral), on which there would be the chief of the marine side of the expedition, an official also known as the *almirante*. Usually, though, there would be six or eight galleons.

Soon the term *galleones* would be used to indicate all vessels leaving for Tierra Firme, that is Venezuela, or Portobello, on the isthmus of Panama, with goods intended for Peru; and the expression *la flota* would mean the ships going to Veracruz and New Spain. When the two fleets sailed outward together, they would travel from Seville to the Canaries and then continue on to the island of Dominica, where the *flota* would detach itself from the *galleones*.

From the beginning of any voyage there were predictable difficulties. For example, it was necessary to sail down from Seville on the river Guadalquivir as it twisted through the marshy lands known to Voltaire, and then manipulate the sand-bar at the town of Sanlúcar de Barrameda, the headquarters of the Medina Sidonia family. During the manoeuvering which was usually necessary, ships frequently became entangled, lost their anchors, or broke their cables.

A cannon would be customarily fired when the ships bound for the Indies set off from Seville, their real starting point. Criers would have announced in the towns of Andalusia the opportunities that lay ahead for young men aged between twenty-five to thirty if they turned their minds to a career on the high seas. But it would be several weeks later that such vessels would expect to leave Sanlúcar, the ship known as the *capitana* in the lead and the *almirante* in the rear. The journey of seven or eight days to the Canary Islands was the first oceanic stage, a voyage of twenty-five to thirty days to reach the Lesser Antilles being the second; a sighting of the island of either Guadalupe or Deseada was the indication that the Atlantic Ocean had actually been crossed.

An ordinance in 1522 specified that a ship of 100 tons burden should have fifteen able seamen on board, eight apprentice seamen, and three cabin boys. Later, larger crews were provided for larger vessels.

From February 1564 the arrangements for the Spanish fleets changed. Instead of two sailings each in March and September, there would be a single voyage in April or May.[10] But then from October of that year (on the recommendation of Juan Rodríguez de Noriega, the well-connected owner of six Seville-based ships) two fleets would again set out the following April, and two after that in August, making for Dominica. From there vessels intended for Veracruz and New Spain, namely the first fleet, would go north, west to Puerto Rico, Santo Domingo, and then San Juan de Ulloa. Some ships would break away to go to Cuba and Honduras. The second fleet, intended for Peru and the mainland of South America, Tierra Firme, would usually stop at Cartagena de Indias, which was well protected and more healthy than the isthmus of Panama, and then at Nombre de Dios. Ships wishing to go to Venezuela and Santa Marta would leave this second fleet as appropriate.

The diet for a crew in, say, 1560 was rough but in normal conditions ample: the daily ration for each member of the crew was 24 ounces of bread and 3.8 ounces of chickpeas or beans. Three times a week there would be a ration of salted beef, twice a week there might be cheese, and twice a week also there would be several ounces of salted cod. Occasionally there might be quince jelly, figs, dates, olives, and hazelnuts. Most days the seamen would also receive a quart of wine each, some vinegar and olive oil. These rations were supplemented by garlic and onions, saffron and pepper, parsley and cloves, mustard and cinnamon. Sometimes sheep, pigs, or chicken would have been taken on board to be killed, to provide variety to the food. Large stocks of horses, cattle, and seeds were also carried, though not for use en route. Meals would be served on wooden plates or saucers laid on a tablecloth spread on the deck. The officers would, of course, sit at a different table from the ordinary hands, and the passengers, who were expected to provide their own supplies, also sat separately.[11] The cabin boys acted as waiters. Two litres of water were issued for washing every day, when feasible.[12]

All passengers were, of course, registered and their birthplaces and parents noted. As a rule, married men could not leave without their wives. Single women could not travel to the Indies unless they were the daughters of families which had already emigrated.

Perhaps the most vivid account of a journey across the Atlantic in the sixteenth century is that of Tomás de la Torre, a Dominican father who with forty-six clergymen accompanied Bartolomé de las Casas on one of his return journeys to the New World in 1544. De la Torre wrote:

> A ship is a very narrow and stout prison from which no one can escape ... even though he wears no shackles nor chains. It makes no distinction in its cruelty to its inmates, confining them all equally.

Closely compressed into its narrow confines, the heat and the suffocation are unbearable. The deck floor is usually one's bed and, though some brought good mats, ours were small, hard and poor, thinly stuffed with dog hair; our bed coverings were wretched blankets of goatskin . . . No one has any desire to eat and one can hardly face anything sweet. The thirst one endures is unbelievable and is increased by the ship's biscuit and salt beef which constitute our chief fare. Wine is drunk by those passengers who happen to have brought it. An infinite number of lice eat one alive and clothing cannot be washed because sea water shrinks eventually. Bad odours pervade everywhere, especially below deck, and the whole ship becomes intolerable when the ship's pump is working, which varies according to whether the ship is sailing well or not. It goes at least four times a day in order to pump out of the hold the water that has leaked in . . . On top of this, when one feels well enough, there is no place where one can study or withdraw to oneself a little . . . one remains eternally seated for there is no place to walk.[13]

The return journey would be similar.

The first stop in the New World on the outward journey was Portobello, on the Caribbean coast of Panama, which was just a small collection of poor houses adorned by a governor's residence and by the Castillo of San Felipe, which seems to have been completed in 1604 and which was the base for fifty soldiers. The waterfront at Portobello was two miles long by half a mile wide, with a deep sandy depth virtually reaching the edge of the shore so ships could enter and leave easily. The port of Nombre de Dios had been abandoned after the attacks of Francis Drake, who nevertheless would die there in January 1596.

The annual fair on the waterfront at Portobello, held in tents made from sails, was a great occasion since the place acted as an entrepôt for the whole of South America. The squares and streets of the town would be temporarily full of stalls and booths with innumerable items for sale. Here the merchants of Seville and Cadiz would meet their Peruvian agents and partners. The fair would last several weeks.

The next halt would have been old Panama, where the seamen of the isthmus assisted by black slaves would have unloaded the treasure brought north from Peru prior to carrying it to the Caribbean coast at

Portobello, where it would be reloaded on the ships bound for Havana and then Spain.[14]

Goods intended for Peru would be carried across the isthmus of Panama by mules close to the eventual route for the Panama Canal opened in 1914. The muleteers would probably be African slaves, sometimes using barges along the river Chagres, sometimes driving mules the whole way. Travel in both ways was dangerous. One had to choose between the use of the perilous river Chagres, a journey along which took about two weeks, or the steep and narrow paths over the hills which only took four days but was far more rough and very risky.

Panama was a dull, unhealthy place, at the mercy of pirates and raids by escaped slaves. There were five convents with gardens, but these were almost the only habitable spots. There were just eight private houses. In 1607 there were a mere 550 male Europeans, of whom about half were married. The white Europeans were heavily outnumbered by the 3,700 black slaves who still seem to have spoken their African languages.[15] There were no *encomiendas* in Panama and few Indians. The port had silted up, so even ships as small as 50 tons could not enter the harbour and had to be unloaded and loaded by lighter. It was astonishing to find that a place of such importance to the Spanish empire was so poorly serviced and indeed so poor.

For the return journey by sea, both the Mexican and the Peruvian fleets would combine at Havana at the beginning of the year, would leave before 10 March, and sail back to Spain via the Bahamas, the route first worked out by Cortés's brilliant pilot, Antonio de Alaminos, of Palos (he had been a cabin boy on Columbus's fourth voyage).[16] From 1565 the *galleones* seem to have set off only every two years. In 1573 it was announced that if the fleets could not for any reason depart from Havana before October, they should be told to winter there.[17] The decision to maintain the fleets at Havana over the winter led directly to the failure of the great fair at Medina del Campo, for the lack of income there was marked.[18] King Philip wanted punctuality in all these undertakings but he never achieved it except accidentally, for the outgoing fleets would usually have to delay their departure.[19]

All these vessels were as a rule a blend of warship and cargo boat. They would be likely to carry not only about thirty soldiers, but also artillery. It was still an era when guns were easier to manipulate on a ship than on land. All these ships were also used to carrying smuggled goods. This trafficking was so frequent that the *bodegas* (holds) were made even bigger to carry the contraband. All the same, these vessels remained so specialized that they were not much employed outside the Atlantic.

A merchantman on these journeys was usually 400 to 500 tons burden. The sandbar at Sanlúcar made the passage of ships of more than 200 tons difficult, and so all bigger vessels were loaded from lighters outside the bar. In both Havana and Sanlúcar, foodstuffs represented an important cargo, for the numbers of sailors, passengers, and slaves grew every year.

We should spare a word for the great city of Havana. Fray Martín Ignacio de Loyola wrote in the late sixteenth century that it was:

> a very good port ... where there is all kind of provision necessary belonging to the fleets and ships, some of which the island doth yield to itself and others brought from other places; but in particular there is a great store of very good timber, as well for repairing of timber as well as for other things with which they do ordinarily ballast the ships which come from Spain. The King's Majesty hath in this a governor and a captain with very good soldiers for the defence thereof and a fort which is in the same harbour, the best that is in all the Indies.[20]

Being a link between the New World and the Old, the harbour in Havana would play a decisive part in Spanish imperial history for three centuries.[21]

Already by 1590 Havana had become the most important shipyard in the New World. This was partly because the ships of the treasure fleets often needed repairs. The splendid forests near Havana offered a marvellous supply of good hardwoods ('the best in the world' according to Governor Tejeda).[22] Contact with Europe made possible the easy shipment to Cuba of iron parts and supplies, sails, cordage, and tar. Skilled shipwrights sometimes visited Havana.[23] There were also, however, many resident shipwrights. The city's main shipyard lay appropriately between the great monastery of San Francisco and the fortress of La Fuerza. In addition, the development of copper mining at El Prado near Santiago de Cuba, and the establishment of a foundry there with royal financing (raising 250,000 *reales* in 1597), made artillery easily available for the royal service. Master smelters and other specialists were employed.[24] Cuba also already had several sugar mills, twenty-five being near Havana in 1610. They were mostly animal-driven. One or two large ones were water-driven, the biggest using over thirty slaves. This was the ex-governor Juan Maldonado's San Diego mill, worth about 20,000 ducats.[25] From the beginning this industry required the employment of African slaves, whose purchase was carried through along the lines which had become traditional in both Spain and Portugal, not to speak of the Canary Islands.[26]

In theory, these great fleets would bring back treasure both for the Spanish Crown and for private persons. But on occasion the Crown would seize private merchandise.[27] Privacy, as the sixteenth century came to know well, had a very modest dominion.

# 23

# Populations Discovered

*I married in this land a woman very much to my liking and, although it may appear severe [recio] to have married an Indian, here one does not lose any honour by such action because it is a nation in which Indians are held in high esteem.*

Andrés García in New Spain to his nephew Pedro Guiñón in Colmenar Viejo, Spain, 10 February 1571

In the early years of the reign of King Philip II, about 1570, the population of Spanish and Portuguese America was probably about 10 million, of whom about 9½ million were indigenous people, 250,000 or so were black, mulatto, or mixed Indian and white (*mestizos*), while a mere 140,000 or so were 'white' or Europeans, half of them having been born in Europe.[1] Much the most populous part of the Indies was New Spain, by then firmly known as such, on Cortés's inspiration, and its population was about 3,555,000.

At the time of the death of King Philip nearly thirty years later, in 1598, the population of the great American empire which he passed on to his son, Philip III, probably totalled 12 million. By then this empire included the Portuguese dominion of Brazil, which had been ruled by the king of Spain since 1580. It also included the population of the remote Spanish colony of the Philippines, the so-called 'Islands of the West'.

These people were far from homogeneous, for the newcomers were Spaniards, Portuguese, Italians, African slaves, and free Africans, alongside a diverse indigenous population which had interbred, if not intermarried, with all of them. Each subdivision had its particular name: thus the children of blacks and whites were *mulattos*, a useful designation which nobody seems to employ in our morally opaque twenty-first century. The concept of a quadroon or an octaroon, a person with a quarter or an eighth of black blood, is nowadays considered even more eccentric. Very few people today talk of *mestizos*, the offspring of Indians and Europeans. But the sixteenth century liked clarity. The children of blacks and Indians were known as *zambos*.[2] The explanation for the disappearance of these interesting words derives from the fact that racial origins are no longer considered important. To specify them as was done in the past is considered in some way discriminatory on grounds of race.

About 250,000 Spaniards seem to have emigrated to the New World in the course of the sixteenth century.[3] Most were Andalusians, and a majority of those were *sevillanos*, though, as we have seen, a substantial number of the leaders of expeditions were *extremeños* or Castilians. Andalusia was at that time one of the richest regions of the Mediterranean, with large vineyards and olive orchards. Its citizens lived on bread made from wheat often grown in north Africa, and they traded wine and oil to much of the world. The riches of the region make the emigration of Andalusians difficult to understand. All the same, Andalusia was the region which had the most contact with the New World. Perhaps the explanation is that riches broadened the minds of potential emigrants who wanted to gamble on an adventure. Julius Klein, in his famous book *The Mesta*, argued that sheep flocks, which were well suited to transhumance along the *cañadas*[4] of Castile, provided a precedent for the convoys of fleets to the New World;[5] the Mesta may also have prepared the minds of Andalusians for transhumance on an altogether different scale.

A harsher financial motive for emigration from Andalusia lay in the fact that the price and availability of bread fluctuated enormously because of the frequent droughts. In 1521 the Venetian ambassador to Spain commented, 'There was such famine in Andalusia that countless animals died and the countryside became deserted. Many people died too. There was such drought that the wheat harvest was lost and not a blade of grass could be found in the fields. That year the Andalusian breed of horses for the most part died out . . .'[6]

Europe in the sixteenth century was also undergoing rapid

demographic changes. The population of the Mediterranean region probably doubled between 1500 and 1600 from about 30 or 35 million to about 60 or 70 million. The population of Castile perhaps rose from just over 3 million in 1530 to nearly 6 million in 1591. The city of Seville increased from about 73,500 in 1530 to about 115,000 by the end of the century.[7]

Seville was the centre of emigration from Spain. The city was full of adventurers hoping for a licence to travel: vagrants, sturdy beggars, the impoverished, gentlemen hoping for a passage to Peru to restore their fortunes, soldiers and thieves, debtors and tramps. The Indies, Cervantes assured his readers in *The Jealous Extremaduran* (*El geloso Extremeño*, 1613), was 'the church of rebels, and sanctuary of murderers', the promised land.[8] On one occasion in 1581 the municipality of Seville assembled all the vagabonds in the city and embarked them for the straits of Magellan, where it was intended that they should work the land. But most of the ships on which these individuals embarked on their journey were lost: about a thousand died.[9]

Every part of Spain seems to have produced emigrants. For example, we learn that 3,076 citizens from the province of Valladolid went to the New World or the Philippines in the century following Columbus's discovery, mostly from the capital city of Valladolid (1,066) or from the nearby great market town of Medina del Campo (639).[10]

Probably about 240,000 Jews remained in Spain after the expulsion of 1492,[11] concentrated in the large cities and especially in ports. Jews and Muslims, even converted ones, were formally prohibited from going to the Indies, but not in practice.[12] There were numerous Jews, rich and poor, in Madeira and São Tomé, and many *conversos* of Portuguese origin. Samuel Abravanel, a Neapolitan Jewish merchant, was a great sugar entrepreneur in Madeira where Jews were so numerous that many practised their religion freely. A small list of conquistadors of Jewish origin could be found in New Spain or Central America, and the same proportion probably in Peru-Chile. The former included the hardy and persistent Pedrarias, governor of Darien and Panama; the latter included two brothers of the famous saint, Teresa of Ávila.

The Basques were numerous in the Indies from the days of Cortés onwards, as shown by the exploits of El Cano, the first captain to complete a circumnavigation of the world (Magellan was killed in the Philippines before his expedition was completed). We should not forget either Juan de Garay, the real founder of Buenos Aires, Aguirre 'wrath of God' on the Amazon, Ercilla the poet of Chile, and Martínez de Irala in Paraguay, all of whom we met variously in previous chapters.[13] The role of another Basque, Miguel López de Legazpi, in the 'Islands of the West' will be discussed later.

About 75,000 black slaves were sold in Spanish America between 1500 and 1600, and perhaps a few more in Brazil.[14] In 1552 the Emperor Charles V had agreed to permit a *negrero* – that was the usual word for a slave merchant – named Ochoa to sell 23,000 African slaves over seven years. Ochoa paid the vast sum of 184,000 ducats for the contract.[15] As early as 1570, the black Africans in the Caribbean exceeded the European or Indian populations there. That would remain the case for the next three centuries, during which the slaves created a world of sugar for the delectation of Old Europe. Slaves represented the most valuable import into Havana in the sixteenth century after wine and textiles – between 1,300 and 1,500 slaves were sold in Havana in the 1590s. Though these are not large numbers, they did represent a substantial increase in the population of blacks in Cuba as a whole.[16] In New Spain, African slaves seem to have been employed especially as shepherds of the new flocks of sheep. There seem to have been more blacks (10,595) than whites (9,495) in the city of Mexico by 1576, by which time there could also have been 1,000 mulattoes.[17] Several indigenous Mexicans told the viceroy that he should recruit African slaves to do some of the hard work which he wanted done. Many slaves seemed at that time to prefer white masters to their indigenous black ones. Most slaves were bought as such, having been enslaved in Africa.

Most of these slaves were men, only a quarter were women. Of those Africans who were shipped to regions of the Spanish empire in the reign of Philip II, most, by now, came from Senegambia, 'the Rivers of Guinea', or the Congo.[18] The Portuguese were obtaining most of their slaves from Angola.

Already the black portion of the population of the New World had its champions: for example, in Cartagena de Indias, an important slave port from the mid-sixteenth century onwards, Alonso de Sandoval, a graduate of San Pablo in Peru, had demonstrated his boundless love for the African. His famous book *De Instauranda Aetopium Salute* – which may be translated *On the Establishment of the Health of Ethiopians [or Africans]* – circulated among Jesuits in particular. Sandoval's famous pupil, Pedro Claver, who was later sanctified, would join him in 1610 from Cataluña, where he had been born.

Some efforts were made to limit excessive reliance on black slave labour. Thus in October 1578 the Jesuit general, Everard Mercurian,[19] instructed the Jesuits of San Pablo in Lima to dismiss all black women from the service of the college. But that was easier said than done, so the Jesuits there continued to have their African slaves.[20] But free blacks and mulattoes were rather unwelcome: Viceroy Villamanrique in New Spain wrote to his successor Luis de Velasco in 1590 that these types were 'damaging and pernicious as you know, since they wandered as vagabonds making thefts and assaults'.[21] Some saw danger in the sheer numbers of black slaves imported to the Spanish Caribbean. For example (as we saw in chapter 14), Menéndez de Avilés wrote in 1558 to King Philip that on the island of Santo Domingo there were over 50,000 blacks but fewer than 4,000 Spaniards. A rebellion of slaves, which might be the consequence of such an imbalance, could herald a terrible tragedy.[22]

By 1600 the Indian population of the Americas had fallen dramatically as a consequence of contact with European diseases,[23] and also, to a lesser extent, because of the unchecked proliferation of European livestock which affected access to land, itself made possible by the decimation of the indigenous population. The departure of some of the Indian population to seek gold was another factor in their demographic decline. Death in battle was a more modest contributor, though it certainly happened, as we know from all the accounts of the bloody siege of Tenochtitlan, the capital of the Mexica's empire, in 1521.

There are doubts about the size of the populations of both ancient New Spain and ancient Peru before the Spanish arrived. Two important historians, Professors Woodrow Borah and Sherburne Friendly Cook, thought that the people of Montezuma's empire totalled 25.3 million.[24] The belief of the present writer is that, on the eve of the conquest, the Indian (Mexica) population in what became New Spain

(Mexico) was probably between 8 and 11 million.[25] But by the end of the sixteenth century, it does not seem as though the indigenous population of all peoples was more than about 2.5 million. Professors Borah and Cook thought that there were only 6.3 million in New Spain in 1548 and as few as 1.9 million there in 1580. Still, a good description of Tenochtitlan/Mexico was written in 1580 by Fray Alonso Ponce, a leading Franciscan. He thought that there were perhaps 4,000 white Spanish residents in that capital, supported by innumerable Indians.[26] The white population of all of New Spain could not have been much more than 30,000.

In Peru there is a similar tale. The Indian population may have been 6 million just before Pizarro and his fellow conquistadors arrived in 1531. Epidemics on a Mexican scale, such as influenza and smallpox, then swept away most of those indigenous peoples. It is unlikely that there were more than 2 million Peruvian Indians by 1600.

European epidemics were the chief enemies of indigenous populations in the New World. These epidemics struck a largely defenceless, immunity-free population. The diseases of Europe spread with amazing speed and inspired large death rates which almost annihilated whole provinces in New Spain, the Caribbean, Peru, and northern South America equally. The indigenous populations recovered only after several generations.[27]

In the Otomí valley of Mezquital close to Tenochtitlan there were occasions when it was supposed that the diseases were weakening, and when the population showed signs of recovery.[28] But then there broke the terrible epidemic known as 'The Great Cocolistle', which raged from 1576 to 1581 in New Spain. It was followed by some kind of outbreak there every ten years or so until 1620, when at last the Indians seem to have found some kind of accommodation with their new enemies.[29]

The most ruinous diseases which flourished in the New World were smallpox, measles, influenza, plague, and tuberculosis. The last named seemed to be especially threatening to people aged between fifteen and forty, that is, the hard-working elements of the population. The indigenous peoples of the New World were often affected by several of these infections at the same time. Contagion was often spread by people fleeing their stricken villages. There were no attempts at quarantine.

In the Caribbean, the collapse of the native population was even more striking, though absurdly high figures were often given for the indigenous peoples of 1492. Thus Fray Martín Ignacio de Loyola, in his best-selling account of his *Journey Round the World* of 1584, insisted that there had been 600,000 Indians in Santo Domingo in Columbus's day.[30] As early as 1519 the prolific Italian letter-writer, the Milanese Peter Martyr, had written:

> ... the natives have been reduced to a very small number. Pitiless wars destroyed many at the beginning, famine killed many others, especially during the year when they tore up their yucca, from which they make the caciques' bread and then they refused to sow maize which serves for their own bread. The survivors have been attacked by the germs of hitherto unknown maladies, especially smallpox which, during the last year 1518, raged among them as if it were an epidemic among cattle ... Let us add that the [Spaniards'] craze for gold was also one cause of their destruction. For these people, who were accustomed, as soon as they had sown their fields, to play, to dance, to sing, and chase rabbits, were set mercilessly to work cultivating the ground, extracting and sifting gold. The Royal Council has, however, decided to restore to them their liberty and, henceforth, they will only occupy themselves with agriculture ... Slaves will be brought into the hard work of mines.[31]

Thus, as the nineteenth-century educationalist Basilio Vadillo thought, there may have been only between 4,500 and 5,000 indigenous natives by 1532 in the Caribbean.[32] In 1556 the governor of Cuba, Diego de Mazariegos, thought that there were fewer than 2,000.[33] By 1570 there seem to have been a mere twenty-five indigenous natives in Hispaniola, all of them old, poor, and without families. Yet there may still have been several thousand Indian slaves.[34]

The connection between these different peoples was complex and became more so. Thus in 1570 the 'Carta Anuale', a report sent from Lima to Rome, mentioned several Indian boys, 'students of our college', taking part in a college play. But by 1618, when the viceroy of Peru, the Prince of Esquilache, tried to establish a school for Indian nobles under the care of the Jesuits, San Pablo's Jesuit school of humanities in Lima was barred to indigenous people.[35]

Another early seventeenth-century viceroy in Lima, Juan Mendoza de Lima, the Marquis of Montesclaros, organized a census in his capital. The total population he discovered to be 26,441, of whom the Spaniards numbered 5,258 men and 5,359 women. A further 820 women lived in convents.[36] These women, cloistered or non-cloistered, were busy passing on to their children and others, including *mestizos*, that passion for Christianity which characterized the early Spanish empire. *Mestizos* were expensive to bring up, since they usually expected to be treated similarly to full Europeans. There was thus in the 1540s a family in Lima headed by a certain Francisca Suárez, 'La Valenciana', who had welcomed a *mestiza* girl into her family. Francesca received from the viceroy a black slave as compensation for the costs of educating her *mestiza*.[37]

Many *mestizas* as well as Spanish women also compensated for the absence or lack of husbands by adopting some domestic role. Thus female bakers were quite common, as were quack doctors (*curanderas*). The shortage of trained doctors encouraged women to take on those healing roles too. Some were skilful in adapting European plants to the conditions of the New World. Normally, *curanderas* were relatively old and experienced and could turn their hands to a variety of tasks – nursing, pottery-making, sail-making, as well as millinery. Some became hatters.

Perhaps 13,000 Spanish women went to the New World in the course of the sixteenth century.[38] From about 1508 wives of governors usually accompanied their husbands there, Diego Colón leading the way with his grand wife, María de Toledo (a niece of the Duke of Alba). Not surprisingly, the arrival of so many women led to a widespread cult of Our Lady, the Virgin Mary, and by 1600, hundreds of Marian sanctuaries decorated the courtyards of Central and South America. Almost every city had at least one *cofradía*, or brotherhood, under the patronage of Our Lady, which attracted not only the *conquistadoras* and their attendants but Indians, black slaves, *mestizos* and *mestizas*. As we saw in chapter 10, the popularity of nunneries was astonishing. Women thereby were enabled to break away from brutal connections with tyrannical men. As the twentieth-century historian Fray Luis Martín pointed out, those convents became 'fortresses of feminism, true islands of womankind'.[39] Mary was seen as the mediator between woman and God.

The most original creation of the Spaniards in the New World was really the *mestizo*, the mixture of European and Indian. It is worth considering, by way of contrast, how rare such a state of affairs was between Anglo-Saxons and the Indians of North America. There are obvious reasons for that rarity of course – not least the lack of an urban society among North American Indians – but that need not have been such a barrier as it in fact turned out to be.

In the next generation, say in 1600, we find the following gradations or castes:

1. A Spaniard mixed with an Indian was a *mestizo*.
2. A *mestizo* mixed with a Spaniard was a *castizo*.
3. A *castizo* mixed with a Spaniard was a Spaniard.
4. A Spaniard mixed with a black was a mulatto.
5. A mulatto mixed with a Spaniard was a quadroon (*cuaterón*).
6. A quadroon mixed with a Spaniard was a *salto atrás*.
7. A *salto atrás* mixed with an Indian was a *chino*.
8. A *chino* mixed with a mulatta was a *lobo*.
9. A *lobo* mixed with a mulatta was a *gibaro*.
10. A *gibaro* mixed with an Indian was an *alvarasado*.
11. An *alvarasado* mixed with an Indian was a *cambujo*.
12. A *cambujo* mixed with an Indian was a *samboya*.
13. An Indian mixed with a mulatto was a *calpamulato*.
14. A *calpamulato* mixed with a *cambuja* was a *tente-en-el-aire*.

Other terms were often substituted.

# BOOK FOUR

# The East in Fee

# 24

# The Conquest of the Philippine Islands

*So without further delay, they weighed anchors and having the wind prosperous for them, sailed all night till, about break of day, they descried the island.*

Garci Rodríguez de Montalvo,
*Amadís de Gaula*, 1508 (trans. Anthony
Munday, ed. Helen Moore, Aldershot 2004, 927)

The archipelago known now as the Philippine Islands, and spoken of in the sixteenth century as 'the Islands of the West' (las Islas del Poniente), entered the imagination of Europeans in 1521, when Magellan's great expedition touched the territory of the so-called Bisaya Group. Magellan christened this previously unknown archipelago 'the islands of San Lázaro'.[1] He reached the island of Cebú (Zebú) in the same archipelago, where he was killed in a foolish skirmish that April. His command eventually passed to a Basque, Juan Sebastián de El Cano, who, with his small crew, demonstrated in this circumnagivation that the earth really was round.[2]

These adventures raised the question of where the Portuguese interest in what they thought of as the Far East ended and where the Spanish responsibility began in what they considered the Far West. The Pope in 1492 and the Treaty of Tordesillas of 1494 had drawn a longitudinal line in the region of Brazil and the Atlantic separating East and West. But no one knew then for certain that the earth was round. Diplomatic difficulties intensified in the 1520s after the return of El Cano. They were only resolved in 1529 by a treaty at Saragossa between Spain and Portugal, by which Spain gave up her claims to the

Spice Islands – 'the Moluccas' – and abandoned all presence beyond the line of latitude 117 degrees east. This ran from Lomboa in what soon became the Dutch East Indies, to Borneo and then Sabah, and entered China at Hsia-men some 100 miles east of Hong Kong. In exchange, Spain received the substantial sum of 350,000 ducats.[3]

This treaty was not popular in the *cortés* of Spain, but it left the Spanish interest in the East Indies and the Philippines still simmering. So both speculation and dreaming continued, which in turn spurred on more adventurers. Thus in the 1540s the apparently immortal warrior, Pedro de Alvarado, known as 'son of the sun' after his conquest of New Spain, organized a fleet there whose aim was to visit and perhaps conquer some of those 'Islands of the West'. He accepted that 'the spice islands' (Moluccas) should be left to Portugal as agreed in 1529, but there were other places known to Magellan for which there was no such agreement. Antonio de Mendoza, the clever viceroy of New Spain, perhaps considering such matters in his palace in Mexico, became interested. The expedition was to have two wings, one in the north led by Juan Rodríguez Cabrillo and one in the south under Ruy López de Villalobos, who seems to have been a cousin of Viceroy Mendoza.[4] The undertaking was to have thirteen vessels, a larger fleet than had ever sailed the Pacific. Rodríguez Cabrillo, an expert in nautical matters, was Portuguese in origin and had been both with Pedro de Alvarado in Cuba and then with Pánfilo de Narváez in New Spain. After that, Cabrillo became a councillor in Guatemala under Alvarado's leadership.

The other commander, López de Villalobos, was a *malagueño* whose family had belonged to the immediate circle of King Fernando the Catholic. López de Villalobos was more a man of letters than of the sword. He was a brother-in-law of Viceroy Mendoza. He had six ships under his command.

Alvarado was to be the commander-in-chief. How could so great a captain be anything less? But then the rebellion of the Chichimec Indians in central New Spain caused the expedition to be postponed. Alvarado felt obliged to return to New Spain in 1540 and to try and save the viceroyalty. But, as will be remembered,[5] in July 1541 his horse slipped in the rain near Guadalajara, he was seriously hurt, and a few days later he died of his injuries.

The expedition to the East Indies had been postponed, but not abandoned. López de Villalobos did set off with his six ships and with 370 men in November 1542. His captains included several men who would later become famous. For instance, Ginés de Mafra, a pilot who had been with Magellan; Guido de Lavezaris ('Labozares' in Santiesteban's spelling), a son of a Genoese bookseller living in Seville, who would eventually become governor of the Philippines; and the Augustinian friar Jerónimo de Santiesteban, who became the voyage's chief chronicler.[6]

López de Villalobos took three months to cross the Pacific. His ships first put in at a group of islands which he named Revillagigedo, presumably after an Asturian nobleman of that name who invested in the expedition; then the Coral Islands, the Marshall Islands, the Matolotes in the Carolinas, and the Palaos.

The pilot Gaspar Rico laid the grounds for the capture of the island of Taongin. Then, López de Villalobos discovered the large Philippine island of Mindanao and that of San Antonio, previously known by the indigenous people as Sarangani, in the far south of the archipelago. They found evidence everywhere of extensive trading relations with China. Most of the expedition then sailed south to the Moluccas. But one of Villalobos's friends, Bernardo de la Torre, went north to discover the volcanic islands of Oceania. Iñigo Ortíz de Retes, a Basque nobleman who was chief magistrate of the fleet, left with Gaspar Rico on the galleon *San Juan* to sail along the north of New Guinea – a large island of the archipelago which had been discovered in 1528 by Alonso de Saavedra, a cousin of Cortés. The *San Juan* sought to return to New Spain but it was damaged in a storm and so made for Tidore in the Moluccas.

Having remained in the region of the Philippines for several months, López de Villalobos reached a sensible if rather humiliating agreement with the Portuguese. The 143 men who were left of his expedition which had set out the previous year were sent home to Spain – not New Spain – in Portuguese ships. They embarked in Ternate in the Moluccas in February 1546. López de Villalobos himself reached neither his old nor his new home, for he died in Amboina (Ambon) in the Moluccas, his last moments being soothed by the care of the great Jesuit missionary Saint Francis Xavier in person. One of his pilots, the

Augustinian friar Andrés de Urdaneta, returned after many adventures in the Pacific to New Spain, which he reached in 1563.

It was López de Villalobos who gave this archipelago of 7,000 islands, spread over an area of 1,000 miles, the name by which it is still known: the 'Philippine Islands', named after the young Spanish Regent, the future Philip II (the island of Leyte was originally called Filipina).[7]

The picture soon changed once more. In 1564 the big-hearted, elegant, and aristocratic Luis de Velasco, viceroy in New Spain, listened with great interest to a report by the aforementioned pilot-friar Urdaneta. Velasco discussed the possibilities of a new expedition to 'the Islands of the West' with the king by letter, and in the autumn of that year he commissioned another Basque, Miguel López de Legazpi de Gurruchateguí, to cross the Pacific and properly establish the Spanish presence in the Philippine archipelago. Both viceroy and king may have been attracted by a recent rise in the price of spices.[8]

Legazpi, who now became an *adelantado*, had been born in 1503 or 1504 in the little town of Zumárraga in Guipuzcoa, between Tolosa and Mondragón. Zumárraga was the same town from which the great first Bishop (later Archbishop) of New Spain took his revered name. Lope de Aguirre ('Wrath of God') and Martínez de Irala, the conquistador of Paraguay, both came from Mondragón.[9]

Legazpi had had a long, albeit conventional, official career before he set off on his remarkable journey across the Pacific. His father, Juan Martínez de Legazpi, had fought for 'el gran capitán' in Italy, and he had been *escribano*, or chief notary, in the village of Areria in the Basque country. His son had succeeded him there, for a year or so in 1527–8.[10]

Legazpi had been in New Spain since 1540, labouring there for twenty years as a chief notary, a similar position to what he had had in the Basque country. He had above all worked for the town hall in Mexico, embarked on numerous lawsuits, and he was accustomed to give evidence against those who spoke ill of the Supreme Court there.[11] He founded the *Cofradía* (brotherhood) of the Sweet Name of Jesus (*El dulce nombre de Jesús*).[12] We hear from Francisco Tello, the Visitor to New Spain (afterwards in the Council of Indies) in the 1540s, that Legazpi was 'a very honourable and gentlemanly person', also 'very prudent and someone who always knew what was going on in the city'. Legazpi was a widower with nine children by his late wife, Isabel Garcés. His chief lieutenant was his grandson, Felipe de Saucedo, an unusual relationship among conquistadors. Legazpi had also been for a time secretary of the Inquisition in New Spain.[13]

The instructions which Velasco formulated for Legazpi were drawn up with the teaching of the great theologian from Salamanca, Francisco de Vitoria, in mind. (Vitoria had been the foremost humane interpreter of law and custom in Salamanca for many years. He was born in Burgos and his mother was from a *converso* family.) Velasco stated to Legazpi that if any *naturales* in the Philippines were to refuse to listen to him, he was to use all reasonable means to overcome them, and to proceed always with 'all manner of discretion, kindness and moderation'. If, as would seem likely, the Spaniards were physically opposed by the Filipinos, the latter should be told that the Spaniards were not trying to settle there in order to do them or others any harm, nor to commit any wrong, nor would they seize their possessions. They only wished to engage with the local population in a spirit of friendship and teach them to live in a civilized manner, to recognize the true God, and to explain to them the law of Jesus Christ by which they would be saved.[14]

Like most journeys of conquest in the sixteenth century, including those of Cortés and Pizarro, Legazpi's expedition was a venture of private enterprise, in which the main investor was Legazpi himself. But the Crown in New Spain also had an interest in this expedition from the beginning. The fleet which Legazpi commanded was built with public money, including the provision of soldiers, priests, and friars, while the food, armaments, and ammunition were all provided by the viceroy. Much of the shipping, however, was Legazpi's responsibility.

After his death Legazpi was the subject of an interesting official obituary. Therein he is described as 'captain-general of the Isles of the West'.[15] He was often referred to as *general*.[16] The memorandum also discussed Legazpi's achievement, describing how his expedition had set off on 21 November 1564 from Navidad, on the north-west coast of New Spain. The commander, who was probably sixty years old, had left many of his followers in New Spain with the impression that he was really going to China, not just the Philippine Islands. That rumour stimulated recruitment to his expedition, for it had been widely reported that the Chinese were more intelligent than the Mexica, therefore easier to rule.[17]

Legazpi's flotilla consisted of the *San Pedro*, of 500 tons; the *San Pablo*, the commander's ship, of 300 tons; and two pinnaces, the *San Juan* and the *San Lucas*. Legazpi also maintained a brigantine as a kind of guard to sail at the stern of the *San Pablo*. On this little flotilla there were 150 sailors, 200 soldiers, and five Augustinian friars, one of whom was the experienced Fray Andrés de Urdaneta mentioned earlier – who confessed himself surprised to find that the actual conquest of the Philippines was mentioned in the instructions given to Legazpi. There were, too, a rather large number of servants, which caused the ships' company to rise to 380 persons. Legazpi sold his office as treasurer of the Casa de Moneda in Mexico to help finance the expedition.

Urdaneta was more than a friar, and more than a pilot, for he was the wise man of the fleet: memorable for more than his holy activity and his maritime knowledge. He had fought in skirmishes with Portugal in the Moluccas and also in the war in New Spain against the Chichimec Indians. Fray Juan de Grijalva, in his history of Mexico, called Urdaneta an 'indefatigable man, as prepared as any ordinary member of the crew for navigation, for fighting, for preaching, or for founding and even designing churches'.[18]

Legazpi and Urdaneta's fleet (as we are tempted to think of it) reached Leyte on the Philippine Island of Cebacac in a section of the archipelago called the Bisayas. They moved in to capture the island of Samar and then, on 27 April 1565, the island of Cebú (Zebú), where Magellan had died forty-four years before. Legazpi conducted himself with subtlety, persuading all the leaders of the places which he visited formally to accept Spanish control. This was at first sight difficult because of the character of the Philippine polity. The islands had been invaded many times before by Japanese, Chinese, and Malays. In addition, the original population, in so far as it had survived, was often nomadic. There was no large, central political entity. Instead local lords would govern their own *barangays* – villages or collections of dwellings of, say, thirty to a hundred families. These lords were usually quite independent of, and were often at war with, their neighbours.

Hernando de Riquel, the notary of the expedition, thought the lords were absolute monarchs (*señores absolutos*) who, within their districts, had great power and authority.[19]

A little later yet another prominent Augustinian, Fray Martín de Rada, from Pamplona in Navarre and educated in Paris, wrote that the Philippines had neither lords nor kings but that every little *pueblo* (*pueblozillo*), however small, was a republic of its own and was managed by a kind of oligarchy.[20] Antonio de Morga, a clever judge, a *sevillano*, and son of an official of the Inquisition, who afterwards served in New Spain and Quito, later had the same impression: 'In these islands,' he wrote, 'there are no lords nor kings who dominate in the style of other monarchies and provinces: but, in every island, there are lords who govern a number of families. In a small number of places, there are political authorities who are superior to the kings.'[21]

'In Philippine society,' Morga went on, 'there were three classes – hidalgos, plebeians and slaves. The first did not pay taxes or tribute but had a responsibility for supporting the *principal* in any conflict. The plebeians did pay taxes, and the slaves were those who did the work of maintaining everything.'[22]

Faced with this difficult situation, Legazpi, in Cebú, began by trying to impose a form of harsh control. The few Portuguese who were lurking in these islands were also persuaded to leave. But Legazpi soon found that the Filipinos who did not want to pay tribute began to leave too. There were also various forms of resistance in the islands. Bishop Miguel de Benavides, a Dominican of relatively humble origin, born in Carrión de los Condes, Palencia, who had left Spain in 1586 and been in the Philippines since 1587, the first Bishop of Nueva Segovia who became Archbishop in Manila a generation later, wrote, 'Seeing that the Spaniards were ... not merchants but soldiers, the indigenous population thought that the best way to get rid of them was by starving them, not fighting them. So they did not sow the land.'[23] For a year or two, though, in specific places such as the Camarines (which became New Cáceres), the resistance was bitter. These Filipinos had bronze culverins – muskets – and even arquebuses, which they had taken from the Portuguese and learned how to use.

After building a fortress on Cebú, and reaching an effective understanding with the local Philippine lord Tupas, Legazpi sent back to

New Spain the biggest of his ships, the 500-ton *San Pedro*. This was captained by Legazpi's eighteen-year-old grandson, Juan de Salcedo, who was accompanied by 400 men. It included as its pilot the ubiquitous Augustinian Fray Andrés de Urdaneta. To find the right route home was a serious challenge for young Salcedo, but he accomplished it triumphantly, largely thanks to the brilliant Urdaneta. They left Cebú on 1 June 1565 and found themselves in northern California in August. They then sailed down south to Acapulco, which they reached on 6 October. From there they were a few days' journey from the city of Mexico. The expedition by then had been reduced to fewer than 200 Spaniards – who had the benefit of needing less food than if they had numbered nearly 400, as earlier.

The late 1560s saw the few Spaniards who had stayed on in the Philippines living for a time in rather harsh conditions. Juan de Salcedo returned from New Spain with some supplies but, on this return voyage, his ship was wrecked at the Pacific island of Guam. The arrival of another galleon from New Spain, the *San Jerónimo*, in the Philippines worsened matters further, for there were not enough supplies to enable a community of this size – now 300 – to survive. No one wanted to live off local products, for they coveted wheat or rye bread, wine, and salted beef.

Legazpi sent one of his deputies, Juan de la Isla, from Cebú back to Spain in the galleon *San Juan*, with a full account of his extraordinary adventures. De la Isla travelled, of course, via New Spain, leaving Cebú on 27 July 1567 and arriving in Acapulco on 16 November. He finally reached Castile on 6 June of the following year – a journey of over ten months. He carried letters from Legazpi to King Philip, which described the monarch's new dominion in glittering terms.[24]

Legazpi changed his tactics. First of all, he sent an expedition under his chief of staff, Martín de Goyte, to Panay, a medium-sized island where the production of rice was good, and where the conquistadors also arranged to buy it at good prices. Goyte then continued to the island of Luzón, where not only rice was available, but also pigs, goats, pepper, bergamot, mint, camphor, and even a little gold. On another island, nearer Baguindemao, there was the much-prized cinnamon.

Goyte was resisted in Luzón by Sultan Suleiman of Manila and by his uncle, Rajah Matandá, who possessed artillery which he had gained from the Portuguese without, however, being able to work it very well. These Muslims were by Philippine standards as much conquistadors as the Spaniards, but they were more brutal, so Legazpi and Goyte found it surprisingly easy to persuade the indigenous people that they were their liberators, as well as their new masters. The Muslim leaders were undoubtedly more formidable than the local chiefs hitherto mentioned.

Paray was conquered by the Spanish in 1569 and, for a time, Spain's Philippine empire consisted of that island, Cebú, and Leyte. Legazpi now proceeded with intelligence. He permitted no unorganized raids and hoped thereby to persuade the *naturales* of his protestations of peaceful intent. In relation to the Muslims, Legazpi's instructions were explicit: 'Under no circumstances whatsoever shall you enslave those Indians who have adopted the worship of Mahomet. But you will endeavour to convert them and persuade them to accept our holy Catholic faith, by good and legitimate means.'[25]

His new tactics worked. The people of Cebú accepted Spanish sovereignty, and also the requirement to pay tribute – in return for protection in the face of their Muslim enemies. In a few years it could be said that Legazpi was adopting a method of conquest quite different from what had been adopted in the Americas. Violence was in large measure replaced by commercial agreements with the *naturales*. The Spaniards paid reasonable prices for the food which they needed – pork, rice, and sweet potatoes. Cebú began to be occupied again by the indigenous people.

True, the Spaniards could not as yet send back to New Spain much more than cinnamon from the Philippines, as Legazpi put it in a letter of 1569 to the viceroy, Martín Enríquez de Almansa; in 1572, Legazpi wrote to Enríquez that all the viceroyalty could expect from the islands in addition to cinnamon were cloaks of cotton, wax, and thread, as well as a little gold.[26]

Long before that, however, Legazpi had received new instructions. For in August 1568 a galleon arrived from New Spain whose commander carried letters to the effect that as soon as the 'pacification' of the islands was complete, new Spanish cities should be founded. Legazpi was nothing if not obedient as well as conciliatory and, within a short time, he had inspired the creation of two new cities on Cebú, which became known as Jesús and Cebú itself. In the meantime Legaz-pi's new chief lieutenant, Martín de Goyte, sailed to Luzón, the largest island in the north of the archipelago, and suggested the bay of 'May-nila' (meaning 'a woody grove' in the indigenous *tagalog* language) as the ideal place for a capital. There was already a commercial centre there with many mercantile links to China, including forty resident Chinese families, and it was (relatively) close to the mainland. On 22 July 1570, Legazpi wrote to King Philip to say that he was leaving Cebú to move there. Legazpi had already been apprised that the land around 'Maynila' was well provided with 'rice, pigs, goats and gold'.[27]

# 25
# Manila

*Rice, pigs, goats, and gold . . .*
Miguel López de Legazpi was so told that
this was a description of the land near Manila

The old port of 'Maynila' in the south-west of the Philippine island of Luzón had been deserted by its former population in 1570, except for the small groups of Chinese who had lived there in the hope of commerce. The city lay on the southern side of the river Pasig just where it enters the bay.[1] There were already fortifications of earthworks and the trunks of coconut palms. It seems that, before 1570, the city had had a population of 2,000 families, or say 6,000 people. The imposition of a large-scale monarchy had begun to be developed under the inspiration of 'the false prophet Mahomet whose perfidious memory was easily extirpated by the holy evangelist of Christ,' wrote Fray Martín Ignacio de Loyola.[2] The lord of Maynila, Suleiman, a Muslim, was related by marriage to the ruling families of Sulin and Borneo. Though Muslims, they were wine-drinkers.

The Spanish occupation of Manila began in 1571. After a confused battle, in the course of which the house of Suleiman was burned, that potentate and his household along with other supporters left across the bay for Tondo.

Manila boasted a magnificent harbour and the agricultural hinterland was rich. Already the Muslim lords had allowed Chinese merchants to settle in the so-called Binondo region, which became a centre of Chinese settlement almost until our own day.[3]

Legazpi formally founded the Spanish city of 'Manila' on 24 June 1571. As with all important Spanish foundations, he immediately created a town council and appointed public officials. Two magistrates were named, as well as twelve town councillors, a constable, and a notary. The conquest of the rest of the large island of Luzón was completed by Martín de Goyte and Juan de Salcedo, the *adelantado*'s resourceful grandson. At the same time, Legazpi established reasonable relations with the surviving Muslim rajahs who were now on the other side of the bay in Cavite. His first intention was to call the new capital after the *cofradía* which he had founded in New Spain – 'The Sweet Name of Jesus'. But then he chose for the city a Hispanicized version of the Philippine name *Maynila*: Manila.

While Legazpi was completing his local pacifications, Martín de Goyte busied himself with the conquest of the Pampangos people. Juan de Salcedo conquered nearby Taytay and then Cainta, south-east of Manila. In both cases, the Spaniards quickly seized the indigenous artillery. Salcedo moved on the town of Paracale on the west coast of Luzón, but found that the gold mines said to have been there yielded nothing. All the same, further Spanish cities began to be founded: Nueva Segovia on the river Cagayán on Luzón island; Nueva Cáceres, Camariñas, also on Luzón; Averalon, on the island of Parrey; and Villa Fernandina, in the province of Ilocos on Luzón. Churches, of course, were soon built in all these places. Gold was found nearly everywhere, if sporadically, sometimes in rivers, sometimes in mines. There were also pearls to be discovered.

After the Spanish conquest of Luzón and the foundation of Manila, three matters had to be resolved: the question of slavery in the islands; the role and power of *encomiendas*; and the question of the islands' relation with New Spain, where for the time being political authority rested.

First, the conquerors were divided on the matter of slavery. Their memory of Bartolomé de las Casas was green, and his ideas were current everywhere in the Spanish dominions, Asiatic as well as American. An Augustinian friar, Diego de Herrera, from San Pedro de Rega near Astorga, returned to Spain from the Philippines to report excesses by settlers:

It is considered a just cause for war if the *naturales* say that they do not want friendship with Spaniards, or if they build forts with which to defend themselves. Such natives can be killed, captured, robbed and their houses burned. For that reason a war of the people known as the Bitis and of the Kubao occurred when their forts were taken by Juan de Salcedo; while in Canuta, an Indian climbed into a tree and cried out 'O Castile, what do you want of us? Why do you make war on us? Why do you demand tribute from us? What do we owe you? What good work have you done for us or for our ancestors?'[4]

The Indian's declamation was considered an occasion for a just war by a Council of War in Manila. It was resolved too that any village which promulgated a view comparable to this one could be legally destroyed, and all those captured could be enslaved if any Spaniard had been killed in the place concerned – 'although the justification that the dead man may have given, or the ways that crimes that he might have committed are not considered'.[5] One of the first petitions, it should be said, submitted by the conquerors to the viceroy in New Spain, was a request for the legality of slaves. This was the theme of a petition even before the Spaniards had left Cebú.[6]

Nevertheless the Council of War deliberated far away. There is no doubt that many slaves were bought, imported, and sold in the Philippines, as in other parts of the Spanish empire. There was what the historian Juan Gil describes as 'a clandestine traffic' in slaves from Portuguese India to the Philippines, as well as to Macao. Most were branded on the face before their sale.[7] In Spanish houses in the Philippines, the slaves were usually Chinese, though a few were black, from Africa.

The second argument in the Spanish conquest of the Philippines concerned *encomiendas*, which were established on Cebú from January 1571. A series of holdings (of land and of people) were founded in the name of the Crown, and about forty-eight in the names of private persons, the largest being that of 3,000 hectares granted on Cebú to Gerónimo de Monzón, one of Legazpi's foremost comrades.[8] In the first years of Spanish settlement, sixteen *encomiendas* were set up on Negros island, twelve on Leyte, eleven on Cibaboa, an island off Luzón, and three on Cebú.[9] When parts of Luzón island were divided up between the settlers, an *encomienda* of 8,000 souls was given to the adventurous Martín de Goyte.

These *encomiendas* were those known in the Americas as *encomiendas suavizadas*, which meant that the *encomenderos* had the right to use *naturales* in return for offering them protection, and instruction in the Christian faith.[10] But the arrangements were modified in the Philippines to ensure that tributes were not converted into personal services. There were soon some interesting discussions as to whether the Filipinos could pay their tribute in kind.[11]

Another modification of the principle of the *encomienda* used in these islands was the so-called *polo*, by which *naturales* were divided up into *repartos* (divisions) to be regularly paid for short periods of work – forty days a year. The application of the *polo* was made easier by the fact that the *naturales* had had a similar system before the arrival of the Spaniards. The old class system of the Philippines could thus be partly maintained so that the *naturales*, if plebeians, would be put to work in such necessary enterprises as cutting wood, building ships, servicing of artillery, and manufacture of rigging. In times of conflict they would also serve in galleys.

As was to be expected, the first *encomiendas* had hardly been granted before arguments began within the Spanish world about the length of time that they were to last: just one lifetime; two lifetimes; or forever. It should be no surprise to the reader to know that the matter was never properly resolved.

The third element in Spanish settlement of the Philippines was a consequence of voyages by the so-called 'Manila Galleon', which began to ply its way remorselessly to and from New Spain from the 1570s and which was essential in maintaining the continued union of New Spain with the Philippines.[12] To begin with, the number of ships which annually crossed the Pacific from Manila to Acapulco varied. Four ships seem to have been the average in the first years, although only three arrived in Acapulco in 1570. The first serious cargo of Chinese goods seems to have been despatched across the Pacific to Acapulco in 1573. The galleons sailed every year thereafter until the eighteenth century.

The ships on this remarkable series of voyages began to transport liquor, drugs, silk, cotton, and porcelain (china) from Manila to

Acapulco, and to bring back olive oil, European and American cloth, wine, lead, tin, gold, and, above all, Mexican silver. On one occasion a galleon arrived in New Spain with all her goods on board but without a living soul, for the ship's company had been lost: 'The ghost ship sailed into port on her own.'[13]

One shipment went on to El Callao, in Peru, in 1581 but was redirected to Acapulco. The high value of Mexican silver, and its popularity in China, assured a constant flow of unusual and much sought-after merchandise from China to New Spain. This no doubt encouraged the Spaniards to concentrate their interests more and more in Manila, which soon became a great multicultural city.[14]

The most obvious consequence of these famous voyages by galleons sailing to Acapulco was the fact that every year the city of Manila became for several months a veritable fairground. There was a large immigration of Chinese on a temporary scale and a great quantity of Chinese vessels in the harbour. Thus as many as fifty Chinese ships were in the harbour in 1595.[15]

In 1593, King Philip, after a long talk with the Council of the Indies, limited the number of ships to two both ways. Why two? Because the Council thought that was the number of voyages which could be guaranteed. The number of men within each crew and their responsibilities also varied considerably, but there was always a captain, usually two second mates, three or four pilots, two boatswains, two assistants to them, and two specialists hired to look after the armaments. As a rule there were also two surgeons. These galleons would usually also boast a notary, a chaplain, a ship's carpenter, an auditor, perhaps a diver and a major-domo. There might also be a general supervisor. The crew might number sixty to a hundred men. On the journey out from Acapulco there would also usually be a silver master (a master craftsman), a lieutenant of the army, and a sergeant major. Sometimes a captain would be designated a mission in the Mariana Islands or the minor islands of the Philippines. A galleon would usually leave Acapulco in late March and would start back from Manila in July.[16] The commander of a galleon would be well paid, anything between 50,000 and 100,000 pesos for a round trip.[17]

Until the late 1570s the Pacific Ocean seemed to Spanish travellers like an immense lake on which no system of defence seemed at all necessary, at least before Sir Francis Drake made his famous journey around the world between 1577 and 1580. Even then, no serious attempts at an arrangement for defence were made until much later.

By the 1580s the trade of the galleons had become the overwhelming *raison d'être* of the Spanish settlers in Manila. Little was done to develop the splendid agricultural possibilities of the region around the city, and even the gold resources of Luzón – which were not negligible – were neglected. The market (in South America) was for Chinese silks, porcelain, and other fine craft products. The Manila galleons were largely manned, of course, by Spaniards, but the Chinese brought to them almost all of the goods to be shipped and did most of the mercantile and skilled craft work in Manila, including making porcelain.

China itself, therefore, was now in the Spaniards' sights. It was known to be a well-managed, vast, rich land with stone-walled cities, many of them much bigger than any in Europe. The first indication of the possible ambition of the Philippine Spaniards appears in a document of July 1569:

> It will be first of all necessary to settle in these islands [that is, the Philippines], because it would not be right to pass among so many islands and depths as these ... on the coast of China with ships so big but with only rowers. For to conquer so big a territory which has such a large population, it will be necessary to have people ready to deal with anything which may happen, even though I have been informed (including by them) that the Chinese are in no way bellicose.[18]

Thus Legazpi himself wrote home to Spain; and thus the intoxicating dream of a Spanish conquest of China began to be formed. Already in 1569 some Spaniards in the Philippines tried to pass themselves off as Chinese. It was not a deception which worked very well.[19] Actually, even before that missive, Legazpi had written to King Philip proposing the building of six galleys to 'run down the coast of China and reach agreements with the mainland'.[20]

On 12 December 1567 the town council in Mexico had also suggested to the king that the Crown divide up not only the Islands of the West (the Philippines) but also those off China.[21] The admirable Catalan historian Manuel Ollé argues that from the beginning of the

Philippine connection, the Spaniards had begun to collect information about China from both Chinese and Philippine merchants, and later from Chinese immigrants and traders in the Philippines known as *sangleyes*.[22] Legazpi was soon showing himself more than ever the conquistador, since he told the king that 'with God's help, and not too many people, we could easily subject them'.[23]

The idea of the Philippines as a stepping stone to China was thenceforth never far away. On 10 August 1571 the Augustinian Fray Martín de Rada (whom we have already met in this chapter) wrote from Manila to the viceroy in New Spain, Enríquez de Almansa,[24] about his efforts to establish a mission in China, for some *sangleyes* had decided to return from the Philippines to near Canton – including one or two who had become Christians. These had agreed to lead two friars to China.[25] Rada had with him in his monastery there for six months a Chinese named Canço, who could not go home because of the monsoon. As they slowly overcame the barrier of language, Rada made himself very well informed about the Chinese political system and civil service both in the late sixteenth century and in previous times. For example, if a man were able enough, he could pass an examination when young and then be appointed to administer a remote province. Such was life in the Ming empire.

A little later, on 22 August 1571, Legazpi wrote to Viceroy Enríquez too, this time about a journey to China which he himself was considering. In his letter he described the Chinese as 'Indios Chinos'.[26] Legazpi had every reason to be optimistic about his chances of being accepted in China, since some of his sailors had saved the crew of a big Chinese junk which had been wrecked off the island of Mindero, south of Manila. The Chinese talked of this act of generosity when they reached home, and many official presents followed.

Eighteen months later, Viceroy Enríquez (who had never hidden his interest in the Philippines) gave instructions of a new kind to Juan de la Isla, one of Legazpi's captains, to carry further the discovery of China. He was to be given three good ships by Legazpi. King Philip had personally approved this plan in what seems to have been a mood of euphoria after the battle of Lepanto in October 1571. These instructions not only endorsed a journey of exploration to the coast of China but also 'a seizure of Chinese lands' (*toma de posesión de las tierras chinas*).[27] This amounted to royal approval of the idea of expansion into China.

These plans were still at a premature stage when Legazpi died of a heart attack in his city of Manila in August 1572, a year after he had written his letter to Viceroy Enríquez. Appropriately Fray Martín de Rada gave the eulogy to Legazpi in the Augustinian church of Saint Fausto in Manila.

One of the most remarkable changes brought about by Legazpi and the first generation of conquistadors in the Philippines was that the islands were now politically unified for the first time. Previously, as we saw in chapter 24, they had been self-organized as hundreds of little independent entities. But the archipelago had now been turned into a province according to the traditional Castilian or Roman model, the viceroyalty of New Spain being the real source of authority, although the supreme authority of course remained the monarchy. There now existed on most of the islands the familiar municipal system organized around town halls and military squares. This was supported in the countryside by friars, whose monastic orders became important as landowners in perpetuity, thus differing from the shorter-term secular *encomiendas*.

Legazpi divided the Philippine islands into twenty-five *alcaldías mayores*. In the main town of each island a small Hispanic population was established, including as a rule a magistrate (*alcalde mayor*) and a small following of councillors. The land nearby had been allocated to *encomiendas*, it is true, but *encomenderos* in the Philippines were expected to live in the *pueblos cabeceros* (head villages) of provinces, unless they were in Manila (or even in New Spain, as some were). Meanwhile the friars used their unique opportunity shrewdly. They defended the indigenous people against the abuse of settlers, but in the process the *naturales* became their congregants – virtually their subjects.[28]

By the end of the sixteenth century, the Spanish presence in the Philippines was firmly enough established for the colony to be a starting point, or springboard, for the penetration of China.

# 26

# The Temptation of China

*The city of Chincheo. The common houses are small, the main streets broad and very beautiful, full of shops of every kind. Every street is like three of the best ones in Spain, because every street is as broad as the principal one. There is a tremendous abundance of food, chicken, capons, duck, pork . . . [and] a great deal of fruit and vegetables, such as cherries, pears, grapes, peppers and many dried fruits as well as nuts and chestnuts. There are also many bakers' shops, grocers, and offices of all kinds such as silversmiths, tailors, shoemakers and sail-mercers.*

Relación del viaje del jesuita Alonso Sánchez a la
China, probably 1582 (AGI, Filipinas, leg. 79, no. 10, 34)

The conqueror Miguel López de Legazpi, as we have seen, died in 1572. His successor as governor of the Philippines was temporarily Guido de Labezanes (Lavezaris), the son of an Italian bookseller established in Seville, who had gone to the New World in 1536. Labezaris had spent some years in the rewarding Moluccas, he had sailed in López de Villalobos's expedition as purser, and he had returned to Europe via India. He was then with Legazpi from the beginning of the Spanish adventure in the Philippines. Like Legazpi he was mature, being over sixty years old when he was called upon to rule in Manila.

During Legazpi's time, Labezaris had subjugated several important islands such as Betis and Lubao. He also founded the Spanish city of Fernandina, in the north of Luzón, which later became known as Vigán. His activities made him the natural successor to Legazpi.

One of the unresolved issues facing Labezaris as governor was how to manage the growing trade with China, which had begun on a regular basis from Fukien in particular, but also the trade from the ports of Emuy and Chincheo. More broadly, Labezaris was also deeply concerned with the so-called 'China project' (*la empresa de China*), as it was known in the Council of the Indies as well as in Manila. That meant essentially an expedition to submit some parts of China, perhaps all of it, to Spanish rule. That Spanish ambitions remained apparently limitless can be seen from reading an extraordinary letter which was sent on 11 January 1574 by the chief notary of Manila, Hernando Enríquez Riquel. Enríquez Riquel, who like Labezaris had been with Legazpi throughout his governorship, thought that China could be conquered by fewer than sixty 'good Spanish soldiers'. Some six months later, on 30 July, Governor Labezaris sent home to Castile two maps – one of China in its relation to Luzón, the other of China and Japan. They were neither detailed nor accurate. But they were optimistic. The governor told the Council of the Indies that he hoped for Spanish expansion into all these rich lands. He added, 'I trust that this work, worthy of gods, to enlarge and increase Your Majesty's dominions and lordships, will, at the same time, carry the true knowledge of the Catholic faith to so many people who are barbarous and blind, as they are in these parts where Heaven (*el Gran Cielo*) may enter.'[1] The Spaniards in Manila were quite aware of the riches that any contact with China might bring.[2]

The prospect of a Spanish invasion of China preoccupied Viceroy Enríquez in New Spain. In October 1574 he reported to King Philip that he had not yet found the right person to lead the expedition against the Ming emperor. He had been looking for a new Hernándo Cortés.[3] Juan Pablo de Carrión, one of Legazpi's first lieutenants and one experienced in the Moluccas, had thought for some time that those 'Islands' (China, that is) were so well provided for, so very rich and so large in comparison with the Philippines that it would be worthwhile doing anything to reduce them to Spanish control. He offered to fit out at his own cost two ships accompanied by two pinnaces to undertake the conquest of China.[4] All he asked for in return was the title of 'admiral of the South Seas and the coast of China'. These were heady proposals. The king was evidently interested. But he was deeply concerned at this time by the problems in which he was still engaged in the Netherlands, despite the departure for that territory of the great Duke of Alba.[5] He hesitated.

Other events overshadowed these magnificent possibilities. Thus in the course of 1574 two fine hospitals were built in Manila, one for Spaniards, the other for Filipinos and Chinese, both being managed by Franciscans. A third hospital, that of San Gabriel, was later established for Chinese alone by the benign Dominicans. Then, in November 1574, Chinese corsairs led by the pirate Lin Fung (known as 'Limahon' to Spaniards) – his base was in Taiwan (Formosa) – heard from the *sangleyes* of Manila how few Spaniards there were in the Philippines. Lin Fung decided to sail immediately to Luzón with an army of about 2,500 men. He was, however, held up, and then pressed back, by Labezaris and Legazpi's grandson and heir, Juan de Salcedo. Two hundred Chinese seem to have been killed and several Spanish ships were burned. But Martín de Goyte, for a long time Legazpi's chief deputy, was also killed. This was a serious setback, for as we have seen in earlier chapters, he had played a major role in the early conquests of the islands. Lin Fung retained a presence in the islands by establishing a stockade on the river Payno near Manila.

Other difficulties delayed action over China. In September 1574, King Philip saw two Augustinian friars, Fray Diego de Herrera and Fray Juan González de Mendoza,[6] who brought complaints about the way that the new *encomenderos* were already committing abuses on Luzón.[7] Fray Martín de Rada had also sent a note to the king attacking unjust conquistadors such as Pedro de Cháves and Juan de Salcedo for telling villagers on Luzón either to submit peacefully and pay appropriate tribute, or to accept war. The *naturales* had refused to yield, and Chávez and Salcedo had attacked the villages. Rada insisted that that was far from being a just war. Then Governor Labezaris sent Philip a counter-declaration to the effect that the splendid pilot-friar Andrés de Urdaneta had sanctioned these wars since they seemed the only way to convert the East to Christianity. King Philip seemed satisfied.

Next year, in March 1575, the ever active Salcedo led a skilful attack on Lin Fung in his stockade outside Manila, with two large ships and six small ones. A long siege ensued. While it was under way, the Chinese sent an official embassy to the Philippines under a member of their imperial court, Wang Wanggoa, and the Spanish governor promised to hunt down and hand over to them Lin Fung, dead or alive. Wang took back to China with him a small delegation of Spaniards whose instruction was to found a commercial enclave on the coast of Fujián, comparable to that which the Portuguese were establishing in Macao. That new colony would be led by two Augustinians, Fray Martín de Rada and Fray Jerónimo de Marín, the first of whom we know,[8] and the second of whom had just come from New Spain; perhaps Marín was a grandson of Cortés's Genoese-born captain, Luis de Marín (Marini). These two friars were served by a small unit of Spanish soldiers headed by an Asturian companion of Legazpi, Miguel de Luarca, an *encomendero* of Otón in the north of Luzón. They were supported by Pedro de Sarmiento, also an *encomendero* of Otón. (Luarca had a large *encomienda* with 1,600 *naturales*; Sarmiento had one with 300 *naturales*.)[9]

This first Spanish expedition to China set off from Manila on 12 June 1575. It was an astonishing enterprise. Some of those on board the vessels believed that they were about to rival Cortés's and Pizarro's extraordinary achievements in New Spain and Peru respectively. Commercial judgements affected matters too. The plan was that the secular members of the expedition, including Luarca and Sarmiento, should return soon to Manila. The friars, left to their missionary work, would seek guarantees for their safety by going to Hangzhou, where they would meet a Chinese military force which would conduct them to the emperor.[10]

On 17 July the Spanish expedition reached Fuzhou in Fujian, where the governor, Lin Yaohiu, received them. He sent on to the emperor in Peking a request from Fray Rada and Fray Marín that they should be allowed to remain in China in order to preach Christianity and learn the language. The governor suggested to the two friars that they should return to Manila to await the emperor's decision. If it was affirmative, the governor would send a ship to bring them back.[11]

In fact, the Chinese had already declared their willingness to allocate the Spaniards an island facing Taiwan in the bay of Amoy or a hillside on the mainland, once they had delivered the pirate Lin Fung to them, for that pirate had done as much damage to the Chinese as to the Spaniards. The Spanish military force returned to Manila.

But the defeat of Lin Fung was more difficult to achieve than the Spanish missionaries had imagined. He managed to flee his stockade in August 1575, apparently with the help of Filipinos who gave him the wood needed to build the junks in which he could escape. Matters were not helped by the new acting governor of the Philippines (after the sudden death of Governor Labezaris), Dr Francisco de Sande Picón, a protégé of Juan de Ovando, the current president of the Council of the Indies. He was undiplomatic and, to begin with, unable to respond to Chinese tactfulness.

But Sande soon showed superior qualities. He had studied law at the university of Salamanca and had been a prosecutor, as well as a magistrate in charge of criminal cases in New Spain, where he meted out harsh justice, as the sons of Cortés and their friends remembered only too well.[12] In the Philippines, Sande learned quickly and, after some initial mistakes, he began to govern with prudence, energy, and wisdom. His five years in power in Manila were a time of consolidation during which he extended a warm welcome to the first Franciscan mission (his brother was a Franciscan in Guatemala) and carried out military conquests on the coasts of the islands of Joló and Mindanao. His instructions included the provision to 'procure communication and secure dealings with the people of China and make them understand the warm faith of the Kingdom of Spain'.[13]

Macao by this time had become a new Portuguese settlement under the authority of distant Goa. The arrangements proposed by China to Spain were similar to those envisaged for Portugal in respect of Macao.[14]

Meantime Wang and his delegation of Chinese had returned to Manila, but they had become irritated by Dr Sande's clumsiness at the beginning of his mandate and again left the Philippines for home. They took with them not only the Spanish merchandise which they had gathered, but also the presents of silk, cotton, and horses which they had intended to present to the late Governor Labezaris. They took with them too Fray Rada and a companion, Alberto de Alburquerque, but decided to abandon them on the (Philippine) island of Bolinaco at the tip of the gulf of Lingayon, near Cape Bojeador.[15]

Yet 'the China project' could not be forgotten. By midsummer 1576, Governor Sande was still full of plans for the conquest of China.

Thus he wrote to King Philip on 6 June that he had devised a plan for the subjugation of the Ming dynasty with four to six thousand men who would be sent from both New Spain and Peru. They would come armed with arquebuses or pikes for which they themselves would pay.[16]

Sande also sent home to Spain a detailed picture of China under the Ming emperors. He knew that the dynasty had been in control of the country for over 200 years. The Ming had restored the independence of China from the Mongols, and they were jealous protectors of it. Under their rule, no foreigner was allowed into the land and such a celestial empire had no need of either trade or imports. The exception was that the Portuguese had in 1557 secured trading facilities in Macao, which allowed European manufactures to reach the fairs in Canton where they were exchanged for Chinese silk. For commercial reasons both that invaluable commodity and European firearms began to be taken once a year on a 'great ship' to Japan.

The emperor, the remarkable Shen Tsung, was as cultivated as he was long-lived. He was famous for many cultural achievements. Peking had been the Ming capital since 1421. The fifteenth century had witnessed many extraordinary expeditions – Chinese naval vessels had even sailed to Africa, for example – but by the sixteenth century the age of such adventure seemed to be over.[17] Governor Sande made several suggestions as to how a Mexican-Peruvian task force could conquer China by means of a very just war ('*una guerra justísima*'). Were not the Chinese soldiery beneath contempt, being 'idolatrous, sodomite, given to robbery and to piracy?' But China had many precious metals and its smallest province had a population greater than that of New Spain and Peru put together. Sande thought that the most intelligent course would at first be to conquer just one province, on the assumption that its population would welcome the conquerors as liberators. Had that not happened in New Spain in respect of Tlaxcala? Spain would then use Chinese collaborators as stepping stones to ensure the subjugation of other provinces.[18]

Sande knew that the ordinary Chinese – the *naturales* of China – were neither simple nor foolish, nor indeed liable to be frightened. They seemed impervious to threats. On the other hand, they could be manipulated by force, he thought, or by gifts of gold or silver: 'If they were in any way comparable to the people of New Spain, Peru, Tierra Firme (Venezuela) or indeed anywhere else in the Americas, sound reasoning could also have a good effect.'[19]

The writer and soldier Bernardino Escalante, in his *Discursos de la navegación* published in 1577, criticized the Spanish plans for the invasion of China. He argued that the despatch of a peaceful embassy there would easily be able to explain to the Chinese the benefits of submission to Spain.[20]

Sande wrote along these lines to King Philip in 1576 and he sent an almost identical letter a day later to the Council of the Indies. But neither king nor Council replied.

Two years later, in 1578 (not in those days a long interval to elapse in international correspondence of this importance), King Philip received another letter from Sande. In it the governor explained, using a comparison which Hernando Cortés too had employed, that merely by the subjugation of the Philippine islands, Spain had conquered 'an empire larger than Germany', which contained much wealth and substantial tributaries, and people accustomed to change their lords.[21] Soon after this letter was sent, seventeen Franciscans reached Manila, led by Fray Pedro de Alfaro, possibly a son of Cortés's moneyed backer, Luis Fernández de Alfaro.[22] There they established the monastery of San Felipe, later renamed as that of Saint Gregory the Great. Pedro de Alfaro then left for China, leaving behind Juan de Plasencia who set to work to compose a grammar and a vocabulary in Tagalog, the Philippine language. Plasencia later claimed that he had converted 250,000 *naturales* in nine years.

Alfaro's achievements were no less remarkable. He wrote a long letter describing his experiences from the walled city of Canton.[23] Several of his fellow Franciscans accompanied him and he had a Chinese interpreter, a *sangley*, whom everyone called 'Juanico'.

Fray Pedro de Alfaro described how he and his fellow friars were detained in Canton by a vast sceptical crowd which pressed so hard on them that they could not move easily. The friars insisted that all they wanted to do was to preach God's word. Alfaro, meantime, had come to the conclusion that the kingdom of China constituted one large well-populated city with a demanding but efficient government.[24] He thought that the Philippines were an archipelago which could become the centre of a vast East Indian (Spanish) empire stretching from Goa in India to Macao in China.

The dream of conquering China was catching on in the Americas. Thus Diego García de Palacio, judge of the *audiencia* (Supreme Court) in Guatemala, proposed in a letter to King Philip of March 1578 that it would be both desirable and easy to recruit 4,000 men in central America and embark them on six galleys to be sent direct to China. The king was asked to assist by contributing a good supply of bronze with which to make guns.[25]

The reaction of the Council of the Indies, like that of the king, to these bold ideas was complex. The Council members had no doubt that they were responsible for whatever decision the Crown took in relation to China. Having read numerous reports, they believed the country to be 1,100 leagues long by about 500 leagues broad; its circumference or border, therefore, was about 3,000 leagues. There were, the Council thought, fifteen provinces in which there were almost 300 cities, over 1,000 walled smaller towns, and presumably a vast number of villages as well. The emperor also had an army of nearly 5 million men which guarded his realm with arquebuses, pikes, and swords, bows and arrows, as well as war machines of different kinds, such as were used in sieges in Europe. So it was possible, the Council argued, that 'the conquest of China might not be quite so easy as Judge García de Palacios had thought'.[26]

The king was also becoming doubtful. On 29 April 1579 he wrote a crucial letter to Governor Sande from San Martín de la Vega, a small town between Madrid and Toledo. 'As for your idea of conquering China which you think we ought to do now, it really seems that this is not the moment to discuss the matter. Rather ought we not to seek to procure good friendship with the Chinese; and you should not act against them nor accompany them with their corsair allies nor give any cause of indignation against us.'[27]

The previous year, in the summer of 1578, Sande had led a journey of reconnaissance from Manila south to Borneo. Fray Martín de Rada had been with him, but he died on the journey. In August, Fray Jerónimo Marín, by now the most experienced of the Augustinian friars in the Philippines, arrived at the court of Spain with letters from Sande. This led the king and the Council of the Indies to consider anew their policy towards Peking. It was not, however, until February 1581 that Marín, backed by Fray Francisco de Ortega and Fray Antonio González de Mendoza, set off from Castile for New Spain and then across the Pacific, with presents for the emperor of China which included pictures by the fashionable Valencian court painter Alonso Sánchez Coello.[28] These included an equestrian portrait of King Philip, another of Philip standing alone, a third of the late Emperor Charles, a fourth of Our Lady, and a fifth of Christ.[29] Sánchez Coello received 400 pesos for these labours. None of these pictures appear to have survived, although Sánchez Coello's work is recognized throughout Spain.[30]

These Chinese schemes were, however, now obstructed by a new viceroy of New Spain, the Count of Coruña,[31] who had the support both of his outgoing predecessor, Martín Enríquez, and of ex-Governor Sande of the Philippines; Sande had returned to New Spain after leaving Manila (en route for Guatemala where he was to become president of the Supreme Court). Effective opposition was also mounted by Gabriel de Ribera, formerly chief magistrate in Cebú in Legazpi's day and currently *procurador general* of the Philippines, who was also temporarily in New Spain. All these grandees (Sande in particular) thought that a Spanish embassy might be snubbed in China and the presents be refused.

Two years after this despatch of presents, King Philip found himself needing to instruct yet another new governor in Manila. Sande had died and his successor, appointed in August 1578, was Gonzalo Ronquillo de Peñalosa.[32] He was the son of a mayor of Valladolid, Rodrigo Ronquillo, who had become famous for his ruthlessness during the rebellion of the *comuneros*. Philip reminded the new proconsul of the law of 1573 governing new conquests – that all slaves, both those taken in territories which the Spanish conquered and those whom they had brought with them, were to be freed. Ronquillo was also to ask the new Bishop of Manila, the enlightened and clever Dominican Domingo de Salazar, whether the new law might be carried out 'more mildly and with less hardship to the Christian community'.[33]

Ronquillo arrived at Manila with a large number of friends, relations, and would-be immigrants – perhaps as many as 600. In 1580, indeed, more Spaniards reached Manila than in any other year in the sixteenth century.[34] Ronquillo expected that his governorship would be a life appointment, and in an inquiry of 1581 he explained how he had spent most of his money fitting himself out for the Philippines. Those who went with him included his nephew Diego, who would succeed him.

Ronquillo was a man who energetically made his presence felt. He established a ghetto for the Chinese at Parian outside Manila, under the shadow of his own heavy artillery. He also conquered the province of Cagayan, whence he despatched Juan Pablo Carrión to dislodge a Japanese pirate who had established himself there. Carrión proceeded to found two more towns, Nueva Segovia and Nuevo Arévalo. Ronquillo also imposed a 3 per cent tax both on imports to and exports from China. That was opposed both by Spaniards and Chinese, but it remained in place (as taxes have a habit of doing).[35] He then instituted a tax of 3 per cent on all goods imported to or exported from the Philippines. This echoed a similar tax paid in Seville, which, however, was lower (2.2 per cent).[36] All these taxes were gradually raised, while sales of pearls incurred their own duty.

Ronquillo's ecclesiastical colleague, Bishop Salazar, was one of Spain's most remarkable holy men. He was born at La Bastida near Salamanca in 1513 and at the university of Salamanca he had been, for a time, a pupil of Francisco de Vitoria, the philosopher of the idea of a just war. In 1546, Salazar was received into the monastery of San Esteban, Valladolid, as a Dominican. Then he went to New Spain where he learned Nahuatl well enough to be able to preach in it. By 1556 he was demanding that the Indians of New Spain should not have to pay tithes. In 1558, Salazar participated in Tristan de Luna's expedition to Florida and in 1561 he became prior of Santo Domingo in the city of Mexico. Judge Alonso de Zurita recalled him as an admirable churchman, 'exemplary in every virtue, an excellent preacher, whose doctrine was substantial and learned'.[37] He became a missionary in Zacatecas, in the centre of what is now modern Mexico, and later presided at the trial of the rebel sons of the conquistadors in 1567.[38] He seems then to have gone briefly to Tierra Firme but soon returned to New Spain.

Inspired directly by Bartolomé de las Casas, Salazar began to write in Latin a book on the history of Spain's rule in the Indies, and the justice of it, which he planned to present in Spain to the Council of the

Indies. No trace of the work can now be found, but all the same Salazar did present in Spain the case for the Indians, and was briefly imprisoned by the papal nuncio for his pains. He preached the cause of the Indians at the monastery of Atocha, where Las Casas had recently died, and there, whatever the nuncio felt, Salazar attracted the attention of the king. Philip was always on the look-out for promising clergymen and he named him Bishop of Manila. Salazar did not arrive at his post in the Philippines until September 1581, where he found his new bishopric to be a place in which 'sheep were without a shepherd'. Predictably, he immediately took up the cause of the indigenous people, but he also antagonized everyone by 'the austerity of his disposition and by his desire to dominate'. One soldier said that he should moderate his language. If he did not, the soldier warned him that he could hit a mitre at fifty yards with an arquebus. Salazar also alienated the Chinese by insisting that converts to Christianity cut off their pigtails.[39] Ronquillo complained to King Philip and instructed Salazar to withdraw. The governor wrote to the king that 'so firm was Salazar in his opinions that he did not call it an opinion but a truth'.[40]

Bishop Salazar held a meeting of all the superiors of the locally based orders. They discussed a series of rather inflammatory questions posed by the bishop. First, 'Is hardship a sufficient reason for the Governor to neglect to proclaim and execute a decree?' Second, did 'a petition presented to the King on behalf of the masters of slaves provide any reason to neglect the law?' Third, 'must the Governor enact laws immediately or could there be a time allowance?' The superiors answered 'no' to all these questions, saying, in particular, that the 'freedom of Indians [the natives] could not be deferred since it was a matter of divine law'.

Had Philip persisted in the plans for the conquest of China, Salazar would surely have been appointed the first Archbishop of Peking.*

---

* I recognize the help in this chapter provided by reading the letters and reports contained in the wonderful Number 10 of the document known in the Archivo de Indias as Filipinas legajo 79. See p. 416, note 18, for a summary of the riches there.

# 27

# The Conquest of China

*It would be easy to reduce them to our faith if we had liberty to preach to them.*

Fray Martín Ignacio de Loyola, 1585

In March 1582, Fray Alonso Sánchez, the son of workers, an able and self-confident Jesuit from the small town of Mondéjar near Guadalajara, who had gone to New Spain in 1579, finally set out in three ships for what he called 'the kingdoms of China' (*los reynos de China*). He was accompanied by a 'brother assistant', Nicolás Gallardo, two Franciscans including Fray Juan Pobre, and twenty-two sailors. The Jesuits in the Far East were rivals of the Dominicans, but they found it easy enough to collaborate with Franciscans.

The expedition encountered a ferocious storm between the Philippines and China and lost their ships near the Chinese port of Zhelin, which was famous for its smuggling. Fray Sánchez, in an absorbing account of this expedition, talked of 'the mountains of water which surrounded our frigate'. 'What a terrible night,' exclaimed the pilot at one point. Sánchez and his colleagues were eventually rescued and deposited in Zhelin.[1]

Fray Sánchez followed his report of this shipwreck with a description of what he and his companions saw next in China. On Palm Sunday, he recalled:

> all the Chinese ships were assembled, each with four large flags of silk on their poops, with many pennants, and much use of pikes and preparation of arquebuses as well as other pieces of iron, and bunting. The

soldiers were massed on either the ships or nearby on land inside a fortress dominated by large war animals [dogs] characterised by clothes of yellow whose justification we could not guess. We could not imagine that they wanted to kill us but about noon we realised what the point of it all was because, on land, they made parade with much attention to detail for even those at sea fired off guns, and showed their arquebuses, and made the biggest noise and show of bravery that they could.

That done, three captains came to tell us that the *supi* (that is, the provincial governor) had sent us for the *lanbo*. We did not know what that was and we clamoured to be sent to Canton saying that we could with difficulty do so in a single frigate. We were offered three boats, one of which was clean and beautiful, and laquered so splendidly as to seem like a sword with no cobweb or insect to be seen. There were wardrobes so large that one could sleep in them.

We came out through one of the big bays of the sea, past many islets . . . we sailed that night and, by Monday of Holy Week, we were already getting ourselves into small carts. We travelled across land where we saw workmen comparable to those of Spain in some beautiful fields, ploughing the land with buffaloes, except for one where there was a camel, with a plough.

The fact that the Chinese had arquebuses, as well as ploughs, thanks to the Portuguese was a disturbing warning.

Sánchez and his companions were then sent to an unidentified fort where they experienced an alarming interrogation with very poor interpreters. The four religious men were allowed to go up to Guangzhou – that is, Canton – while the sailors were detained at Zhelin for seven months.[2] The churchmen travelled across many rivers, thereby submitting their horses to a serious challenge, and then they were stopped at Huizhou for further interrogation about their purposes. There they met the local governor, who allowed them to go on to Guangzhou, where they met some Portuguese merchants and some Jesuits. They were able to stay in the ample dwelling of a Neapolitan Jesuit, Miguel Ruggiero from Salerno, being saved from imprisonment – or worse – by a Portuguese captain, Maca Matias Panela, who by then knew some Chinese, and who had many Chinese girls at his beck and call.[3]

While this epic journey (so it seemed since it was the first land journey by Spaniards in China) was under way, a meeting of the Spanish clergy in Manila was discussing the legality of plans for the absorption of the entire archipelago of the Philippines as well as the reform of the *encomiendas* in those islands.[4] Early in 1582, Governor Ronquillo sent a ship from Manila south to the Moluccas under Francisco Dueñas to tell the Portuguese on the island of Tidore of the recent union of Spain and Portugal, and also to gather information about the island of Ternate.[5] Meanwhile in the Philippines the governor concentrated the Spanish forces in New Segovia, a new town which had been created to the north-east of Luzón, as a platform for future expansion towards China.

In May 1582, Fray Alonso Sánchez arrived in Macao after his hard months of journeying. There he met Fray Alessandro Valignano, the able Neapolitan and Jesuit 'Visitor' who was at that time on his way from Nagasaki to Europe. Valignano came from a rich Italian family in Chieti near Pescara, in the southern Abruzzi. His parents had been friends of the formidable Pope Caraffa (later Pope Paul IV), formerly their local bishop. Valignano himself was an abbot by the time he was eighteen and a canon when he was twenty. Then he was promoted to become master of novices in Rome and soon rector of the Jesuit college at Macerata near Ancona. He was named Visitor to the Jesuit missions in India by the fourth general of the Jesuit order, the Dutch Everard Mercurian. For Mercurian's purpose, 'India' included Japan.

Valignano was the father of the Jesuit colonization of the Far East. It was he who told his brilliant disciple, Matteo Ricci, who in 1582 had arrived in Macao from Italy, to learn Chinese, having himself been in Macao for ten months in 1577–8. Valignano had a low opinion of the imperial Mogul government in India; he also thought the Indians no better than beasts. Having been at first impressed with, and then disillusioned by, the character of Japan, Valignano was left with China as the focus for any enthusiasm for colonization that he might still have in the Far East. In 1578 he wrote, accordingly, to Mercurian's successor, Fray Claudio Aquaviva. He believed that the Japanese could help the Spaniards conquer China ('the people of Japan could do much to help what His Majesty was planning to do in China').[6]

A Chinese official from Macao told Fray Alonso Sánchez that he understood the deceitful conduct of Valignano and others accompanying the friar, so Sánchez thought it best to hide. He embarked for Japan in early July 1582, in a large junk commanded by a Portuguese merchant, Bartolmeu Vaz Landeiro, but he was wrecked off Formosa. Sánchez and a Portuguese fellow Jesuit, Francisco Pérez, eventually made a boat which enabled them to return to Macao by early October of that same year.

High politics, however, had remained as active as ever. In June 1582 the royal agent – or high official – in Manila, Juan Bautista Román, sent a letter to King Philip in which he urged full commercial relations with China, but that, if they could not be peacefully established, he would now favour the use of military force to impose them.[7] Governor Ronquillo, however, told the king that military forces in the Philippines were at that time inadequate for an invasion of China. That could only be achieved, as others had said, by the despatch of a large body of troops from New Spain.[8] Ronquillo had also sent Fray Alonso Sánchez back to Macao to see whether there were any signs there of activity on behalf of Don Antonio de Crato, the claimant to the Portuguese throne, and moreover to secure the submission of Macao to Portugal's new Spanish king, Philip II. Sánchez was also to gain information about Chinese morale in case an eventual military operation should be decided upon.

An expedition led by the resolute Portuguese captain Matías Panela had gone north from Macao to Zhaoqing in April 1582. Another, directed by Jerónimo de Burgos and accompanied by seventeen Franciscans and a unit of soldiers, followed in June. Panela was asked by the local magnate in Zhaoqing, Chen Riu, to sell him silver. Instead, Panela gave him a watch, a rare present at that time, which turned out to be a great success.[9] Macao was further consolidated as a Portuguese enclave. Permission for a Jesuit mission in China was agreed and the brilliant and inventive Italian Matteo Ricci would soon embark on his extraordinary twenty-seven years as a Jesuit in the country.[10]

In Manila the death of Governor Gonzalo Ronquillo in February 1583 had a tragic aftermath. At his funeral in the new, makeshift cathedral, high wax tapers were lit on his catafalque. A strong wind blowing through these set fire to the timber roof of the building. The cathedral burned. Only the Holy Sacrament was saved. Most of the bamboo-built houses in Manila, thatched as they were with tinder-like leaves, burned down. The new bishop's palace was also consumed by fire, as were the main parish church, with its organ, a warehouse full of goods waiting to be taken to New Spain on the next Manila galleon, many books from the library of Bishop Salazar, and the small fort with all its weapons. Artillery and other bronze guns melted in the heat. Most of the 700 Spaniards were rendered homeless and ruined. The 3,000 or so Chinese (*sangleyes*) in Manila also suffered.

It was left to Diego Ronquillo, the nephew of Governor Gonzalo, to set about the rebuilding of the city. Diego assumed the role of temporary governor. An important part in the recovery was also played by a determined Jesuit, Fray Antonio de Sedeño, who taught the Filipinos to make tiles and bricks and who was responsible for the first stone fort as well as the first lime kiln in the new colony. At this stage in Spanish imperial history the Jesuits were the driving force behind most innovations.

Now it is that we start to see the beginning of a distinctive Spanish-Philippine architecture, characterized in Manila by the Augustinian and Franciscan monasteries, the fine hospital of San Clemente, the great Dominican church the Real Colegiata de San José, and the church-fortress of Nuestra Señora de Guia. A new market was also soon built, including 150 shops in which 600 Chinese lived. Other outbreaks of fire, however, ruined these reconstructions at the end of the century.

In Manila, Bishop Salazar and the new governor rarely saw eye to eye. The bishop was humane and just, whereas the governor was a narrow-minded bureaucrat. But in early 1583 they did agree on one matter: that 8,000 Spaniards and a fleet of about twelve galleons would be enough to enable the king of Spain to take over the Chinese empire. The bishop admitted that in the past he had supported the contention of most learned men in Spain and the empire which condemned the conquering of Indian peoples. But, since his arrival in the Philippines, where he had been able to consult further well-informed and God-fearing persons, he had changed his mind. Cortés would have agreed.[11]

On 27 March 1583 the resolute Jesuit Fray Alonso Sánchez returned to Manila from China to agree with Bishop Salazar. It was impossible, Sánchez said, to preach the gospel in China without further military backing. He talked confidently of the startling benefits, both commercial and political, which the affair of China (*la empresa de China*) could yield. He himself thought, though, that as many as 10,000 men would be needed to complete the conquest, many more than Ronquillo and Salazar had suggested. But to seize Canton a mere 200 men would be adequate. Thereafter the Chinese cities would quickly adapt to the new power. Fray Sánchez easily convinced Governor Ronquillo of his point of view because of his direct experience of China.[12] He spoke of Matteo Ricci as so close to the Chinese that he seemed almost to be one of them.[13]

In the spring of 1583 a meeting was held in Manila of a committee responsible for the 'China project', at which the king of Spain's right to proceed with a conquest of China was discussed in detail.[14] Bishop Salazar began what he called a 'juridical theological process' on the conquest, which he sent to Pope Gregory XIII (Ugo Buoncompagni) as well as to King Philip. The bishop formulated a questionnaire containing eighteen questions which he wanted to put to eight witnesses. The questionnaire was influenced by the memory of Francisco de Vitoria, the theologian of Salamanca under whom Salazar had studied. There was a discussion by the committee as to whether any such conflict could be described as 'a just war': Salazar now thought that it could be, but considered that the moment had not yet arrived to proclaim that. Shortly afterwards a new Supreme Court was established in Manila to oversee not only the Philippine archipelago but also the mainland of China ('whether discovered or yet to be discovered'). Officials attached to this somewhat improbable institution began to function the following year. On 9 June 1583, Fray Sánchez sent a long letter to Claudio Aquaviva, still the general of the Jesuits, asking for ecclesiastical backing for the idea of a military force to be sent to China.[15]

Two weeks later, Governor Diego Ronquillo wrote home to Madrid that the character and grandeur of China was such that, though it contained some of the richest and most fertile places in the world, conquering the country would provide little difficulty. He again thought that a mere 8,000 men would be necessary.[16] In early 1584, Bishop Salazar seems to have changed his mind again about the wisdom of an invasion, but on 25 June of that year Francisco Cabral, a Portuguese Jesuit, wrote a letter from Macao to King Philip giving unconditional support for the plans to invade and conquer China. Since China was an empire, the conquest could be as easily assimilated as the Mexican and Inca empires had been. The Spaniards would seize the emperor in Peking as they had seized Montezuma and Atahualpa, and everything would then fall into place. In both spiritual and material ways, the conquest would be beneficial. Cabral thought that 10,000 soldiers would probably be necessary, but 2,000 would be easy enough to recruit in Japan. The Jesuit fathers already there could recruit them.[17] It was assumed that the Chinese already in Manila would welcome such arrangements.

Despite the heightened expectations of an invasion and subsequent conquest, more pacific plans already under way were still pursued. Thus, on the same day that Cabral wrote his letter, 25 June, the royal agent in Manila, Juan Bautista Román, proposed to send to the emperor in Peking the presents which had been collected for him years before – namely a grand suit of velvet and brocade, a Flemish tapestry, as well as some Venetian glass, some half-boot mirrors, curiosities from Milan, hogsheads of red and white wine, a few swords, and the paintings by Sánchez Coello previously mentioned.[18] Alas, these presents would confuse rather than delight the Chinese.

A few weeks later, however, Fray Alonso Sánchez repeated that any idea of a peaceful evangelization of China was impossible and that it was necessary, even urgent, that a conquest be swiftly embarked upon. Everyone who knew the Chinese agreed that the discussions under way 'had to end with China sharing the fate of New Spain and Peru'.[19]

The Chinese traders in Manila were incidentally now moved to a special Chinatown – called Baybay or the Parian – inside the city walls. This quarter was becoming a thriving place of orderly streets surrounding a lake accessible by ships from the sea. In the middle of the lake, there was an island reserved for punishments. There were then about 4,000 *sangleyes* in Manila, and there was a Catholic church in Baybay from 1589.[20] The Chinese, who dominated all trades for many generations, from bookbinding to baking, from tavern-keeping to stone masonry, were sometimes removed from this area for short periods, but essentially they remained there till the nineteenth century. The collaboration of two enemies, or cultures, seemed to work perfectly.

Some Spaniards were nonetheless unhappy at the tide of bellicosity which seemed to be rising in the Philippine colony. The Portuguese thought that war would ruin their commercial interests. The Portuguese Jesuits distanced themselves as far as they could from Fray Alonso Sánchez, and disapproved of his comments about what seemed their relaxed way of life. Fray Antonio de Mendoza, *provincial* of the Jesuits in New Spain, wrote to Aquaviva in January 1585, pointing out that Alonso Sánchez was really saying that 'with pacific methods we could do nothing in China and that it was not only legal but necessary to send an army to conquer it'.[21] It was plain that Mendoza was critical.

So too was the great Fray Alessandro Valignano, who also wrote to Aquaviva in alarm about the ideas of Alonso Sánchez who, he said, 'with his fantastic and wandering spirit', had committed 'so many indiscretions that I remain shocked'.[22] Aquaviva eventually wrote back to Mendoza that Sánchez had made many mistakes in respect 'to China and writing about the need for war against it'. He suggested that Sánchez should perhaps be sent home where, in some different circumstances, he would be more serviceable and less inconvenient.[23]

About this time Fray Martín Ignacio de Loyola, a Dominican who, as we have seen, was a resourceful traveller and great-nephew of the founder of the Jesuits, wrote that though the Chinese

> commit many mistakes, it would be easy to reduce them to our faith if we had liberty to preach to them. If there is an eclipse of the sun or the moon they hold it for certain that the Prince of Heaven wants them to quit their lives and out of pure fear, they place themselves in that way of thinking . . . even though they both believe that the sun is a man and that the moon is a woman. They believe in the immortality of the soul and that, in another life, they will receive the prize, or the punishment, which they deserve, according as to how they have lived on earth . . .'[24]

In the spring of 1586 a committee of all the religious orders in the Philippines was called together by Dr Santiago de Vera, the president of the Supreme Court. Vera had been a judge in Santo Domingo and in Nueva Galicia, New Spain, and he had been the magistrate most concerned with crime in that viceroyalty. He was himself undecided on the matter of the '*empresa de China*'.[25] Despite that, he could not prevent Fray Alonso Sánchez becoming the representative who would report back to Spain what the *provinciales* had decided and who harangued the meeting about the many benefits of securing China for

Spain. But perhaps haranguing was not necessary, for the *provinciales* were generally persuaded of the benefits of these audacious plans.

They thought that China could be prised open by a relatively small force led by the governor of the Philippines. The soldiers were to be recruited from anywhere in the king's realms, although Basques were to be preferred. Had not the Philippines been conquered by a Basque, Miguel López de Legazpi? Had not El Cano been a Basque? Six thousand indigenous fighters could also be recruited from the Philippine Islands themselves. Five hundred slaves would be useful to the enterprise, as would 6,000 Japanese soldiers.

Some Japanese had allowed it to be known that they too would favour a Spanish invasion of China. The powerful *daimyo* (feudal lord) Konishi Yukunaga, indeed, offered 6,000 men to Spain for use in war in either China, Borneo, or the Moluccas.[26]

Careful attention would have to be paid to the arms needed. Money would also have to be found to suborn certain mandarins who could be expected to rebel against their emperor if they were properly financed. The form of invasion would have to be carefully devised, and certainly it should not be like the conquest of Cuba (allowing the west of the island to be forgotten while the east was developed).[27]

Bishop Salazar, back in the fold on these matters, wanted the spirit of Vitoria to characterize the conquest. Matteo Ricci and Michele Ruggieri from Salerno, the Italian Jesuits now established in China, thought that they should remain where they were till the eve of the invasion. But then they would be asked to inform the Spanish invaders what reaction to expect from the Chinese. Salazar meanwhile was beginning to reveal himself as no friend of the Chinese and believed that, in the Philippines, 'they were introducing the *naturales* to sin and corruption'.[28]

Ricci was of a different frame of mind. He and Ruggieri had gone to Chao-ch'ing near Canton on the invitation of the governor there and the viceroy of the province. They had been offered land on which to build a church, freedom to travel, and a promise of protection. Thus began, in 1588, one of the most remarkable European adventures. Ruggieri went home and would try to persuade the Pope to send an ambassador to China. But Ricci remained in China, establishing Jesuit houses first at Chao-ch'ing, then at Nan-ch'ang, the capital of Kiangsi province, next at Nanking, the southern capital, and finally at Peking. This stay was made possible by another visit from Ruggieri during which he gave to the Chinese viceroy the present of a remarkable watch – 'a beautiful little machine made of brass which struck the hours without anyone touching it'. He also presented him with several kaleidoscopes. These objects, wrote Hugh Trevor-Roper, were 'to prove powerful engines for the spiritual conquest of China'.[29]

The resolution of the *provinciales* ended in March 1587 with an acknowledgement of the large number of new *encomiendas* which would be available in China, not to speak of the new judges, dukes, marquises, and viceroys who would be named, as well as the universities, monasteries, and military orders which would be established. From the beginning the conquest would be openly dedicated to *mestizaje* (mixing blood), since Chinese women were 'extremely serious, honest, retiring, faithful and humble subjects of their husbands, and usually of great grace, beauty and discretion'. The conquest of China, the *provinciales* thought, would surely be followed by that of India, Cochin China, Cambodia, Siam, the Moluccas, Borneo, and Sumatra. Spain seemed thus to be embarking upon a triumphant procession!

Those who knew anything of the politics of the Spanish empire recognized that it would take some time to gain royal approval for any such plans; and so Governor Ronquillo began to make preparations in a very leisurely fashion for his military entry into China. Fray Antonio Sedeño began to build a defensive wall around Manila. Three hundred men commanded by Martín Pérez de Olzabal arrived in April in Manila from New Spain. This meant that there were then over 900 arquebusiers in the islands. Francisco de Luján then arrived from Bayamo (the third-largest city of Cuba) with ninety would-be soldiers for the intended war in China. One of the ubiquitous Rojas family, Juan Bautista, was his lieutenant. These were the earliest contingents of the planned Spanish army of invasion. Perhaps Rojas would soon become Marquis of the Yellow River, and Luján would become the Duke of Peking!

At the end of December 1587, Fray Alonso Sánchez, the representative of the monastic orders, at last returned home and had an audience with King Philip at the Escorial which lasted two hours. It was a sensational occasion which must rank high in the annals of the history of the Society of Jesus. Sánchez gave the king a memorandum entitled 'On the quality and state of the Philippines in general'. The paper included positive descriptions of the archipelago and gave an imaginative impression of the riches which might be expected in the future. The islands could of course be an important staging point for trade with China. In this first talk, Father Alonso followed the instructions of the general of his order, Claudio Aquaviva, and was silent about the 'China project'. But he did leave with the king a paper entitled '*De la entrada de China en particular*'. He told Bishop Salazar and others such as the Dominican Juan Volante and the Franciscan Jerónimo de Burgos that he did not discuss the idea of entering China in the form of an invasion nor even mention it, 'but I did give my secret paper to the King'.[30] That document, alas, does not seem to have survived.

The consequence was that in March 1588, King Philip established a committee (*junta*) specifically to study the despatches of Fray Alonso Sánchez and his recommendations, along with the proposals of the religious men of Manila. Fray Miguel de Benavides, a Dominican, begged that his order might be represented on the committee. But in the end the body which was to decide what to do about China consisted of the president of the Council of the Indies, Hernando de la Vega, in whose veins public service flowed; four members of the Castilian Council of War; Alonso de Vargas; Juan de Cardona, an admiral, who had played a part in the great victory of Lepanto and for a time had commanded the galleys of Sicily; Juan Idiáquez, an experienced secretary; and Cristóbal de Moura, Philip's chief Portuguese adviser. On the committee there was also Pedro Moya de Contreras, who had been Chief Inquisitor in New Spain as well as the archbishop there. Of these men, Idiáquez had already been won over by Fray Alonso Sánchez to the idea of an invasion of China. Moya was open to persuasion. Vega, however, was a career civil servant from whom nothing in the way of interesting ambitious proposals could be expected.

The remarkable Father Sánchez now wrote a third memorandum for the king entitled '*Relación de las cosas particulares de la China*'. In this he talked of the great wealth of China which it would be desirable to harness to Spain. He called the plan to invade and conquer China 'the greatest enterprise which has ever been proposed to any monarch in the world'.[31] It would seem that even now, Sánchez did not go into details, but he spoke rather of the importance of military protection for the planned missionary endeavours.

In the discussion by the *junta* in Madrid, there was considerable talk of the legitimacy of conquest. The *junta's* deliberations were then interrupted by the arrival of the Franciscan Jerónimo de Burgos and the Dominican Juan Volante. They participated in a new debate on the relation between preaching and military power. There is no exact record of what was said, but we know that Father Alonso again insisted that successful missionary work in China necessitated military commitment. In the remote past, he admitted, the gift of tongues had produced miracles, but now armed force was called for. One had only to consider the success of arms in carrying the cross to the Americas earlier in the century.[32]

In early August 1588, Fray Alonso Sánchez had a second audience with the king at the Escorial. But this coincided with news of the defeat of the Armada Invencible on 8 August, an eventuality which necessitated the king's sudden return to Madrid. A third audience was prepared, but the Jesuit realized that this was not the moment to talk to his king of another great maritime expedition.

A new governor of the Philippines, Gómez Pérez Dasmariñas, was told that he was not to make war till he had consulted 'the churchmen and lawyers as well as captains and other experienced men on matters of law and theology'. Yet Pérez Dasmariñas was a *gallego* nobleman of a military frame of mind and a strong character who had begun his government career as a protégé of Bishop Antonio de Pazos when he was president of the Council of Castile. Pérez Dasmariñas had commanded coastal ships against the corsairs of Barbary and had been *corregidor* (municipal councillor appointed by the Crown) first of Cartagena and then of Murcia. He was apparently named to the governorship in Manila on the recommendation of Fray Alonso Sánchez himself, who would have liked to accompany him back to the archipelago. But Aquaviva, still general of the order of the Jesuits, wanted Sánchez to go instead to Rome to talk about his remarkable plans with the Pope.

Who could have resisted such an invitation? Sánchez went to Rome where, by pure chance, in a mere eighteen months he was received by no fewer than four pontiffs: Sixtus V, who died on 27 August 1590;

Gregory XIV, who died on 16 October 1591; Innocent IX, who died on 30 December 1591 after only two months in office; and Clement VIII, who survived till March 1605. Long before that, in October 1593, Governor Pérez das Mariñas had been murdered by Chinese oarsmen interested in jewels while he was on a boat setting off for the Moluccas. Despite a long-running feud with Bishop Salazar about matters of protocol, he had been among the most benign of Spanish governors, as his publication, *Ordenanzas sobre las vexaciones de los Indias* (*Rules of the Problems of the Indies*), showed in 1592.[33]

The scheme of a military expedition to conquer China was never explicitly abandoned. Had it been approved, it would have amounted to the grand climax of a hundred years of Spanish conquests and struggles. Had it happened, it would surely have brought less deprivation to China than occurred under the Manchu dynasty and certainly less than under the terrible communist era in the twentieth century. After the Mongols, China had become used to living under a dynasty of foreign origins. The Manchus were not Han Chinese. Alas, though, on his return from Rome, Fray Alonso Sánchez seems to have moderated his opinions, in the interest of maintaining the unity of the Jesuits, and Bishop Salazar wrote, falsely, to warn the king that Father Sánchez had never really represented the views of the *juntas generales* of the orders. The idea of establishing an entrepôt, a Spanish Macao, on the Chinese mainland continued, and Manila remained a thriving market city of its own.[34]

King Philip refrained from approving any further Chinese adventures. Had England been defeated in 1588, the Spaniards would no doubt have had a new policy. In 1600, Luis Pérez de las Marinas proposed a scheme to Philip III for conquering China, to be preceded by the conquest of Thailand.[35]

Fray Alonso Sánchez is a perplexing figure, not least because he abandoned as an older man the vehemence of his views early in life. It seems that he never really ceased to advocate conquest as a way of securing the conversion of China but he came to think that he needed general Jesuit approval or support. Bishop Salazar was a great man for whom, as a prince of the Church, equivocation came naturally.

At the end of the sixteenth century the Philippines seemed much as the Caribbean had been a hundred years before. There were many criminals, plebeians were enabled to live in greedy prosperity, and there were innumerable footloose soldiers of fortune and of Castilian origin. Probably 200 Spaniards lived in Nueva Segovia, about the same number in Santísimo Nombre de Jesús, 100 in Nuevo Cáceres, 80 in nearby Nuevo Arévalo, and about 700 in Manila.[36] The Jesuit historian Pedro Murillo Velarde wrote: 'The Spaniards in the Philippines who settled into the archipelago look on it as an inn, not as a permanent home.' Manila offered the enticements of many gambling dens, luxurious goods, exoticism, and rich living. Silk was the most important item brought from China, but also cattle, horses, and even chicken, fruit, and vegetables were imported. Many types of porcelain were available too.[37] Manila was a city of many peoples, not just Spaniards and Filipinos but also Malays, Chinese, and Japanese. The Chinese staged comedies and the ever-active Fray Alonso Sánchez even went to one before the Inquisition suddenly prohibited them in 1592.

The governor was not only captain-general of the islands but president of the Supreme Court.[38] The system of justice functioned reasonably well, being a copy of Spanish practices. In the provinces, the Indian *pueblos* were governed by *gobernadorcillos* – petty rulers. From 1589, there was a protector of the 'Indians', a post associated with the Bishop of Manila.[39] But the Chinese also often suffered. The Dominican Miguel de Benavides, already Bishop of Nueva Segovia and soon to be the second Archbishop of Manila, wrote to King Philip about mistreatment of the Chinese and added that there were 'no worse enemies of Christian behaviour than many of your Majesty's representatives'.[40]

Benavides was a typical member of the Spanish elite in the first generation after the conquest of the New World. Born in 1553, he came from a comfortably wealthy agricultural family in Castile and had studied at the university of Valladolid as at the Dominican college of San Pablo in that city. He became a Dominican aged fifteen. He studied further at the famous college of San Gregorio next to San Pablo. In 1586 he became chief nurse in the monastery of Santo Domingo in Valladolid. The next year he set off for New Spain and then in 1590 for the Philippines. He went to China with Juan de Castro. He returned briefly to Castile in the 1590s. In 1601 he was named Archbishop of Manila, and he died in that post in 1603. Competent, conventional, noble, but unimaginative, he was a characteristic empire-builder such as was often created by Europeans to administer territories which greater men had earlier won.

Our history of Spanish adventures in the Far East ends with the tale of the beautiful *gallega* Isabel de Barreto, a reminder that the enterprises in the Pacific and the New World were sometimes undertaken by women. In 1586 aged about twenty she married Admiral Álvaro Medaña, renowned as the most eligible bachelor in Peru and a man who then led an expedition which included forty women. They had set off from Lima in four boats in June 1595. Some 350 passengers were on board, heading for the so-called island of Guadalcanal, named after a village in the Sierra Morena which they all knew. They were then to search for the 'Solomon Islands', so called by Medaña for reasons that remain unclear. Because of Isabel's close friendship with the viceroy's wife, Teresa de Castro, Marchioness of Cañete, to whom she had been a favoured lady-in-waiting, Medaña named a new archipelago which he discovered en route the Marquesa Islands – a name they retain to this day. Isabel was haughty and high-handed, attributes which inspired her companions on the expedition to mock her as the queen of Sheba – an appropriate comparison since they were, after all, looking for the Solomon Islands. When Medaña died, Isabel took command, continuing to seek the Solomon Islands; but instead, in 1595 her expedition reached Manila.

She remained there a year before marrying Fernando de Castro, the nephew of a previous governor of the Philippines, who since 1593 had been commander of the Manila–Acapulco galleon and fleet. They announced their intention of seeking anew the Solomon Islands and jointly set out from Manila on 10 April 1597 with new ships, cattle, seeds, and even colonists. They sailed first for Acapulco and then Peru, to seek approval for their governorship of the elusive Solomons. The crew, however, signed a document demanding a return to New Spain. Isabel tore it up and declared that anyone who signed anything similar would be hanged But Isabel's project to go eastwards foundered, and ultimately she died in Spain in her native Galicia, leaving an imperishable memory.[41] She was not the only great adventurer in the sixteenth century to die at home.

# 28

# Epilogue: The Age of Administration

*We would not venture to describe Alexander the Great as a 'traveller'.*

Melchor Cano, *De dominio indorum*
(Biblioteca Vaticana MS Lat. 4648, 1540, f. 39v),
cited in Anthony Pagden, *Spanish Imperialism
and the Political Imagination*, 24

*Colonies are like fruits which cling to the tree only when they ripen.*

Anne-Robert-Jacques Turgot, Baron de l'Aune,
quoted in J. R. Seeley, *The Expansion of England*, 17

*There never was a Spanish Empire.*

Anthony Pagden, *Spanish Imperialism
and the Political Imagination*, 3

*Under Philip we pass from the epoch of conquerors to that of
the organization of conquered territories.*

Fernández Álvarez, *Felipe II y su tiempo*, 361

The greater part of the first printing of Cervantes's *Don Quixote de la Mancha* was apparently shipped to the New World in 1605. (It seems likely that Mateo Alemán's novel *Guzmán de Alfarache* reached Lima and Mexico at much the same time.) The entrepreneur Juan Ruiz de Gallardo from Ayamonte told his friends in the New World that he had amused himself in 1605 reading *Don Quixote* on his way in his galleon, *Nuestra Señora de los Remedios*.[1] Thereafter the book was a great success in the Americas, whose new masters, as we have amply seen, were determined to give the conquered inhabitants their own, distinctly Spanish, institutions, language, religion, and culture. In this, as in so many other ways, Spain conceived herself as the heir of Rome.

Spain in 1600, after all, controlled the largest collection of territories the world had seen since the fall of the Roman empire. In respect of size, it was an enterprise superior to that founded by Rome. The Piedmontese writer Giovanni Botero, an ex-Jesuit who became secretary to Cardinal Carlo Borromeo and tried to destroy the reputation of Niccolò Machiavelli, wrote in 1607 that the Spanish dominions surpassed every empire which had ever been. There was 'such a variety of peoples, divided by language, customs, religion and by every other quality'.[2] This enterprise was also, of course, divided by distance.

Spain itself had been united in its peninsula since the seizure of Navarre in 1510, and Aragon and Castile had had the same monarchs since 1479. Granada had ceased to exist as an independent emirate in 1492. As we saw in chapter 19, Spain had also been united with the still unwearied Portugal and its variegated intercontinental empire since 1580.[3] Spain also dominated Italy, where a Spanish viceroy ruled Naples and Sicily. The Spanish king was the hereditary Duke of Milan, while Tuscany, even if grand-ducal, and formally independent, and Medicean, was almost a Spanish dependency. Thanks to Alessandro Farnese, King Philip's nephew, Spain had also maintained her mastery of at least the southern Netherlands, the ancestor of modern Belgium.[4] The twentieth-century thinker José Ortega y Gasset said that the unity of the peninsula had been 'achieved in order to hurl the energy of Spain to the four winds'.[5] Whether or not he was right as to any conscious purpose, that spreading of Spanish energy around the globe certainly occurred.

In the New World, Spain governed a whole combination of dependencies and colonies which constituted kingdoms (*reinos*) of their own, or parts of Greater Spain, *Magnae Hispaniae*, no different from Aragon or Naples. The meticulous French historian of the Atlantic Pierre Chaunu called the Spanish empire a 'dynastic grand alliance of seventeen crowns'.[6] The French, it is also true, had already made piratical sallies into both Brazil and Florida, while the English would soon discover an interest in North America which thereafter never flagged.

Not all these Spanish possessions were in good shape. Thus a political scientist from Genoa, Paolo Mattia Doria, said of Naples that it seemed 'like a human stomach filled with ulcers'.[7] A famous bandit, Mario Sciarra, maintained there a virtual army of well-armed malefactors. But by 1600, despite these rickety European corners, the whole of the empire in the New World had been enriched by a vast number of remarkable religious buildings – cathedrals, monasteries, churches, convents, and places of burial – which showed that the conquerors expected to remain where they were for ever. Although the original conquests had been astonishingly swift, they had produced architectural monuments on the grandest scale.

The philosophy which governed the Spanish empire is not difficult to unravel. The great theological writers of the sixteenth century, Fray Francisco de Vitoria, Fray Domingo de Soto, and Bishop Bartolomé de las Casas, thought that they knew exactly the nature of the Spanish dominions. The two works by Vitoria, *De Indis*, from a lecture given in 1539, and *De justitia et iure*, another from 1556, make that evident. But these writings revolved around a discussion of what rights the indigenous Indians had in their own lands before the arrival of the Spaniards and what rights the Spaniards had after the conquests. As has been indicated throughout this book and its predecessors, the Spaniards went to great lengths to analyse the moral basis of their conquests.[8] Vitoria argued that Spaniards had every right to settle in the Indies, and trade there too, so long as they did not ill-treat the *naturales*. They also had a duty to seek to convert them. But if the Indians refused conversion, the conquistadors had no right to impose Christianity by force. Only if the Indians wantonly attacked Spaniards – as it was claimed that pioneer conquerors, such as Francisco Hernández de Córdoba and Juan de Grijalba in Yucatan, respectively in 1517 and 1518, had been attacked – were the conquistadors entitled to fight back and even enslave them.

The indigenous population was supposed to fit into a larger whole. Dante's idea of the desirability of a universal monarchy was much discussed in the sixteenth century, despite the fact that his *De*

*Monarchia* (1312–13) was soon on the Index of Forbidden Books. That work was a philosophical argument about the necessity of a single world monarchy. Book II argued that the Holy Roman Empire was best equipped to fulfil that role. Peace, Dante insisted, could be most successfully secured by a single all-powerful monarch.[9] A German writer, Georg Sauermann, who was in Spain in 1520, had also argued the case for a universal Christian monarchy in his *Hispaniae consolatio*. That book had been dedicated to Bishop Ruiz de la Mota, who had served and advised the Emperor Charles;[10] Ruiz de la Mota had spoken in 1520 of his one-time pupil as the emperor of the world.[11] The idea of Christian unity was also a preoccupation of Erasmus and Juan Luis Vives. Giovanni Botero too thought that the human race would live most happily if it were all brought together under a single prince. How excellent if one could travel everywhere using the same language and the same money![12] The new empire in the Americas could surely be seen as a step towards this desirable consummation.

King Philip II's tutor and Las Casas's enemy Ginés de Sepúlveda wrote two clever essays, *Democrates Primus* and *Democrates Secundus*, about the Emperor Charles's universalist claims. The first, however, was essentially an argument for resisting the Turks, the second a defence of Spanish conquest in the Americas. Even Las Casas, often seen as the enemy of empire, thought it right that the kings of Castile should be 'universal lords, emperors ruling over many lands'.[13] In 1563 it was rumoured that Philip would be proclaimed King of the Indies and of the New World in its entirety, and the idea remained in the air.[14]

The notion of empire was not well developed in the sixteenth century. The best historian of the concept was indeed Ramón Menéndez Pidal, the director of the Spanish Academy of Letters, who lectured on the imperial ideas of Charles V in 1937. In exile from Spain because of the civil war, Menéndez Pidal sought to establish the Emperor Charles as the leading spokesman of a Spanish crusade against Islam. Through Charles, all Europe would be Hispanicized. This, Menéndez Pidal insisted, was the emperor's own idea, not that of his far-sighted chancellor, Mercurino Gattinara. Its transfer to the New World was proclaimed by a preceptor of Charles, Bishop Pedro Ruiz de la Mota, in the Cortes in Corunna in 1520 – an appropriate authorship since the bishop, a *converso* from Burgos, was a first cousin of one of Hernando Cortés's brigantine captains who were so important in the final battle for Tenochtitlan.[15]

These new Spanish dominions had been conquered and converted by a variety of leaders: an Italian of course, Columbus; several *extremeños*, such as Ovando, Cortés, Sandoval, Tapia, the Alvarados, the Pizarros, Soto, and Valdivia; a *sevillano* in the shape of Ponce de León; and a Castilian, Diego Velázquez. The explorer of the Amazon Francisco de Orellana was also an *extremeño*. There was the Montejo family from Salamanca. In Paraguay and Argentina, there were Basques such as Martínez de Irala and Juan de Garay, a kinsman of the conqueror of Jamaica. Miguel López de Legazpi, conqueror of the Philippines, was also a Basque, as was El Cano, Magellan's lieutenant. In the northern part of the new continent of Latin America there were Córdobans, such as Jiménez de Quesada and his indefatigable nephew, Antonio de Berrio.

The diverse regions from which these conquerors originated are a reminder that the Spanish empire in the Americas was a great undertaking from most parts of Spain, not one driven by a single province, even though Andalusians provided most of the emigrants of the first generation. In Fernández de Oviedo's history we read of Spaniards from different parts of the mother country who eventually realized their common ancestry in the Panamanian jungle.[16]

Portuguese, Flemings, Greeks, Florentines, and Frenchmen were also particularly to be found on most of the great expeditions. Magellan of course was Portuguese, and everywhere in the great journeys of his time his compatriots were to be found. Pedro de Valdivia had Germans with him in Chile. The early Franciscans in New Spain included many remarkable Frenchmen and Flemings.

The Spaniards also usually had the help of indigenous allies in their conquests. The Maya, the Totonaca, and above all the Tlaxcalteca played an essential part in the conquests of Cortés. Nor in New Spain should one forget the assistance of the Otomí. In Peru, the Cañari Indians were also helpful to Pizarro and the Spanish cause.

Soon after the conquests, in all parts of the Indies, marriages or associations began between conquistadors and the daughters of native noblemen. Thus in New Spain, Leonor, a daughter of Montezuma, married the conquistador Juan Paz and then Cristóbal de Valderrama. She received Ecatepec in the neighbourhood of the city of Mexico as an *encomienda* in 1527; thereafter her daughter, another Leonor, and her son-in-law, Diego Arias de Sotelo, enjoyed it until 1568.[17] Another daughter of Montezuma, the apparently beautiful Techuipo who, after being one of Cortés's mistresses, allowed her name to dwindle eventually into 'Isabel', married Alonso de Grado, next Pedro Gallego, and finally the *extremeño* Juan Cano of Cáceres. In 1526 she received the *encomienda* of Tacuba, which remained in the hands of the Canos till the end of the colonial era.[18] There is a poem which recalls Techuipo:

> Who are you who sits beside the Captain General?
> Ah, it is Doña Isabel, my little niece,
> It is true she brings me prisoners.
>
> (Quien eres tú, que te sientas junta al capitán general?
> Ah es doña Isabel mi sobrinita!
> Ah es verdad, prisioneros son los reyes)

A son of Montezuma, Pedro, founded what became a grand *criollo* family with a Spanish title (Count of Montezuma) and the *encomienda* of Tula, which eventually became converted into a prosperous estate (*estancia*).[19]

The explorer-captains were accompanied by enlightened men of the Church such as the *sevillano* Las Casas and the Basque Zumárraga in New Spain; the semi-royal Fray Pedro de Gante with his hospital next to the convent of San Francisco in Tlatelolco; the austere Motolinía, also active in New Spain; and Fray Domingo de Salazar, Bishop of Manila, who had an active career both in New Spain and the Philippines. The scholar Fray Bernardino de Sahagún, Julián Garcés, the benign Bishop of Tlaxcala, and the first enlightened bishops of Mexico, Michoacan, and Lima (Zumárraga, Quiroga, and Vicente Valverde respectively), were the doyens and intellectual fathers of a new American Church. Nor should we forget the first Spanish speaker of Nahuatl (the language of the Mexica), Fray Andrés de Olmos, who had the reputation of being able to preach in ten local languages.

The first generation of Franciscan pioneers in the New World – not just Motolinía – were remarkable men. Many were both brave and creative. They and their colleagues compiled lives of saints, sermons, selections from the New Testament, grammars, dictionaries, and manuals for preaching the catechism, all in Nahuatl. Over a hundred books in that tongue were circulating in the late sixteenth century, passing from one monastery to another. All three of the great mendicant orders (Franciscans, Dominicans, and Augustinians) made an impact and many Indians declared that they loved their friars. By 1600, there were about 1,500 friars in the New World.[20] But by then the Jesuits were making the biggest impression on the life of Spanish America. The next century would especially prize the life and work of Pedro Claver, a Catalan Jesuit, who worked for forty years at Cartagena de Indias as the 'apostle of the slaves'.[21]

Friar-architects, inspired improvisers not professionals, were responsible for about 270 religious monuments big and small in New Spain in the sixteenth century. Typically these were monasteries with a barrel-vaulted church and a walled atrium in front.[22] As Sir Nicholas Cheetham says, they represented a creative outburst comparable to what occurred in Europe in the Middle Ages, when a 'white mantle of churches seemed to cover the whole earth'. In Europe these churches looked like castles, of the spirit no doubt, but castles all the same.[23]

As important as these churchmen were, great architects were instrumental in carrying the ideas behind Spanish churches and palaces to the New World. Typical among them was Francisco Becerra from Trujillo, whose grandfather had worked on the final stages of the cathedral at Toledo and whose father was responsible for many buildings in Trujillo, Badajoz, and Guadalupe in Old Spain. Becerra himself went on to design the cathedral at Puebla in New Spain as well as the monastery of Santo Domingo in the capital, before proceeding to Peru and Quito, Cuzco, and finally Lima, where he designed the great cathedral. Town planners also translated the rectangular classical influences of old Europe to the centres of the main Indian cities in the New World. Many of the older towns had the beauty of symmetry which echoed not only Tenochtitlan but also Vitruvius's ideas, which had inspired the Renaissance in Italy.

In New Spain, the most remarkable development after the building of churches was the policy of *congregación*, the 'congregating' of the indigenous population in medium-sized towns, where they could be more easily cared for but also supervised.

The old agrarian system under which the land of a peasant would be held communally and allotted in plots to individuals was usually maintained, although those who had received the allocations had less time for their private farming activity than before the conquest. For most Indian farmers or peasants had to offer their tribute and labour to Christian missions as well as to the *encomenderos*, where these survived, and to the survivors among the old Mexican upper class.

Although the empire was diverse, it was held together spiritually by a series of feasts and celebrations. The religious processions which formed such a big part of life in Spain itself, whether in Holy Week or at the feast of Corpus Christi, or the celebration of a much-respected local martyr, were transported with devotion and energy to the New World. The Spaniards with Cortés celebrated Easter with a procession even before they had left the coast at Veracruz.[24] 'The Christian year,' wrote the historian Alejandro de la Fuente in his fine book about Havana, 'had its own rhythms and these rhythms were similar in all parts of the Empire.'[25] These events, religious by definition but with many elements of carnival and festivity, had a strong Castilian flavour whether they occurred in Madrid or Havana, Toledo or Veracruz. There were theatrical performances and games such as *juegos de cañas*, in which horsemen fought with wooden pikes. There were even bullfights. During these festivities the people honoured the king or the royal family as well as popular saints. The variety within the celebrations was as impressive as the similarity between them. But all were held in the newly built main squares of the new Spanish American cities.

By the time of King Philip the friars had realized, throughout the Indies but perhaps especially in New Spain, that their message of Christianity could be more easily accepted if it were clothed in ceremonial behaviour which echoed ancient practices. Thus Indian and European festivities and music would be cleverly blended. Indigenous colours would decorate Christian patterns. Such syncretism was consciously sought. But there were difficulties too: the friars generally condemned the drinking habits of the *naturales*. In New Spain the Indians' addiction to *pulque* was a scandal for the churchmen to attack. Nor did the Indians approve of the Spanish Church's insistence that they could have only one wife, especially in Paraguay where they saw how many Spaniards enjoyed a veritable harem of women.

Not far behind the architects or friar-architects in importance were the interpreters, of whom, during the conquest itself, Marina in New Spain must take pride of place, though she was followed by the clever but sometimes treacherous '*lenguas*' of Peru such as Felipillo.[26] By 1550 there were also many Spaniards who spoke indigenous languages – not simply Jerónimo de Aguilar in New Spain, whose linguistic facility had once been so essential to Cortés.

Finally there were the administrators, of whom the viceroys Mendoza, Velasco, and Enríquez were outstanding in New Spain, as was Francisco de Toledo in Peru. The Spanish Crown had no idea in 1500 that it would soon be called upon to provide courageous and determined administrators of the quality of those men. But the country rose magnificently to this extraordinary challenge. Sometimes these valiant men were assisted by remarkable judges (*oidores*).

The Spanish empire has been consistently denigrated in the rest of the world. Consider the case of the Cambridge professor J. R. Seeley, the historian of the British empire whose *The Expansion of England* sold so well in late Victorian Britain. Queen Victoria's daughter, another Victoria ('Vicky'), wrote to her mother in 1884, 'How I wish, dear Mama, that you would read that admirable little book *The Expansion of England* by Prof Seeley. It is wonderful and so statesmanlike, so far sighted and so fair.'[27] Seeley was the historian who reflected that the British empire seemed to have 'conquered and peopled half the world in a fit of absence of mind'.[28]

Yet whatever one thinks of Seeley's reflections on the British empire, his judgements about Spain are wrong. He talks only of 'the cruelty and rapacity of the [Spanish] empire'. He has not a word to say about Las Casas or Motolinía, nor about the noble activities of Franciscans in the sixteenth century. He has apparently not heard of Sahagún. The fact that Spaniards tried to explain in noble language the justification for their conquests passed him by. On this subject Seeley appears an ignorant and parochial ideologue.

Yet there were similarities in the two methods of government. This is a matter which Sir John Elliott has illuminated in his admirable book contrasting the Spanish and British empires. For example, in the late nineteenth century, wives of members of the political service in the British protectorate of Sudan were not allowed to go out to that country until their husbands had completed five years of service, and the same kind of rule had existed in New Spain.[29] We even find, also in the Sudan, that blue shirts could not be worn in the territory until the public servant in question had been there for two years. White shirts were considered more formal.[30] The judges of Peru with their prohibition of silk would have understood.

In this epilogue, the great achievements of the conquistadors should be recalled. Who better than Sir Walter Raleigh to bring to mind:

> the patient virtue of the Spaniards: we seldom or never find any nation hath endured so many misadventures and miseries as the Spaniards have done in their Indian discoveries; yet persisting in their enterprises, with invincible constancy, they have annexed to their kingdom so many goodly provinces as bury the remembrance of all dangers past. Tempests and shipwrecks, famine, overthrows, mutinies, heat and cold, pestilence and all manner of diseases, both old and new, together with extreme poverty and want of all things needful, have been the enemies wherewith every one of their most noble discoverers, at one time or another, hath encountered.[31]

Raleigh's political judgement was bad, but here however he managed to show both wisdom and justice.

The great American historian of Granada, Washington Irving, also made much the same point:

> The extraordinary actions and adventures of these men, while they rival the exploits recorded in chivalric romance, have the additional interest of verity. They leave us in admiration of the bold and heroic qualities inherent in the Spanish character which led that nation to so high a pitch of power and glory and which are still invincible in the great mass of that gallant people by those who have an opportunity of judging them rightly . . .[32]

The mention of chivalric romance is correct. As we have seen, the conquistadors were influenced by their reading of such novels as *Amadís de Gaula* or *Sergas de Esplandián*.[33] The fact that Bernal Díaz del Castillo compared his vision of Mexico/Tenochtitlan to a scene in *Amadís de Gaula* is interesting in itself. Bernal Díaz was a native of the well-known commercial city of Medina del Campo, and his father was, like Montalvo (the author of *Amadís*), a councillor there, so the conquest of New Spain could suddenly appear to him a dazzling illustration in a book opening onto one more great market.

Spanish adventurers and settlers in the New World were fascinated in those days by the realm of fantasy, sometimes appealing, often threatening. We have mentioned often enough the role of the Amazons. They were frequently rumoured to be nearby. Cortés mentions them at least twice, once in his fourth letter to the Emperor Charles, once in an instruction to his cousin Francisco.[34] Were they perhaps an attractive idea to the conquistadors? Martín de Salinas, a Spanish official who was charged with telling the emperor's brother Ferdinand, in Vienna, what was going on in Spain, once wrote to him an engaging letter which read:

> I can hardly exaggerate how much credence has been given to the report that seventy large ships have come into the harbours of Santander and Laredo bringing ten thousand Amazon women who have come to mate with Spaniards because of the reputation for valour and virility of our men. The arrangement was that any Amazon who became pregnant would give fifteen ducats to any man concerned for his labours and she would remain to give birth. If the offspring were male, the Amazons would leave them here; if female, they would carry them away.

This report caused the rates of the local 'ladies of pleasure' to fall, because of 'such a large and wealthy competition and because their male customers are so well remunerated for their trouble. And rest assured that this news has been considered so well founded that nothing else has been or is talked about.'[35] Salinas went on to comment intelligently enough about the general gullibility of the average citizen in the sixteenth century. What he does not notice is the fact that the conquistadors and many others wanted these fantasies to be true.

By the time the chivalric novels ceased to be popular, we have reached the end of the reign of Philip II and also an end to the era of spectacular conquest such as had characterized his time as monarch.

The heroic age in the history of Spain, and its expansion in the Americas, was at an end.

The speed with which the sixteenth-century conquistadors conquered such large territories on two vast continents, and the comparable success of the missionaries with large populations of Indians, stands as one of the supreme epics of both valour and imagination by Europeans. Spain supported those conquests with the charting of trade routes on an unprecedented scale. The home country's rapid construction of an administrative structure in the New World, which plainly derived from Mediterranean models, is remarkable.

The Spanish empire lasted three centuries, from the early sixteenth to the early nineteenth century. Its last remnants only fell in 1898, following the Spanish–American war in Cuba, over 400 years after Columbus had embarked for the Caribbean. Spain had left behind a Catholic religion and innumerable monuments, a tradition and much literature. Above all, it had created dependencies which matured successfully into the new independent countries of Latin America. Wars in this region are rare. In comparison with the rest of the world, Latin America now seems an oasis of peace.

Professor Roger Merriman spent some time in the last chapter of his history of the empire, *The Rise of the Spanish Empire in the Old World and in the New*, confessing himself uncertain as to why Spain declined. In his judgement, it was the 'very continuity of Spain's imperial tradition that furnishes the chief explanation of the suddenness of her rise and of her fall', and that fall was 'the product of a complex of different causes; and we are still quite as far from having reached any general agreement as to the relative importance of those that have already been assigned as we are in the case of those that have been given for the fall of Rome'. Perhaps the explanation derives from the fact that in many respects Spain did not decline.[36] Both New Spain and Peru in the seventeenth century were, as Octavio Paz put it in his splendid life of the poet Sor Juana Inés de la Cruz, 'peaceful, stable and relatively prosperous . . . The city of Mexico became larger, richer and more beautiful than Madrid.' It was a society stronger and more civilized than New England.[37] If one visits Latin America today, it is certainly reasonable to wonder whether the empire did ever end. It did not continue to expand after 1600 – that much is true. Brigands multiplied on the roads, shipwrecks were frequent on the high seas, one whole treasure fleet would soon be lost (in 1628). All the same the great empire remained the empire even though neither Philip III nor Philip IV called themselves emperors. Spain did not conquer China or Japan. But she retained a vast territory: from the Philippines to Cuba, from California to the straits of Magellan. In Europe she remained a great power if no longer predominant. Spain in the seventeenth century was a most cultivated country, as the work of Velázquez and Murillo, not to speak of Cervantes and Calderón, Tirso de Molina and Góngora, Quevedo and Lope de Vega, vividly reminds us. So does the palace of Buen Retiro of which so much remains.[38] One should not forget the poetry of Sor Juana. Pierre Vilar described even the eighteenth century in Spain as 'un très grand siècle colonial'.[39] Was there really decline? Decline from what and of what, Sir John Elliott pertinently remarks in his admirable memoir, *History in the Making*, adding that Spain was not really faced with decline but the 'perception of decline'.[40] In the seventeenth and eighteenth centuries, at least, there was not much by way of decline, in the sense that Gibbon saw it in Rome. The loss of Jamaica to Oliver Cromwell's navy in the 1650s might perhaps be an example, but that mild diminution was scarcely a catastrophe. In return there was the continued Spanish dominion in the Philippines, whose trade from China enabled the *criollo* elite of New Spain 'to enjoy Chinese porcelains and silks, and to think of themselves as the centre of the world, facing not only across the Atlantic to Europe but also across the Pacific to the fabled lands of Asia'.[41]

King Philip died in 1598, eaten away by fever, a tumour on his leg, and by gout – which had affected his hands – and other infirmities such as septicaemia, after a reign which had lasted in practice since 1542 when his father had first entrusted him with the Regency. He continued to work until 1 September 1598, his chief minister then being the able Portuguese nobleman Cristóbal de Moura.[42] The king died on 13 September in the Escorial, where he had been taken on 30 June in an articulated chair invented by his valet, Jean l'Hermite. His will was longer than that of his imperial father, but he demanded the same number of masses to be said for his soul: 30,000.[43]

Philip had imposed his dedicated and cultivated personality on his country, which has never forgotten him. He died as he had lived, and as so many had lived in the New World, a man of religion who hoped for help from the Virgin Mary as from other saints, above all Saint Anne and La Magdalena. He was in part a friar as well as a bureaucrat and his admiration for Saint Teresa of Ávila is something for which he is rightly remembered. But he was also a great lover of the paintings of Titian, whom he befriended and employed. He was, too, an architect-king and his Escorial remains an extraordinary achievement. His works and those of his deputies in the New World were many and noble. Both should be remembered by all Europeans as well as Latin Americans with pride. He died after a peace with France had already been made, at Vervins in May 1598, and while one with England was in the making. King Philip is at once considered as 'the Prudent King' but also the bureaucratic king, '*el rey papelero*', a king dominated by memoranda and paper. He took seriously his immense task of ruling an American as well as a European empire. He was from the beginning, as the Bishop of Limoges wrote, 'wholly devoted to his affairs, never losing an hour for he is all day among his papers'.[44] The king wanted to read everything and his wishes were respected. He spent the last three days of his life confessing his mistakes. Fernand Braudel, at the end of the greatest book written up till now about Philip and the sixteenth century, rightly commented that the king saw his task 'as an unending succession of small details. This is a man who sits silently reading at his desk annotating reports, distant and pensive . . . He was the sum of all the weaknesses and all the strengths of his empire.'[45] Both the strengths and weaknesses survive in our own and, let us hope, judicious remembrance.

Perhaps the greatest achievement of Philip was his inspiration which created a new Christian world in the Americas. Can one imagine in any other age the creative novelty which led to the construction of so many convents, monasteries, and churches? In 1586 the famous convent of San Jerónimo was built in the city of Mexico – solid, austere, and large, covering 14,000 square yards. There the poet Sor Juana Inés de la Cruz would later live the best years of her life, and there would be wonderful celebrations. Old Europe had had similar monuments to faith, but in the New World they were an astonishing innovation which articulated the good life for several hundred years. Sor Juana wrote a brief theatrical piece, a *loa*, which is a prologue to a play, usually performed on a royal anniversary. This *loa* was intended to celebrate the birthday of the queen of Spain, Marie Louise d'Orléans. Three faculties – Intellect, Will, and Memory – and three eras speak about music:

> Memory: I call upon Time Past,
> World's protocol, the roll where Fate,
> Through bodies of magistrates,
> All the ancient writings has analysed.
> Will: And I invoke Time Present
> So swiftly passing, pliant instant
> That he who praises you
> Starts in the present but in the past concludes!
> Intellect: I sing of Time Future
> Impregnable wall, lofty structure,
> To the Angel yet unknown,
> Whose secrets are reserved for God alone.[46]

# Appendix 1

## Some Statistics

The monetary unit most widely used was the real (34 or 35 maravedís). The maravedí was much used in Spain.

| | |
|---|---|
| 1 real = 34 maravedís | 350 maravedís = 1 ducat |
| 1 peso = 8 reales | 400 maravedís = 1 escudo |
| 1 peso de plata = 10 reales | 11 reales = 1 ducat |

1 quintal = 100 kg = 220.5 lbs

Source: La Fuente, 59

### THE ESTIMATED WEALTH
### OF COUNTRIES, *c.* 1600

| | |
|---|---|
| 9 million ducats in Castile | 3.9 million ducats in Venice and her empire |
| 5 million ducats in France | 6 million ducats in the Turkish empire |

Source: Braudel, I, 451

### STATE REVENUES IN SPAIN

Under Charles V ordinary expenditure (not counting war costs) exceeded revenue by 2 million ducats;
in 1566 the excess was 10,9443,000 ducats;
in 1577 the excess was 13,048,000 ducats;
in 1619 the excess was 26,000,000 ducats.

Note: A ducat in 1580 was worth approximately £100 in the money of 2014.

Source: Braudel, I, 533; II, 671n62

# Appendix 2

## Income from the Indies (in maravedís)

|  | Crown | private persons | total |
|---|---|---|---|
| 1556–1560 | 1,500,000 | 6,500,000 | 8,000,000 |
| 1560–1565 | 1,800,000 | 9,400,000 | 11,200,000 |
| 1565–1570 | 3,800,000 | 10,300,000 | 14,100,000 |
| 1570–1575 | 3,300,000 | 860,000 | 11,900,000 |
| 1576–1580 | 6,600,000 | 10,600,000 | 17,200,000 |
| 1581–1585 | 7,500,000 | 21,800,000 | 29,300,000 |
| 1586–1590 | 8,000,000 | 15,700,000 | 23,700,000 |
| 1591–1595 | 10,000,000 | 25,100,000 | 35,100,000 |
| 1596–1600 | 10,900,000 | 23,500,000 | 34,400,000 |

Source: Fernández Álvarez, *Felipe II*, 120

# Appendix 3

## Population of *Iberoamérica* towards 1570

### (According to Ángel Rosenblatt)

| territory | whites | blacks, mulattos, mestizos | indigenous | total |
|---|---|---|---|---|
| New Spain | 35,000 | 25,000 | 3,500,000 | 3,555,000 |
| Central America | 15,000 | 10,000 | 550,000 | 575,000 |
| Santo Domingo | 5,000 | 30,000 | 500 | 35,500 |
| Cuba | 1,200 | 15,000 | 1,350 | 17,550 |
| Puerto Rico | 1,000 | 10,000 | 300 | 11,300 |
| Jamaica | 300 | 1,000 | extinguished | 1,300 |
| Lesser Antilles | — | — | 20,000 | 20,000 |
| Colombia | 10,000 | 15,000 | 800,000 | 825,000 |
| Venezuela | 2,000 | 5,000 | 300,000 | 307,000 |
| Guaiana | — | — | 100,000 | 100,000 |
| Ecuador | 6,500 | 10,000 | 400,000 | 416,000 |
| Peru | 25,000 | 60,000 | 1,500,000 | 1,585,000 |
| Bolivia | 7,000 | 30,000 | 700,000 | 737,000 |
| Paraguay | 3,000 | 5,000 | 250,000 | 258,000 |
| Argentina | 2,000 | 4,000 | 300,000 | 306,000 |
| Uruguay | — | — | 5,000 | 5,000 |
| Brazil | 20,000 | 30,000 | 800,000 | 850,000 |
| Chile | 10,000 | 10,000 | 600,000 | 620,000 |
| TOTALS | 138,000 | 260,000 | 9,827,150 | 10,225,150 |

# Appendix 4

## Regional origins of the emigration to the Americas

| | percentages | |
|---|---|---|
| origin | 1509–1538 | 1540–1579 |
| Andalusia | 34.1 | 36.9 |
| Old Castile | 18.5 | 12.7 |
| New Castile | 11.8 | 17.5 |
| Extremadura | 16.7 | 17.7 |
| Leon | 8.8 | 5.4 |
| Vizcaya | 3.1 | 3.4 |
| Galicia | 1.5 | 1.0 |
| Murcia | 1.0 | 0.5 |
| Aragon | 0.8 | 0.5 |
| Asturias | 0.5 | 0.5 |
| Navarre | 0.5 | 0.7 |
| Valencia | — | — |
| Cataluña | 1.0 | 0.6 |
| Baleares | — | — |
| Canaries | — | 0.6 |
| Total Spanish | 98.3 | 97.8 |
| foreigners | 1.7 | 2.2 |
| Total | 100.0 | 100.0 |

Figures by Magnus Mörner

# Appendix 5

Total of the treasures, public and private, brought from each region of america

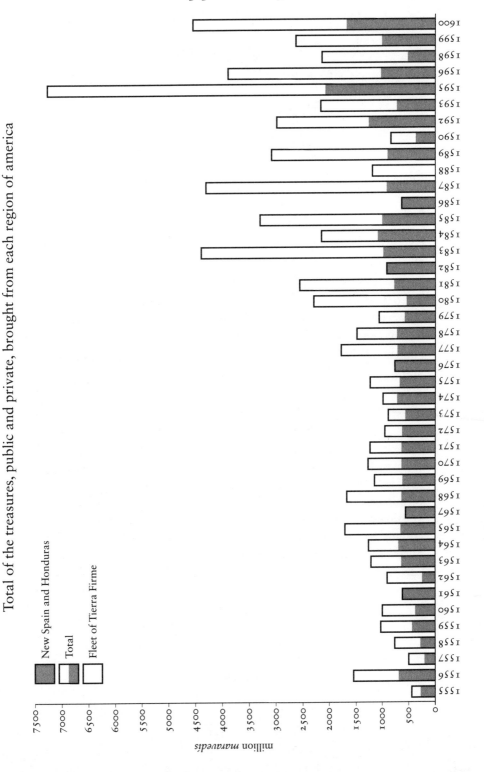

# Appendix 6

## Viceroys and Governors

### GOVERNORS OF THE PHILIPPINES

| | |
|---|---|
| Miguel López de Legazpi | 1564–1572 |
| Guido de Labezaris | 1572–1575* |
| Francisco de Sande | 1576–1580 |
| Gonzalo Ronquillo | 1580–1583 |
| Diego Ronquillo | 1583–1584* |
| Santiago de Vera | 1584–1590* |
| Gómez Pérez Dasmariñas | 1590–1593 |
| Pedro de Rojas | 1593* |
| Luís Pérez Dasmariñas | 1593–1595* |
| António de Maga | 1595–1596* |
| Francisco de Tello de Guzmán | 1596–1602 |

*acting governors

### VICEROYS IN NEW SPAIN

| | |
|---|---|
| Antonio de Mendoza | 1535–1549 |
| Luis de Velasco | 1549–1564 |
| Gastón de Peralta, Marquis of Falces | 1566–1567 |
| Martín Enríquez de Almansa | 1568–1580 |
| Lorenzo Suárez de Mendoza, Count of Coruña | 1580–1583 |
| Álvaro Manrique de Zúñiga, Marquis of Villamanrique | 1585–1589 |
| Luis Velasco the younger, later Marquis of Salinas | 1589–1595 |
| Gaspar de Zúñiga y Acevedo, Count of Monterrey | 1595–1603 |

## VICEROYS IN PERU

| | |
|---|---|
| Andrés Hurtado de Mendoza, Marquis of Cañete | 1553–1559 |
| Diego López de Zúñiga y Velasco, Count of Nieva | 1558–1564 |
| Francisco de Toledo | 1568–1580 |
| Martín Enrique de Almansa | 1580–1583 |
| Fernando Torres y Portugal, Count of Villadompardo | 1584–1588 |
| García Hurtado de Mendoza | 1588–1595 |
| Luis de Velasco | 1593–1603 |

# Appendix 7

## Slave Ships from African Ports

| year | total | Cape Verde | Guinea | São Tomé | Angola | other | Canaries |
|------|-------|------------|--------|----------|--------|-------|----------|
| 1551 | 5 | 5 | | | | | |
| 1552 | 3 | 3 | | | | | |
| 1553 | 4 | 4 | | | | | |
| 1554 | 3 | 3 | | | | | |
| 1556 | 1 | 1 | | | | | |
| 1557 | 2 | 2 | | | | | |
| 1558 | 7 | 7 | | | | | |
| 1559 | 2 | 2 | | | | | |
| 1560 | 3 | 3 | | | | | |
| 1561 | 2 | 2 | | | | | |
| 1562 | 11 | 11 | | | | | |
| 1563 | 4 | 4 | | | | | |
| 1564 | 2 | 2 | | | | | |
| 1565 | 6 | 6 | | | | | |
| 1567 | 3 | 3 | | | | | |
| 1569 | 4 | 4 | | | | | |
| 1570 | 2 | 2 | | | | | |
| 1571 | 2 | 1 | | 1 | | | |
| 1572 | 2 | 1 | 1 | | | | |
| 1573 | 1 | 1 | | | | | 1 |
| 1574 | 8 | 5 | 3 | | | | |
| 1575 | 3 | 3 | | | | | |
| 1578 | 1 | 1 | | | | | |
| 1580 | 1 | 1 | | | | | |
| 1581 | 1 | 1 | | | | | |
| 1582 | 8 | 8 | | | | | |
| 1583 | 4 | 3 | 1 | | | | |
| 1584 | 5 | 2 | 1 | | | 2 | |
| 1585 | 4 | 2 | | 1 | | 1 | |

| year | total | Cape Verde | Guinea | São Tomé | Angola | other | Canaries |
|------|-------|-----------|--------|----------|--------|-------|----------|
| 1586 | 16 | 2 | 5 | | | 8 | 1 |
| 1587 | 11 | 1 | 3 | | | 3 | 4 |
| 1588 | 19 | 2 | 13 | | | 3 | 1 |
| 1589 | 11 | 1 | 4 | 3 | 1 | 2 | |
| 1590 | 7 | 1 | | | | 6 | |
| 1591 | 18 | 7 | 9 | | | 2 | |
| 1592 | 22 | 3 | 4 | | 4 | 10 | 1 |
| 1593 | 17 | 6 | 2 | | 2 | 6 | 1 |
| 1594 | 9 | | | | | 9 | |
| 1595 | 38 | 2 | 11 | | | 24 | 1 |

Source: Lorenzo Sanz, II, 585

# Genealogies

# Genealogy I
## Some Relations of King Philip II

Fernando King of Aragon d. 1516 = Isabel Queen of Castile d. 1504

Children: Infante Juan d. 1498; Catherine of Aragon d. 1540; Juana 'La Loca' d. 1555

Catherine of Aragon d. 1540 = 1. Prince Arthur of England; 2. King Henry the VIII

Mary Duchess of Burgundy = Maximilian I Emperor 1493–1519

Children: Philip I 'The Handsome' d. 1506; Margaret Archduchess d. 1530

Margaret Archduchess d. 1530 = 1. Infante Juan of Castile d. 1498; 2. Philibert of Savoy d. 1504

Juana 'La Loca' d. 1555 = Philip I 'The Handsome' d. 1506

Children: Charles V (I) King of Spain 1516–56, Emperor 1519–56, d. 1558; Ferdinand Emperor 1556–64

Charles V (I) = Isabel of Portugal d. 1540

Ferdinand Emperor 1556–64 = Anne of Bohemia

Children of Ferdinand: Maximilian Emperor 1564–76; Ferdinand Count of Tyrol; Charles of Styria

Philip II b. 1527 King 1556–98, married:
1. María Manuela of Portugal
2. Mary Tudor Queen of England
3. Isabel (Elisabeth) of Valois
4. Ana

'Don Carlos' d. 1568

Isabel 1566–1633 = Albert Habsburg

Catalina 1567–97 = Charles Emanuel of Savoy

four children who died young

María = Maximilian Emperor 1564–76

Children: Rudolph Emperor 1576–1612; Albert; Matthias Emperor 1612–1637; Philip III King 1598–1621

Ferdinand Count of Tyrol = Philippa v. Welser

Charles of Styria

Children: Ferdinand III Emperor 1619–37; Leopold

Philip III = Margaret → Later Spanish Habsburgs

Ferdinand III, Leopold → Later Austrian Habsburgs

# Genealogy II
## The Portuguese Succession 1580

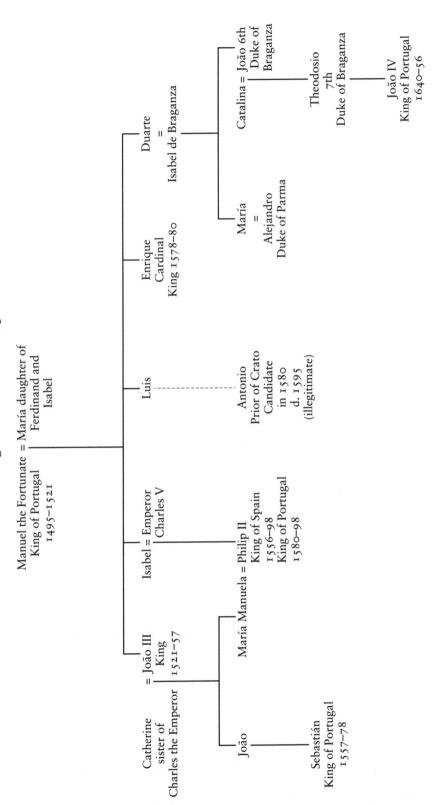

# Genealogy III
## The Last Valois Kings of France

FRANCIS I = Claude
King of France
1515–47

Catherine = HENRY II
de' Medici   King of France
1547–59

Charles
Duke of Orleans

Margaret
m. Emmanuel Philibert
Duke of Savoy

1. Madeleine & KING JAMES V = 2. Mary of Guise
d. 1537            of Scotland
                   1513–42

FRANCIS II
King of France
1559–60

CHARLES IX
King of France
1560–74

Francis
Duke
of Alençon

HENRY III
King of France
1574–89

Elizabeth = KING PHILIP II
of Spain

Margaret = KING HENRY IV = Marie de' Medici
          of France
          (9th cousin of the
          Valois brothers)

Mary Queen of Scots = Henry Stuart
1542–67              Lord Darnley

KING JAMES VI of Scotland
& I of England
1567–1625

KING LOUIS XIII = Anne of Austria

# Genealogy IV
## The Habsburgs in the Sixteenth Century

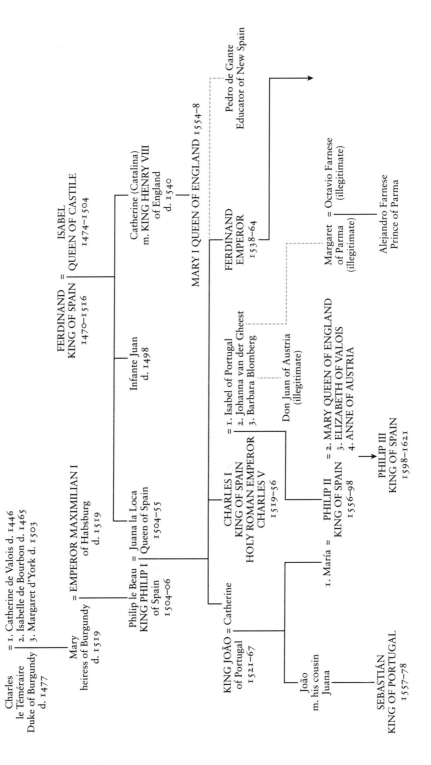

*Maps*

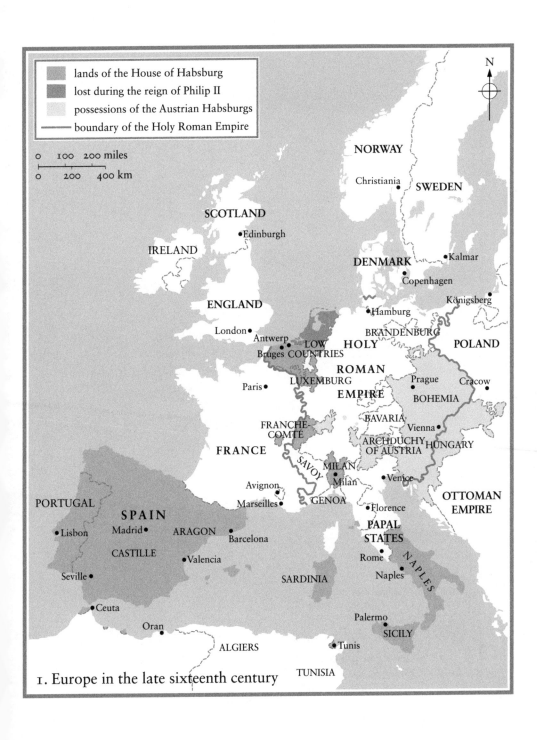

lands of the House of Habsburg
lost during the reign of Philip II
possessions of the Austrian Habsburgs
boundary of the Holy Roman Empire

0   100   200 miles
0   200   400 km

NORWAY

Christiania   SWEDEN

SCOTLAND

Edinburgh

IRELAND

DENMARK   Kalmar

Copenhagen

Königsberg

ENGLAND

Hamburg

London

BRANDENBURG

POLAND

Antwerp   LOW   HOLY
Bruges   COUNTRIES   ROMAN

Paris   LUXEMBURG   EMPIRE   Prague   Cracow

BOHEMIA

BAVARIA

FRANCHE-
COMTE   Vienna

FRANCE   ARCHDUCHY   HUNGARY
OF AUSTRIA

SAVOY   MILAN

Avignon   Milan   Venice

Marseilles   GENOA

PORTUGAL   Florence   OTTOMAN
EMPIRE

SPAIN   PAPAL
STATES

Lisbon   Madrid   ARAGON

Barcelona   Rome   NAPLES

CASTILLE   Naples

Valencia

Seville   SARDINIA

Ceuta

Oran   Palermo

ALGIERS   SICILY

Tunis

TUNISIA

1. Europe in the late sixteenth century

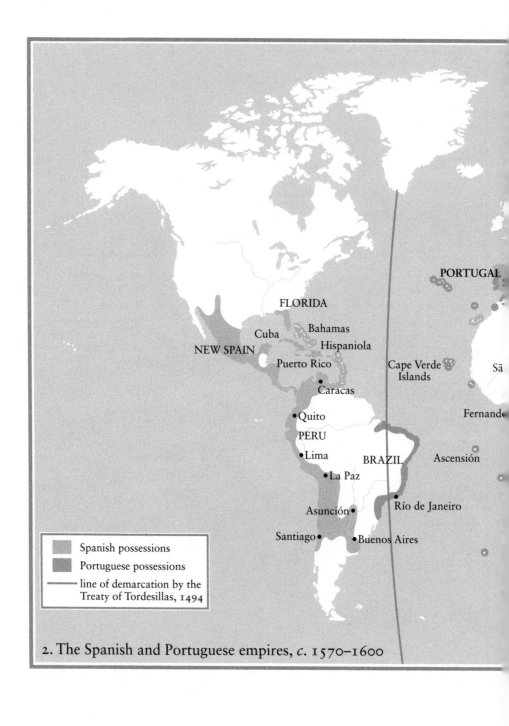

FLORIDA

Cuba  Bahamas
NEW SPAIN  Hispaniola
Puerto Rico
•Caracas
•Quito
PERU
•Lima
•La Paz
Asunción•
Santiago•  •Buenos Aires

PORTUGAL

Cape Verde
Islands  Sã

Fernand

Ascensión

BRAZIL

•Río de Janeiro

Spanish possessions
Portuguese possessions
—— line of demarcation by the
Treaty of Tordesillas, 1494

2. The Spanish and Portuguese empires, *c.* 1570–1600

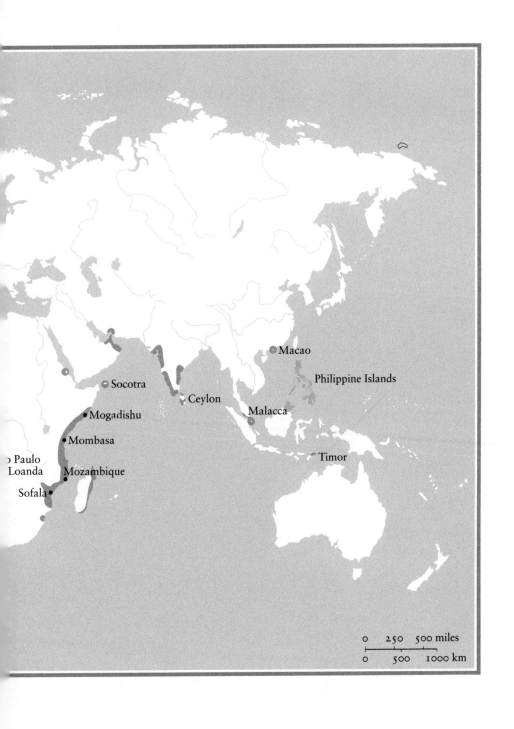

Macao

Philippine Islands

Socotra

Ceylon

Mogadishu

Malacca

Mombasa

Paulo
Loanda    Mozambique

Timor

Sofala

0    250    500 miles

0    500    1000 km

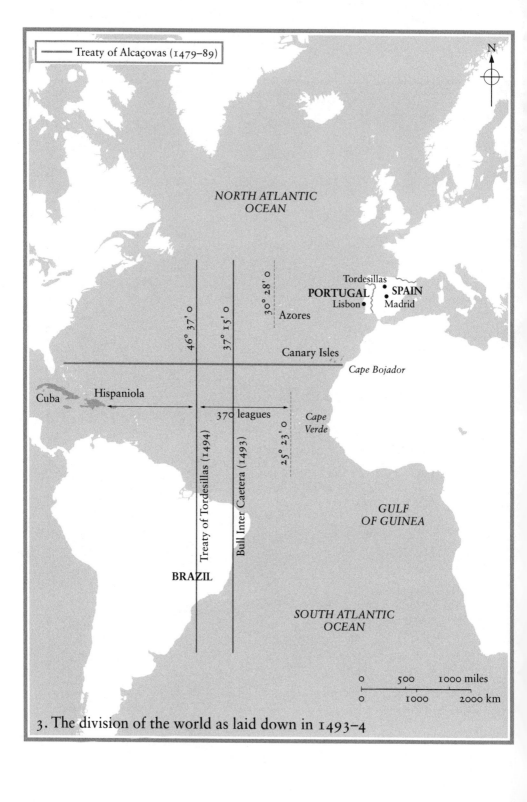

N

NORTH ATLANTIC
OCEAN

30° 28' O

46° 37' O

37° 15' O

Tordesillas

PORTUGAL  SPAIN
Lisbon•  Madrid

Azores

Canary Isles

Cape Bojador

Cuba  Hispaniola

370 leagues  Cape
Verde

25° 23' O

Treaty of Tordesillas (1494)

Bull Inter Caetera (1493)

GULF
OF GUINEA

BRAZIL

SOUTH ATLANTIC
OCEAN

0  500  1000 miles

0  1000  2000 km

3. The division of the world as laid down in 1493–4

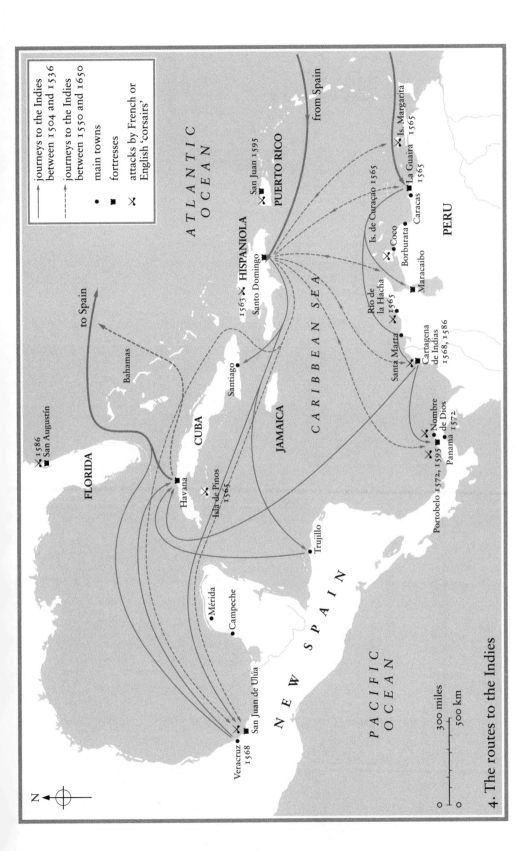

**4. The routes to the Indies**

Legend:
- journeys to the Indies between 1504 and 1536
- journeys to the Indies between 1550 and 1650
- main towns •
- fortresses ■
- attacks by French or English 'corsairs' ✕

*ATLANTIC OCEAN*

*CARIBBEAN SEA*

*PACIFIC OCEAN*

N

FLORIDA

✕ 1586 San Augustin

San Juan 1595 ✕

PUERTO RICO

HISPANIOLA

1563 ✕ Santo Domingo

Is. Margarita 1565 ✕

La Guaira 1565

Caracas

Is. de Curaçao 1565

Coco

Borburata ✕ 1565

PERU

Maracaibo

Río de la Hacha ✕ 1565

Santa Marta

Cartagena de Indias 1568, 1586 ■

Nombre de Dios

Portobelo 1572, 1595 ✕

Panamá 1572 ■

to Spain

Bahamas

Santiago •

CUBA

JAMAICA

Isla de Pinos ✕ 1565

Havana ■

Trujillo •

Mérida •

Campeche •

San Juan de Ulúa ■

Veracruz ✕ 1568

*N E W   S P A I N*

from Spain

0     300 miles
0     500 km

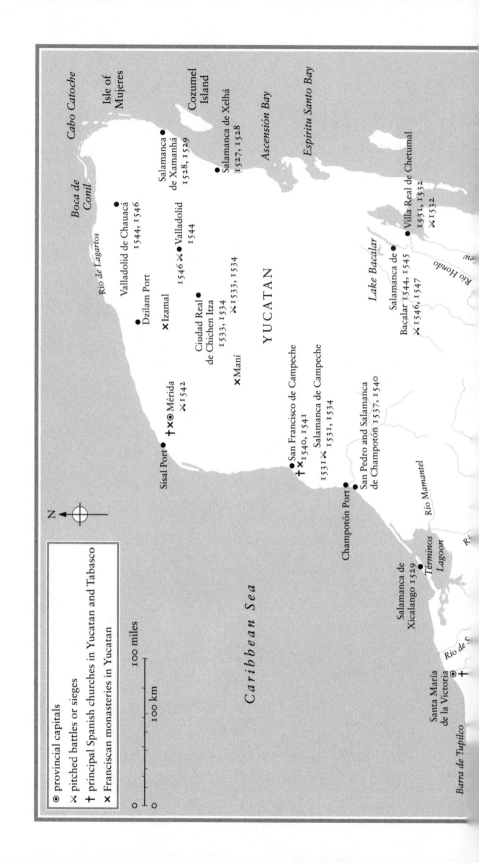

N

100 miles

100 km

⊙ provincial capitals
✕ pitched battles or sieges
✝ principal Spanish churches in Yucatan and Tabasco
✕ Franciscan monasteries in Yucatan

*Caribbean Sea*

*Barra de Tupilco*

Santa María de la Victoria ⊙ ✝
Río de S~

Salamanca de Xicalango 1529
*Terminos Lagoon*
Río Mamantel
R~

Champotón Port ●

San Pedro and Salamanca de Champotón 1537, 1540

San Francisco de Campeche ●
✝✕ 1540, 1541
✕ 1531 Salamanca de Campeche
1531, 1534

Sisal Port ●
✝✕⊙ Mérida
✕ 1542

✕ Maní

Ciudad Real de Chichen Itza
1533, 1534
1533, 1534
✕ 1533, 1534

Dzilam Port ●
✕ Izamal
1546 ● Izamal
1533, 1534

Valladolid de Chauacá ●
1544, 1546

1546 ✕● Valladolid
1544

*Río de Lagartos*

*Boca de Conil*

Isle of Mujeres

*Cabo Catoche*

YUCATAN

Salamanca de Xamanhá
1528, 1529

Salamanca de Xelhá
1527, 1528

Cozumel Island

*Ascensión Bay*

*Espiritu Santo Bay*

*Lake Bacalar*

Salamanca de Bacalar 1544, 1545
✕ 1546, 1547

Villa Real de Chetumal
1531, 1532
✕ 1532

Río Hondo
m~

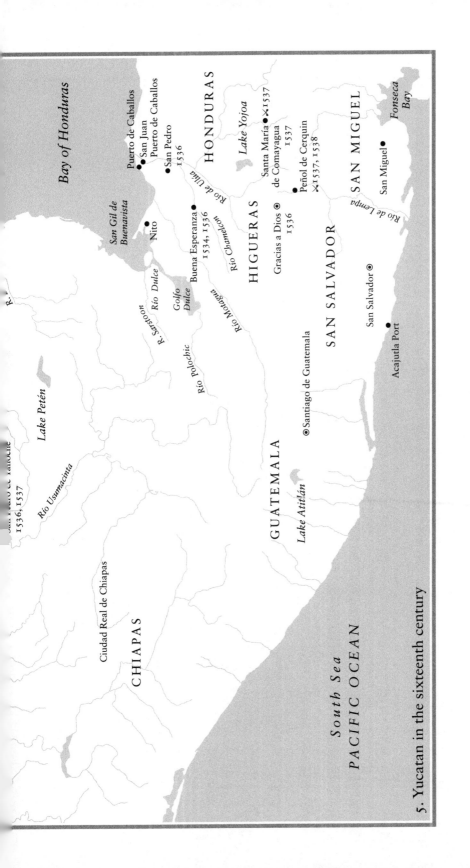

5. Yucatan in the sixteenth century

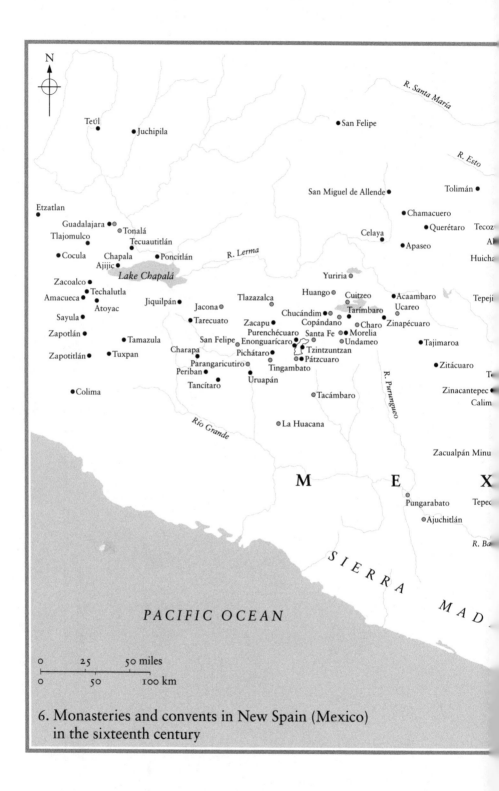

N

Teúl
Juchipila
San Felipe
R. Santa María
R. Esto
Etzatlan
Guadalajara
Tlajomulco
Tonalá
Tecuautitlán
Cocula
Chapala
Ajijic
Poncitlán
R. Lerma
San Miguel de Allende
Tolimán
Chamacuero
Querétaro
Tecoz
Celaya
Apaseo
A
Huicha
Zacoalco
Techalutla
Amacueca
Atoyac
Jiquilpán
Jacona
Sayula
Tarecuato
Zapotlán
Zapotitlán
Tuxpan
Tamazula
Charapa
San Felipe
Pichátaro
Parangaricutiro
Periban
Tancítaro
Uruapán
Colima
Lake Chapalá
Tlazazalca
Huango
Yuriria
Cuitzeo
Acaambaro
Tepeji
Chucándim
Tarímbaro
Ucareo
Zacapu
Copándano
Charo
Zinapécuaro
Purenchécuaro
Santa Fe
Morelia
Enonguarícaro
Undameo
Tajimaroa
Tzintzuntzan
Pátzcuaro
Zitácuaro
Tingambato
Tacámbaro
La Huacana
R. Purungueo
Zinacantepec
Calim
Zacualpán Minu
M      E      X
Pungarabato
Tepec
Ajuchitlán
R. Ba
Río Grande
SIERRA
MAD
PACIFIC OCEAN
0      25      50 miles
0      50      100 km

6. Monasteries and convents in New Spain (Mexico)
in the sixteenth century

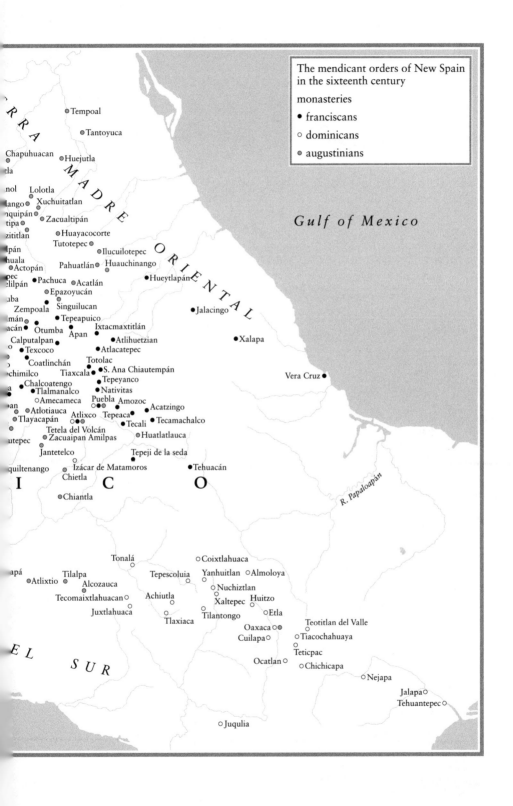

**The mendicant orders of New Spain in the sixteenth century**

monasteries

- ● franciscans
- ○ dominicans
- ● augustinians

*Gulf of Mexico*

Tempoal

Tantoyuca

Chapuhuacan

Huejutla

tla

nol   Lolotla

lango   Xuchuitatlán

nquipán

tipa   Zacualtipán

zititlan

Huayacocorte

Tutotepec

lpán

huala   Ilucuilotepec

Actopán   Pahuatlán   Huauchinango

pec

lilpán   Pachuca   Acatlán   Hueytlapán

Epazoyucán

uba

Zempoala   Singuilucan

mán   Tepeapuico

acán   Otumba   Ixtacmaxtitlán   Jalacingo

Calputalpan   Apan

Texcoco   Atlihuetzian   Xalapa

Coatlinchán   Atlacatepec

Totolac

chimilco   Tiaxcala   S. Ana Chiautempán

Chalcoatengo   Tepeyanco   Vera Cruz

a   Tlalmanalco   Nativitas

Amecameca   Puebla   Amozoc

an   Atlotiauca   Atlixco   Tepeaca   Acatzingo

Tlayacapán   Tecali   Tecamachalco

Tetela del Volcán   Huatlatlauca

utepec   Zacuaipan   Amilpas

Jantetelco   Tepeji de la seda

quiltenango   Izácar de Matamoros   Tehuacán

Chietla

Chiantla

*R. Papaloapán*

Tonalá   Coixtlahuaca

apá   Tilalpa   Tepescoluia   Yanhuitlan   Almoloya

Atlixtio   Alcozauca   Nuchiztlan

Tecomaixtlahuacan   Achiutla   Xaltepec   Huitzo

Juxtlahuaca   Tilantongo   Etla

Tlaxiaca   Teotitlan del Valle

Oaxaca   Tlacochahuaya

Cuilapa   Teticpac

Ocatlan   Chichicapa   Nejapa

Jalapa

Tehuantepec

Juqulia

I   C   O

EL   SUR

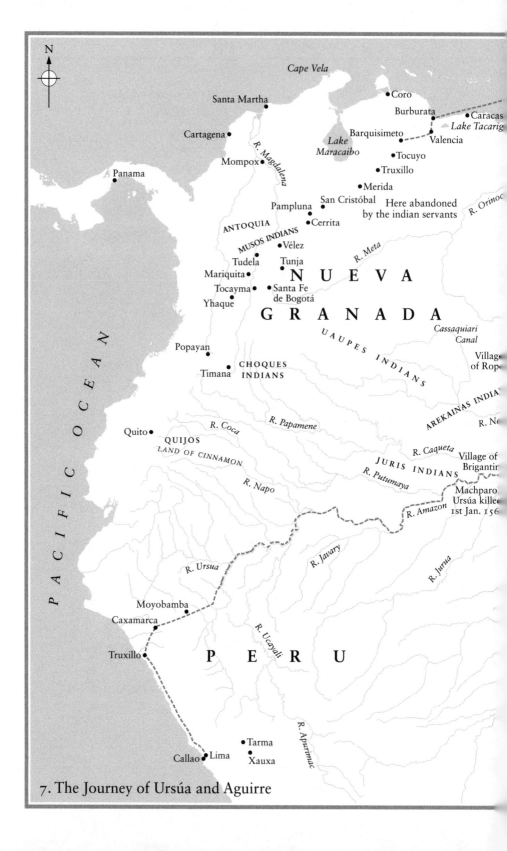

N

*Cape Vela*

Coro

Santa Martha

Burburata
Caracas
*Lake Tacarig*

Cartagena
Barquisimeto
Valencia

Mompox
Lake
Maracaibo
Tocuyo

Panama
Truxillo

R. Orinoc

Merida

Pampluna
San Cristóbal
Here abandoned
by the indian servants

ANTOQUIA
Cerrita

R. Meta

MUSOS INDIANS

Vélez

Tudela
Tunja

Mariquita
N U E V A

Tocayma
Santa Fe
de Bogotá
Yhaque

G R A N A D A

Cassaquiari
Canal

U A U P E S
Popayan

Villag
of Rop

Timana
CHOQUES
INDIANS

I N D I A N S

AREKAINAS INDIA

P A C I F I C   O C E A N

R. Coca
R. Papamene

R. N

Quito
QUIJOS
LAND OF CINNAMON

R. Caqueta
Village of
Brigantir

JURIS INDIANS

R. Napo
R. Putumaya

Machparo
Ursúa kille
1st Jan. 156

R. Amazon

R. Ursua
R. Javary

R. Jurua

Moyobamba

Caxamarca

R. Ucayali

Truxillo
P E R U

Tarma

Callao Lima
Xauxa

R. Apurimac

7. The Journey of Ursúa and Aguirre

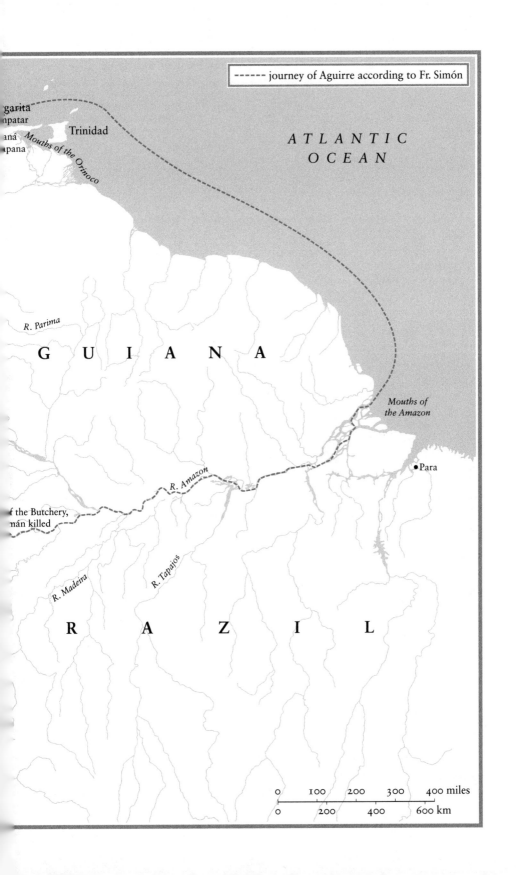

garita
npatar
Trinidad

aná
apana

*Mouths of the Orinoco*

ATLANTIC
OCEAN

*R. Parima*

G U I A N A

*Mouths of
the Amazon*

•Para

*R. Amazon*

f the Butchery,
nán killed

*R. Tapajos*

*R. Madeira*

R A Z I L

| 0 | 100 | 200 | 300 | 400 miles |
|---|-----|-----|-----|-----------|
| 0 | 200 | 400 | 600 km | |

N

shaded territories idicate zones where *audiencias* had authority

Mexico 1527
•Mexico

VICEROYALTY
OF NEW SPAIN

Santo Domingo

Santa Domingo 1511
NEW CREATION 1526

ATLANTIC OCEAN

Guatemala
•

Guatemala 1543
1563 RE-ESTABLISHED

Panamá
•

Panamá 1535
1542 SUPPRESSED

•Mérida
VENEZUELA

Porto
Buenaventura

•Santa Fe de Bogotá
•Popayán

GUAYANA

•Quito

Line of
Tordesillas

Limits of Peruvian
Viceroyalty

Quito 1556
INAUGURATED IN 1561

Santa Fe de Bogotá 1549
INAUGURATED IN 1550

Paita•

Lima•
Lima 1542

Charcas 1559
INAUGURATED IN 1551

•La Plata

PACIFIC

OCEAN

Chile 1565
1573 SUPPRESSED
1609 RE-ESTABLISHED

CUYO

SOUTH

ATLANTIC

OCEAN

Concepción•

0      500     1000 miles

0     500    1000 km

8. Supreme courts (*audiencias*)
of the Spanish Empire
in the sixteenth century

*Straits of Magellan*

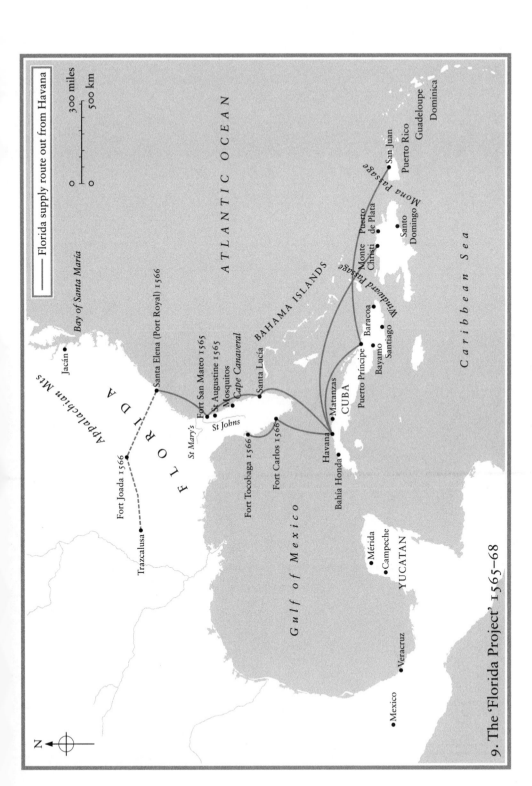

N

Florida supply route out from Havana

300 miles
500 km

*Bay of Santa María*

Santa Elena (Port Royal) 1566

Jacán

*Appalachian Mts*

F L O R I D A

Fort Joada 1566

Trazcalusa

Fort San Mateo 1565
St Augustine 1565
*St Mary's*
Mosquitos
*Cape Canaveral*
St Johns
Santa Lucía

Fort Tocobaga 1566

Fort Carlos 1566

Bahía Honda

Havana

Matanzas

Puerto Principe

Baracoa

Bayamo

Santiago

CUBA

*Windward Passage*

Monte
Christi
Puerto
de Plata
Santo
Domingo

San Juan

Puerto Rico

*Mona Passage*

Guadeloupe

Dominica

A T L A N T I C   O C E A N

BAHAMA ISLANDS

*C a r i b b e a n   S e a*

*G u l f   o f   M e x i c o*

Mérida
Campeche
YUCATAN

Veracruz

Mexico

9. The 'Florida Project' 1565–68

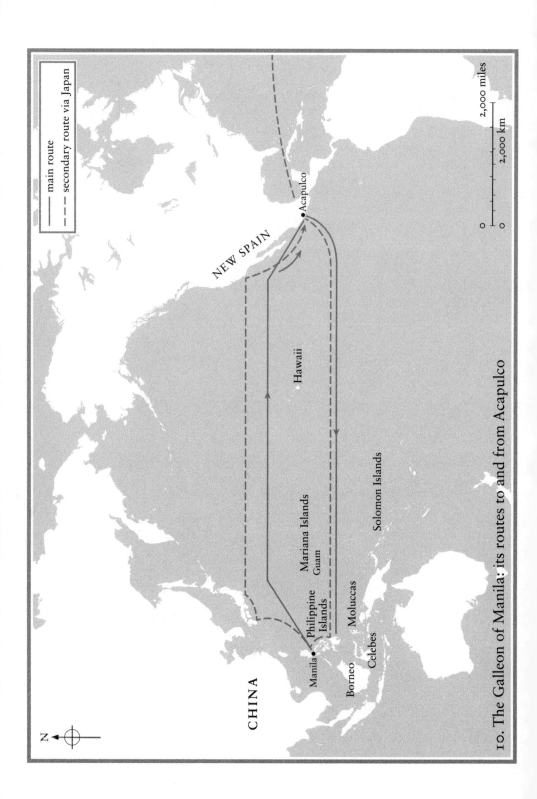

10. The Galleon of Manila: its routes to and from Acapulco

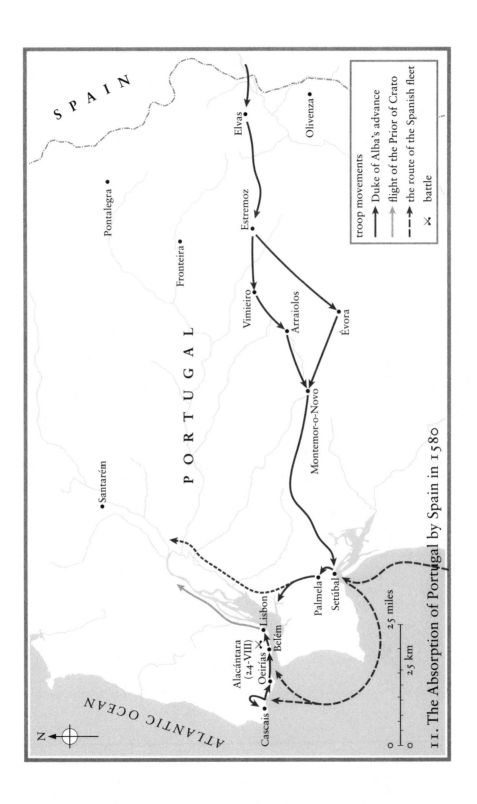

SPAIN

PORTUGAL

ATLANTIC OCEAN

N

Elvas

Olivenza

Pontalegra

Fronteira

Estremoz

Vimieiro

Arraiolos

Évora

Santarém

Montemor-o-Novo

Palmela

Setúbal

Lisbon

Belém

Oeiras

Alacántara
(24-VIII)

Cascais

troop movements

Duke of Alba's advance

flight of the Prior of Crato

the route of the Spanish fleet

battle

0       25 miles

0       25 km

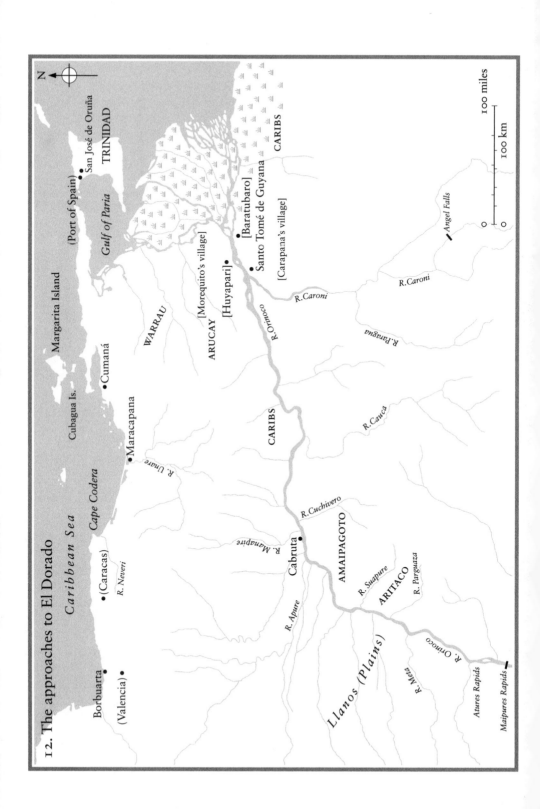

12. The approaches to El Dorado

Chichuahua
Carichi
NEW SPAIN
Zacatecas
San Luis de Potosi
Morelia Guanajuato
Tepotzotlán City of Mexico
Puebla
Oaxaca

ATLANTIC OCEAN

CUBA

HISPANIOLA

Cartagena de Indias

Tópaga
Bogotá

Quito

PERU          BRAZIL

Trujillo

Lima
Ayacucho              Salvador da Bahía
Pisco    Cuzco
Nazca   Andahuaylillas
Arequipa  Juli
Potosi  Sucre   San Francisco Javier

PACIFIC OCEAN

São Miguel

Córdoba

Buenos Aires

SOUTH
ATLANTIC
OCEAN

Achao

0    500    1000 miles
0   500  1000 km

13. Jesuit establishments in Spanish America and Brazil, c. 1600

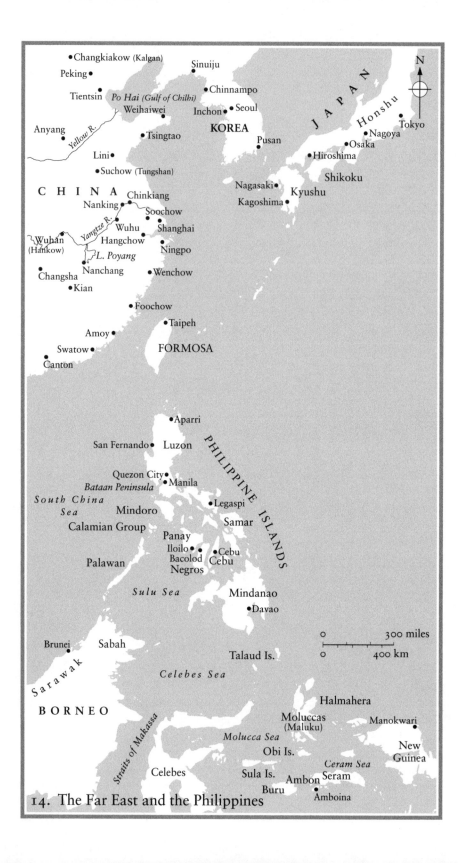

14. The Far East and the Philippines

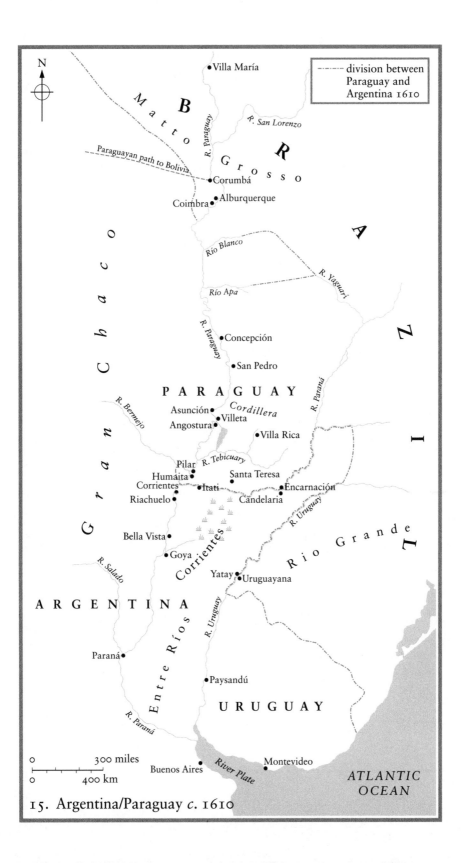

N

•Villa María

division between
Paraguay and
Argentina 1610

B R A Z I L

M a t t o   G r o s s o

R. San Lorenzo

R. Paraguay

Paraguayan path to Bolivia

•Corumbá

Coimbra•  •Alburquerque

Río Blanco

R. Yaguari

Río Apa

R. Paraguay

•Concepción

•San Pedro

P A R A G U A Y

Cordillera

Asunción•  •Villeta

Angostura•

R. Bermejo

R. Paraná

•Villa Rica

G r a n   C h a c o

Pilar•  R. Tebicuary

Humaita•  Santa Teresa

Corrientes•  •Itati

Riachuelo•  Candelaria  •Encarnación

Bella Vista•

C o r r i e n t e s

R. Uruguay

•Goya

R. Salado

Yatay•  •Uruguayana

R i o   G r a n d e

A R G E N T I N A

E n t r e   R í o s

R. Uruguay

Paraná•

•Paysandú

U R U G U A Y

R. Paraná

300 miles

400 km

Buenos Aires•  River Plate  •Montevideo

ATLANTIC
OCEAN

15. Argentina/Paraguay c. 1610

# Bibliography

## ABBREVIATIONS

*AEA – Anuario de Estudios Americanos*
AGI – Archivo General de las Indias
BAE – Biblioteca de Autores Españoles
BN – Bibliothèque Nationale
*BRAH – Boletín de la Real Academia de la Historia*
CDI – *Colección de documentos inéditos relativos al descubrimiento, conquista y organización de las antiguas posesiones españolas en América y Oceania*
CDIHE – *Colección de documentos inéditos para la historia de España*
DBE – *Diccionario Biográfico Español*
*HAHR – Hispanic American Historical Review*
Indif. Gen. – Indiferente General
leg. – legajo
*R de I – Revista de Indias*

## PRIMARY SOURCES

Printed documents, first-hand accounts, and sixteenth- and seventeenth-century books. Unpublished papers are marked with an asterisk (*).

Acosta, Fr José de, *Historia natural y moral de las Indias*, Eng. tr. by Edward Grimston 1604, published in the Hakluyt Society, 1st series, vols. 60 and 61, London 1880

Acuña, René, ed., *Relaciones geográficas del siglo XVI*, 10 vols., Mexico 1984

Aguilar, Fr Francisco, *Relación breve de la conquista*, written *c.* 1565, first edn Mexico 1892; new edn by Germán Vázquez in *La Conquista de*

*Tenochtitlan, Historia* 16, *Crónicas de América* 41, Madrid 1988; Eng. tr. by Patricia de Fuentes, foreword by Ross Hassig, Norman 1993

Alba, Duke of, *Epistolario del III duque de Alba*, 3 vols., Madrid 1952

Alberi, Eugenio, *Relazione degli ambasciatori veneti al senato*, Florence 1839–40

Albret, Pierre d' (Pedro de Navarra), *Diálogos de la preparación de la muerte*, in *Diálogos muy sutiles y notables*, Tortosa 1565

Altadonna, Giovanna, *Cartas de Felipe II a Carlos Manuel, duque de Saboya*, in *Cuadernos de investigación histórica* 9 (1986)

Álvar Ezquerra, Alfredo, *Antonio Pérez: relaciones y cartas*, 2 vols., Madrid 1986

Alvarado, Pedro de, *Proceso de Residencia*, ed. José Fernando Ramírez, Mexico 1847

—, *Juicio a un conquistador*, ed. José María Vallejo García-Hevia, 2 vols., Madrid 2005

*Álvarez, Rodrigo, *Información de servicios y méritos*, AGI, Patronato, leg. 900

Álvarez, Vicente, *Relation du beau voyage que fit aux Pays-Bas en 1548 le Prince Philippe d'Espagne*, ed. M.-T. Dovillée, Brussels 1964

Anales de Tlatelolco, *Colección de fuentes para la Historia de México*, Mexico 1948

Andrews, Kenneth, ed., *English Privateering in the West Indies, 1588–1595*, Cambridge 1995

Ávila, Santa Teresa de, *Obras completas*, Madrid 1984

*Azamour, Juana de, Probanza de, AGI, Mexico, leg. 983

Barrientos, Bartolomé, *Pedro Menéndez de Avilés: su vida y hechos*, 1567, in Génaro García, *Dos antiguas relaciones*, Mexico 1902

Benzoni, Girolamo, *Historia del Mondo Novo*, 1565. There is a new Spanish translation by Manuel Carrera, *Historia del Nuevo Mundo*, Madrid 1989

Bernáldez, Andrés, *Cura de Los Palacios*, ed. Manuel Gómez-Moreno and Juan de M. Carriazo, *Memorias del Reinado de los Reyes Católicos*, Madrid 1962.

Bornate, C., *Miscellanea di storia italiana*, 3rd series, xvi, Turin 1915

Borregán, Alonso, *Crónica de la conquista del Perú*, ed. Rafael Loredo, Seville 1948

Bouza Álvarez, Fernando, *La Corte de Felipe II*, Madrid 1986

—, *Cartas de Felipe II a sus hijas*, Madrid 1988

—, *Locos, enanos y hombres de placer en la corte de Los Austrias*, Madrid 1991

Brantôme, Pierre de, Abbé de Bourdeille, *Mémoires*, ed. P. Lalanne, Paris, 12 vols., 1864–96

Cabeza de Vaca, Álvaro Núñez, *Naufragios y comentarios*, ed. Roberto Ferrando, Madrid 1984. An excellent English edn of *Naufragios* only is published as *Castaways*, ed. Enrique Pupo-Walker, Berkeley 1993

Cabrera de Córdoba, Luis, *Historia de Felipe*, II, 4 vols., Madrid 1874–7

Calvete de Estrella, Juan Cristóbal, *El felicísimo viaje del muy alto y muy poderoso príncipe don Felipe*, Antwerp 1552

—, *Rebelión de Pizarro en Perú*, ed. Paz y Mela, Madrid 1889

*Cárdenas, Juan de, *Problemas y secretos maravillosos de las Indias*, Mexico 1591, facsimile edn, Madrid 1945

Cartas de Indias, Madrid 1877 (BAE, vol. 264)

Casas, Bartolomé de las, *Apologética Historia Sumaria*, ed. Juan Pérez de Tudela, 2 vols., BAE, vols. 95 and 96, Madrid 1957

—, *Los tesoros de Perú*, ed. Angel Losada, Madrid 1958

—, *Tratado de las doce dudas*, BAE, Madrid 1958

—, *Tratado sobre los hombres que han sido hechos esclavos*, in *Opúsculos, cartas y memoriales*, BAE, Madrid 1958

—, *Historia de las Indias*, 3 vols., Mexico 1986, edn of Agustín Millares Carlo. The edition I used was that of Millares Carlo, to which Lewis Hanke wrote an introduction. It is based on the MSS now in the Biblioteca Nacional de Madrid. It is incomprehensible that there has never been a translation into English or any other language that I know.

*Castillo, Andrea del, Probanza de, AGI, Mexico, leg. 974

Cervantes, Miguel de, *Don Quijote de la Mancha*, 1st edn, Madrid 1606, new edn of Francisco Rico, 2 vols., Barcelona 1998

—, *Novelas Ejemplares*, ed. Francisco Rodríguez, Madrid 1943

Cervantes de Salazar, Francisco de, *Crónica de la Nueva España*, written 1558–66, first published by the Hispanic Society of America, Madrid 1993

Chagny, A. de, *Correspondance politique et adminstrative de Laurent de Gorrevod*, 1517–1520, Lyons 1913

Cieza de León, Pedro, *Descubrimiento y conquista del Perú*, edn of Carmelo Sánz de Santa María, *Crónicas de America* 17, Historia 16, Madrid 1986. There is an English translation of Part 3, ed. by Alexandra Parma Cook and Noble David Cook, Durham, NC, 1998. The last few chapters are a translation of Herrera's chapters which he copied from a lost MS of Cieza.

*Colección de documentos inéditos para la historia de España*, 112 vols., Madrid 1846 onwards

*Colección de documentos inéditos relativos al descubrimiento, conquista y organización de las antiguas posesiones españoles en América y Oceania*, eds. Joaquín Pacheco and Francisco Cárdenas, 42 vols., Madrid 1864–89; 25 vols., Madrid 1880–1932

Colín, Francisco, *Labor evangélica de la compañía de Jesús en las Islas Filipinas por el padre Francisco Colín*, 1660, ed. Pablo Pastells, Barcelona 1904

Colón, Cristóbal, *Textos y documentos completos*, edn of Consuelo Varela and Juan Gil, 2nd edn enlarged, Madrid 1992. Many of the important letters, including the *relaciones* of the four voyages, were translated by J. M. Cohen in his *The Four Voyages of Cristopher Columbus*, Harmondsworth 1969.

Colón, Fernando, *The Life of the Admiral Christopher Columbus, by his Son*, trans. by Benjamin Keen, New Brunswick 1958

Córdoba, Fr Martín de, *Jardín de las nobles mujeres*, Valladolid 1500; also ed. H. Goldberg, Chapel Hill, 1974.

Cortés, Hernán (Hernando), *Cartas de relación*, ed. Angel Delgado Gómez, Madrid 1993 (English trans. by Anthony Pagden, New Haven 1986).

—, *Cartas y memoriales*, ed. María del Carmen Martínez, Salamanca 2003

*Cortes de los antiguos reinos de León y de Castilla*, vol. 4, 1476–1537, Real Academia de la Historia, Madrid 1882

Cuevas, Mariano, S. J., *Documentos inéditos del siglo XVI para la historia de México*, Mexico 1914

Chirino, Pedro, *Relación de las Islas Filipinas y de lo que en ellas han trabajado los padres de la compañía de Jesús 1604*, reprinted Manila 1890

Dante Alighieri, *De monarchia*, Oxford 1916

Delicado, Francisco, *La Lozana Andaluza* (a novel), Venice 1528, ed. Bruno Damiani, Madrid 1970

Díaz, Fr Juan, *Itinerario de la armada del Rey Católico a la Isla de Yucatán, en la India, en el Año 1518*. A Spanish edn by Joaquín García Icazbalceta in his *Colección* (see above under Aguilar)

Díaz del Castillo, Bernal, *Historia verdadera de la Nueva España*, 2 vols., Madrid 1982; *The True History of the Conquest of New Spain*, trans. by A. P. Maudslay, 5 vols., the Hakluyt Society, 2nd series, 23–5, 30, 40, London 1908–16. J. M. Cohen prepared an abbreviated edition for the twentieth century.

Dorantes de Carranza, Baltasar, *Sumario de la relación de las cosas de la Nueva España*, new edn, Mexico 1970

Douais, C., ed., *Dépêches de M. Raimond de Beccarie, seigneur de Fourquevaux, 1565–1572*, 3 vols., Paris 1896–1904

Enríquez de Guzmán, Alonso, *Libro de la vida*, ed. H. Keniston, BAE, Madrid 1960. Clements Markham published an abbreviated and very bad English translation for the Hakluyt Society (1st series, vol. 29) in 1862.

Ercilla y Zúñiga, Alonso de, 3 vols., *La Araucana*, Madrid 1569–89. There seems never to have been an English translation except for that of Canto 1 by Walter Owen, Buenos Aires 1945.

Estete, Miguel de, *El descubrimiento y la conqusta del Perú*, Quito 1918

Federmann, Nicolaus, *Indianische Historia, eine schöne kurtz-weilige Historia*, Hagenau 1557, trans. by Juan Friede, in Joaquín Gabaldón Márquez, *Descubrimiento y conquista de Venezuela*, Caracas 1962

Fernández Álvarez, Manuel, *El corpus documental de Carlos V*, 7 vols., Salamanca 1973

Fernández de Navarrete, Martín, *Collección de viajes y descubrimientos que hicieron por mar los españoles*, ed. Carlos Seco Serrano, BAE, vols. 75–77, Madrid 1954. An admirable edition of invaluable material.

Fernández de Oviedo, Gonzalo, *Historia general y natural de las Indias*, ed. Juan Pérez de Tudela, BAE, vols. 117–121, Madrid 1959

—, *Las quinquagenas de los generosos e illustres e no menos famosos reyes . . .* vol. 1 (the only one published), Madrid 1880

Florentine Codex, *The General History of the Things of New Spain*, by Fr Bernardino de Sahagún, trans. by Charles Dibble and Arthur J. Anderson, 12 vols., New Mexico 1952 onwards. Spanish edn trans. by Fr Angel Garibay, 4 vols., Mexico 1956

Friede, Juan, *Documentos inéditos para la historia de Colombia*, Bogotá 1955

—, *Gonzalo Jiménez de Quesada a través de documentos históricos: estudio biográfico*, I, 1509–1550, Bogotá 1960. No other volume published.

Gabrois, M., *Descripción de la villa y minas de Potosí*, Madrid 1603, republished Madrid 1992

Gachard, M., *Correspondance de Philippe II sur les affaires des Pays-Bas*, 5 vols., Brussels 1848–79

—, *Relations des ambassadeurs vénitiens sur Charles V et Philippe II*, Brussels 1855

—, *Correspondance de Charles V et d'Adrien VI*, Brussels 1859

Galíndez de Carvajal, Lorenzo, *Anales breves de los reyes católicos*, BAE, vol. 30, Madrid 1851

García, Género, *Documentos inéditos o muy raros para la historia de Mexico*, Mexico 1907

García Bravo, Alonso, *Alarife que trazó la ciudad de Mexico, información de méritos y servicios de García Bravo*, ed. Manuel Toussaint, Mexico 1956

García Icazbalceta, Joaquín, *Colección de documentos para la historia de México*, 2 vols., Mexico 1980

García Mercadal, J., ed., *Viajes de extranjeros por España y Portugal*, 2 vols., Madrid 1952

Garcilaso de la Vega, El Inca, *Royal Commentaries of the Incas and General History of Peru*, trans. by Harold Livermore, 2 vols., Austin 1960

Gasca, Pedro de la, *Descripción del Perú*, 1553, ed. Josep M. Barnadas, Caracas 1976

Gómez de Castro, Álvar, *De las hazañas de Francisco Jiménez de Cisneros*, ed. José Oroz, Madrid 1984

González, Tomás, *Retiro, estancia y muerte del emperador Carlos Quinto*, c. 1835. An account with letters.

González Alonso, Benjamín, *El corregidor castellano*, Madrid 1970

González de Mendoza, Juan, *The History of the Great and Mighty Kingdom of China*, published in 1585 as *Historia de las cosas, más notables ritos y costumbre del gran reino de China*. The book had a famous appendix in the shape of Martin Ignacio de Loyola's journey around the world.

Granvelle, Cardinal de, *Papiers d'état du Cardinal de Granvelle*, ed. C. Weiss, 9 vols., Paris 1841–52

—, *Correspondance, 1567–1586*, ed. E. Poullet and C. Piot, 12 vols., Brussels 1877–96

Guiccardini, Francesco, *The History of Italy*, abbrev. and trans. by Sidney Alexander, New York 1969

Hakluyt, Richard, *The principal navigations, voyages, traffiques and discoveries of the English nation*, ed. Sir Walter Raleigh, 12 vols., the Hakluyt Society, Glasgow 1903–5. A useful short version in one volume is Richard Hakluyt, *Voyages and Documents*, ed. Janet Hampden, London 1956

Hanke, Lewis, with Celso Rodríguez, *Los virreyes españoles en América durante el gobierno de la casa de Austria*, 5 vols., BAE, vol. 273, Madrid 1976

—, *Perú*, 7 vols., Madrid 1978

Hans Kraus Collection of Hispanic American MSS, Library of Congress, Washington 1974, 116 letters and documents mostly from the archive of Archbishop Zumárraga and his successors. It includes some Verrazzano material.

Harkness Collection of Calendar of Spanish Manuscripts Covering Peru, 1531–1651, Library of Congress, Washington 1932

—, Documents from Early Peru: The Pizarros and the Almagros, 1531–1578. US Government Printing Office, Washington 1936

—, MSS concerning Mexico. A guide with selected transcriptions and trans. by J. Benedict Warren, Library of Congress, Washington 1974. These include what has been christened the Huejotzingo Codex, a lawsuit between Cortés and the first *audiencia*; some papers relating to the conspiracy of 1566–8 of Martín Cortés, etc.; and the grant of Cortés's arms in 1525.

Hernández, Francisco, *The Mexican Treasury*, Stanford 2000

Hernández, Pedro, *Comentarios*, Madrid 1954

Herrera, Antonio de, *Historia general del mundo, del tiempo del señor rey don Felipe II el prudente*, 3 vols., Madrid 1601

Herrera Heredia, Antonia, *Catálogo de las consultas del Consejo de Indias*, I, *1529–1591*, Madrid 1972

Hojeda, Fr Diego de, *La Christada*, Seville 1611

Hurtado de Mendoza, Diego, *De la guerra de Granada*, Madrid 1949, English trans. by Martin Shuttleworth, London 1982

Jiménez de Quesada, Gonzalo, *Memoria de los descubridores y conquistadores que entraran conmigo a descubrir y conquistar este nuevo Reino de Granada*, c. 1566, in Joaquín Acosta, *Compendio histórico*, Paris 1848, and trans. by C. R. Markham, *The Conquest of New Granada*, London 1912

Khevenhüller, Hans, *Diario de Hans Khevenhüller*, ed. Félix Labrador Arroyo, Madrid 2001

Ladero Quesada, Miguel Angel, *Las Indias de Castilla en sus primeros años. Cuentas de la Casa de la Contratación, 1503–1521*, Madrid 2008

Lalaing, Antoine, *Relation du premier voyage de Philippe le Beau en Espagne, en 1501*, Brussels 1876

La Marche, Olivier de, *Le Chevalier délibéré*: see Clavería in secondary sources.

Landa, Fr Diego de, *Relación de las Cosas de Yucatán*, edn of Miguel Rivera, Madrid 1985. See Anthony Pagden's translation of 1975.

La Peña y de la Camera, José María de, *A List of Spanish Residencias in the Archivo de Indias, 1516–1775*, Library of Congress, Washington 1955

La Torre, Antonio de, *Documentos sobre relaciones internacionales de los reyes católicos*, 3 vols., Madrid 1952

*Lazarillo de Tormes*, Antwerp 1553

León-Portilla, Miguel, *La visión de los vencidos*, Madrid 1985; English trans. as *The Broken Spears*, New York 1992

Levillier, Roberto, *Gobernantes del Perú, siglo XVI*, documentos del Archivo de Indias, 3 vols., Madrid 1921

—, *Biografías de conquistadores de la Argentina*, Madrid 1933

López Rayón, Ignacio, *Documentos para la historia de México*, Mexico 1852

López de Ayala, Pedro, *Crónica del rey don Pedro*, BAE, vol. 66, Madrid 1953

López de Gómara, Francisco, *Historia general de las Indias*, Saragossa 1552, new edn in BAE, vol. 22, Madrid 1846

—, *La conquista de México*, Saragossa 1552, new edn of José Luis Rojas, Madrid 1987, English trans. by L. B. Simpson, Berkeley 1964

López de Jerez, Francisco, *Verdadera relación de la conquista del Perú, y provincia del Cuzco, llamada Nueva Castilla . . .* Seville 1534; new edn, BAE, vol. 26, Madrid 1853

López de Mendoza, Íñigo, Count of Tedilla, *Correspondencia del Conde de Tendilla*, vol. I, Madrid 1974

Loyola, Ignacio de, *Powers of Imagining: The Collected Works*, ed. Antonio T. de Nicholas, Albany 1986

Lucía Megiás, José Manuel, *Antología de libros de caballerías castellanos*, Alcalá de Henares 2000

Magellan, F., *The First Voyage Around the World*, trans. from Antonio Pigafetta et al., the Hakluyt Society, London 1874

March, José María, *Niñez y juventud de Felipe II, documentos inéditos*, 2 vols., Madrid, 1941–2

Marineo Siculo, Lucio, 'Don Hernando Cortés', *De Rebus Hispaniae memorabilibus libri*, vol. 25, Alcalá de Henares 1530, new edn of Miguel León-Portilla, *Historia 16*, April 1985

Marte, Roberto, *Santo Domingo en las MSS de Juan Bautista Muñoz*, transcribed by Roberto Marte, 2 vols., Santo Domingo 1981

Martín, Esteban, *Relación de la expedición de Ambrosio Alfinger*, Coro 1534. In the edn of Joaquín Gabaldón Márquez, it is called *Descubrimiento y conquista de Venezuela*, Caracas 1962

Martorell, Joannot, and Martí, Loan de Galba, *Tirant lo Blanch*, first published in Catalan 1490, first published in Castilian 1511, and translated into English by David H. Rosenthal, London 1984

Martyr, Peter, *De Orbe Novo*, trans. by Francis MacNutt, New York 1912. The translation is eccentric and the names are sometimes misleading. There is a good new Spanish edition by Ramón Alba, *Décadas del Nuevo Mundo*, Madrid 1989.

—, *Epistolario*, vol. 9, *Documentos inéditos para la historia de España*, Madrid 1953.

—, *Cartas sobre el Nuevo Mundo*, Madrid 1990

Maura, V., *Antecedentes de la recopilación de Indias*, Madrid 1906 (for the *visita* of 1571)

Medina, José Toribio, *Descubrimiento del Río de las Amazonas*, 1894. An English edition with many invaluable appendices was published as *The Discovery of the Amazon* by the American Geographical Society in 1934. It includes an English translation of the work of Galíndez de Carvajal (see above).

—, *Cartas de Pedro de Valdivia, tipografico*, Seville 1929. The letters to Charles V were translated by R. B. Cunninghame Graham in his life of Valdivia. See Secondary Sources.

Mena, Cristóbal, *La conquista del Perú, llamada la Nueva Castilla*, New York Public Library, 1929

*Montejo, Francisco de, AGI, Justicia, leg. 244

Monumenta Centroamérica e Histórica, *Colección de documentos y materiales para el estudio de la historia y de la vida de los pueblos de la América central*, eds. Federico Argüello Solorzano and Carlos Molino Argüello, Managua 1997

Morales Padrón, Francisco, ed., *Primeras cartas sobre América*, Seville 1990

Morel-Fatio, Alfred, *Historiographie de Charles Quint*, includes a French translation of the autobiography of Charles (as well as the 1620 edition in Portuguese), Paris 1913. There are also here essays by Morel-Fatio about other histories of Charles V: Giovio, Lorenzo de Padilla, Páez de Castro, etc.

Morga, Antonio de, *Sucesos de las Filipinas*, Mexico 1609, reprinted Madrid 1997

Motolinía, Fr (Fr Toribio de Benavente), *Memoriales*, ed. Eduardo O'Gorman, Mexico 1971

Muñoz, Juan Bautista, *Catálogos de la colección*, edn in *Real Academia de la Historia*, 2 vols., Madrid 1955

Muñoz Camargo, Diego, *Historia de Tlaxcala*, new edn, Madrid 1988

Münster, Sebastián, *Cosmografía*, 1545. This, the most widely read history of the sixteenth century, gave only desultory attention to America.

Murúa, Fr Martín de, *Historia general de Perú*, in *Crónicas de America* 35, ed. Martín Ballesteros, 1987. The conquest is confined to chapters 58 to 77.

Navagero, Andrea, *Il viaggio fatto in Spagna*, Venice 1563

Núñez Cabeza de Vaca, Álvar, *Naufragios y comentarios*, Madrid 1984. There is an English translation by Enrique Pupo-Walker, Berkeley 1992.

Ortiguera, Toribio, *Jornada del Río Marañón, con todo lo acaecido en ella y otras cosas notables dignas de ser sabidas acaecido en las Indias Occidentales del Perú*. This was based on the testimony of several participants. For an English version see Medina, *Descubrimiento del Río de las Amazonas*, 310.

Otte, Enrique, *Cartas privadas de emigrantes a las Indias*, Seville 1988

Palencia, Alfonso de, *Crónica de Enrique IV*, 4 vols., Madrid 1904–8

Paso, Francisco del, *Epistolario de Nueva España*, especially vols. 1 to 6, Mexico 1939 onwards

Pastells, Pablo, et al., *Historia general de las Filipinas, catálogo de los centros relativos a las islas Filipinas existentes en el archivo de Indias de Sevilla*, 9 vols., Barcelona 1925–36

Paz y Mélia, A., *Nobilario de conquistadores de Indias*, Madrid 1982

Pérez de Guzmán, Fernán, *Generaciones y Semblanzas*, London 1965

Pizarro, Francisco, *Dos documentos esenciales sobre Francisco Pizarro*, in *Revista Histórica* 17, Lima 1948. This includes (a) *La información . . . en 1529*; (b) *El acta perdida de la fundación de Cuzco*

—, *Testimonio, documentos oficiales*, ed. Guillermo Lohmann Villena, Madrid 1986

Pizarro, Hernando, *Carta a los oidores de Panamá*, 23 November 1533, published in Fernández de Oviedo, op. cit., bk 46, chap. 16, trans. by Markham in Hakluyt, vol. 47, 113–27

Pizarro, Pedro, *Relación del descubrimiento y conquista de los reinos del Perú*, in *Colección de documentos para la historia de España*, ed. Martin Fernández de Navarrete, vol. 5, Madrid 1844, 201–388. English trans. by Philip Ainsworth Means, Cortés Society, New York 1921

Polavieja, General Camilo, *Hernán Cortés, copias de documentos existentes en el archivo de Indias . . . sobre la conquista de Mexico*, Seville 1889

*Popol Vuh*, the Maya book of the Dawn of Life, trans. by Dennis Tedlock, New York 1996

Pulgar, Hernando de, *Crónica de los reyes católicos*, ed. Juan de Mata Carriazo, 2 vols., Madrid 1943

Quiroga, Vasco de, *La Utopia en America*, ed. de Paz Serrano Gassent, Madrid 2002

Raleigh, Sir Walter, *The History of the World*, 6 vols., at the end of which is 'Voyages of Discovery of Guiana', Edinburgh 1820. The latter is more conveniently available in *The Discovery of Guiana*, London 1928.

Ramusio, Giovanni Bautista, *Della navigazioni e viaggi*, first published 1555. It includes a letter from Oviedo to Cardinal Bembo, about Orellana's journey and visit to Santo Domingo, dated 20 January 1543.

Riba García, Carlos, *Correspondencia privada de Felipe II con su secretario Mateo Vázquez 1567–1591*, Madrid 1959

Rodríguez, Pedro and Justina, *Don Francés de Álava y Beamonte. Correspondencia inédita de Felipe II con su embajador en París, 1564–1570*, San Sebastián 1991

Rodríguez Villa, Antonio, *El emperador Carlos V y su corte, según las cartas de don Martín de Salinas*, Madrid 1903

Rodríguez de Montalvo, Garcí, *Amadís de Gaula*, ed. Juan Bautista Avalle-Arce, Madrid 1991

Rojas, Fernando de, *La Celestina*, ed. and trans. by L. B. Simpson, Cambridge, Mass., 1955

Ruiz de Arce, Juan, *Relación de servicios*, BRAH 1102 (1934)

Sahagún, Fr Bernardino de, *Historia general de las cosas de Nueva España*, Mexico, 1585ff (The *Florentine Codex*)

Salazar, Eugenio de, *Cartas de Eugenio de Salazar*, BAE, Madrid 1926

San Agustín, Fr Gaspar, *La conquista de las islas filipinas*, Madrid 1698

Sánchez, Diego, Probanza of, AGI, Patronato, leg. 69, R 8

Sancho de la Hoz, Pedro, *Relación para su majestad de lo sucedido en la conquista . . . de la Nueva Castilla, colección de libros referentes a la historia del Perú*, vol. V, Lima 1917; trans. by Philip Means, Cortés Society, New York 1917

Sandoval, Fr Prudencio de, *Historia de la vida y hechos del emperador Carlos V*, 2 vols., Valladolid 1604–6, in BAE, vol. 82, Madrid 1956

Santa Cruz, Alonso de, *Crónica del emperador Carlos V*, 5 vols., Madrid 1920–25

Santillana, Marqués de, *Obras*, Madrid 1852

Schmidl, Ulrich, *Voyage to the Rivers la Plata and Paraguay*, in *The Conquest of the River Plate*, the Hakluyt Society, 1891 (voyage with the Welsers and Pedro de Mendoza); *Derrotero y viaje a España y las Indias*, trans. by Edmundo Wernicke, Buenos Aires 1944

Serrano, Luciano, ed., *Correspondencia diplomática entre España y la Santa Sede*, 4 vols., Madrid 1914

Sigüenza, Fr José, *Historia de la Orden de San Jerónimo*, Madrid 1595–1606

Simón, Fr Pedro, *Noticias historiales de las Conquistas de Tierra Firme en las Indias Occidentales*, Cuenca 1627

— *The Expedition of Pedro de Ursúa and Lope de Aguirre*, trans. by William Bollaert, the Hakluyt Society, 1st series, vol. 28, London 1861

Solís de Merás, Gonzalo, *Pedro Menéndez de Avilés*, trans. by Jeannette Thurber Connor, Gainesville 1964

Soto, Fernando de, *The Narrative of the Expedition of Hernando de Soto, by the Caballero de Elvas*, 1907

Stendhal (Marie-Henri Beyle), *Promenades dans Rome*, Paris 1829

Suárez de Peralta, Juan, *Tratado del descubrimiento de las Indias y su Conquista*, ed. Giorgio Perissinotto, Madrid 1990

Tapia, Andrés de, *Relación de algunas cosas de lo que acaecieron al muy illustre señor Hernando Cortés*, first edn in Joaquín García Icazbalceta, *Colección de documentos para la historia de México*, 2 vols., Mexico 1866. New edn by Germán Vázquez, see Francisco de Aguilar, English trans. in Patricia de Fuentes, *The Conquistadors*, Norman 1993

Thevet, André, *Les singularités de la France antarctique*, Paris 1555; *Vie des hommes illustres*, 1584 (favourable to Colón)

Tlaxcala, *Relación de Tlaxcala*, Mexico 1876

Toledo, Francisco de, *Disposiciones gubernativas*, 2 vols., Seville 1986

Toribio Medina, José, *Cartas de Pedro de Valdivia*, Seville 1929

Torre, Fr Tomás de la, *Desde Salamanca, España, hasta Ciudad Real, Chiapas: diario de viaje, 1540–1545*, ed. Franz Blom, Mexico 1945

Trujillo, Diego de, *Relación del descubrimiento del Reino del Perú, 1571*, ed. Rafael Porrás Barrenechea, Seville 1948

Tudela de la Orden, José, ed., *Manuscritos de América en las bibliotecas de España*, Madrid 1954

Ungerer, Gustav, *A Spaniard in Elizabethan England: The Correspondence of Antonio Pérez's exile*, 2 vols., London 1974–6

Valdés, Alfonso de, *Diálogo de las cosas acaecidas en Roma*, Venice 1546 (?); new edn Madrid 1982

Valera, Diego de, *Crónica de los reyes católicos*, Madrid 1927

Vandenesse, Jean de, *Journal des voyages de Philippe II*, in L. P. Gachard, *Collection des voyages des souverains des Pays-Bas*, vols, 2 and 4, Brussels 1882

Van der Wyngaerde, Anton, *Ciudades del siglo de oro. Las vistas españoles de Anton van der Wyngaerde*, ed. Richard Kagan, Madrid 1986

Van Male, Guillaume, *Lettres sur la vie intérieure de l'empereur Charles Quint*, Bruxelles 1843

Vargas Ugarte, Ruben, *Manuscritos peruanos en las bibliotecas extranjeras*, 3 vols., Lima 1935

Vázquez de Tapia, Bernardino, *Información de servicios y méritos* in Aguilar; see above

Vivar, Jerónimo de, *Crónica de los reinos de Chile*, ed. Angel Barral Gómez, Madrid 2001

Warren, J. Benedict, ed., *La conquista de Michoacán, 1521–30*, trans. by Agustín García Alcaraz, Morelia 1979

Weiditz, Christoph, *Trachtenbuch*, in the Deutsches Museum, Nuremberg, of which there was a facsimile in 1927

Weiss, Charles, *Papiers d'état du Cardinal de Granvelle*, 9 vols., Paris 1841–52

Wicki, Josef, ed., *Documenta Indica*, 18 vols., Jesuit Institute, Rome 1948–present

Zárate, Agustín de, *Historia del descubrimiento y conquista de la provincia del Perú*, BAE, Madrid, vol. 26

Zúñiga, Francesillo de, *Cronica 1504–1527*, and *Epistolario*, BAE, Madrid, vol. 36

## SECONDARY SOURCES

Abulafia, David, *The Discovery of Mankind*, New Haven 2008

Acosta Saignes, Miguel, *Los Caribes de la costa venezolana*, Mexico 1946

Addy, George M., *The Enlightenment in the University of Salamanca*, Durham, NC, 1966

Aguirre Beltrán, Gonzalo, 'The Slave Trade in Mexico', *HAHR* 24 (1944)

Aiton, Arthur Scott, *Antonio de Mendoza*, Durham, NC, 1927

Alcalá, Ángel, *El proceso inquisitorial de fray Luis de León*, Salamanca 1991

Alcalá, Luisa Elena, *Fundaciones jesuíticas en Iberoamérica*, Madrid 2002

Alcázar, Cayetano, *Las origenes del correo moderno en españa*, 5 vols., Madrid 1928

Alegre, F. J., *Historia de la Compañía de Jesús en Nueva España*, 3 vols., Mexico 1842

Alegría, Ricardo E., 'Origin and Diffusion of the Term "Cacique"', in *Acculturation of the Americas Proceedings and selected papers of the 29th International Congress of Americanists*, ed. Sol Tax, Chicago 1952, 313–15

Altamira, Rafael, *Felipe II, hombre de estado*, with a new introduction by José Martínez Millán, Alicante 1997

Altolaguirre, Angel, *Vasco Núñez de Balboa*, Madrid 1914

*Andalucia y América en el siglo XVI*, 2 vols., Seville 1983

Angulo, Íñiguez, D., and Bautista Antonelli, *Las fortificaciones americanas del siglo XVI*, Madrid 1947

Aparicio la Serna, Arturo, *Mar de sangre*, Bogotá 2010

Argenti, P., *The Occupation of Chios by the Genoese*, 3 vols., Cambridge 1958

Aritso, Luis Blas, *Vasco Núñez de Balboa y los cronistas de Indias*, Panama 2013

Arranz, Luis, *Don Diego Colón*, vol. 1, Madrid 1982

—, *Repartimientos y encomiendas en la isla española*, Madrid 1991

Arroniz, Othón, *La influencia italiana en el nacimiento de la comedia española*, Madrid 1969

Aubespine, Sébastien de, *Négociations, lettres et pièces diverses relatives au règne de François II*, Paris 1945

Auke, Pieter Jacobs, *Pasajeros y polzones sobre la emigración española en el siglo XVI*, Seville 1983

Ávila, Carlos Lázaro, 'Un freno a la conquista: la resistencia de los cacizagos indígenas', *R de I* 52 (1992)

Avilés Moreno, Guadalupe, 'El arte mudéjar en Nueva España, en el siglo XVI', *AEA* 37 (1980)

Azcona, Tarsicio, *Isabel la Católica*, Madrid 1964

Baer, Yitzak, *History of the Jews in Christian Spain*, New York 1961–6 (translation)

Ballesteros, Antonio, ed., *Historia de América*, 1952; see esp. Amando Melón, *Los primeros tiempos de la colonización*, vol. 6

Ballesteros Gaibrois, Manuel, *Descubrimiento y fundación de Potosí*, Saragossa 1950

—, *La idea colonial de Ponce de León: un ensayo de interpretación*, San Juan 1960

—, *La fundación de Buenos Aires y los indígenas*, Buenos Aires 1980

Barghahan, Barbara von, *Age of Gold, Age of Iron: Renaissance Spain and Symbols of Monarchy*, 2 vols., New York 1985

Baron, Hans, *The Crisis of the Early Italian Renaissance*, Princeton 1966

Bataillon, Marcel, *Novo mundo e fim do mundo*, *Revista de Historia* 18 (São Paolo 1954)

—, *Érasme et l'Espagne*, new edn by Daniel Devoto, Geneva 1991

Baudot, G., *Utopie et histoire au Mexique. Les premiers chroniqueurs de la civilisation mexicaine*, *1520–1569*, Toulouse 1977

Bazarte Martínez, Alicia, *Las cofradías españoles en la ciudad de Mexico, 1526–1869*, Mexico 1989

Benison-Wolff, Inge, *El Juez comisario en el Alto Perú*, *AEA* 39 (1962)

Benítez, Fernando, *La vida criolla en el siglo XVI*, Mexico 1953; English translation, ed. Joan Maclean, Chicago 1962

Benítez, José R., *Alonso García Bravo, primer planeador en la ciudad de México*, Mexico 1933

Bennassar, Bartolomé, *Valladolid au siècle d'or*, Paris 1967

—, *Historia de la tauromaquía*, Ronda 2000

Bennett, Charles E., *Laudonnière and Fort Caroline*, Gainesville 1964

—, *The Settlement of Florida*, Gainesville 1968

Bermúdez de Plata, Cristóbal, *Catálogo de pasajeros a Indias*, 3 vols., Seville 1946

Bernal, Antonio-Miguel, *La financiación de la carrera de Indias, 1492–1824*, Seville 1992

Blair, Emma, and James Robertson, *The Philippine Islands, 1493–1898*, 55 vols., Cleveland, Ohio, 1903–9

Bleichman, Daniela, 'Latin America: The Background of Art', *The New York Review of Books*, February 2012

Bolton, Herbert E., *The Spanish Borderlands: A Chronicle of Old Florida* New Haven 1921

—, *Coronado, Knight of Pueblos and Plains*, New York and Albuquerque 1949

Borah, Woodrow and S. F. Cook, 'The Aboriginal Population of Central Mexico', *Ibero-Americana* 38 (1958)

Borderje y Morencos, Fernando de, *Tráfico de Indias y política oceánica*, Madrid 1991

Borrego, María Carmen, *Cartagena de Indias en el siglo XVI*, Seville 1963

—, *Locos, enanos y hombres de placer en la corte de los Austrias*, Madrid 1991

Bowse, W. B., *Organización del correo en España y las Indias Occidentales*, Buenos Aires 1942

Boxer, C. R. M., *The Portuguese Seaborne Empire*, London 1969

—, *The Christian Century in Japan, 1549–1650*, Manchester 1993

Boyd-Bowman, Peter, *Indice geobiográfico de más de 56 mil pobladores de la América Hispánica*, Mexico 1985

Boyden, James M., *The Courtier and the King, Ruy Gómez e Silva*, Berkeley 1995

Brading, David, *The First America*, Cambridge 1991

Brandi, Karl, *The Emperor Charles V*, trans. by C. V. Wedgwood, London 1939

Bratianu, G. I., *Recherches sur le commerce génois dans l'outre-mer*, 2 vols., Paris 1973–80

Braudel, Fernand, *The Mediterranean and the Mediterranean World in the Age of Philip II*, 2 vols., New York 1973

Brotton, Jerry, *A History of the World in Twelve Maps*, London 2012

Brown, Jonathan, *Felipe II coleccionista*, 4th Centenario del monasterio del Escorial, Madrid 1986

Brown, Lloyd A., *The Story of Maps*, New York 1959

Brumar, Henry, *The Cultural History of Mexican Vanilla*, HAHR 28 (1948)

Burke, Peter, *The Renaissance Sense of the Past*, New York 1970

Burke, M. B., and Peter Cherry, *Documents for the History of Collecting: Spanish Inventories 1, Collections of Painting in Madrid, 1601–1755*, Turin and Los Angeles 1997

Busto Duthurburu, J. A. del, *La tierra y la sangre de Francisco Pizarro*, Lima 1993

—, *Los Trece de las Fama*, Lima 1989

—, *Pizarro*, 2 vols., Lima 2001

Butterfield, Andrew, *Titian and the Birth of Tragedy*, in *The New York Review of Books*, 23 December 2010

Cadenas y Vicent, Vicente, *Carlos I de Castilla, señor de las Indias*, Madrid 1988

Calderón Quijano, José Antonio, *Colón, sus cronistas e historiadores en Menéndez Pelayo*, Seville, XVIII (1956)

—, *Toponomía Española en el Nuevo Mundo*, Seville 1988

*The Cambridge History of China*, vol. 8, Cambridge 1998

Camín, Alfonso, *El Adelantado de Florida, Pedro Menéndez de Avilés*, Mexico 1944

Campos y Fernández de Sevilla, S. J., *La mentalidad en Castilla la Nueva en el siglo XVI*, Madrid 1986

Cantera Burgos, F. Álvar García de Santa María, *Historia de la judería de Burgos y de sus conversos más egregios*, Madrid 1952

Carabias Torres, Ana María, *Los colegiales mayores salamintinos en el gobierno de las Indias*, in *Res Gesta* 13 (January–June 1983)

Carande, Ramón, *Cartas de mercaderes, moneda y crédito*, Madrid, 9 (June 1944)

—, *Carlos V y sus banqueros*, 3 vols., 3rd edn, Barcelona 1987

Carlos V, *Homenaje de la Universidad de Granada*, Granada 1958

Caro Baroja, Julio, *Los Judíos en la España moderna*, 3 vols., Madrid 1961

—, *Los Moriscos del reino de Granada*, Madrid 1976

Carril, Bonifacio del, *Los Mendoza*, Buenos Aires 1954

Carro, Venancio D., *Domingo de Soto y su doctrina jurídica*, Salamanca 1944

Castañeda Delgado, Pauline, *El mestizaje en Indias*, Madrid 2008

Castilla Urbana, Francisco, 'Juan Ginés de Sepúlveda en torno de una idea de civilización', *R de I* 52 (1992)

Castillo Utrilla, María José, 'Temas iconográficos en las fundaciones Franciscanos en América y las Filipinas en el siglo XVI', *AEA* 38 (1981)

Castro, Americo, trans. by Edmund L. King, *The Structure of Spanish History*, Princeton 1954

Cebrían Franco, Juen José, *Obispos de Iria Flavia y arzobispos de Santiago*, Santiago de Compostela 1997

Cedillo, Conde de, *El Cardenal Cisneros, gobernador del Reino*, 2 vols., Madrid 1921 (vol. 2 is composed of documents)

Céspedes del Castillo, Guillermo, *La Avería en el comercio de Indias*, Seville 1945

Chabod, Federico, *Carlos Quinto y su imperio (Carlos I e il suo imperio)*, Spanish trans. by Rodrigo Riza, Madrid 1992

Chamberlain, Robert S., *The Conquest and Colonisation of Yucatan, 1517–1550*, Washington 1948

Chaunu, Pierre and Huguette, *Séville et l'Atlantique, 1540–1650*, 10 vols., Paris 1955–9

—, *L'Espagne de Charles Quint*, Paris 1973

Checa Cremades, Fernando, *Felipe II, maecenas de las artes*, Madrid 1993

—, *Carlos V: la imagen del poder en el Renacimiento*, Madrid 1999

Cheetham, Sir Nicholas, *New Spain*, London 1974

Chevalier, François, 'Les cargaisons des flottes de la Nouvelle Espagne vers 1600', *R de I* 12 (1943)

—, *La formation des grands domaines au Mexique*, Paris 1952

Chipman, Donald, *Nuño de Guzmán*, Glendale, CA, 1967

—, *Moctezuma's Children*, Austin 2005

Cipolla, Carlo, *The Economic Decline of Empires*, London 1970

Ciudad Suárez, María Milagros, *Los Dominicos, un grupo de poder en Chiapas y Guatemala, siglos XVI y XVII*, Seville 1996

Clavería, Carlos, *Le chevalier délibéré de Olivier de la Marche y sus versiones españoles del siglo XVI*, Saragossa 1950

Clendinnen, Inga, *Ambivalent Conquests*, Cambridge 1987

Coello de la Rosa, Alexandre, 'Mestizos y criollos en la Compañía de Jesús (Perú, siglos XVI – XVII)', *R de I* 77, no. 243 (May–August 2008)

Colín, Francisco, *Labor evangélica de la compañía de Jesús en las Islas Filipinas*, Barcelona 1904

Congreso Historia del Descubrimiento, *Actas*, 4 vols., Madrid 1992

Cook, Noble David, *Demographic Collapse in Indian Peru, 1520–1620*, Cambridge 1981

Cooper, Edward, *Castillos señoriales de la Corona de Castilla*, 3 vols., Salamanca 1991

Cortés Alonso, Vicenta, 'La producción documental en España y América en el siglo XVI', *AEA* 41 (1984)

—, 'El imagen del otro, blancos, indios, negros', *R de I* 51 (1991)

Costa, Horacio de la, *The Jesuits in the Philippines, 1581–1768*, Cambridge, Mass., 1967

Cotarelo y Valledor, A., *Fray Diego de Deza*, Madrid 1902

Coury, Charles, *La médecine de l'Amérique précolombienne*, Paris 1969

Crane, Nicholas, *Mercator*, London 2002

Cronin, Vincent, *The Wise Man from the West: Matteo Ricci and his Mission to China*, New York 1955

Crosby, Alfred, 'Virgin Soil Epidemics as a Factor in Aboriginal Depopulation', *The William and Mary Quarterly* 33 (1976)

Cuesta, Luis, 'Una documentación interesante sobre la familia del conquistador de Perú', *R de I* 8 (1947), 866–71. Hernando Pizarro's will is on pages 879–891.

Cunninghame-Graham, R. B., *Pedro de Valdivia*, London 1926

*Curso de conferencias sobre la política africana de los reyes católicos*, Madrid 1953

Cushner, Nicholas P., *Spain in the Philippines*, Manila 1971

Danvila, Alfonso, *Don Cristóbal de Moura 1538–1613*, Madrid 1900

Deagan, Kathleen, 'El impacto de la presencia europea en la Navidad', *R de I* 47, no. 3 (1987)

Deive, Carlos Esteban, *La Española y la esclavitud del Indio*, Santo Domingo 1995

Delgado Barrado, José Miguel, 'Las relaciones comerciales entre España y las Indias durante el siglo XVI', *R de I* 50 (1990)

Delmarel, Guy, *Los Honores: Flemish Tapestries for the Emperor Charles V*, Mecheln (Malines) 2000

*Diccionario de Historia Ecclesiástica de España*, ed. Quintín Aldea Vaquero et al., 4 vols., Madrid 1972

Dickens, A. G., *The Courts of Europe*, London 1977

Domínguez, L. L, ed., *The Conquest of the River Plate*, London 1891

Domínguez Ortiz, Antonio, *La clase social de los conversos en Castilla en la edad moderna*, Madrid 1955

—, *Los Judeoconversos en España y América*, Madrid 1988

Doria, Paolo Matta, *Massime del governo spagnolo a Napoli*, Naples 1973

Doussaingue, José María, *Fernando el católico y el cisma de Pisa*, Madrid 1946

Drescher, Seymour, 'Jews and Christians in the Atlantic Slave Trade', in Paolo Bernardini, ed., *Jews and the Expansion of Europe to the West, 1450–1825*, New York 1999

Duncan, David Ewing, *Hernando de Soto*, New York 1995

Durme, M. Van, *El Cardenal Granvela, Imperio y revolución bajo Carlos V y Felipe II*, Barcelona 1957 (the first edition was in Flemish)

Duviols, J. Paul, *L'Amérique espagnole vue et rêvée*, Paris 1985

*Dworski, R. J., *The Council of the Indies in Spain, 1524–1558*, unpublished, Columbia University thesis, 1979

Édouard, Sylvène, *Le Corps d'une Reine*, Rennes 2009

Edwards, John, *The Spain of the Catholic Kings, 1474–1520*, Oxford 2000

—, *Mary Tudor*, Oxford 2011

Einaudi, Luigi, ed., *Paradoxes de Malestroiet touchant les monnoyes*, Turin 1937

Eisenstein, Elizabeth L., *The Printing Revolution in Early Modern Europe*, Cambridge 1983

Elizalde, María Dolores, Josep M. Pradera, and Luis Alonso, *Imperios y naciones en el Pacífico, I, La formación de una colonia*: Filipinas, Madrid 2001

Elliott, Sir John, *Imperial Spain*, London 1963

—, 'La ética en la conquista de América', Madrid, Corpus Honorum de Pace, 1984. This includes Agueda María Rodríguez Cruz's *Alumnos de la Universidad de Salamanca en la conquista de America*.

—, *Empires of the Atlantic World*, London 2006

—, *Spain, Europe and the Wider World, 1500–1800*, London 2009

—, *History in the Making*, London 2012

— (with Jonathan Brown), *A Palace for a King*, London 2003

Eugenio Martínez, María Angeles, *Tributo y trabajo del Indio en Nueva Granada*, Seville 1977

Evans, Mark, *The Sforza Hours*, London 1992

Feldman, Lawrence, *Lost Shores and Forgotten Peoples*, Salt Lake City 2004

Felix, Alfonso, *The Chinese in the Philippines*, 2 vols., Manila 1966

Fernández Álvarez, Manuel, *Tres embajadores de Felipe II en Inglaterra*, Madrid 1951

—, *La sociedad española del Renacimiento*, Salamanca 1970

—, *Copérnico y su huella en la Universidad de Salamanca del Barroco*, Salamanca 1974

—, *El corpus documental de Carlos V*, 5 vols., Salamanca 1973–82

—, *El testamento de Felipe II*, Madrid 1997

—, *Felipe II y su tiempo*, Madrid 1998

—, *Carlos V, el Caesar y el hombre*, Madrid 1999

—, *El imperio de Carlos V*, Madrid 2001

— and Luis Suárez Fernández, *La España de los reyes católicos*, a volume in the series *Historia de España*, ed. Ramón Menéndez Pidal, Madrid 1969

Fernández-Armesto, Felipe, *The Canary Islands after the Conquest*, Oxford 1982

—, *Before Columbus*, London 1987

—, *Columbus*, Oxford 1992

Fernández Asis, Victoriano, *Epistolario de Felipe II sobre asuntos de mar*, Madrid 1943

Fernández del Castillo, Francisco, *Doña Catalina Xuárez Marcayda*, Mexico 1920

Fernández Pérez, Isacio, *Studium* 29 (1984)

Fernández Sanz, Eufemio, *Cuatro mil vallisoletanos y cien poblaciones en América y Filipinas*, Valladolid 1995

Fernando el Católico, *Pensamiento Político*, V Congreso de historia de la corona de Aragón, Saragossa 1956. Essays by, for example, Manuel Ballesteros Gabrois on Fernando and America, Alfonso García Gallo on the title 'Virrey', and the Baron de Terratieg on the Valencian contribution to the diplomacy of Fernando el Católico.

Ferrara, Orestes, *Philippe II*, Paris 1961

Fontana, Michela, *Matteo Ricci, 1552–1610*, Paris 2005

Foronda, Manuel de, *Estancias y viajes de Carlos V*, Madrid 1895

Fortea Pérez, José Ignacio, *Córdoba en el siglo XVI, las bases demográficas y ecónomicas de una expansión urbana*, Salamanca 1979

Freund, Scarlett, and Teofilo Ruiz, *Jewish-Christian Encounters Over the Centuries*, 1994

Friede, Juan, *Vida y viajes de Nicolás Fédermann*, Bogotá 1964.

Frost, Elsa Cecilia, 'Fray Andrés de Olmos en la relación de Alonso Zurita', *R de I* 51 (1991)

Gachard, M., *Don Carlos et Philippe II*, Paris 1867

Gandia, Enrique de, *Historia de la conquista del río de la Plata y del Paraguay*, Buenos Aires 1931

—, *Crónica del magnífico adelantado don Pedro de Mendoza*, Buenos Aires 1936

García, Casiano, *Vida del comendador Diego de Ordáz, descubridor del Orinoco*, Mexico 1952

García-Abasolo, Antonio, ed., *España y el Pacífico*, Córdoba 1982

—, *Martín Enríquez y la reforma de 1568 en Nueva España*, Madrid 1983

García Baquero, González A., *La carrera de Indias*, Sevilla 1992

García Bernal, Manuela Cristina, *Yucatán, población y encomienda bajo los Austrias*, Seville 1978

García, Casiano, *Vida del comendador Diego de Ordás, descubridor del Orinoco*, Mexico 1952

García de Prodián, Lucía, *Los Judios en América*, Madrid 1966

García del Pino, César, with Alicia Melis Cappa, *El libro de los escribanos cubanos de los siglos XVI, XVII y XVIII*, Havana 1982

García Granados, Rafael, *Historia gráfica del Hospital de Jesús*, Mexico 1956

García Hernán, David, *Historia sin complejos*, essays in honour of Sir John Elliott, Madrid 2010

García Icazbalceta, Joaquín, *Don Fray Juan de Zumárraga*, Mexico 1881

García Oro, J., *El cardenal Cisneros, vida y empresas*, 2 vols., Madrid 1992–3

García Sánchez, Francisco, *El Medellín extremeño en América*, Medellín 1992

García Valdecasas, Alfonso, *El Hidalgo y el honor*, Madrid 1948

Gardiner, Harvey, *Naval Power in the Conquest of Mexico*, Austin 1956

Garrido Atienza, M., *Las capitulaciones para la entrega de Granada*, Granada 1910

Gerhard, Peter, *Geografía histórica de la Nueva España, 1519–1821*, trans. by Stella Maestrangelo, Mexico 1988

—, *La frontera sureste de la Nueva España*, Mexico 1991

Gibson, Charles, *The Aztecs under Spanish Rule*, Stanford 1964

Gil, Juan, 'Marinos y mercaderes en Indias, 1499–1504', *AEA* 42 (1985)

—, *Mitos y utopias del descubrimiento*, 3 vols., Seville 1989

—, 'Sobre la vida familiar de Vicente Yáñez Pinzón', *R de I* 47 (1987)

—, *Una familia de mercaderes sevillanos: los Cisbón, Studi storici in memoria di Alberto Boscolo*, vol. 3, Rome 1993

—, *Los conversos y la Inquisición sevillana*, 8 vols., Seville 2000–2003

—, *Los Chinos en Manila, siglo XVI y XVII*, Lisbon 2011

Gilman, Stephen, *The World of Humanism*, New York 1962

—, *The Spain of Fernando de Rojas*, Princeton 1972

Giménez Fernández, Manuel, *Bartolomé de las Casas*, 2 vols., Seville 1953, 1961

—, *Bartolomé de las Casas, Bibliografía crítica*, Santiago 1954

—, *Breve biografía de Fray Bartolomé de las Casas*, Seville 1966

Giroud, Nicole, *Une mosaïque de fray Bartolomé de las Casas*, Fribourg 2002

Glete, Jan, *War and the State in Early Modern Europe: Spain, the Dutch Republic and Sweden as Fiscal-Military States, 1500–1660*, London 2002

Gómez-Centurión Jiménez, Carlos, *La invencible y la empresa de Inglaterra*, Madrid 1988

Gómez de Cervantes, Gonzalo, *La vida económica y social de Nueva España al finalizar el siglo XVI*, Mexico 1944

Gómez Pérez, María del Carmen, *Pedro de Heredia y Cartagena de Indias*, Sevilla 1984

Góngora, Mario, *Los grupos de conquistadores en Tierra Firme, 1509–1530*, Santiago de Chile 1962. A study of *los de Panama*.

González de Amezúa y Mazo, Agustín, *Isabel de Valois*, 3 vols., Madrid 1949

González, Julio, *Repartimiento de Sevilla*, Madrid 1951

González, Tomás, *Censo de población de las provincias y partidos de la corona de Castilla en el siglo XVI*, Madrid 1829

González de la Calle, Pedro Urbano, *Elio Antonio de Lebrija*, Bogotá 1945

González Novalín, José Luis, *El Inquisidor-General Fernando de Valdés*, 2 vols., Oviedo, 1968–71

González Olmedo, Félix, *Humanistas y Pedagogos españoles: Nebrija, debelador de la barbarie*, Madrid 1942

González Palencia, Angel, *Gonzalo Pérez*, 2 vols., Madrid 1946

González-Trevijano, Pedro, *La Mirada del poder*, Madrid 2004

Goodman, David C., *Power and Penury: Government, Technology and Science in Philip II's Spain*, Cambridge 1988

Gounon-Loubens, J., *Essais sur l'administration de la Castille au XVIe siècle*, Paris 1860

Goulding, Michael et al., *The Smithsonian Atlas of the Amazon*, Washington 2003

Greenleaf, R. E., *The Inquisition in New Spain*, Oxford 1969

Griffin, Clive, *The Cromberger of Seville*, Oxford 1988

Grunberg, Bertrand, *L'univers des conquistadors*, Paris 1993

Guerra, Francisco, 'La epidemía americana de influenza en 1493', *AEA* 45 (1985)

Gussaert, Ernest, *Espagnols et Flamands*, Brussels 1910

Gutiérrez, Luis, *The Synod of Manila, 1582–86*, Manila 1990

Gutiérrez Escudero, Antonio, *Pedro de Alvarado*, Madrid 1988

Haebler, Konrad, *Prosperidad y decadencia económica de España durante el siglo XVI*, Madrid 1899

Hale, Edward E., *The Queen of California, the Origin of the Name California*, San Francisco 1945

Hale, Susan, *Titian*, London 2012

Hamilton, Earl J., 'Wages and Subsistence on Spanish Treasure Ships 1503–1660', *The Journal of Political Economy* 37 (August 1929)

—, *American Treasure and the Price Revolution in Spain, 1501–1650*, Cambridge, Mass., 1934. Few will not be moved by the statement in the Preface that the author and his wife worked jointly for 30,750 hours on the book, carrying out 3 million computations.

Hampe Martínez, Teodoro, *Don Pedro de la Gasca*, Lima 1989

—, *Don Pedro de la Gasca, 1493–1567: su obra política en España y América*, prólogo de Juan Pérez de Tudela, Lima 2000

*Handbook of the Middle American Indians*, Austin 1984–2000

*Handbook of the South American Indians*, Washington 1946

Hanke, Lewis, *The Spanish Struggle for Justice in the New World*, Philadelphia 1949

—, *Aristotle and the American Indians*, London 1959

—, *All Mankind is One*, Philadelphia 1974

—, *Los virreyes españoles en América durante el gobierno de la casa de Austria*, Madrid 1976

— and Gunnar Mendoza, *Guía de las fuentes en Hispanoamérica para el estudio de la administración española mexicana, 1535–1700*, Washington 1980

Haring, C. H., *Trade and Navigation between Spain and the Indies in the Time of the Hapsburgs*, Cambridge 1918

—, *The Spanish Empire in America*, New York 1947

Harrisse, Henry, *The Discovery of North America*, London 1892.

Harth-Terre, Emilio, 'Esclavas blancas en Lima, 1537', *El Comercio*, Lima (3 June 1963)

Harvey, L. P., *Islamic Spain, 1250 to 1500*, Chicago 1990

—, *Muslims in Spain, 1500–1614*, Chicago 2006

Hauser, Henri, in Louis Halpen and Philippe Sagnac, *Peuples et civilisations*, IX, *La préponderance espagnole, 1559–1660*, Paris 1948

Hazañas, Joaquín, *Maese Rodrigo*, Seville 1909

Headley, John M., *The Emperor and his Chancellor*, Cambridge 1983

Heers, Jacques, *Gênes au XVème siècle*, Paris 1961

—, *Christophe Colomb*, Paris 1991

Hemming, John, *The Conquest of the Incas*, London 1970

—, *Red Gold*, London 1978

—, *The Search for El Dorado*, London 1978

Herrera Oria, Enrique, *Felipe II y el Marqués de Santa Cruz en la empresa de Inglaterra*, Madrid 1946

Hidalgo Nuchera, Patricio, *Encomienda, tributo y trabajo en Filipinas, 1570–1608*, Madrid 1995

Hillgarth, Jocelyn, *The Spanish Kingdoms, 1250–1518*, 2 vols., Oxford 1976–8

Himmerich y Valencia, Robert, *The First Encomenderos of New Spain*, Austin 1996

Hinojosa, R., *Los despachos de la diplomacía pontífica en España*, 2 vols., Madrid 1896

Hinz, Felix, 'The Process of Hispanisation in Early New Spain', *R de I* 68, no. 243 (2008)

Huizinga, J., *The Autumn of the Middle Ages*, trans. by Rodney J. Payton and Ulrich Mammitzsch, Chicago 1996. The first edition is still in some ways superior.

Humboldt, Alexander V. and Aimé Bompland, *Personal Narrative of Travels to the Equinoctial Regions of America during the Years 1799–1804*, ed. Thomasina Ross, 3 vols., London 1894

Hurtado, Publio, *Los Extremeños en América*, Seville 1992

Icaza, Francisco de, *Diccionario autobiográfico de conquistadores y pobladores de la Nueva España*, Madrid 1923

Íñiguez Almech, Francisco, *Casas reales y jardines de Felipe II*, Madrid 1952

Insansti, Sebastián, *Miguel López de Legazpi, escribano de Areria in Boletín de la Real Sociedad Vascona de Amigos del País*, San Sebastian 1974

Irving, Washington, *The Life and Voyages of Christopher Columbus*, New York 1863

Iwasaki, Fernando, 'La evangelisación en Perú y Japón', *R de I* 48 (1988)

Jacquot, Jean, ed., *Les Fêtes de la Renaissance, II, Fêtes et céremonies au temps de Charles Quint*, Paris 1960. This includes Bataillon's essay, 'Plus Oultre: La Cour découvre le Nouveau Monde'.

Jensen, J. de Lamar, *Diplomacy and Dogmatism: Bernardino de Mendoza and the Catholic League*, Cambridge, MA, 1964

Jones, R. O., *The Golden Age: Prose and Poetry*, London 1971

Jongh, Jane de, *Margaret of Austria*, trans. from the Dutch by M. D. Herter Norton, London 1954

Kagan, Richard, ed., *Students and Society in Early Modern Spain*, Baltimore 1974

—, *Lucrecia's Dreams: Politics and Prophecy in Sixteenth-Century Spain*, Berkeley 1990

—, *Anton van der Wyngaerde: ciudades del siglo de oro*, Madrid 1994

Kamen, Henry, *Crisis and Change in Early Modern Spain*, Aldershot 1993

—, *Philip of Spain*, London 1997

—, *The Spanish Inquisition*, New Haven 1997

—, *The Duke of Alba*, New Haven 2004

—, *Imagining Spain*, New Haven 2008

Kellenbruz, Hermann, *Los Fugger en España y Portugal hasta 1560*, Salamanca 1999

Kelsey, Harry, *Sir Francis Drake*, New Haven 1996

Kendrick, T. D., *St James in Spain*, London 1960

Keniston, Hayward, *Garcilaso de la Vega*, New York 1922

—, *Francisco de los Cobos*, Pittsburgh 1958

Klein, Julius, *The Mesta: A Study in Spanish Economic History, 1273–1836*, Cambridge, Mass., 1920

Knecht, Robert J., *The French Renaissance Court*, New Haven 2008

Koebel, W. H., *Paraguay*, London 1917

Koenigsberger, H. G., *The Government of Sicily under Philip II of Spain*, London 1951

Konetzke, Richard, *El imperio español: origenes y fundamentos*, Madrid 1946; trans. from the German

—, *La emigración española al Río de la Plata*, in vol. 3 of *Miscelánea Americanista*, Madrid, 1953. About the preparations for the expedition of Cabeza de Vaca to Buenos Aires, etc.

Kriegel, Maurice, 'La Prise d'une décision, l'exclusion des Juifs d'Espagne', *Revue Historique* CCLX (1978)

Kubler, George and Martin Soria, *Art and Architecture in Spain and Portugal and in their American Dominions, 1500 to 1800*, Harmondsworth 1959

—, *La obra del Escorial*, Madrid 1983

Kwarteng, Kwasi, *Ghosts of Empire*, London 2010

La Fuente, Alejandro de, *Havana and the Atlantic in the Sixteenth Century*, Chapel Hill 2008

*Lagomarsino, Paul David, *Court Factions and the Formulation of Spanish Policy towards the Netherlands, 1559–1567*, Cambridge unpublished thesis, 1973

Laínez Alcalá, Rafael, *Pedro Berruguete, pintor de Castilla*, Madrid 1935

Lamb, Ursula, *Una biografía contemporánea y una carta de fr. Nicolás de Ovando . . . [al rey, November 1509]*, *Revista de Estudios Extremeños* 3–4, Badajoz 1951, 693–707

—, 'Cristóbal de Tapia vs. Nicolás de Ovando', *HAHR* 33, no. 3 (August 1953), 427–42

—, *Fr. Nicolas de Ovando with comentarios preliminares of Miguel Muñoz de San Pedro*, Madrid 1956

Lapeyre, Henri, *Une famille de marchands: les Ruiz*, Paris 1955

—, *Géographie de l'Espagne morisque*, Paris 1960

Lasero Quesada, Miguel Angel, *Castilla y la conquista de Granada*, Granada 1993

—, *La incorporación de Granada en la corona de Castilla*, Actas de symposium, Granada 1993

—, *La edad media hispánica: en torno da cuatro centenarios*, Madrid 2012

Laso de la Vega, M., *Doña Mencia de Mendoza, marquesa del Cenete, 1508–1554*, Madrid 1942

Lavallé, Bernard, *Francisco Pizarro*, Paris 2004

Lawley, Alethea, *Victoria Colonna*, London 1889

Lea, H. C., *The Inquisition of Spain*, 3 vols., New York 1907

Lebroc Martínez, Reynerio, *Episcopologio cubano*, vol. 1, Caracas 2001; vol. 2, Miami 2003.

Leddy Phelan, John, *The Hispanization of the Philippines, 1565–1700*, Madison 1959

León Portilla, Miguel, *Aztecas-Mexicas Desarollo de una civilización originaria*, Madrid 2005

—, *Hernán Cortés y el mar del sur*, Mexico 2005

Leonard, Irving, *Romances of Chivalry in the Spanish Indies*, Berkeley 1933

—, *Books of the Brave*, New York 1964

Levillier, Roberto, *Don Francisco de Toledo, su vida, su obra*, Madrid 1935

—, *Anexos* [to the above], Madrid 1935

—, *América la bien llamada*, 2 vols., Buenos Aires, n.d.

—, 'Gobernantes del Perú', in *Cartas y Papeles*, 14 vols., Madrid 1921–6

Lewis, Samuel, 'The Cathedral of Old Panama', *HAHR* 1 (1918)

Lida de Malkiel, María Rosa, *La idea de la fama en la edad media castellana*, Mexico 1952

Lisón Tolisano, Carmelo, *La imagen del rey. Monarquía, realeza y poder ritual en la casa de las Austrias*, Madrid 1991

Liss, Peggy, *Isabel the Queen*, Oxford 1992

Lissón, Emilio, *La Iglesia en el Perú*, 5 vols., Seville 1943–56

Llorente, Juan Antonio, *Historia crítica de la inquisición en España*, 10 vols., Madrid 1822; 4 vols., Paris 1817

Lobo Cabrera, Manuel, 'Esclavos negros a Indias a través de Gran Canaria', *AEA* 45 (1985)

Lockhart, James, *Spanish Peru 1532–1560*, Madison 1968

—, *The Men of Cajamarca*, Austin 1972

Lohmann Villena, Guillermo, *Enrique García, descubridor del mercurio en el Perú*, Seville 1948

—, *Las minas de Huacavelica en los siglos XVI y XVIII*, Sevilla 1949

—, *Les Espinosa*, Paris 1968

—, *Los americanos en las ordenes militares*, 2 vols., Madrid 1980

López de Cogulludo, *Historia de Yucatán*, Mexico 1957

Lorenzo Sanz, Eufemio, *Comercio de España en la época de Felipe II*, 2 vols., Valladolid 1986

Lovell, W. George, *Conquest and Survival in Colonial Guatemala*, Montreal 1992

Lovett, A. W., *Early Habsburg Spain, 1517–98*, Oxford 1986

Lowry, Martin, *The World of Aldus Manutius: Business and Scholarship in Renaissance Venice*, Oxford 1979

Loyola, Martín Ignacio de, *Itinerario. Viaje alrededor del mundo*, Rome 1883; new edn Madrid 1989

Lynch, John, *Spain under the Habsburgs*, 2 vols., Oxford 1954–69

—, *Spain, 1516–1598*, London 1991

Lynn, Caro, *A College Professor of the Renaissance*, Chicago 1937

Lyon, Eugene, *The Enterprise of Florida: Pedro Menéndez de Avilés and the Spanish Conquest of 1565–1568*, Gainesville 1976

Magalhaes Godinho, Vitorino, *Mito e mercadería, utopia e practica do novegar*, Lisbon 1990

Mallett, Michael, *The Borgias: Rise and Fall of a Renaissance Dynasty*, London 1969

Maltby, William S., *Alba: A Biography of Fernando Álvarez de Toledo, Third Duke of Alba*, Berkeley 1983

—, *Rise and Fall of the Spanish Empire*, Madrid 2009

Manzano, Juan, *Cristóbal Colón, Siete años decisivos de su vida, 1485–1492*, Madrid 1964

Marañón, Gregorio, *Antonio Pérez*, 2 vols., Madrid 1958

Maravall, José Antonio, *Carlos V y el pensamiento político del Renacimiento*, Madrid 1960

March, J. M., *Niñez y juventud de Felipe II*, 2 vols., Madrid 1941

—, *El comendador Mayor de Castilla, Don Luis de Requesens*, Madrid 1943

Mariejol, J. H., *The Spain of Ferdinand and Isabella*, trans. by Benjamin Keene, New Brunswick 1961

Mariluz Urquijo, José María, 'Ensayo sobre los juicios de residencia indi-anos', *Hispano-Americanos* 70 (1952).

Marlet, L., *Le comte de Montgomery*, Paris 1890

Martin, C. and G. Parker, *The Spanish Armada*, London 1988

Martín, Luis, *Daughters of the Conquistadors*, Albuquerque 1983

—, *The Intellectual Conquest of Peru*, New York 1968

Martínez del Peral, Rafael, *Las armas blancas en España e Indias*, Madrid 1992

Martínez Mendoza, Jerónimo, *La leyenda de el Dorado*, Caracas 1957

Martínez Millán, José, with J. Esquerra Revilla, *Carlos V y la quiebra del humanismo político en Europa, 1530–1558*, 4 vols., Madrid 2001

—, *La monarquía de Felipe II*, 2 vols., Madrid 2005

—, ed., *La corte de Carlos V*, 5 vols., Madrid 2000

Matienzo, Juan de, *El gobierno del Perú*, Madrid 1580

Mattingly, Garrett, *The Defeat of the Spanish Armada*, London 1939

—, *Renaissance Diplomacy*, London 1955

Maura Gamazo, Gabriel, *El príncipe que murió de amor*, Madrid 1944

—, *El designo de Felipe II y el episodio de la Armada Invencible*, Madrid 1957

Medina, José Toribio, *Escritores americanos celebrados por Cervantes en el canto de Calliope*, Santiago 1926

Melis, F., *Mercaderes italianos en España, siglos XIV–XVI*, Seville 1976

Mellafe, Rolando and Sergio Villalobos, *Diego de Almagro*, Santiago 1954

Mena García, María de Carmen, 'El traslado de la Ciudad de Nombre de Dios a Portobelo', *AEA* 40

—, *Sevilla y las flotas de Indias*, Seville 1998 (This is based on the accounts of the flota of Pedrarias which Carmen Mena García found in the AGI, Contratación 3253.)

—, *Pedrarias Davila*, Seville 1992

Méndez Bejarano, M., *Histoire de la juiverie de Séville*, Madrid 1922

Menéndez Pidal, Ramón, *La idea imperial de Carlos V*, Buenos Aires 1941

Menzies, Gavin, *1421*, New York 2002

Merriman, Roger B., *The Rise of the Spanish Empire in the Old World and in the New*, 4 vols., New York 1918–34

Meyerson, Mark D., *The Muslims of Valencia in the Age of Fernando and Isabel*, Oxford 1991

Mier y Teran Rochas, Lucía, *La primera traza de la ciudad de México*, Mexico 2005

Milhou, Alain, 'Las Casas frente a las reivindicaciones de los colonos de la Isla Española', *Historiografía y Bibliografía Americanistas* 19–20, 1975–6

Mintz, Sidney W., *Sweetness and Power*, New York 1985

Mira Caballos, Esteban, 'Las licencias de esclavos negros a Hispanoamérica, 1544–50', *R de I* 54 (1994)

—, *Hernán Cortés, el fin de una leyenda*, Madrid 2010

Modica, Anne-Marie, *Discussions actuelles sur l'origine de la syphilis*, Marseilles 1970

Molina Martínez, Miguel, 'El soldado cronista', *AEA* 41 (1984)

*Monografías historiales sobre la historia de Lima*, 2 vols., Lima 1935

Moorhead, Max, 'Hernán Cortés and the Tehuantepec Passage', *HAHR* 29 (1949)

Morales Padrón, Francisco, *Jamaica Española*, Seville 1952

Morison, S. E., *Admiral of the Ocean Sea*, 2 vols., Boston 1942

—, *The European Discovery of America: The Northern Voyages*, Oxford 1971

—, *The European Discovery of America: The Southern Voyages*, New York 1974

Morner, Magnus, *La mezcla de razas en la historia de América Latina*, Buenos Aires 1969

Moulin, Anne-Marie and Robert Delort, 'Syphilis: le mal américain', *L'Histoire* 63 (1984)

Mulcahy, Rosemarie, *Philip II, Patron of the Arts*, Dublin 2004

Muñoz, Andrés, *Viaje de Felipe segundo a Inglaterra*, ed. P. Gayangos, Madrid 1877

Muñoz de San Pedro, Miguel, *Francisco de Lizaur, hidalgo indiano de principios del siglo XVI*, Madrid 1948

—, 'Francisco Pizarro debío apellidarse Díaz o Hinojosa', *Revista de Estudios Extremeños* 6 (1950)

—, 'Doña Isabel de Vargas, esposa del padre del conquistador de Perú', *R de I* 11 (1951)

—, *Tres testigos de la conquista del Perú*, Madrid 1964

—, 'Información sobre el linaje de Hernando Pizarro', *Revista de Estudios Extremeños* 22 (1966)

Muriel, Josefina, *Hospitales de la Nueva España*, 2 vols., Mexico 1956–60

Muro, Gaspar, *La vida de la princesa de Éboli*, Madrid 1877

Muro, Luis, Bartolomé de Medina, 'Introductor del beneficio de plata en Nueva España', *Historia Mexicana* 52 (1962)

Nader, Helen, *The Mendoza Family in the Spanish Renaissance*, New Brunswick 1979

Netanyahu, Benzion, *The Marranos of Spain*, New York 1966

—, *The Origins of the Inquisition in Fifteenth-Century Spain*, New York, 1995

—, *Toward the Inquisition*, Cornell 1997

—, *Isaac Abravanel*, Philadelphia 1972

Nieto, J. C., *El renacimiento y la otra España*, Geneva 1990

Nordenskjöld, E., 'The Guaraní Invasion of the Inca Empire in the Sixteenth Century', *The Geographical Review* (1917)

Norton, F. J., *Printing in Spain, 1501–1520*, Cambridge 1966

—, *A Descriptive Catalogue of Printing in Spain and Portugal, 1501–1520*, Cambridge 1978

Novalín, José Luis G., *El inquisidor general Fernando de Valdés*, 2 vols., Oviedo 1968–71

Núñez Jiménez, A., *El almirante en la tierra más hermosa. Los viajes de Colón a Cuba*, Cadiz 1985

Ochoa Brun, Miguel-Ángel, *Miscelánea diplomática*, Madrid 2012

O'Gorman, Edmundo, *La idea del descubrimiento de América*, Mexico 1951

Ojer, Pablo, *Don Pablo de Berrio, Gobernador del Dorado*, Caracas 1960

Olachea Labatón, Juan B., 'El aceso de los mestizos a las encomiendas', *R de I* 51 (1991)

Olarte, Teodoro, *Alfonso de Castro*, San José 1946

Ollé, Manuel, *La empresa de China*, Barcelona 2002

Olschidi, Leonardo, 'Ponce de León's Fountain of Youth', *HAHR* 21 (1941)

Orozco y Berra, Manuel, *Historia antigua de la conquista de Mexico*, 4 vols., Mexico 1880

Ortega y Gasset, José, *España invertebrada*, Madrid 1921

Ortiz Belmonte, Miguel A., *Los Ovando y Solís de Cáceres*, Badajoz 1932

Ortiz, Fernando, 'La "leyenda negra" contra Bartolomé de las Casas', *Cuadernos Americanos* 65, no. 5 (1952)

Ortiz de la Tabla Ducasse, Javier, *Los encomenderos de Quito, 1534–1660: origen y evolución de una elite colonial*, Sevilla 1993

Otte, Enrique, 'Cartas de Diego de Ordaz', in *Historia Mexicana*

—, 'Aspiraciones y actividades heterogéneros de Gonzalo Fernández de Oviedo, cronista', *R de I* 71 (1958)

—, 'Documentos inéditos sobre la estancia de Gonzalo Fernández de Oviedo en Nicaragua', *R de I* 18 (1958)

—, *Die Negersklavenlizenz des Laurent de Gorrevod*, Spanisches Forschungen der Görresgesellschaft, Erste Reihe 22, 283–320, Munster 1965

—, *Las perlas del Caribe*, Caracas 1977

—, *Cartas privadas de emigrantes a Indias*, Seville 1988 and Mexico 1993

—, 'Los mercaderes transatlánticos bajo Carlos V', *AEA* 47 (1990)

—, *Sevilla y sus mercaderes a fines de la Edad Media*, Seville 1996

Ovideo y Baños, José, *Historia de la conquista y población de la provincia de Venezuela*, Caracas 1967

Padilla, S. with M. L. López Arellano and A. González, *La encomienda de Popayán*, Seville 1977

Pagden, Anthony, *Spanish Imperialism and the Political Imagination*, New Haven 1990

—, *Peoples and Empires*, London 2001

Parker, Geoffrey, *The Army of Flanders and the Spanish Road, 1567–1659*, Cambridge 1972

—, *The Dutch Revolt*, London 1977

—, *Philip II*, Boston 1978

—, *The Grand Strategy of Philip II*, New Haven 1998

Parry, John, *The Establishment of the European Hegemony*, London 1961

—, *The Spanish Seaborne Empire*, London 1966

Pastells, Pablo and Pedro Torres Lanzas, *Catálogo de los documentos relativos a las Islas Filipinas*, 9 vols., Barcelona 1925

Pastor, Ludwig von, *History of the Popes*, trans. by Frederick Ignatius Antrobus, and Ralph Kerr, vols. 5 to 20, London 1898–1930

Paz, Octavio, *México en la obra de Octavio Paz*, 3 vols., Mexico 1987

Pereda López, A., *Conquistadores y encomenderos burgaleses en Indias, 1492–1606*, Burgos 2001

—, *La emigración burgalesa a América durante el siglo XVI*, Burgos 2009

Pereyra, Carlos, *Historia de la América*, 8 vols., Mexico 1924–6

Pérez, Joseph, *Carlos V*, Madrid 1999

—, *La rebelión de los comuneros*, Madrid 2001

Pérez Bustamente, Ciriaco, 'Cuando nací Legazpi', *R de I* 32 (1971)

Pérez de la Riva, Juan, *El Barracón y otros ensayos*, Havana 1975

Pérez de Tudela, Juan, *Las armadas de Indias y los orígenes de la política de la colonización*, Madrid 1956

Pérez López-Portillo, Raúl, *Aztecas-México*, Madrid 2012

Pérez-Mallaína, Pablo Emilio, 'Juan Gutiérrez Garibay, vida y hacienda de un general de la Carrera de Indias en la segunda mitad del siglo XVI', *R de I* 70, no. 249 (2010)

Pfandl, Ludwig, *Felipe II, bosquejo de una vida y de una época*, Madrid 1942

Phelan, John Leddy, *The Millennial World of the Franciscans in the New World: A Study of the Writings of Gerónimo de Mendieta*, Berkeley 1956

Phillips, Carla Rahn, *Ciudad Real, 1500–1750*, Cambridge, Mass., 1979

—, *Six Galleons for the King of Spain*, Baltimore 1986

Pierson, Peter, *Philip II of Spain*, London 1975

Pike, Ruth, *Enterprise and Adventure: The Genoese in Seville*, Ithaca 1966

—, *Aristocrats and Traders*, Ithaca 1972

Pirenne, Jacques, *Les grands courants de l'histoire universelle*, 3 vols., Neuchâtel 1948–53

Pohl, Frederick J., *Amerigo Vespucci*, London 1966

Porrás Barrenechea, Raúl, *Cedulario del Perú*, Lima 1944–8

—, 'Dos documentos esenciales sobre Francisco Pizarro', *Revista Histórica* 17 (1948)

—, *Cartas del Perú 1524–1543*, Lima 1959

—, *Las relaciones primitivas de la conquista del Perú*, Lima 1967

—, *El nombre del Perú*, Lima 1968

—, *Pizarro*, Lima 1978

Porrás Camunez, José Luis, *Sínodo de Manila de 1582*, Madrid 1988

Porrás Muñoz, Guillermo, *El gobierno de la ciudad de México en el siglo XVI*, Mexico 1982

Powell, P. W., 'Portrait of an American Viceroy: Martín Enríquez, 1568–1583', *The Americas* 14, no. 1 (July 1957)

Prescott, William H., *The Art of War in Spain: The Conquest of Granada, 1481–1492*, ed. Alfred D. McJoynt, London 1995 (the chapters dealing with war in Prescott's *History of the Reign of Ferdinand and Isabella*)

*Presencia italiana en Andalucía, siglos XIV–XVII*, Sevilla 1985 (articles by Otte, Carande, Pike, Heers, etc.)

Pulido Rubio, José, *El piloto mayor de la Casa de la Contratación de Sevilla*, Seville 1950

Pursell, B., 'Gondomar: A Spaniard in King James's Court', *North American Society for Court Studies*, occasional pamphlets

Quenun, Alphonse, *Les églises chrétiennes et la traite atlantique du XVe au XIXe siècles*, Paris 1993

Ramos Gómez, Luis, 'Los Lucayos guias naúticas', *R de I* 49 (1986)

Ramos Pérez, Demetrio, 'Castillo del Oro', *AEA* 37 (1980)

—, *El conflicto de las lanzas jinetes*, Santo Domingo 1982

—, 'El repudio al tratado de Tordesillas', *Congreso Nacional de Historia*, Salamanca 1992

—, *Hernán Cortés, mentalidades y propósitos*, Madrid 1992

Ranke, L. von, *The Ottoman and Spanish Empires in the Sixteenth and Seventeenth Centuries*, London 1843

Redondo, A., 'Luther et L'Espagne de 1520 à 1536', *Mélanges de la Casa de Velázquez* (1965)

—, *Antonio de Guevara et l'Espagne de son temps*, Geneva 1976

Redworth, Glyn, *The Prince and the Infanta*, New Haven 2003

Reiss, S. and D. Wilkins, *Beyond Isabella: Secular Women Patrons of Art in Renaissance Italy*, Kirksville, Missouri, 2001

Reitz, Elizabeth J., 'Dieta y alimentación hispano-americana en el Caribe en el siglo XVI', *R de I* 51 (1991)

Remedios Casamar, María, *Los dos muertos del rey Don Sebastián*, Granada 1995

Remesal, Agustín, *La raya de Tordesillas*, Salamanca 1994

Ricard, Robert, *The Spiritual Conquest of Mexico*, trans. by Leslie Byrd Simpson, Berkeley 1966

Rivera, Javier, *Juan Bautista de Toledo y Felipe II*, Valladolid 1984

Rivero Rodríguez, Manuel, *Felipe II y el gobierno de Italia*, Madrid 1998

—, *Gattinara, Carlos V y el sueño del imperio*, Madrid 2005

—, *La edad de oro de los virreyes*, Madrid 2011

Robertson, William A., *History of America*, 3 vols., Dublin 1777

Rodríguez, Isacio, *Historia de la provincia agustiniania del santísimo nombre de Jesús de Filipinas*, 22 vols., Manila 1965

Rodríguez, Lorenzo, 'El Galeón de Manila', *R de I* (1944)

Rodríguez Demorizi, Emilio, *Los dominicos y las encomiendas en la Isla Española*, Santo Domingo 1971

Rodríguez Moñino, A., *Los pintores badajoceños del siglo XVI*, Badajoz 1956

Rodríguez Prampolini, Ida, *Amadíses en America, la hazaña de Indias como empresa caballeresca*, Mexico 1948

Rodríguez Salgado, María José, *Armada, 1588–1988*, a catalogue for the Armada exhibition in Greenwich, London 1988

—, *The Changing Face of Empire: Charles V, Philip II and Habsburg Authority, 1551–1559*, Cambridge 1988

Rodríguez Sánchez, Angel, *La población cacereña en el siglo XVI*, Salamanca 1976

Rodríguez Villa, Antonio, *El Emperador Carlos V y su corte según las cartas de Don Martín de Salinas, embajador del infante Don Fernando, 1522–1539*, Madrid 1903

—, *Etiquetas de la casa de Austria*, Madrid 1913

Rojas, Pedro, *Historia general del arte mexicano*, Mexico 1963

Romero de Terreros, M., *Pedro Romero de Terreros, el primer español que pisó el continente americano*, Mexico 1941

Romier, Lucien, *Les origines politiques des guerres de religion*, Paris 1913–14

Romoli, Kathleen, *Balboa of Darien*, New York 1953

Rosenblatt, Ángel, *La población indigena y el mestizaje en América*, 2 vols., Buenos Aires 1954

—, *La población de América de 1492*, Mexico 1967

Rubio Mañé, J. I., *Mexico 1955, introducción al estudio de los virreyes de Nueva España*, 3 vols., Mexico 1955

Rublé, Alphonse, *Le traité de Cateau-Cambrésis*, Paris 1889

Ruidiaz y Caravia, Eugenio, *La Florida: su conquista y colonización por Pedro Menéndez de Avilés*, 2 vols., Madrid 1893–4

Ruiz Martín, Felipe, *El siglo de los Genoveses en Castilla*, Paris 1973

—, *La monarquía de Felipe II*, Madrid 2003

Rumeu de Armas, Antonio, 'Colón en Barcelona', *Anuario de Estudios Hispano-Americanos* (1944), 461

—, 'Piraterías y ataques navales contra las Islas Canarias', Instituto Jerónimo Zurita, vol. 1, Madrid 1947

—, *Alonso de Lugo en la corte de los reyes católicos, 1497–1497*, Madrid 1952

—, 'Cristóbal Colón y doña Beatriz de Bobadilla', *AEA* 28 (1954)

—, *Itinerario de los reyes católicos*, Madrid 1974

Russell, Sir Peter, *Prince Henry the Navigator*, New Haven 2000

Sáenz de Santa María, Carmelo, 'La hueste de Alvarado en Perú', *AEA* 43 (1983)

Salas, Alberto, *Tres cronistas de Indias*, Mexico 1986

Sale, Kirkpatrick, *The Conquest of Paradise*, London 1991

Salomon, Noël, *La vida rural castellana en tiempos de Felipe II*, Barcelona 1973

Sánchez, Carlos José Hernando, *Castilla y Napolés en el siglo XVI: el virrey Pedro de Toledo*, Salamanca 1994

Sánchez Blanco, Francisco, 'Descubrimiento de la variedad humana . . . el impacto del nuevo mundo', *AEA* 45 (1985)

Sánchez González, Antonio, *Medinaceli y Colón*, Madrid 1995

Sánchez Ochoa, Pilar, 'Poder y conflicto de autoridad en Santiago de Guatemala durante el siglo XVI', *AEA* 49 (1992)

Santamaría, Alberto, *The Chinese Parian in the Philippines, 1570–1770*, Manila 1966

Sarabia Viejo, María Justina, *Don Luis de Velasco*, Seville 1978

—, 'Historia española en torno de Hernán Cortés', *R de I* 50 (1990)

Sauer, Carl, *The Early Spanish Main*, Berkeley 1966

Sayous, A. E., 'Les débuts du commerce de l'Espagne avec l'Amérique d'après des minutes inédites des archives notariales de Séville', *Revue Historique* (1934)

Schäfer, Ernesto, *El consejo real y supremo de las Indias*, 2 vols., Seville 1935. New edn with prologue by Antonio-Miguel Bernal, Madrid 2003.

Schick, León, *Un grand homme d'affaires au début du XVIe siècle: Jacob Fugger*, Paris 1957

Scholes, France and Eleanor Adams, *Don Diego Quijada, alcalde mayor de Yucatán*, 2 vols., Mexico 1938

Schurz, William Lette, *The Manila Galleon*, New York 1939

Serrano, F. Luciano, *Los conversos Don Pablo de Santa María y Don Alfonso de Cartagena*, Madrid 1942

Serrano Sanz, Manuel, *Las orígenes de la dominación española en Indias*, Madrid 1918

—, *Los amigos y protectores aragoneses de Cristóbal Colón*, Madrid 1918, reissued Barcelona 1991

—, 'El Licenciado Juan de Cervantes y Don Íñigo López de Mendoza, cuarto duque del Infantado', BAE 13 (1926)

Serrera, Ramón María, *La América de los Habsburgos, 1517–1700*, Seville 2011

Shergold, N. D., *A History of the Spanish Stage*, Oxford 1967

Sicroff, Albert A., *Les controverses des statuts de 'pureté de sang' en Espagne du XVème au XVIIème siècle*, Paris 1960

Sigüenza, Fray José de, *Historia de la orden de San Jerónimo*, 2 vols., Madrid 1907–9

Simpson, L. B., *The Encomienda in New Spain*, Berkeley 1934

Soustelle, Jacques, *La vie quotidienne des Aztèques à la veille de la conquête espagnole*, Paris 1955

Spivakovsky, Erika, *Son of the Alhambra: Diego Hurtado de Mendoza*, Austin 1970

Spreti, Marchese Vittorio, *Enciclopedia histórica nobilare italiana*, 8 vols., Milan 1928–35

Stella, Alessandro, *Histoire des esclaves dans la péninsule ibérique*, Paris 2000.

— and Bernard Vincent, 'L'esclavage en Espagne à l'époque moderne; Colloque du GIREA, Naples 1997

Stirling-Maxwell, Sir William, *The Cloister Life of the Emperor Charles V*, London 1851

Stradling, Robert, *Philip IV and the Government of Spain, 1621–1665*, Cambridge 1988

Suárez Fernández, Luis, *Isabel I, reina*, Barcelona 2000

Super, John C., *Food, Conquest and Civilisation in the Sixteenth Century*, Albuquerque 1988

Tardieu, Jean-Pierre, *Cimarrones de Panamá: la forja de una identidad afroamericana en el siglo XVI*, Madrid 2009

Taviani, Paolo Emilio, *Cristoforo Colombo*, 2 vols., Novara 1974

Teixera, Manuel, *Macau no século XVI*, Macau 1951

Telleacha Idigoras, J. L., *El arzobispo Carranza y su tiempo*, 2 vols., Madrid 1968

Tena Fernández, Juan, *Trujillo histórico y monumental*, Trujillo 1967

Thayer Ojeda, Tomás, *Formación de la sociedad chilena y censo de la población de Chile en los años de 1540 a 1565*, 3 vols., Santiago 1939–41

—, *Valdivia y sus compañeros*, Santiago 1950

Thomas, Henry, *Spanish and Portuguese Romances of Chivalry*, Cambridge 1920

Thomas, Hugh, *The Conquest of Mexico*, London 1993

—, *Quién es quién de los conquistadores*, Barcelona 2000

—, *Rivers of Gold*, London 2003

—, *The Golden Age*, London 2010

Thomson, I. A. A., *War and Society in Habsburg Spain*, Aldershot 1992

*Tordesillas 1494*, Madrid 1994

*Tra Siviglia e Genova: notaio, documento e commercio nell'eta Colombina*, Milan 1994

Touissant, Manuel, *La catedral de México*, 2 vols., Mexico 1924

—, *La conquista de Pánuco*, Mexico 1948

Tracy, James D., *Emperor Charles V, Impresario of War*, Cambridge 2002

Tremayne, Eleanor E., *The First Governess of the Netherlands, Margaret of Austria*, London 1908

Trevor-Roper, Hugh, *From Counter-Reformation to Glorious Revolution*, London 1992

—, *History and the Enlightenment*, New Haven 2010

Turrel, Denise, *Bourg-en-Bresse au XVIe siècle, les hommes et la ville*, Bourg-en-Bresse 1986

Twitchett, Dennis and Frederick Mote, *The Cambridge History of China*, *VIII, The Ming Dynasty, 1368–1644*, Part 2, Cambridge 1998

Ullibari, Saturnino, *Piratas y corsarios en Cuba*, Tortuga 2004

Ulloa, Modesto, *La hacienda real de Castilla en el reinado de Felipe II*, Madrid 1986

Vaille, E., *Histoire générale des postes françaises*, 2 vols., Paris 1949

Valdeón Baruque, Julio, ed., 'Isabel la Católica y la política', *Instituto de Historia Simancas*, Valladolid 2001

Valgoma y Díaz Varela, Dalmiro, 'Sangre de Legazpi', *R de I* (1946)

—, *Norma y ceremonia en los reinos de la casa de Austria*, Madrid 1958

Vallee-Arizpe, Artemio de, *Virreyes y virreinas de la Nueva España*, Mexico 2000

Van der Essen, L. *Alexandre Farnèse, Prince de Parme, 1545–1592*, 5 vols., Brussels 1933

Van Durne, M., *El cardenal Granvela, 1517–1586*, Barcelona 1957

Varela, Consuelo, *Cristóbal Colón, retrato de un hombre*, Madrid 1992

Vargas, José María, *Fr Domingo de Santo Tomás*, Quito 1937

Vázquez Fernández, Luis, *La presencia de la merced en América*, Madrid 1991

Ventura, Pietro Tacchi, *Opere storiche del P. Matteo Ricci*, 2 vols., Macerata 1913

Vergès, Françoise, *Abolir l'esclavage, une utopie coloniale*, Paris 2000

Vernon, Ida Stevenson Weldon, *Pedro de Valdivia*, Austin 1946

Vicens Vives, J., *Política del rey católica en Cataluña*, Barcelona 1940

Vilacorta Bañõz, Antonio, *La Emperatriz Isabel*, Madrid 2009

Vila Vilar, Enriqueta with Jaime J. Lacueva Muñoz, *Familia, viajes y negocios entre Sevilla y las Indias*, Madrid 2003

—, *Mirando las dos orillas*, Sevilla 2012

Vilar, Pierre, *Histoire de l'Espagne*, Paris 1968

Vocht, Henry de, *John Dantiscus and his Netherlandish Friends as Revealed by their Correspondence*, Louvain 1961

Wagner, Henry R., 'Francisco Ulloa Returned', *California Historical Society Quarterly* 19 (September 1940)

—, *The Rise of Fernando Cortés*, Berkeley 1944

Walser, Fritz, *Die spanischen Zentralbehörden und der Staatsrat Karls V*, Göttingen 1959

Warren, J. Benedict, *La conquista de Michoacán, 1521–1530*, Morelia 1977

—, *Vasco de Quiroga y sus pueblos: hospital de Santa Fe*, Morelia 1990

Wedgwood, C. V., *William the Silent*, London 1945

Whitaker, Arthur P., *The Huancavelica Mercury Mine*, Cambridge 1941

Wicki, Josef, *Documenta Indica*, 18 vols., Rome 1948–88

Wilkinson Zerner, Catherine, *Juan de Herrera, Architect of Philip II*, New Haven 1993

Wilson, Edward M. and Duncan Noir, *A Literary History of Spain: The Golden Age: Drama*, London 1971

Wright, I. A., *The Early History of Cuba*, New York 1916

Yuste López, Carmen, *El comercio de la Nueva España con Filipinas, 1590–1785*, Mexico 1949

Zavala, Silvio, *Las instituciones jurídicas en la conquista de América*, 3rd edn, Mexico 1988

—, *Recuerdo de Vasco de Quiroga*, Porrúa 1965. This unites all the articles, etc., by Zavala about the matter.

Zimmerman, T. C. Price, *Paolo Giovio*, Princeton 1995

Zinny, Antonio, *Historia de los gobernantes de las provincias argentinas*, vol. 1, Buenos Aires 1920

Zubillaga, Félix, *Monumenta mexicana*, Rome 1956–81

# Glossary

**adelantado** – An official with both judicial and political authority named to represent the King's interest in frontier areas

**adarme** – A weight of 3 **tomines**, equivalent to 179 cg approximately

**alcabala** – A tax levied on goods as an excise

**alcaide** – A commander of a fort

**alcalde** – A magistrate

**alférez** – A lieutenant

**alguacil** – Magistrate, hence **alguacil mayor**

**almojarifazgo** – Customs duty

**armador** – A shipbuilder

**arroba** – A weight of *c.* 25 lbs. If used as a liquid measure, it is equivalent to 16 litres or 3.5 gallons

**asiento** – A contract

**audiencia** – A supreme court

**avemaría** – Each of the small beads in a rosary

**aviso** – Information

**ayuntamiento** – Municipal council

**bando** – An official proclamation

**barco** – Any water craft

**bergantín** – A brigantine, a small two-masted sailing ship usually with **lateen** sails

**caballero** – A knight

**cabildo** – A municipal council, generally synonymous with **ayuntamiento**

**cacique** – A local chief

**cadenilla y media cadenilla** – Pearls distinguished by their size

**capitulación** – A contractual arrangement agreed by the Crown

**carabela** – A caravel, a three-masted vessel, light and narrow. Also **caravela**

**carrera de Indias** – The journey to the New World

**casa de la contratación, la** – A judicial administrative body arranged to deal with commercial, judicial arrangements with the New World

**cedula** – A decree

**chalupa** – A small, decked ship usually with two masts. Rowed by six to eight oarsmen. A shallop

**codo** – A linear measure, *c.* 0.57 metres or 1.87 feet

**cofradía** – An association of like-minded Christians in support of a favoured saint or Virgin

**conquistador** – A Spanish conqueror who made available conquests to the Crown

**consulado de la universidad de mercaderes** – A guild of merchants in the Spanish trade.

**contaduría** – An accountant or auditor's office at the exchequer

**converso** – a converted Jew or Muslim

**corregidor** – Official charged by the Crown to participate in municipal councils

**curandera** – A benign witch

**encomendero** – One who has an **encomienda**

**encomienda** – Arrangement whereby a grantee might have rights to the services of Indians in return for his protecting them and bringing them into Christianity

**escudo** – A type of coin. In Spain there were gold escudos worth two dollars or forty **reals,** and silver pieces or escudos of eight and of ten **reals**

**entrada** – An expedition into an unknown territory

**entrerredonda** – Type of round pearl similar to the **asiento**

**escribano** – A notary

**excusado** – Exempted or privileged

**extremeño** – A native of Extremadura

**factor** – An official concerned with carrying out policies

**fanega** – A measure of grain, about 100 lbs, 55.5 litres or 1.5 bushels

**fiscal** – A prosecutor

**galeota** – A galiot or small galley, usually with oars as well as sails

**gobernadorcillo** – Petty ruler

**governador** – A governor usually in charge of a province

**grano** – Twelfth of a **tomin,** equivalent to 48 mg; when related to precious stones, a quarter of a carat

**hidalgo** – Someone of upper-class origins

**juro** – An annuity given by the Crown from some royal revenue

**labrador** – Someone who cultivates pasture or raises livestock

**lateen** – A triangular sail on a long yard at an angle of 45 degrees to the mast

**licenciado** – Someone who has obtained a doctor's degree

**maestre** – An official whose responsibility it was to control other groups

**maestre de campo** – One in charge of a **tercio**

**maravedí** – the smallest unit of Spanish currency in the sixteenth century

**mayorazgo** – an entailed estate

**merced** – A grant

**mestizaje** – The mixing of blood between European and Indian

**mestizo** – One of mixed Indian and Spanish blood

**el mozo** – The younger

**mulatto** – One of mixed Spanish and black blood

**nao** – A three-masted ship

**natural** – A native

**ochava** – Eighth of a silver mark, equivalent to 75 grains, which means 359 cg

**oidor** – A supreme court judge

**onza** – A weight of 16 **adarmes**, equivalent to 28.7 g, or a sixteenth of a Castilian pound

**patache** – A pinnace, a small sailing ship usually with two masts

**peso** – A Spanish colonial monetary unit. The most common was a silver peso of eight **reals'** value, worth 272 **maravedís**

**poder** – A power of attorney

**procurador** – Representative in a parliamentary sense

**quintal** – a weight equivalent to 100 Castilian pounds, *c.* 46 kg or 101.5 lbs.

**quinto** – The royal fifth – a sum collected by the Crown on bullion and goods obtained in trade

**real** – A Spanish monetary unit worth 34 **maravedís**

**repartimiento** – A division made by an official

**requerimiento** – A formal request such as that served by the colonial Spaniards on the Indians

**residencia** – The examination of the functioning of a Spanish official after the end of his term of office. Often performed by his successor

**sangley** – A Chinese in the Philippines

**tercio** – A Spanish military formation comprising twelve to fifteen infantry companies

**tomines** – One third of an **adarme**, which in turn was a sixteenth of a Castilian ounce, so there were 48 tomines to the ounce. It is equivalent to 596 mg (0.596 g)

**urca** – A large capacious vessel, useful for carrying freight across shallow bars

**vecino** – A citizen of a municipality

**veedor** – An inspector of a ship or a journey of conquest

**visita** – An investigation of the behaviour of an official, carried out by a 'Visitor'. It might lead to a **residencia,** a more formidable enquiry

**zabra** – A small vessel comparable to a **bergantín**

# Notes

The full titles of works cited can be found in the Bibliography (pp. 339–76).

## INTRODUCTION

1. See Leonard, *Books of the Brave*, 27.
2. Antonio Pigafetta in *Primer viaje alrededor del mundo*, ed. Leonicio Cabrero, Madrid 1985.
3. Quoted in Hugh Thomas, *The Golden Age*, 413.
4. Díaz del Castillo, 311.
5. Leonard, *Books of the Brave*, 29.
6. Diego Clemencín (ed.), *El ingenioso hidalgo don Quijote de la Mancha*, Madrid 1833, 8 vols., I, xiii.
7. E. Allison Peers, *Studies in the Spanish Mystics*, London 1927, 2 vols., I, 8.
8. *La vida de la Santa Madre Teresa de Jesús ... por ella misma* in BAE, Madrid 1861, vol. 53, 24.
9. Leonard, *Books of the Brave*, 78; Henry Thomas, 152–3.

## PROLOGUE: A JOURNEY TO PARIS

1. In the Montmorency family, Anne could be a masculine Christian name.
2. See Romier I, 299, and Rublé, 14.61.
3. Cavalli to the Doge, 16 December 1558, cited in Braudel, II, 945.
4. Cf González de Amezúa, I, 38, for the role of Cristina of Denmark, niece of the Emperor Charles V.
5. See Braudel, II, 105.
6. Alba, I, 501. This letter, of 3 April, was to the licentious Duke of Feria.
7. Calendar of State Papers, Venetian, 1558–80, 49.
8. Stendhal, *Promenades dans Rome*, II, M1.
9. Braudel, I, 165 n 238.

10. 'Un présent magnifique', says the princesse de Clèves, 118. The *coffret à bijoux* is mentioned by Édouard, 119. In his essay on Charles V, Brantôme talks of a pear-shaped pearl brought by Cortés for the emperor.

11. I know of this conversation only from Wedgwood, 29.

12. He had been christened 'Henry' not 'Henri', for his godfather had been Henry VIII of England.

13. Who does not remember Sir Walter Scott's great novel *Quentin Durward* about the Scotch guard in the days of Louis XI? For Montgomery, there is Marlet, *Le Comte de Montgomery*.

14. For Vesalius see C. E. Daniels, *André Vésale*, Amsterdam 1905. His most famous work, *De humani corporis*, had been published in 1543. For Paré, see M. Broussais, *Ambroise Paré*, Paris 1900.

15. See, for a good account, Knecht, 241–3.

16. King Louis XII had also died in this palace.

17. Jean-Marc Houasse, *Victor Hugo*, Paris 2001, I, 467. Montgomery like Hugo became a refugee in Jersey.

18. Alba, I, 509–12.

19. Qu. Braudel, II, 946.

20. Qu. Braudel, II, 948. This letter is not in Alba's *Epistolario*.

21. Thus he missed the terrifying spectacle of the famous *auto-de-fe* in Valladolid on 20 May 1559, presided over by the Infanta Juana and Prince Carlos.

22. Parker, *Philip II*, 63.

23. I take this figure from Fernández Álvarez, *Felipe II*, 87. That historian suggests that only 12,000 to 15,000 of these were Spaniards.

24. 'Il re d'Espagna e principe potentissimo e arbitro del mundo', in Gachard, *Relations des ambassadeurs vénitiens*, 558.


I KING PHILIP II THE ENLIGHTENED DESPOT

1. Josse de Courteville cited in Gachard, *Don Carlos et Philippe II*, 51.

2. See Hakluyt, *Voyages and Documents*, 365. Eufrasia was a daughter to Gonzalo Franco de Guzmán, lord of Préjano and Villafuerte, who had been tutor to the Infante Fernando, the brother of the Emperor Charles V and future Emperor Ferdinand. Eufrasia's mother was María Porres, maid of honour to the Empress Isabel. Eufrasia also seems to have borne Philip a son, who sailed with the Armada Invencible in 1588.

3. Bautista de Toledo was born in Madrid in the early years of the century and travelled, going to Rome where he studied mathematics, philosophy,

Latin, Greek, and sculpture, as well as architecture. Juan de Herrera was his pupil and successor. Toledo died in 1567.

4. There seems to be only one portrait of her, that by Titian now in the Museo del Prado, painted after her death. It emphasizes the empress's good looks. The emperor loved it. Antonio Villacorta Baños, *La emperatriz Isabel*, Madrid 2009, 308, 355; for the portrait see Sheila Hale, *Titian*, London 2012, 497ff.

5. Pedro González de Mendoza worked as a close assistant to the Emperor Charles.

6. The name was originally Stúñiga.

7. In his own time he was referred to as 'Hernando', not 'Hernán'.

8. Giménez Fernández, *Bartolomé de las Casas*, II, 35.

9. See Hugh Thomas, *Rivers of Gold*, and Giménez Fernández, *Bartolomé de las Casas*, II, 757.

10. Charles the Emperor in Fernández Álvarez, *Corpus Documental*, III, 225.

11. Cobos to Charles in Keniston, *Francisco de los Cobos*, 271.

12. Enríquez de Guzmán, 399.

13. Charles was away from Spain 1520–22, 1529–34, 1539–40, 1543–51, and 1554–56.

14. Silíceo was the author of a well-known work of mathematics, *Liber aritmétice práctice astrologíi*, Paris 1513. Another member of that household translated Erasmus's magnificent *Enchiridíon: The Education of a Christian Prince* (Antwerp 1516).

15. No relation to Pánfilo Narváez, the conqueror of that name.

16. The *vihuela* was a plucked chordophone of the viol family on which the gut strings were arranged in six or seven courses, each probably paired in unison. It was thus similar to the lute. Narváez introduced into Spanish music the principle of variation. See *Luis Millán and the Vihuelistas*, Oxford 1925, 54, 64.

17. The only *vihuela* to survive appears to be in the Musée Jacquemart-André, in Paris.

18. Giovanni Pierluigi da Palestrina (c.1525–94) was born in the town from which he took his name. He studied in Rome. He was chapel master at the Lateran in 1555, and of Santa Maria Maggiore in February 1561.

19. His account of events between 1545 and 1549 compensates for the loss of the papers for those years of the Council of the Indies, especially those relating to the rebellion in Peru of Gonzalo Pizarro.

20. See his book *Rebelión de Pizarro en Peru*, completed in January 1567, edited by Paz y Mela, Madrid 1889. Calvete (1510–1593) was the son of a surgeon in Estella, Navarre. An uncle, Juan Quintana, was a confessor of the

emperor. Calvete himself met the emperor in Bologna in 1533. He spent most of his life as Latin adviser to Philip. For the Council of the Indies, see chapter 3.

21. Enríquez de Guzmán, 399.

22. Ibid., 137.

23. See Keniston, *Cobos*, 270, and Novalín, I, 2.

24. The Spanish Inquisition was, of course, the secret religious investigating bureaucracy set up in the late fifteenth century to ensnare heresy, especially among Jews who presented themselves as Christian converts.

25. This disease was common in women after giving birth, owing to the genital tract being exposed in septic surroundings. The mortality of those pregnant with this condition was much reduced due to the work of the tragic Hungarian I. P. Semmelweis (1818–1865).

26. Remarkably, Philip was spoken of as 'King Philip' in the 'addresses to the Sovereign' in Westminster Hall on the occasion of the celebration of the Diamond Jubilee of Queen Elizabeth II in 2012.

27. Federico Badoaro was born in 1518 and became the Venetian ambassador to Spain in 1556. His account is in García Mercadal, especially 1113.

28. Ibid. Later, Gian Francesco Morosini described Philip's skin as being completely white, 'of a perfect allure, combined with a constant gravity' (Eugenio Alberi, cited García Mercadal, *Viajes de extranjeros por España y Portugal desde los tiempos más remotos, hasta fines del Siglo XVI*, Madrid 1952, 602–5). This Antonio Tiepolo had been already in Spain in 1567.

29. Baodero report in García Mercadal, 1114.

30. See Hugh Thomas, *The Golden Age*, 522.

31. García Mercadal, 1434.

32. Pastor was a man who, being born in 1854, was Austrian ambassador of the Papacy in 1920 and so straddled two centuries.

33. The Moriscos were Muslims who had accepted Christian baptism.

34. Diego Espinosa y Arévalo (1512–1572) became a clergyman aged twelve. His rise was as abrupt as his fall.

35. Parker, *Philip II*, 54. Perhaps that exception was *Amadís de Gaula*, his favourite among chivalrous novels?

36. Azpilcueta was a Navarrese, born near Pamplona and famous for a *Manual de Confesores* (1552).

37. Fray Bernardo was born Bernardino de Alvarado, in 1509. He was not of the family of conquistadors of that name and was known as Fresneda since he was born in the town of that name near Burgos. Educated at Alcalá de Henares, he caught the attention of Philip's secretaries, Francisco de Eraso and Ruy Gómez de Silva, and accompanied the king to England in 1554, later to the Netherlands.

38. Diego Rodríguez de Chaves was an *extremeño*, born in Trujillo in 1507. A Dominican, he was at Trent in 1547, afterwards in Salamanca. He was in Rome in 1572.

39. He was the son of Cosimo I by Eleonora de Toledo, daughter of the Viceroy of Naples, and so was half-Spanish.

40. Lucian Freud called these the most beautiful of pictures (Andrew Butterfield, 'Titian and the Birth of Tragedy' in *The New York Review of Books*, 23 December 2010). Philip first met Titian in Augsburg in 1550. He commissioned a painting from him every year till that master died in 1576. The *Poesie* were based on Ovid's *Metamorphoses*, translated by Lodovico Dolce. The two masterpieces mentioned above are now in the Scottish National Gallery (Edinburgh); the others of the series are *Danae* and *Venus and Adonis*, both in the Prado (Madrid), *Perseus and Andromeda* in the Wallace Collection (London), and the *Rape of Europa* in the Isabella Stewart Gardner Museum (Boston), as well as the *Death of Actaeon* in the National Gallery (London). Perhaps Philip was the prince in the garden with Venus, in the two pictures by Titian in the Prado. See Sheila Hale, *Titian*, London 2011, 518.

41. Ibid., 512.

42. Ibid., 531.

43. Juan's mother was a young German from Ratisbon, Barbara Plumberger (or Blomberg). Don Juan was probably born in 1547.

44. Margaret's mother was Juana van den Gheynst of Oudenarde.

45. Parker, *Philip II*, 8.

46. Pope Pius V issued a Bull, *De salute gregis dominici*, in 1570 which declared it to be a mortal sin worthy of excommunication to attend a bullfight. Pope Gregory XIII ameliorated the punishment but when Pope Sixtus V tried to return to Pius's policy, King Philip, despite his personal dislike of bullfighting, protested against what he denounced as 'the great violence which had been visited on his realm' and began negotiations with the Papacy. Clement VIII limited the excommunication to priests who attended *corridas*. For all this see Bennassar, *Historia de la tauromaquía*, 107ff.

## 2 KING PHILIP THE BUREAUCRAT MONARCH

1. Quoted in Ferrara. I had the pleasure of meeting Orestes Ferrara, sometime Foreign Minister of Cuba, in Rome in 1963, and he gave me this biography.

2. A new edition was published in 1986, *Ciudades del siglo de oro*. Wyngaerde was a native of Brussels, who worked first in the Low Countries. In 1552–3 he was in Italy, and he became official artist to Philip in 1557. Most of his Spanish sketches were done in 1570. He retired, crippled in his hands, in 1572.

3. Francisco Domínguez went to Yucatán in 1576. His survey was not published.

4. There is an excellent new edition in ten volumes edited by René Acuña for UNAM in 1982.

5. Juan Ignacio Gutiérrez Nieto, 'En torno al problema del establecimiento de la monarquía hispánica en Madrid', *Revista de Occidente* 27–29 *extraordinario VIII* (1983), 52–65.

6. Sofonisba Anguissola was an Italian painter of the epoch who was made a painter of the court by Philip II.

7. Alonso Sánchez Coello was born in Benifairó, Valencia, in 1531, and died in 1588 in Madrid. He worked in Lisbon with Moro in 1550 and he later became principal court painter.

8. Juan Pantoja de la Cruz (1545–1610), a Madrileño, disciple and pupil of Sánchez Coello. His splendid portraits include an unknown lady, and the *Virgin and the Birth of Christ*, both in the Prado.

9. Kamen, *Philip of Spain*; see Martínez Millán, with Esquerra Revilla, *Carlos V y la quiebra del humanismo político en Europa, 1530–1558*, III, 331. Pérez was born in 1500 in Segovia, son of Bartolomé Pérez, secretary to the Inquisition, a citizen of Monreal de Ariza (Saragossa). Pérez does not, however, figure in Juan Gil's wonderful work on *conversos*, *Los conversos y la Inquisición sevillana*.

10. Parker, *Philip II*, 28, quoting from Tomás de Armenteros, a citizen of Brabant but a child of a Spanish family, who was secretary and *consejero* to Margaret of Parma, 30 June 1565.

11. Zayas was born in Ecija in 1526 and worked for King Philip from 1546.

12. See Marañón.

13. See Hugh Thomas, *Rivers of Gold*, 20–21.

14. See page 41.

15. Albanio seeks love because his love ('*amor insano*') for the shepherdess Camila has been rejected.

16. Lives of Alba include an excellent one by Henry Kamen and another older one by William Maltby (see Bibliography). Alba's letters were splendidly published in three volumes by his descendant, the tenth Duke of Alba (*Epistolario del III Duque de Alba*, Madrid 1952).

17. Kamen, *Philip of Spain*, 214.

18. Floris de Montmorency, Baron de Montigny, was a Castilian Flemish aristocrat who served Charles V against France in his youth.

19. Carmen Iglesias develops these ideas in her fine essay 'El gobierno de la monarquía' in *La Monarquía de Felipe II*, ed. Ruiz Martín, 501ff.

20. The adjective 'polisinodial' was coined by Manuel Fernández Álvarez for a governmental system based on many councils.

21. Juana to Philip II, 11 October 1558, in Fernández Álvarez, *corpus documental*, IV, 451.

22. The embassies cost: Rome, 12,000 ducats; Vienna, 8,000; Paris 6,000; London, Venice, Genoa, Lisbon, 4,000 each.

23. The *Cortes* had to vote on taxes, to oversee the succession to the throne, and present grievances. There was no *Cortes* for all Spain. That for Castile continued to have two representatives (*procuradores*) from the eighteen main cities, namely León, Toro, Zamora, Salamanca, Valladolid, Burgos, Soria, Segovia, and Ávila in the north; Toledo, Madrid, Guadalajara, and Cuenca in the centre; and Murcia, Jaén, Córdoba, Seville and Granada in the south. Galicia, Asturias, Extremadura and Cantabria were not represented. So Zamora was called on to stand for Galicia, León for Asturias, Burgos for Santander, and Salamanca for Extremadura. The *Cortes* were summoned by the king, and Philip II summoned them twelve times in his reign. The *Cortes* of Aragón usually met in Monzón, and was summoned in three chambers – nobility, clergy, and cities – and was divided as to Aragonese, Catalans, and Valencians.

24. The finances of the Crown are well discussed in Fernández Álvarez, *Felipe II*, chap. 4.

25. The Conde-Duque de Benavente refused the Golden Fleece on the grounds that he did not want a Burgundian honour. See Sandoval, III, 172.

## 3 KING PHILIP AND HIS EMPIRE

1. For a biographical study, see Martínez Millán, ed., *La corte de Carlos V*, 212–20. There are also essays by E. Meneses García, 'Luis Hurtado de Mendoza, marqués de Mondéjar 1489–1522', in *Hispania* 36 (1976), 525–66, and the same in *Cuadernos de la Alhambra* 18 (1982), 148–77.

2. The architect was Pedro Machuca, from Toledo, who had briefly worked with Michelangelo. The Royal Council had wanted to make the building a traditional one. Don Luis was able successfully to insist on a Renaissance scheme – which might seem an appropriate achievement for the family that brought more of the Italian Renaissance into Spain than any other.

3. Álvaro de Bazán y Manuel (c.1495–1555) was son of Álvaro de Bazán, *comendador* of Castroverde, and María Manuel. The younger Álvaro fought for the king against the *germanías* of Valencia and in 1523 became captain of the royal galleys. He too was at Tunis with the emperor in 1535 and commander of the fleet at the west coast of Spain in 1544.

4. Remarkably, these Mendozas were brothers to the famous María Pacheco, wife of Juan de Padilla, the leader of the Comuneros, in the rebellion of 1520. María took refuge in Portugal and Luis spent much time trying, without success, to secure her pardon by the emperor.

5. For whom, see below page 54.

6. For Carranza, see page 46.

7. See Gil, *Los conversos y la Inquisición sevillana*, V, 377. Deza was also of *converso* stock.

8. See Hugh Thomas, *The Golden Age*, 505.

9. This controversy was discussed in *The Golden Age* and revolved round Las Casas's desire to treat Indians humanely and Sepúlveda's feeling that that was dangerous or impossible.

10. See Philip Kerr's comments about life in Washington under FDR. In the present author's experience, the same was true of Downing Street under Margaret Thatcher.

11. The organization and functions of the Casa de la Contratación with its treasurer, comptroller, factor, and chief pilot, have been amply discussed in Hugh Thomas, *Rivers of Gold*, 203–5. Its functions were to supervise trade, exploration, and conquest.

12. Graciáno's actions need to be differentiated from those of his brother Juan, who was also a member of the royal bureaucracy. See *DBE*, IX, 478.

13. Suárez de Peralta, 173–83.

14. Fernando Benítez, 183.

15. Lockhart, *Spanish Peru, 1532–1560*, 7.

16. See Hugh Thomas, *The Golden Age*, 279–81. Almagro had been the partner, then the rival, of the Pizarros in the conquest of Peru.

17. Hemming, *The Conquest of the Incas*, 294.

18. See Lockhart, *Spanish Peru, 1532–1560*, 37. Earlier he had been with Valdivia and for a time commanded a royal squadron off Peru. He had been received by Charles V at Yuste in 1557. Valdivia gave him a good *encomienda* near Villarica.

19. Noble, 62.

20. He had been a judge in Valladolid, *consejero de Indias*, and a graduate of Salamanca. He was a protégé of Juan Sarmiento.

21. See Hugh Thomas, *The Golden Age*, 286. Hernando was in prison, for it was held that he had killed Almagro.
22. These others were Diego de Porrás, Pizarro's *majordomo* in Panama, the priest Juan de Asensio, an expert in selling horses, Pedro Pinehard, Pedro Cataño, of Genovese origin, and Domingo de Soraluce, a Basque.
23. *Siete Partidas*, law 6, title 4, part 3.
24. These enquiries form a collection of primary sources from which the patient historian can learn a great deal about life in the Spanish Indies. These are almost indistinguishable from the *visitas*, which were more a spot check at the end of an official's turn of duty. See Mariluz Urquijo, 'Ensayo sobre los juicios de residencia indianos', *Hispano-Americanos*, 70. See also De la Peña y de la Camera, *A List of Spanish Residencias in the Archivo de Indias, 1516–1775,*.

## CHAPTER 4 AN IMPERIAL THEOCRACY

1. Cuevas, 388, and Ricard, 80.
2. Antonio Bonet Correa, *Monasterios Iberoamericanos*, Madrid 2000.
3. Ghiberti, 1498–1585, was born in Toulouse of a family from Florence. One cannot resist wondering whether he was related to the designer of the great baptistery in Florence, Lorenzo Ghiberti.
4. Also Observantines. A term referring to friars in exact adherence to the rule of Saint Francis. The movement began in Italy in 1368.
5. Discussed in Cheetham, 144.
6. Hanke, *The Spanish Struggle for Justice in the New World*, 81.
7. See Hugh Thomas, *The Golden Age*, chap. 30.
8. Ricard, 189.
9. Ibid., 244.
10. Ibid., 242.
11. Motolinía, 119.
12. For Sepúlveda, see Santiago Muñoz Machado, *Sepúlveda, cronista del emperador*, Barcelona 2012.
13. See Hugh Thomas, *The Golden Age*, chap. 44.
14. The *requerimiento* was a statement of Christian beliefs which was read out to Indians to try and ensure their acceptance of Christian principles and vassalage to the emperor or king. The popular poem *Cortes de la Muerte*, by Luis Hurtado de Toledo and Micael de Carvajal (BAE, XXV, 1–41), was seen by Juan Antonio Ortega y Medina as a reflection of the dispute between Las Casas and Sepúlveda in Valladolid. See his 'El Indio absuelto y las Indias condenadas en las Cortes de la Muerte', *Historia*

*Mexicana*, IV (April–June 1955). Hurtado de Toledo was *párroco* at San Vicente Toledo. Carvajal was a playwright from Plasencia, where he had been born in 1500. He descended from an old *extremeño* family. His great success was *La Tragedia llamada Josefina* of 1535.

15. Hanke, *All Mankind is One*, 116.
16. Argote, who died in Córdoba in 1604, was the son of a municipal councillor of that city. He was a humanist with a large library, and was a well-known judge of *residencias*.
17. Hanke, *The Spanish Struggle for Justice in the New World*, 117.
18. Pastor, XIV, 278–9.
19. See above, page 14.
20. Charles was still intellectually active. Thus he wrote in September 1557 from Yuste to Juan Vázquez de Molina, the cousin and *criado* of Cobos, about the arrival of the American treasure fleet.
21. Stirling-Maxwell, 186.
22. In June 1557, Pope Paul IV used the most violent language against the emperor to Navagero, the Venetian ambassador, calling Charles V 'this heretic and schismatic who has always favoured false doctrine in order to oppress the Holy See'. If the emperor tried to reinstate Carranza, 'we shall raise the whole world against him, deprive him of his imperial dignity, and declare that the devil had chosen him to paralyse papal efforts at reform'.
23. Gil, *Los conversos*, I, 338.
24. Discussed critically by Kamen, *Imagining Spain*, 172.
25. See Wilson and Noir.
26. *CDI*, XLII, 466–7. At Ocaña, 14 April 1531. The emperor was at that time in Italy.
27. These questions are admirably discussed as usual by Leonard in his *Books of the Brave*, chap. 7.
28. Cuevas, I, 1914, 322.
29. Ricard, 81.
30. Ibid., 244.
31. Pastor, XIII, 303.
32. Ricard, 270.
33. Ibid., 81.
34. Kubler and Soria, *Art and Architecture in Spain and Portugal and in their American Dominions, 1500 to 1800*, 66.
35. Pastor, XVIII, 344.
36. Ibid.
37. Ibid., 345.
38. Pastor, XX, 501–2.

39. Qu. Ricard, 173.

40. García Icazbalceta, *Colección de documentos para la historia de México*, II, 509–12.

41. Corresp. Dipl., I, 437ff, cit. Pastor, XVIII, 330, where there is further discussion.

42. Ricard, 321. See too Hugh Thomas, *The Golden Age*, 40, and Cheetham, 136ff.

43. Sahagún was a learned Franciscan who, arriving in New Spain in 1529, devoted himself to a study of what had transpired in the old days before the Spaniards' arrival. He began to publish his masterpiece, the *Historia General de las cosas de Nueva España*, in 1585. It became known as the *Codex Florentino* because the original is in the Laurenziana Medicean library in Florence. The work is written in Spanish with a Nahuatl translation facing it. The Danish writer Henrik Stangerup wrote a novel about Sahagún's remarkable life.

44. Hanke, *Aristotle and the American Indians*, 83.

45. Egaña qu. Hanke, *The Spanish Struggle for Justice in the New World*, 133.

46. *CDIHE*, XIII, 425ff.

47. The *Bull Exponi Nobis* of 1567 approved this change. (This Bull essentially continued the concession of Pope Adrian VI that friars should be able to hear confession and offer communion, without seeking permission of the bishop. These privileges gave friars a power which they never possessed in Europe.) Ricard, 109; see Pastor, XV, 363, for a summary of conclusions.

48. Pastor, XVII, 210.

49. Note there was also the Mercedarian order whose work in the Americas is well summarized in Vázquez Fernández.

## 5 THE JESUIT CHALLENGE

1. The Jesuit college in Valencia was founded in 1544, Valladolid, Gandia, and Barcelona in 1545, and Alcalá the next year. Salamanca dated from 1548, Burgos from 1550, Medina del Campo 1551, Oñate 1552, Córdoba 1553. In 1554 Ávila, Cuenca, Palencia, Seville, Granada, Simancas and Sanlúcar de Barrameda all saw Jesuit colleges established. In 1555, Murcia and Saragossa followed, and in 1556 Monterrey in Galicia.

2. Ignatius signed himself 'Íñigo' until 1537, afterwards till 1543 alternately 'Íñigo' and in a Latin version 'Ignacio'. From 1543 he was almost always 'Ignacio' or 'Ignatius'.

3. Pastor, XII, 21–2.
4. We have met him before as a turbulent genius; see chap. 4.
5. *Spiritual Exercises*.
6. Martín, *The Intellectual Conquest of Peru*, 10.
7. Pastor, XX, 504.
8. Ibid., 476.
9. Ibid., 477.
10. Ibid., 454.

## 6 TROUBLE IN MEXICO

1. See Hanke, *Los virreyes españoles en América durante el gobierno de la casa de Austria*, I, México.
2. Gibson, 175.
3. Ibid., 187.
4. See C. H. Haring, *Trade and Navigation between Spain and the Indies in the Time of the Hapsburgs*.
5. Schäfer, I, 9.
6. See Leonard, *Books of the Brave*, 97–8, for a summary.
7. As depicted in the Los Angeles County Museum of Art, 'Contested visions in the Spanish colonial world'.
8. See Bleichman.
9. The year 1559 was the one in which Las Casas made his wild prediction that Hispaniola would become a realm greater even than Spain, 'the very thought of which would make the king of France tremble', and in which Philip decided in Spain to lodge the tireless Las Casas in 'a manner which befits his standing in consideration of the services to the emperor and to him'. Las Casas's hold over both Charles V and Philip II shows that his magnetism was of no uncommon order.
10. Gibson, 25.
11. Felix Hinz, 'The Process of Hispanisation in Early New Spain', *R de I* 243 (2008).
12. Gibson, 160.
13. See Gerhard, *Geografía histórica de la Nueva España, 1519–1821*, 144–6.
14. The expression is Gibson's in *The Aztecs*, 57.
15. See Soustelle.
16. Gibson, 57.
17. Ibid., 174.

18. See Hugh Thomas, *The Golden Age*, 494ff. The admirable biography by María Justina Sarabia Viejo, *Don Luis de Velasco*, deserves attention.
19. Hanke, *Los virreyes españoles en América durante el gobierno de la casa de Austria*, 128.
20. Gibson, 257.
21. The collapse of the Otomí seems to have been in 1395 when they apparently fled to the eastern shore of Lake Xaltucan, as well as to Tlaxcala and Meztitlan.
22. Gibson, 309.
23. A *fanega* is generally a measure of arable land of 400-fathom square.
24. Gibson, 323.
25. Ibid., 324. See too Walter V. Scholes, *La visita de Diego Ramírez*, Columbia, 1946.
26. L. B. Simpson, *The Exploitation of Lands in the Sixteenth Century*, Berkeley 1952, 1–2. Simpson was a great Californian historian of the mid-twentieth century.
27. See Herman Konrad, *A Jesuit Hacienda in Colonial Mexico: Santa Lucia 1576–1767*, Redwood, 1980.
28. Gibson, 277.

## 7 THE SONS OF THE CONQUISTADORS ASK TOO MUCH

1. Gibson, *The Aztecs under Spanish Rule*, 231, thought that Cortés had really many more than 23,000 dependants.
2. 'Martín Cortés first of whose name was the second duke'.
3. Gibson, 83.
4. Ibid., 36.
5. See below, page 186.
6. Some of the English sailors, such as Job Hislop captured in Vera Cruz in 1570, were sent to *obrajes*.
7. La Fuente, 30.
8. Fernando Benítez, 82.
9. Suárez de Peralta, 189.
10. See *CDI*, XXV, 273.
11. The word *criollo* had already come to indicate a Spaniard or other European who had been born in the New World – as opposed to Spaniards born in Castile.
12. Fernando Benítez, 186.

13. AGI, Patronato, 203 r1 f3; María Justina Sarabia Viejo comments that the friendship of the marquis with Valderrama 'darkened the last months of Viceroy Velasco'.

14. Fernando Benítez, 46.

15. Hanke, *Los virreyes españoles en América durante el gobierno de la casa de Austria*, 155.

16. These brothers were the sons of Gil González de Ávila (Benavides), who had received the *encomienda* of Cuautitlan from the first Alonso de Ávila in 1522.

17. Paso, X, 45.

18. See Gibson, 123.

19. Fernando Benítez, 186; Gerhard, *Geografía histórica de la Nueva España, 1519–1821*, 66.

20. This *criollo* crisis seemed much the most serious of the troubles in New Spain in the 1560s, but there were some other colonial anxieties. For example, in a memorial to the *audiencia* on 11 October 1565, Archbishop Montúfar, the second of New Spain's archbishops and formerly the Inquisition's chief in Granada, together with the other bishops of New Spain, denounced the apparent survival of the ancient religions: 'the great readiness with which these newly converted Indians revert to their idolatries, rites, sacrifices and superstitions is notorious'. Sometimes, as in Chalma, 'the believers would gather in caves difficult of access; sometimes, as at Cholula, they would hide their old gods beneath our crosses. These groups of old believers were led not only by *caciques* but old priests and sorcerers.' See Fernando Benítez, 199, and Ricard, 270.

21. Fernando Benítez, 200.

22. They can be seen in Hanke, *Virreyes*, 168, and were signed by King Philip on 10 March 1566. Much of the document is the same as that given in 1550 to Luis de Velasco. But there was an original passage about fostering cochineal and silk, which in the 1550s were being grown so extensively that Motolinía thought that 'the region would soon become the principal place [for the cultivation of silk] in the Christian world'. *Historia de los Indios*, published as *Memoriales*, 89. Cortés seems to have been the father of the Mexican silk industry.

23. Suárez de Peralta, 208.

24. These included Luis de Castilla, Pedro Lorenzo de Castilla, Bernardino Pacheco de Bocanegra, Nuño de Chávez, Luis Ponce de León, Hernando de Córdoba, Francisco Pacheco, Lope de Sosa, Alonso de Estrada, Alonso de Cabrera, Hernán Gutiérrez de Altamirano, and Juan de Guzmán.

25. Gibson, 63.
26. He was also the first viceroy to be formally addressed as 'Excellency' rather than 'señor'. See Hanke, *Virreyes*, 163, and Paso, X, 161–209.
27. Gaspar de Jarava, Licenciado Alonso Muñoz, and Dr Luis Carrillo.
28. This is in AGI, Indiferente, leg. 1424, and also in Hanke, *Virreyes*, 169ff.
29. Schäfer, II, 54; Hanke, *Virreyes*, 169.
30. Hanke, *Virreyes*, 170.
31. Mostly Suárez de Peralta, 230, as treated by Fernando Benítez, 220ff.
32. We should not forget the black Africans who of course constituted a third race.


## 8 NEW SPAIN IN PEACE

1. See P. W. Powell, 'Portrait of an American Viceroy: Martín Enríquez, 1568–1583', *The Americas* 14, no. I (July 1957); also Hanke, *Los virreyes españoles en América durante el gobierno de la casa de Austria*, the viceroy's instructions being on pp. 188–202, and García-Abasolo, ed., *Martín Enríquez y la Reforma de 1568 en Nueva España*.
2. Hanke, *Virreyes*, 188.
3. Fernán González de Eslava was an Augustinian friar born in Toledo, of *converso* origin. He went to New Spain in 1558 and became known as a poet and playwright in the 1560s, allowing his prose to be full of localisms and aztequisms.
4. *CDI*, III, 480.
5. This English defeat is well discussed in Arturo Aparicio Laserna, *Mar de Sangre*, Bogotá 2010, 248ff.
6. Hanke, *Virreyes*, 294.
7. See chapter 26 for an estimate of numbers.
8. Alberto M. Carreño, ed., *Gonzalo Gómez de Cervantes: la vida económica y social de Nueva España al finalizar el siglo XVI*, Mexico 1944, 99–101.
9. Francisco Becerra (1545–1601) was the grandson of the architect Hernán González de Lara, the chief architect of the cathedral of Toledo.
10. Claudio de Arcienaga (1524–1593) was the son of a Burgundian, Juan de Miaus, and a Spanish lady. He had some difficulties with the Inquisition owing to the bigamy of a brother-in-law. He began work as one of the French *entalladores* (sculptors) of León. His first important work was on the Alcázar in Madrid, then on the facade of the university of Alcalá. He worked in the 1550s on the church of Santiago in Guadalajara. He left Spain in 1554 and was with the *corregidor* Luis de León Romano in

Puebla, Mexico. Thereafter he carried out a multitude of architectural projects of which the most important were the adaptation of the Casas Viejas of Cortés, then the cathedral at Pátzcuaro, the *conventos* of San Agustín and Santo Domingo, the tomb of the Emperor Charles in Mexico, and the hospital de Jesús where Cortés's remains are said to be, also in the Mexican capital. His biography in the *DBE* is admirable.

11. The best book on the cathedral is that by Manuel Toussaint, *El catedral de México*, 2 vols., Mexico 1924. Pereyns was born in Antwerp in 1530. He travelled widely in Europe before coming to New Spain with Viceroy Falces in 1566. But he was eventually accused by the Inquisition. See *Anales de el UNAM*, 1938. He is considered the master of high art in New Spain. He painted innumerable pictures.

12. See above, page 58.

13. Gibson, 329.

14. Ibid., 93.

15. See Hamilton, *American Treasure and the Price Revolution in Spain, 1501–1650*.

16. By now this revolutionary method had become accepted as something essential and was the main use of quicksilver.

17. See Francisco Hernández.

18. *DBE*, XVIII, 296.

19. The archbishop gave a hostile sketch of Cervantes's personality: 'Canon Francisco Cervantes is sixty years old with twenty-five in this country, to which he came reputed as a great Latinist though with age he has lost some of this ... He likes to be praised and is partial to flattery. He is fickle and changeable and has no reputation for chastity or morality; he is ambitious for distinction and is convinced he will become a bishop and they joke to him about this ...' *Cartas de Indias*, BAE, vols. 95–96, Madrid 1957, 305.

20. Rojas is only the presumed author. See the excellent English edition by L. B. Simpson.

21. See Braudel, I, 55.

22. Coruña is a small *pueblo* in Castile near Aranda de Duero and has nothing to do with the great port of La Coruña in Galicia.

23. The *residencia* is described on page 37.

24. See instructions in Hanke, *Virreyes*, I, 202.

25. Quicksilver was needed primarily for its use in the silver trade.

26. See Parry, *The Spanish Seaborne Empire*, 194.

27. Both were discussed in Hugh Thomas, *The Golden Age*.

28. Gibson, 120.

29. For Sahagún see Hugh Thomas, *The Conquest of Mexico*, London 1993, pp. 777–8. Sahagún was asked by the new *provincial* of the Franciscans, Rodrigo de Sequera, to send a copy of his book to the Council of the Indies. He made his copy but it was not published until the mid-nineteenth century.
30. Mendieta spoke good Nahuatl, it seems.
31. Leonard, 103. It is of interest that the son of the author of *Don Florisel of Niquea*, Diego de Silva, was a conqueror of the Incas and lived for a time at Cuzco.
32. For a chronological list of these publications see Henry Thomas, 147–8.
33. See below, page 123.
34. The translator was apparently Andrés Pescioni from Seville.

## 9 VICEROY TOLEDO AT WORK IN PERU

1. Hanke, *Los virreyes españoles en América durante el gobierno de la casa de Austria*, 294.
2. Toledo, I, xiii.
3. *CDHI*, XVII, 51ff.
4. Leonard, *Books of the Brave*, 88.
5. See chapter 26 for an analysis of how this time may have been spent.
6. Acosta went to Peru in 1570 and became *provincial* aged thirty-five. He embarked on a long and difficult journey through the country, amused by Aristotle's idea that all equatorial regions must be blazing hot, because the ancient philosopher neglected that one can be cold if at an altitude. Acosta was in New Spain in 1587. His *De Procuranda Indorum Salute* (1588) was the first work on the Americas by a Jesuit. His first chapter is called 'Why there is no reason to give up hope for the salvation of Indians' and the second 'Why the salvation of Indians seems difficult and unimportant to many persons'. He refutes the idea that wars can be justly waged against barbarians because of their crimes against nature. Essentially he supported Las Casas but does not cite him – perhaps because a fellow Jesuit, Luis López, was then under investigation in Peru for holding similar ideas. Acosta's *Natural and Moral History of the Indies* (1590) asserted that the Indians 'have a natural capacity to be taught, more so than many of our own people' and denounced the 'false opinion generally held that the Indians are a brutal and bestial people without understanding'. He wrote to King Philip protesting against the unjust taxes levied on the Indians and referred to the colonists as 'the refuse of Spain' ('Hispanaiae faeces'). In 1587 he was named *superior* to Alonso

Sánchez with the aim of avoiding that father's advocacy of the invasion of China. See Acosta's 'Parecer sobre la guerra de la China breve y conciso' (15 March 1587) and 'Respuesta de los fundamentos que justifican la guerra contra la China' (23 March 1587), which were directed to Acquaviva, then general of the Jesuits. They amounted to a complete rejection of Alonso Sánchez's views. See chapter 28. In 1588, Acosta had several audiences with King Philip and gave him his *On the Salvation of the Indians*, published in 1584.

7. For whom see AGI, Patronato, leg. 127, no.3, R5.

8. Fray José de Acosta, like so many interesting men of the age, had been born in Medina del Campo, Valladolid, about 1540, the son of a merchant. Four of his brothers became Jesuits and two sisters nuns, one of whom became an abbess. José became a Jesuit aged twelve. He became known for his *Historia Indiana* (1596).

9. María Escobar, wife of Francisco de Chaves, could possibly have been responsible for this innovation. See Martín, *Daughters of the Conquistadors*, 57.

10. AGI, Patronato 55, leg. 27, qu. Kamen, *Philip of Spain*, 61.

11. Cardinal Borgia, as we know, had had a long career as a courtier and royal administrator before he entered the Jesuit community in the 1550s.

12. Bernardo Bitti (1548–1610) was a Jesuit painter born in Amerino, Ancona, the son of Pablo and Cornelia Bitti. He had worked in Rome before being sent to Lima in 1575. He also worked in Cuzco and at Lake Titicaca.

13. See Alexandre Coello de la Rosa, *De mestizos y criollos en la Compañía de Jesus, Perú*, in *R de I* 77 (2008).

14. Quinine derives from a bark of the Rubiacaeae found in Peru. Its use against malaria was discovered in 1638 when it was recommended to the Countess of Chinchón, wife of a senior administrator in that country, by the *corregidor* of Loxa, who had experienced its value eight years before. Quinine was disseminated in Europe by the Jesuits and so it became known as 'Jesuits' bark'. The extraction of the bark in the forest is very hard work.

15. See Appendix A in Martín, *The Intellectual Conquest of Peru*, 173ff. This appendix also cites seventeenth- and eighteenth-century investments.

16. Martín, *The Intellectual Conquest of Peru*, 56.

17. For seventeenth-century intellectual fathers such as Pedro de Oñate and Diego de Avendaño, a master of eloquent Latin, see ibid., 6.

18. Ibid., 67, 173.

19. *CDI*, XLVII.

20. Lohmann Villena, *Los americanos en las ordenes militares*, II, 218–20, also 459–61.

21. Schäfer, II, 50.

22. Levillier, 'Gobernantes del Perú', in *Cartas y Papeles*, VII, 96.

23. Hanke, *The Spanish Struggle for Justice in the New World*, 136.

24. It was asked whether servile 'yes-men' had been chosen specifically to give the bleak picture which Toledo was anticipating. But the best historian of Toledo's era, Roberto Levillier, believed that it was an honest inquiry carried out by a master proconsul; see Levillier, 'Gobernantes del Perú'.

25. Ibid., II, 11–12.

26. Matienzo, Chap. 2.

27. See Garcilaso de la Vega.

28. Ibid.

29. The people of Cuzco said that the *cabildo* questioned whether their dominion was based upon such just and reasonable titles. The territory of France and Germany and other places 'have their rights to possession written in the bones of men'. The *cabildo* declared that they envied such places 'for they do not have to reply to scruples because nobody raises them. We, the inhabitants of this land, have been less fortunate.' They said that of the 1,000 *encomenderos* appointed in Peru by the king, as many as 800 had been killed putting down rebellions. Levillier, 'Gobernantes de Peru', 115–30.

30. Schäfer, II, 370.

31. Ibid., 36. Valenzuela had married a sister of the first Archbishop of Lima, García de Loaisa.

## 10 CONVENTS AND BLESSED ONES

1. *CDI*, VIII, 412.

2. See above, pages 87–8, for a discussion of his family.

3. Emilio Lisson, *La Iglesia en el Perú*, Seville 1943–56, 5 vols., III, 41.

4. This was the abbreviated name of the Jesuit scheme of studies issued in 1599. It was based on the best educational theories, and Jesuit secondary education for the next two centuries was grounded in it.

5. Arriaga died en route to Rome in 1622.

6. See Toribio Medina, *Cartas de Pedro de Valdivia*.

7. Leonard, *Books of the Brave*, 217. The first printer in Peru was an Italian, Antonio Ricardo.

8. The first copies of *Don Quixote* began to appear in book lists arriving in the Indies in 1605, and indeed the boxes containing the book had been opened en route, on board for example a ship commanded by Gaspar de

Maya. Other ships to carry the first edition were the *Nuestra Señora de Remedios* and the *San Cristóbal*. See Leonard, *Books of the Brave*.

9. Medina's work was one of the essential volumes to guide sea captains at that time.

10. I have used the words 'Indian' and 'Inca' as if they were synonyms, which in *many* ways they were not.

11. Vargas Ugarte, I, 245.

12. This section is based on Fray Luis Martín's admirable *Daughters of the Conquistadors*, Albuquerque 1983.

13. Ibid., 178.

14. Ibid., 207. This was much later, in the eighteenth century.

15. A *beaterio* was a house inhabited by pious women who were not quite nuns.

16. There have been those who have compared *La Cristada* with Milton's *Paradise Lost*, though, to an English ear, it has a much less sonorous dignity.

## 11 CHILE AND ITS CONQUERORS

1. For the definition of the role of an *adelantado*, see above, page 65.

2. See Hugh Thomas, *The Golden Age*, chap. 45.

3. It was Alderete, treasurer to Cortés, who in 1521 insisted on torturing Cuahtémoc to find the treasure of Montezuma.

4. Alonso de Ercilla, *La Araucana*, rendered into English verse by Walter Owen, Buenos Aires 1945, 7.

5. See chap. 19.

6. William Knapp Jones, 'America's First Epic', in *Poet Loves* (Autumn 1942).

7. It is astonishing that there is no translation into English.

8. See *Don Quixote*, I, chap. VI, 86, in the edition of Francisco Rico, Barcelona 1998.

9. Agustín de Zárate, 'Historia del descubrimiento y conquista del Perú', book 3, chap. 11, in BAE, vol. 26, *Historiadores primitivos de Indias*, 485.

## 12 THE CONQUEST OF YUCATAN

1. Qu. Hanke, *All Mankind is One*, 60.

2. Bienvenida was in Tierra Firme, or the isthmus of Panama, from 1542. He was the first custodian of the monastery of Izmal. He went later to Costa Rica and returned to Spain in 1564 to explain to the king the dif-

ficulties of conversion in the Indies. That conversation was a success and Bienvenida went to Cartago as guardian to the *convento* there.

3. Fray Nicolás de Albalate, Fray Angel Maldonado, Fray Miguel de Vera, and Fray Juan de la Puerta. The last named was asked to be the new commissary and went on to Mérida, by then the largest city of Yucatan, where he met Lorenzo de Bienvenida.

4. *Cartas de Indias*, 64.

5. Hanke, *The Spanish Struggle for Justice in the New World*, 66.

6. *El Mozo* was the son of Francisco de Montejo, the leader of the expedition, by Ana de León.

7. Probanza of Andrea del Castillo, in AGI, Mexico, leg. 974.

8. See Gerhard, 252–3.

9. See below, page 240.

10. AGI, Mexico, leg. 299.

11. Clendinnen, 29.

12. Chamberlain, *The Conquest and Colonisation of Yucatan, 1517–1550*, 201.

13. Ibid., 198.

14. Ibid., 206.

15. Ibid., 204.

16. Probanza of Diego Sánchez in AGI, Patronato, leg. 69, no. 8.

17. AGI, Mexico, leg. 966, and Patronato, leg. 80.


## 13 CONCLUSION IN YUCATAN

1. López de Cogulludo, 3–7. See too Chamberlain, *The Conquest and Colonisation of Yucatan, 1517–1550*, 216.

2. One should of course consider the estimated figure of 60,000 with some suspicion; López de Cogulludo, 3–7.

3. Information from Rodrigo Álvarez, in AGI, Mexico, leg. 900.

4. *Relación de Valladolid*, cited in Chamberlain, *The Conquest and Colonisation of Yucatan, 1517–1550*, 231.

5. Bienvenida to the Crown, 10 February 1548, cited in ibid., 235.

6. Ibid., 43.

7. Ibid., 241.

8. Clendinnen, 41.

9. Probanza of Juana de Azamor in AGI, Mexico, leg. 983.

10. See Chamberlain, *The Conquest and Colonisation of Yucatan, 1517–1550*, 252.

11. Residencia of Montejo, in AGI, Justicia, 244.
12. *CDI*, XIII, 283ff.
13. For Catalina see *CDI*, XXIV, 453, 455.

## 14 A GREAT CONQUISTADOR FROM ASTURIAS

1. Menéndez de Avilés to a Jesuit friend in Cadiz, 1566, in Díaz, II, 155–6.
2. See Hugh Thomas, *Rivers of Gold*, 282.
3. See chap. 36 in Hugh Thomas, *The Golden Age*.
4. The text of this document of 20 March 1565 is in *CDI*, XXIII, 242–58.
5. See Wright. She is the only historian to have written a poem about the Archivo de las Indias.
6. It is worth noting that the emissary of the Spaniards who negotiated with Sorès was himself a Frenchman – a sign of the internationalization of the island.
7. See La Fuente, the best study of the subject.
8. Ibid., 13.
9. See La Fuente.
10. See Lapeyre, *Une famille de marchands*, 402.
11. García del Pino and Melis Cappa, 9; see too Pérez de la Riva, 304.
12. A *galeas* (or *galleas*) was a heavy, low-built vessel rather larger than a galley but propelled by both oars and sails.
13. AGI, Indif. Gen., leg. 1093, and *CDI*, XIII, 315.
14. A galiot was a small oar-powered boat which could also have a sail.
15. They included twenty-one sailors, fifteen carpenters, ten shoemakers, ten stonemasons, eight smiths, three barbers, two surgeons, as well as some winemakers and mortar-makers, tanners, farriers, wool carders, hat-makers, embroiderers; even some booksellers, three sword-makers, a gunsmith, a crossbow repairer, several coopers, bakers, gardeners, flaxworkers, blanket-makers, a silk dealer, an apothecary, and, of course, a notary.
16. The Huguenots were French Protestants, who took their name from a medieval tale about King Hugues.
17. Menéndez de Avilés to a Jesuit friend in Cadiz, 1566, in Díaz, II, 155–6.
18. That was a new day decided at the Council of Trent.
19. A full account of the expedition was written, as so often, by a chaplain who was part of it, Francisco López de Mendoza Grajales, in *CDI*, III, 442–79.
20. AGI, Escribanía de Cámara, leg. 1024A.
21. See Lyon.
22. Douais, I, 72.

23. Wright, 280.
24. See Hakluyt, *Voyages and Documents*.
25. The journey of John Oxenham was used by Charles Kingsley in his novel *Westward Ho!* (1855).
26. Wright, *The Early History of Cuba*, 291. For the Montalvo family and modern survivors see Hugh Thomas, *Cuba or The Pursuit of Freedom* (London 1973), appendix I. We should not forget that *Amadís de Gaula* was rewritten by Garci Rodríguez de Montalvo and that the first wife of Simón Ruiz of Medina del Campo was a Montalvo. See Lapeyre, *Une famille de marchands*, 75. The same was true of the wife of the last sugar king, Julio Lobo, in the twentieth century as well as the cultivated Countess of Merlin in the nineteenth century. In the 1560s, Antonio Ramírez de Montalvo became a page and courtier of the Grand Duke Cosimo in Florence, being allocated a palace in that city in Via del Corso Burgo d'Albizzi as well as two country houses.
27. Menéndez de Avilés, *La Florida Conquista y colonización*, Madrid 1893.

## 15 FRANCISCANS IN YUCATAN

1. A flageolet is a wooden flute with finger holes instead of keys.
2. Landa, 71–4. Anthony Pagden's translation of 1985 is excellent.
3. See Chamberlain, *The Conquest and Colonisation of Yucatan, 1517–1550*, 321, and the Probanza in AGI, Patronato, leg. 64, no. 7.
4. See above, page 134.
5. *CDIHE*, XI, 70.
6. Ibid., VI, 319ff.
7. Clendinnen, 161.
8. Landa, 61. They did not use six of our letters: D, F, G, Q, R, and S. But they had doubled up some others; so, while PA meant 'to open', PPA meant 'to break'. TAN normally meant 'lime', but TAN spoken harshly between tongue and upper teeth meant 'to talk'.
9. *CDIHE*, XIII, 237.
10. Petition by Landa to Diego Quijada, in Scholes and Adams, I, 222–5.
11. *CDIHE*, XIII, 238.
12. On Sahagún's book see page 397, note 29, above.
13. Scholes and Adams, I, 71.
14. Ibid., I, 200.
15. *CDIHE*, XIII, 236.
16. Clendinnen, 98.
17. Ibid., 177.

18. Scholes and Adams, I, 294.
19. Ibid., I, 62.
20. *Cartas de Indias*, 407–10.
21. *CDI*, XVI, 301.
22. For *residencia* see above, page 37.
23. González de Cicerio, *Perspectiva religiosa*, 238–42, 235–6, qu. Clendinnen, 107.
24. Clendinnen, 109.
25. See Landa.
26. Clendinnen, 182.
27. Ibid., 159.

## 16 THE RIVERS PLATE AND PARAGUAY

1. See Koebel, chap. 1; see Hugh Thomas, *Rivers of Gold*, 437–8.
2. Hugh Thomas, *Rivers of Gold*, chap. 36.
3. Diego García de Moguer (1471–1535) was probably of Portuguese origin. He was master of one of the caravels in Díaz de Solís's fleet. He was also with Magellan and on his return journey he discovered the island of Diego García in the Indian Ocean, which is now British.
4. Cabot had been a companion of the aforementioned conquistador who was killed on the river Plate, Díaz de Solís.
5. W. H. Hudson, *Far Away and Long Ago*, London 1918, 94.
6. See Hugh Thomas, *The Golden Age*, 423.
7. Juan de Ayolas (c.1510–1538) was one of the great Burgos merchants of his time.
8. A brigantine was a two-masted sailing ship ideal for river exploration because its keel was so short.
9. See the chronicle of Ulrich Schmidl, translated into English by Luis L. Domínguez.
10. Schmidl, 45.
11. Mondragón became famous for its cooperative movement founded in 1956.
12. Saint Blaise was one of the so-called 'fourteen Holy Helpers' who fought disease in the Rhineland. He was allegedly Bishop of Sebaste in Armenia and was put to death under the Emperor Licinius in the early fourth century. He is believed to have been torn by wool combs before being beheaded and so was the patron of the wool combers.
13. See Pedro Hernandez.

14. Ibid., 69.
15. An arquebus was the first type of portable gun, supported in the field of battle by a tripod or trestle. The name in German meant originally a hook-gun by which it was attached to its carriage.
16. Felipe de Cáceres had been born in Madrid and joined Pedro de Mendoza in 1534 for his expedition to the river Plate. He returned to Spain but went back to the Indies again, with Cabeza de Vaca to Asunción.

## 17 THE MAD ADVENTURE OF LOPE DE AGUIRRE

1. Gómez de Alvarado had accompanied his brother Pedro in 1534, but he remained in Peru after Pedro's withdrawal. Gómez at first followed Gonzalo Pizarro, but he turned to support Pedro de la Gasca.
2. Díaz de Armendáriz had been at the College of San Bartolomeo in Salamanca. He became a judge in New Granada (Colombia) in 1544. He died a canon of Sigüenza in 1552.
3. Simón, *The Expedition of Pedro de Ursúa and Lope de Aguirre*, 6.
4. See E. Jos, *Ciencia y osadía sobre Lope de Aguirre el Peregrino*, Seville 1950.
5. Guzmán was the son of Alvarez Pérez de Esquital, member of an enormous aristocratic family. He reached Peru with Hurtado de Mendoza in 1556. See *CDI*, IV, 193ff, also 215ff.
6. Simón, *The Expedition of Pedro de Ursúa and Lope de Aguirre*, 230–31.
7. Ibid., 49.
8. Ibid., 187.
9. Ibid., 189.
10. Diego García de Paredes (1506–1563) had one of the most interesting careers in the Spanish imperial service. He was the son of a colonel of the same name (illegitimate) who, because of his great strength, became known as the Samson of Spain. The family came from Paredes (Cáceres). Diego's mother, Mencía de Vargas, was related to the Pizarros. He went to the Indies in 1524 with Francisco de Lizaur, and he was then secretary to Nicolás de Ovando, governor of Panama. He took part in Pizarro's expedition in 1531, and he was among those who captured Atahualpa. He returned to Spain with Hernando Pizarro in 1533 and joined the imperial army in Italy, but he subsequently joined Francisco Orellana in the creation of New Andalusia. Paredes later established himself in Venezuela, of which territory he became the effective ruler in 1556. After the

battle with Aguirre, he ruled as governor of Popayán (Colombia). He was killed by Indians near Cabo Blanco in 1563.

11. Simón, *The Expedition of Pedro de Ursúa and Lope de Aguirre*, 191–4.


## 18 GUIANA AND EL DORADO

1. Hemming, *The Search for El Dorado*, 146.
2. Loc. cit.
3. See Pereda López, *La emigración burgalesa a America durante el siglo XVI*, and the same author's *Conquistadores y encomenderos burgaleses en Indias 1492–1606*.
4. Hemming, *The Search for El Dorado*, 147. A marquis was, as in England, the second most important Spanish title, ranking after a dukedom but above a count.
5. Hemming, *The Search for El Dorado*, 145.
6. Manuel Lucena Salmoral, in *DBE*, XXXI, 498.
7. See *CDI*, IV, 462ff.
8. *DBI*, XXIII, 207.
9. See Hemming, *The Search for El Dorado*, 151. Also *CDI*, IX, 437. I am grateful to Jaime Olmedo for finding a biography of Berrio, which has appeared in the *DBE*.
10. See below, chap. 19.
11. Irving Leonard argues (*Books of the Brave*, 18) that the constant references to Amazons by conquistadors suggest that the novel *Las Sergas de Esplandián*, in which there is talk of those heroines, must have been more widely read than is generally supposed.
12. *Relación de lo que Juan de Salas hizo y descubrió en la isla de Margarita*, in Jerónimo Martínez-Mendoza, *La leyenda de el Dorado*, Caracas 1967, 39–40. For Salas, see too *CDI*, IV, 462. Could there be a connection here with the Dozmary pool into which King Arthur threw Excalibur as he lay dying?
13. See Ojer.
14. Berrio to the king in Raleigh, 'Voyages of Discovery of Guiana'. See too Simón, *Noticias historiales de la conquista de Tierra Firme en las Indias Occidentales*, and the Hakluyt Society.
15. Ojer, 197.
16. Berrio in Ojer, loc. cit.
17. Loc. cit.
18. Rodrigo Carranza, *Traslado bien y fielmente sacado de una escritura de posesiones que parece tomó Domingo de Vera Ibargoien*, qu. Ojer, 95.

19. Cieza de León, *The Travels of Pedro Cieza de León*, in Hakluyt Society publications, series 1, London 1864, 280.
20. Raleigh, 'Voyages of Discovery of Guiana', 13. Among Raleigh's many mistakes was a comment that Diego de Ordaz was allowed to use a burning volcano in his coat of arms to commemorate taking sulphur out of the volcano Popacatepetl, whereas in fact he brought snow down from the mountain.
21. Ojer, 151.
22. 'The shepherd of the Ocean (quoth he)/Unto to that Goddess's grace me first enhanced.'
23. It can be seen in Volume VI of his history of the world, whose title is much more ambitious than the text.

## 19 PORTUGAL JOINS SPAIN

1. Sebastián was Sebastião in Portuguese.
2. 'O grandes, o riquísimas conquistas/de las Indias de Dios, de aquel gran mundo/tan escondido a las mundanas vistas!' Aldana was born in 1537 in Naples, the nephew of a famous cavalry commander (Bernardo de Aldana) and son of a commander in Italy (Antonio Villela de Aldana). He was a member of the Duke of Alba's circle. He was still just thirty years old but had written love sonnets, religious poems, and mythological ones. It is said that his work reflects his Neapolitan connections. His vocabulary was original and Cervantes called him 'el Divino'.
3. Alba, III, 640.
4. Parker, *Philip II*, 143.
5. The Braganzas were also illegitimate in origin, being descendants of Alfonso the first duke, the natural son of King João I, himself a bastard son of Pedro I.
6. Braudel, II, 1180. Cristóbal de Moura (1538–1613) had as a young man joined the secretariat of King Philip's sister, Doña Juana. He had become a friend of both the Prince of Éboli and of Antonio Pérez.
7. But carts had been used in New Spain, with wheels.
8. Braudel, I, 284.
9. An excellent account of this campaign is in the life of Alba by Maltby, 280ff.
10. Mulcahy, 53.
11. See Bouza Álvarez, *Cartas de Felipe V a sus hijas*.
12. See chap. 20 and Pirenne, II, 449.
13. The letters were translated very well into French by L. P. Gachard as *Lettres de Philippe II à ses filles les infantes Isabelle et Catherine écrites*

*pendant son voyage en Portugal, 1581–1583,* Paris 1884, and they appeared in Spanish in the volume by Bouza Álvarez.

14. Braudel, II, 1185.
15. See Gounon-Loubens, 43.
16. The establishment of a Portuguese dependency in Brazil is brilliantly analysed in the early chapters of *Red Gold* by John Hemming.

## 20 THE MONEY BEHIND THE CONQUESTS

1. Fernández de Alfaro and Juan de Córdoba were both *conversos,* according to Juan Gil. Maluenda was also a *converso.* See Gil, *Los conversos y la inquisición sevillana.*
2. Fernández de Alfaro was a captain who made himself a merchant. He appears often in the collection of documents from the Casa de la Contratación, 1503–1521, prepared by Miguel Ángel Ladero Quesada (Madrid 2008). See Hugh Thomas, *Rivers of Gold.*
3. A *quintal* is a fifth part of a hundred, equivalent to a hundredweight.
4. Charles V gave Cristóbal de Haro a coat of arms representing five ships, the Pillars of Hercules, and spices. Haro had this placed on a chapel in the church of San Lesmes de Burgos, which he endowed.
5. See Gil, *Los conversos y la inquisición sevillana,* I, 345 and 548.
6. Braudel, I, 439, fn 448.
7. See E. Vaillé, *Histoire générale des postes françaises,* 2 vols., Paris 1949.
8. See Alcázar.
9. Lapeyre, *Une famille de marchands,* 166. The summary of postal activity in both France and Spain by Lapeyre cannot be bettered.
10. Ibid., 235. Lapeyre (p. 236) comments: 'La belle époque du trafic des assurances à Burgos paraît avoir duré jusque vers 1569.'
11. See Putzger's *Historische Schulatlas,* 73rd edn, Berlin 1958, map 102, 'Zur Geschichte der deutschen Post, 1506–1521'.
12. See *DBE,* XVII, 296.
13. See in particular Felipe Ruiz Martín, *El siglo de los genoveses en Castilla,* Paris 1973.
14. Braudel, I, 343.
15. Ibid., 391.
16. Lapeyre, 478, points out that the history of Medina has been neglected, as has the history of the fairs of Medina de Rioseco and Villalón.
17. See Cervantes, *Don Quijote,* Part 2, 1009.
18. See genealogy 3 in Hugh Thomas, *The Conquest of Mexico.*
19. See *CDHI,* XIV, 46ff.

20. Lorenzo Sanz, II, 34.

21. Lapeyre, *Une famille de marchands*, 66.

22. Qu. Braudel, I, 356.

23. Ibid., 358.

24. Ibid., 356.

25. Carande, *Cartas de mercaderes*.

26. These fairs were the successors to those held from 1534 in Besançon or Lons-le-Saunier in France. At that time Lyons was a contender to be the centre of world wealth. Piacenza was in the duchy of Parma.

27. Braudel, I, 393.

28. Lapeyre has a fine chapter dealing with these French products, 'Les Toiles', in *Une famille de marchands*, 505–28.

29. Braudel, I, 478.

30. 'In the land of Holland,' wrote the geographer Martín Fernández de Enciso, 'they make the best and finest linens in all of Europe which are called *Holanda* after the name of the land.' Qu. La Fuente, 26.

31. Lorenzo Sanz, I, 469.

32. Gonzalo Fernández de Oviedo, *Historia general y natural de las Indias*, edition of Juan Pérez de Tudela, Madrid 1992.

33. See François Chevalier, 'Les cargaisons des flottes de la Nouvelle Espagne vers 1600', in *R de I*, II, 1943.

34. Luis Muro and Bartolomé de Medina, 'Introductor del beneficio de patio en Nueva España', *Historia Mexicana* 52, Mexico 1964, 520.

35. Boteller was probably born in Tarragona in 1530. It seems that he was in New Spain as a metal specialist by 1529. He died bitter and unsuccessful in 1566.

36. Their names are in Lorenzo Sanz, I, 484.

37. See Guillero Lohmann, *Enrique Garcés, descubridor del mercurio en el Peru*, Seville 1948, 453. Enrique Garcés (1522–1596) came from an upper-class family. He went to the Indies very young, in 1545 or thereabouts, with his brother Garci Gómez. Garcés was in Lima, Guayaquil, as a bookbinder. He discovered mercury in 1558 in Huamarga. That enabled him to take 400 *martes* of silver to the Marquis of Nieva. Garcés continued at Huamarga. He was an inventor and an alchemist. Cervantes praises him in his *Canto de Calipso* (1583). Garcés reached Lima in 1589 and died in Madrid in 1596, being a remarkable example of a poet, inventor, and chemist: a real Renaissance man.

38. Lorenzo Sanz publishes statistics as to who paid for mercury, in Lorenzo Sanz, I, 509.

39. See Hugh Thomas, *The Golden Age*.

40. Philip II gave Potosí another slogan: 'For the powerful Emperor, for the wise King, this lofty mountain of silver could conquer the whole world.'

41. The eighteenth-century Scottish historian William Robertson dismissed interest in such matters as beneath the attention of serious historians: 'To describe the nature of the various ores, the mode of extracting them from the bowels of the earth and to explain the several processes by which the metals are separated from the substances with which they are mingled, either by the action of fire or the attractive powers of mercury, is the province of the natural philosopher or chemist, rather than of the historian', in *History of America*, Dublin 1777, III, 243.

42. *Historia Económica del Río de la Plata*, cited in Hanke, *Los virreyes*, 96.

43. Vargas Ugarte, 15–21.

44. Granvelle, *Correspondance 1567–1586*, VII, 2.

45. See Lapeyre, *Une famille de marchands*, 66.

46. See Vila Vilar on the Jorge family. In the 1560s the king tried for a few years to establish a monopoly of trade in Seville. The idea was not a success since the well-established *sevillano* families, who would have been asked to raise a quarter of the capital, did not consider the Crown a partner who could assist them. (An exception was Hernán Vázquez, who would have been the general administrator.)

47. Braudel, I, 377.

48. See Hugh Thomas, *The Slave Trade*, London 1997, 21ff.

49. See Hugh Thomas, *The Golden Age*, 156–7.

50. His actual figure seems to have been 38,250.

51. This famous book was published by Harvard University Press, Cambridge, Massachusetts (1934). Those at the time who pointed out the influence of precious metals on prices included Noël du Fail (1585), Marc Lescabot (1612), and Gerard Malynes (1601).

52. See Einaudi.

## 21 PIRACY AND BUCCANEERING

1. Many such payments are listed in Braudel, I, 489–93. The largest single consignment was 2,200,000 crowns in a convoy in June 1598: 200,000 in gold, 1,300,000 in silver ingots, 700,000 in *reales*.

2. Braudel, I, 496.

3. See Kelsey; also Hakluyt, *Voyages and Documents*, 138–40.

4. See Hakluyt, *Voyages and Documents*, 279.

5. See Andrews for the Hakluyt Society. Most of the documents presented there come from the records of the High Court of Admiralty, some from the Hakluyt records, and a few from Spanish sources.

6. A lateen sail was a triangular sail on a long yard at an angle of 45 degrees to the mast. The word derives of course from a 'Latin' sail.

7. A pinnace was a vague term used to indicate any vessel that could carry up to 50 tons.

8. A saker was a small cannon, a culverin was a bit bigger.

9. See Andrews, loc. cit.

10. See Angulo Íñiguez.

11. Hakluyt, *Further English Voyages*, 301.

12. Andrews, 37.

13. '*Gagner le Pérou*' is still a phrase in French meaning 'to win a great fortune', and '*ce n'est pas le Pérou*' means 'it is no great catch'.

14. AGI, Guatemala, 10, 63–6, qu. Andrews, 306.

15. Ibid., 330. Geare landed close to where the British under Albemarle would land in 1762.

16. Ibid., 28.

17. Rafael Álvarez Estévez and Marta Guzmán Pascual, *Holandeses en Cuba*, Havana 2008.

## 22 THE GALLEON, A VERY NARROW PRISON

1. Qu. Braudel, I, 226.

2. See Céspedes del Castillo.

3. See above, page 221.

4. These questions are explored by Braudel, I, 298.

5. See Chaunu, I, 127.

6. This was George, Third Earl of Cumberland (1558–1605), who sought to make up for his wastefulness at home by adventures at sea. He won the queen's favour by his conduct as captain of the *Elizabeth Buonaventura* in the battle against the Armada. He was said to have been a man of personal beauty despite three warts on his left cheek.

7. Braudel, I, 302.

8. Braudel is also helpful on this matter, I, 306.

9. See Leonard, *Romances of Chivalry in the Spanish Indies*, Appendix IV.

10. Discussed in Bernal, 129.

11. A passenger to the river Plate in the second half of the sixteenth century was expected to provide for himself or herself four hundredweight of

ship's biscuit, one hogshead of flour, eight arrobas of wine, three bushels of beans and chickpeas, four arrobas of olive oil, six arrobas of vinegar, one arroba of rice, two arrobas of dried fish, together with a good supply of bacon, garlic, onions, olives and figs, raisins and almonds. The list continues with a recommended quantity of clothes and concludes with a half arroba of soap.

12. For these supplies see the summary by Hamilton, 'Wages and Subsistence on Spanish Treasure Ships, 1503–1660'.

13. La Torre, *Desde Salamanca, España, hasta Ciudad Real, Chiapas: Diario de viaje, 1540–1545*. Another vivid account, by a judge who went with his family to Santo Domingo in 1573, can be seen in *Cartas de Eugenio de Salazar*, in BAE, vol. 62, Madrid 1926, 291.

14. See in particular Tardieu.

15. *Descripción corográfica de Puertobelo*, 1607, in CDI, IX, 108–20.

16. See Hugh Thomas, *Who's Who of the Conquistadors*, London 2000, 3.

17. La Fuente, 52.

18. Lapeyre, *Une famille de marchands*, 497.

19. Schäfer, II, 326–7.

20. See González de Mendoza, II, 220, and Loyola, 117; the Hakluyt translation.

21. The best introduction to the history of this great city is in the book by La Puerta often cited.

22. Qu. La Fuente, 130. These woods were mahogany (*swietenia mahagonia*), cedar (*cederela odorata*), and oak (*tabebuia calcicola*). Pine trees (*pinus caribaea*) were used to make masts.

23. The most interesting visitor of this kind was Tomé Cano of the Canary Islands, who in 1611 published an important treatise on shipbuilding, *Arte para fabricar, fortificar y aparejar naos de Guerra*.

24. La Fuente, 134ff.

25. It was co-owned by his nephew, another Juan Maldonado.

26. There is an excellent chapter 6 on slavery by La Fuente, 147–85.

27. Braudel, II, 959.

## 23 POPULATIONS DISCOVERED

1. Angel Rosenblatt, *La población de América de 1492*, Mexico 1967. Rosenblatt remains the great historian of population in Latin America. See too Serrano, 162.

2. See below, p. 238.

3. Fernand Braudel gives half this figure, basing himself on *Geografische Zeitschrift*, 1940, 209.

4. A *cañada* is a sheep path.

5. See Klein.

6. Navagero, 27–8.

7. These are Braudel's conclusions, I, 404–5.

8. Cervantes, *Novelas ejemplares*, II, 87ff.

9. Braudel, II, 741.

10. See Fernández Sanz, 17. Other similar volumes include the one by Hurtado. There is much interesting information about Andalusians in the Americas in *Andalucía y América en el siglo xvi*, 2 vols., Seville 1983; the last chapter in vol. 2 (535–55) discusses American Indians who reached Andalusia in various unexpected ways. None were slaves but they were often treated as if they were so. The most famous of these were the Totonaca sent back to Spain by Cortés in 1520, but there were also Indians from Santo Domingo, Cuba, and later Brazil. Those from Santo Domingo were sent to Spain by the treasurer of that settlement, Miguel de Pasamonte, to whom King Fernando had written saying that he wanted to see what kind of people were these Caribbeans who ate meat (op. cit., 538).

11. Caro Baroja, *Los Judeos en la España moderna*, 220.

12. The question of Muslim or Arab influence in Latin America has been discussed by Carlos Pereyra.

13. See chapters 11, 16, and 17. Garay appears in chapter 16.

14. See Lutgardo García Fuentes, 'La introducción de esclavos en Indias desde Sevilla en el siglo XVI', in *Andalucía y America en el siglo XVI*, Seville 1983, 249ff.

15. Fernández Álvarez, *La sociedad española del Renacimiento*, 182.

16. La Puerta, 35, 40.

17. Aguirre Beltrán, 412–31.

18. La Puerta, 41.

19. For whom, see chapter 5 above.

20. Martín, *The Intellectual Conquest of Peru*, 67.

21. For the viceroy, see *DBE*, XXXII, 117–18.

22. Menéndez de Avilés to King Philip, 15 June 1558, cited in Fernández Álvarez, *corpus documental*, I, 165.

23. For the impact of disease see Rosenblatt *passim*.

24. See Borah and Cook.

25. This was discussed in my *The Conquest of Mexico*, Appendix I, 609ff.

26. See above, pages 89–90.

27. Crosby, 289–9.
28. See Borah and Cook, 6.
29. See Gibson, 458–61. Other material can be found in Motolinía (Fr. Toribio de Benavente), *Historia de los Indios de la Nueva España*, Madrid 2001, 302.
30. Ignacio de Loyola, *Viaje alrededor del mundo*, 113.
31. Martyr, *Cartas sobre el Nuevo Mundo*, II, 52.
32. See his *El Campanario*, published posthumously in 1939.
33. Wright, 185.
34. Wright, 194. Diego de Mazariegos was named governor of Cuba in succession to Pedro de Angulo on 31 March 1555. Mazariegos was shipwrecked en route (in which disaster he lost the lieutenant-governor Licenciado Martínez) and he only reached Havana on 7 March 1557. He quickly took the *residencia* of Angulo and established himself in Havana too. He lived with, then married, Francisca de Angulo, daughter of the late governor. His nephew, Francisco Mazariegos, proved to be one of his headaches. But Mazariegos was a very active governor and held off French attacks much more successfully than his predecessor. Later he became governor of Venezuela.
35. Martín, *The Intellectual Conquest of Peru*, 36.
36. *Monografías históricas sobre la historia de Lima*, Lima 1935, I, 408–40.
37. Martín, *Daughters of the Conquistadors*, 564.
38. According to Langa Pizarro of the University of Alicante. There was a fine exhibition, 'No fueron solos', in the Museo Naval in 2012. See *El país semanal*, 20 May 2012.
39. Martin, *Daughters of the Conquistadors*, 20.


## 24 THE CONQUEST OF THE PHILIPPINE ISLANDS

1. Lazarus was the brother of Martha and Mary and a friend of Jesus, who raised him from the dead. He is said later to have been a bishop in Cyprus.
2. See Hugh Thomas, *Rivers of Gold*, 436.
3. The curious entanglements between Spain and Portugal, including the negotiations at Badajoz and Elvas, are very well treated in Brotton, 186–217, though the admirable author may underestimate the significance of Charles V's marriage to his rich Portuguese princess.
4. *CDI*, XIV, 165ff.
5. See Hugh Thomas, *The Golden Age*, 442.
6. *CDI*, III, V, 117–220.
7. *CDI*, XVI, 151–65.

8. Earl Hamilton thought that there was a possible connection with the great rise in the price of spices between 1558 and 1565 and the decision by the viceroy and king. See Hamilton, *American Treasure and the Price Revolution in Spain, 1501–1650*, 233, n. 2. Braudel also noted the point, I, 553. See too *CDI*, VIII, 36ff.

9. See chapters 16 and 17 above.

10. See Insansti, 257.

11. Paso, II, 138.

12. Spanish and Spanish American religious life was marked then as now by numerous brotherhoods which did good works in the name of a special saint or the Virgin Mary. There are about sixty such at present in Seville.

13. Paso, IV, 223.

14. *CDI*, VI, 375, and XIII, 527ff.

15. Capitán General de las Yslas del Poniente; AGI, Patronato, leg. 52, r 1 (7 October 1578).

16. For example, he is called 'el general Miguel López de Legazpi' in a letter to the king of 28 May 1566; see Hanke, *Los virreyes españoles en América durante el gobierno de la casa de Austria*, 156.

17. See the reflections of Fray Betanzos quoted in Hugh Thomas, *The Golden Age*, 484–5.

18. Qu. Pérez de Tudela, 106.

19. Riquel in Isacio Rodríguez.

20. Rada to Alonso de la Veracruz in 1577, *CDI*, XLI, 41.

21. Comparable to what occurred to the Yahoos in the land of the Houyhnhnms, in Jonathan Swift's *Gulliver's Travels*.

22. The Spaniards believed that the *naturales* customarily worshipped the devil and 'made unto him many sacrifices in recompense for the great quantity of gold which he had given them', Ignacio de Loyola, 261.

23. Benavides in *CDI*, XXXIV, 89–101. Miguel de Benavides y Añoza, who was born in Carrión de los Condes (Palencia), was a Dominican son of the soil who worked for a time in San Gregorio in Valladolid. He went to China in 1590 with Fray Juan de Castro. He was admired in Manila for his cultivation of poverty (*DBE*). How marvellous that a labourer's son from Palencia could have had such a varied life!

24. *CDIHE*, III, 325. There was also a report by Viceroy Falces in March 1567 to the effect that in New Spain they had by then no news of the Isles of the West.

25. See *R de I*, 25 (1946), in which can be found Dalmiro de la Valgoma's 'Sangre de Legazpi', and also Ciriaco Pérez Bustamante's 'Cuando nací Legazpi', *R de I* 32 (1971), 123–4.

26. AGI, Filipinas, leg. 79 no. 1, n. 1.
27. Gil, *Los Chinos en Manila, siglo XVI y XVII.*

## 25 MANILA

1. *CDI*, XIII, 529ff.
2. Loyola, 148.
3. See Santamaría. Alfonso Felix, ed., *The Chinese in the Philippines, 1570–1770*, 2 vols. (Manila 1966), I, 67–118, cites testimonies from 1640 by an aged son of the former Muslim king of Manila (106).
4. Loc. cit.
5. Blair and Robertson, 253.
6. Memorial cited in Hidalgo Nuchera, 51.
7. Gil, *Los Chinos en Manila, siglo XVI y XVII*, 390–91.
8. He signed a letter to the king in 1665, in *CDI*, XIII, 530.
9. Hidalgo Nuchera, 42.
10. See page 67 above.
11. Later in 1602 that became obligatory.
12. Félix Álvarez Martínez, *Galeón de Acapulco. El viaje de la misericordia de Dios*, in Schurz.
13. Qu. Braudel, I, 378.
14. See Yuste López.
15. Gil, *Los Chinos en Manila, siglo XVI y XVII*, 83 and 89.
16. See Schurtz.
17. See John Wills, 'Relations with Maritime Europeans, 1514–1662', in *The Cambridge History of China*, Cambridge 1998, VIII, chap. 7, 354.
18. AGI, Filipinas, leg. 79, I, 1 July 8 1569. This file is full of extraordinary documents about China, mostly written in beautiful handwriting by Augustinians or Jesuits. The key sentences read 'para conquistar una tierra tan grande y de tanta gente, es necesario tener cerca el socorro y acogida para qualquier caso que sucediese . . .' and 'la gente de China es nada belicosa'.
19. AGI, Patronato, leg. 263, no. 1, 1ff–2A, cited in Gil, *Los Chinos en Manila, siglo XVI y XVII*, 20.
20. AGI, Patronato, leg. 24, R.2. But it is also in Ollé, 40.
21. Hidalgo Nuchera, *Los primeros de Filipinas* (Madrid 1995), 3: 'Repartir la tierra de las dichas Islas del Poniente y de la China . . .'.
22. For the origin of this interesting word see Gil, *Los Chinos en Manila, siglo XVI y XVII*, xv. Governor Sande thought that it indicated someone who came and went. Berthold Laufer, 'The Relations of the Chinese to the Philippine Islands', Smithsonian Institution, miscellaneous quarterly issue

(Washington 1908), 208, thought the word derived from the Emuy dialect of Chinese Senghi meaning 'commerce'.

23. AGI, Filipinas, leg. 79, no. 1, 8 July 1569.
24. Enríquez de Almansa, a Navarrese, was distantly related to the royal Enriquezes.
25. AGI, Patronato, 24, N 22, cited in Ollé, 46.
26. Ollé, 49.
27. AGI, Patronato, 24, 4, 9, qu. Ollé, 49.
28. Hidalgo Nuchera, 98ff.

## 26 THE TEMPTATION OF CHINA

1. AGI, Patronato, leg. 24, Ramo 6, qu. Ollé, 52.
2. See Gil, *Los Chinos en Manila, siglo XVI y XVII*, 24–5.
3. AGI, Mexico, leg. 69 r, 190.
4. '*para acometer la conquista de China*'.
5. Alba was succeeded by Luis de Requesens in 1573.
6. Juan González de Mendoza (1545–1618) was an Augustinian friar who became Bishop of Lipari (Sicily), Chiapas, and Popayán. Born in Torrecillas en Cameros, in La Rioja, he went to the Indies in 1562, where he remained till 1574. In 1580 he was chosen to lead an embassy to China. He wrote a *History of the Kingdom of China*, a country which in the end he never visited, but the book was published in Rome in 1585 and became a best-seller.
7. Juan González de Mendoza, *Historia del reino de China* (Madrid 1991), 151.
8. See above, page 245.
9. See Hidalgo Nuchera, 320. The largest *encomienda* in Otón was that of Luis de Haya, with 6,000 souls.
10. *Relación de viaje*, in BN, MS 2902 and MS 3042. These are reprinted in Fernández de Navarrete, II, 273. There is also useful material in Ollé, 59.
11. Pastells and Torres Lanzas, II, xliii–xliv.
12. See Hugh Thomas, *The Golden Age*, chap. 7.
13. AGI, Philippines, leg. 339, I, 46–7.
14. When it came to Japan, Francisco Cabral, who then led the Jesuit mission there, wrote to the general of the order, now Fray Claudio Acquaviva (of a Neapolitan aristocratic family), that several thousand Japanese were being converted to Christianity every year. Cabral believed that he himself had converted 20,000 souls in the kingdom of Omura, including sixty entire monasteries and their bonzes. But there was all the same a fearful shortage of preachers. Who could preach in any indigenous tongue?

15. Ollé, 72.
16. AGI, Filipinas, leg. 6, V, 28.
17. See Menzies, 1421.
18. Isacio Rodríguez, xiv, doc. 76.
19. Hanke, *The Spanish Struggle for Justice in the New World*, 143.
20. AGI, Patronato, leg. 24, r 37, cited in Pastells and Torres Lanzas, ii, xlix.
21. AGI, Filipinas, leg. 79, no. 2, 8 June 1577.
22. Pastor, X, 478. Members of the Alfaro family were to be found throughout the Spanish empire in the sixteenth century. Leaving aside the financier/merchant mentioned in the text (for whom see Hugh Thomas, *Quien es quien*, 293, and also *DBE*), there was a curate in Santo Domingo called Alfaro, who became a canon in New Spain; there was Alfonso Alfaro, a companion of Espinosa in Tierra Firme; Diego and Francisco Alfaro were both to be found in Santo Domingo; there was another Francisco Alfaro, who was *fiscal* in Panama; and Melchor Alfaro was an *encomendero* in Tabasco.
23. AGI, Filipinas, leg. 79, no. 6, November 1579.
24. 'Una sola ciudad populosísima cercada y murada', in AGI, Filipinas, leg. 79, no. 5, 13 October 1579.
25. AGI, Patronato, leg. 24, r 47. Diego García de Palacio (1542–1595) was born in Ambrucero, Cantabria, and went as a judge (*oidor*) to Guatemala in 1573. He was in New Spain as *alcalde del crimen* and busied himself with preparing ships for Manila.
26. AGI, Patronato, leg. 47, qu. Pastells and Torres Lanzas, II, xlix.
27. AGI, Patronato, leg. 24, r 37.
28. Mulcahy, 258, 256.
29. Ibid.
30. Alonso Sánchez Coello (1531–1588) may have had Portuguese *converso* blood. See *DBE*. He worked in the studio of Antonio Moro as a young man and went with him to both Flanders and Lisbon. In 1555 he was named painter to Don Carlos and he made four portraits of him. He also painted the new French queen, Elisabeth, in 1559. Thereafter he gained full recognition as court painter.
31. He was not a Coruña of the Mendoza family.
32. *CDI*, VI, 465.
33. García-Abasolo, *España y el Pacífico*, 61. The *residencia* of the outgoing Governor Sande found that proconsul guilty of illegal trading, especially in white silk. Gil in *Los Chinos en Manila, siglo XVI y XVII*, 32, has an admirable summary. All the same, Sande went on to become president of the *audiencia* of Guatemala (1594) and then of Santa Fe (1597).

34. See Hugh Thomas, *The Golden Age*, 356.
35. Ollé, 30.
36. Gil, *Los Chinos en Manila, siglo XVI y XVII*, 81.
37. García Icazbalceta, *Nueva Colección*, III, xxxiii.
38. Suárez de Peralta, 208.
39. See Gil, *Los Chinos en Manila, siglo XVI y XVII*, 429.
40. Hanke, *The Spanish Struggle for Justice in the New World*, 124.

## 27 THE CONQUEST OF CHINA

1. AGI, Filipinas, leg. 79, no. 10. This remarkable letter is seventy-seven quarto pages long. On page 1, Sánchez uses the expression 'Ronquillo gobernador de las Filipinas', I believe, for the first time.
2. Evidence of the sailor Juan Bautista Berragán and the pilot Alonso Gómez appears in the *Información de servicios y méritos* of Bishop Salazar.
3. See Teixera, 5–7, and a letter of Panela to Ronquillo of 10 February 1583 in Colín, 302.
4. Ollé, 35, and see too José Luis Porrás Cameranz, *Sínodo de Manila de 1582*, Madrid 1982, as well as Lucio Gutiérrez, 'The Synod of Manila, 1581–1586', in *Filippina sacra*, XXV, 74, Manila 1990, 195.
5. Hubert Jacobs, *Documenta Malucensia*, Rome 1974, II, 7.
6. Letter from Gonzalo Ronquillo written in Macao on 14 December 1582, cited by Gil, *Los Chinos en Manila, siglo XVI y XVII*, 401.
7. AGI, Filipinas, leg. 79, Isacio Rodríguez, cited *CDI*, XV, 147, n. 586.
8. Blair and Robertson, 1973, V, 25–7.
9. See Neil MacGregor, *Shakespeare's Restless World*, London 2012, chap. 16.
10. The best work on Ricci is by Michaela Fontana. See also Vincent Cronin.
11. Pastells and Torres Lanzas, II, 184.
12. 'Relación breve de las jornadas hizo el P Alonso Sánchez la segunda vez que fue a la China año de 1584', in AGI, Filipinas, leg. 79, n 13.
13. 'Tan semejante en todos a los Chinos que parece uno de ellos en lo hermoso rostro y en la delicadeza.'
14. Ollé, 35.
15. Archive of the Jesuits, Rome, Phil. 9, 16. It is desirable to consult the summary of the synod of Manila of 1582 to be found in a volume edited by José Luis Porras Camúñez, Horacio Santiago-Otero, and José María Soto Rábanos, *Sínodo de Manila de 1582*, Madrid 1988.
16. Pastells and Torres Lanzas, II 184–5.
17. See Biblioteca Nacional de Madrid, ms 7094, ff. 13–18, qu. Ollé, 158.

18. AGI, Patronato, leg. 25, no. 22.

19. Pietro Tacchi Venturi, *Opere storiche del Matteo Ricci SJ*, Macerata 1913, II, 426. This second letter of Sánchez is to be seen in AGI, Filipinas, leg. 79, n 13. This *legajo* has invaluable material from 1569 to 1590 from Jesuits (Alonso Sánchez, Cristóbal Velázquez, Miguel Rogerio, and Francisco Pasio), Franciscans (Pedro de Alfaro and Agustín de Tordesillas), and Augustinians (Martín de Rada, Francisco Manrique, Andrés de Aguirre, Mateo de Mendoza, and Francisco Ortegaz).

20. Isacio Rodríguez, XIV, 1965.

21. Cited in Ollé, 164.

22. Wicki, XIV, 9.

23. Zubillaga, 131–2.

24. Loyola, 169.

25. Schäfer, II, 95, 386.

26. Boxer, 181.

27. See Wright, *The Early History of Cuba*, 123.

28. AGI, Filipinas, leg. 74, 27 June 1588, qu. Gil, *Los Chinos en Manila, siglo XVI y XVII*, 485.

29. Trevor-Roper, *From Counter-Reformation to Glorious Revolution*, 32.

30. Colín, II, 368–74. These matters are admirably summarized by Ollé, 200.

31. This paper is in BN, MS 287, ff 198–226.

32. Ollé, 217.

33. Pérez Dasmariñas also abolished obligatory *repartimientos* and substituted for them free rents of land, but in 1609 the *repartimiento* was revived.

34. Twitchett and Mote, VIII, 358.

35. Gil, *Los Chinos en Manila, siglo XVI y XVII*, 402.

36. Antonio de Morga, *Sucesos de las Filipinas*, Mexico 1609, republished Madrid 1997, 295–7. Morga had been a judge of the Supreme Court in Manila.

37. Morga, 269, 270.

38. The *audiencia*, created in 1583, was abolished in 1589 but revived in 1597.

39. See Hidalgo Nuchera, 113–14.

40. AGI, Filipinas, leg. 18B, 787, cited in Gil, *Los Chinos en Manila, siglo XVI y XVII*, 417.

41. For Isabel de Barreto, see Luis Martín SJ, *Las hijas de los conquistadores, mujeres del virreinato de Perú*, Barcelona 2000.

## 28 EPILOGUE: THE AGE OF ADMINISTRATION

1. Archivo General de la Nación, Mexico, Inquisición, tomo 276, no. 13.

2. *Discorso dell eccelenza della monarchia*, qu. Pagden, *Spanish Imperialism and the Political Imagination*, 2. Botero had been preceptor to the sons of Carlo Emanuel, Duke of Savoy, and was also Abbot of San Miguel de la Chiusa. He resigned his membership of the Society of Jesus to become secretary to Cardinal (later Saint) Carlo Borromeo.

3. In his will King Philip mentioned the need to keep Portugal alongside Castile as essential. See Fernández Álvarez, *Felipe II y su tiempo*, 927.

4. Farnese was the son of Margaret of Parma, the clever illegitimate daughter of the Emperor Charles by a girl from Oudenarde.

5. Ortega y Gasset, 51.

6. Qu. Kamen, *Imagining Spain*, 96.

7. Doria, 38, qu. Pagden, 40.

8. See Hugh Thomas, *The Golden Age*, Book V.

9. See Dante Alighieri, *De monarchia*.

10. See Bataillon, 395ff.

11. See the record of the Cortes, 1520, where he made a speech in honour of Charles. A cousin of his was with Cortés in New Spain.

12. Botero, 237.

13. Giménez Fernández, *Bartolomé de las Casas*, II, 790.

14. See Braudel, II, 675.

15. For his family and connections, see Hugh Thomas, *The Conquest of Mexico*, 470; also *DBE*.

16. Oviedo, *Historia general y natural de las Indias*, I, 52. The matter was also discussed by Peter Martyr, II, 12, and also in Hugh Thomas, *Rivers of Gold*, 31.

17. The second Leonor's son, Fernando Sotelo de Moctezuma, held the *encomienda* afterwards and died in 1607. There were a tangle of *encomenderos* of this family until the end of the colonial area. See Gerhard, *Geografía histórica de la Nueva España, 1518–1821*, 233.

18. See ibid., 254, and Gibson, 431ff.

19. We read in Gerhard, *Geografía histórica de la Nueva España, 1518–1821*, 341, that '*En el siglo XVII los descendientes de don Pedro tenían las estancias de Tepeitec y Tulengo en encomienda privada*'.

20. Cheetham, 149.

21. Saint Pedro Claver (1580–1654), from Verdú in Gerona, studied at Barcelona and was sent to Cartagena in 1610, where he was ordained in 1615. Pedro worked with Fray Alfonso de Sandoval at first but devoted

his life to tending the slaves who might arrive half dead off ships in the harbour. He was canonized in 1888.

22. See Pedro Rojas.

23. Cheetham, 150.

24. See Hugh Thomas, *The Conquest of Mexico*, 171. Martín Vázquez recalled taking part in a procession on Palm Sunday 1520, with branches, a cross, and a picture of the Virgin Mary. See *CDI*, XXVII, 333.

25. La Fuente, 219.

26. For Marina see *Arqueología mexicana*, XX, no. 115, 88.

27. J. R. Seeley, *The Expansion of England*, republished Chicago 1971, xi.

28. Ibid., 12.

29. Kwarteng, 242.

30. Ibid., 243.

31. Raleigh, *The Discovery of Guiana*, 236.

32. Washington Irving, III, introduction, xv.

33. This is of course the theme of Irving Leonard's great study, *Books of the Brave*.

34. Fourth letter; *instrucciones dadas por Hernando Cortés a Francisco Cortés su lugarteniente en la villa de Colima*, in *CDI*, XXVI, 153.

35. Rodríguez Villa, *El Emperador Carlos V y su corte según las cartas de Don Martín de Salinas, embajador del infante Don Fernando, 1522–1539*, Madrid 1903, 529.

36. Merriman, IV, 680, 671.

37. Octavio Paz, *El peregrino en su patria, Historia y política de México*, I (Mexico 1987), 246; also *Sor Juana Inés de la Cruz o las trampas de la fe* (Barcelona 1982), 478.

38. See Elliott and Brown, *A Palace for a King*.

39. Vilar, 48.

40. Elliott, *History in the Making*, 131.

41. Elliott, *History in the Making*, 207.

42. Other close associates at the end of King Philip's life were the Count of Chinchón (Pedro Fernández de Cabrera), the Marquis of Velada, and Juan de Idiáquez, while the president of the Council of the Indies was Licenciado Paulo de Laguna, afterwards Bishop of Córdoba. Philip's last confessor was Fray Diego de Yepes (DBE).

43. The will of Philip II is carefully analysed by Fernández Álvarez in *Felipe II y su tiempo*, 921. It was printed in the same *Codicilio y ultima voluntad de Felipe II*, Valencia 1997.

44. The Bishop of Limoges to the Cardinal of Lorraine, 26 September 1560, in Aubespine, 49.

45. Braudel, II, 1236.
46. This is poem 379 in Sor Juana's works edited by Alonso Méndez Plan-carte, 4 vols. (Mexico 1951–7). Marie Louise (María Luisa) was the daughter of Philip, Duke of Orléans ('Monsieur'), and Henrietta, the sis-ter of King Charles II of England (the delightful 'Minette').

# Index

## ABOUT THE AUTHOR

HUGH THOMAS studied history at Cambridge and Paris. His career has encompassed both America and Europe, and history and politics, as a professor at New York and Boston Universities and as chairman of the Centre for Policy Studies in London. He was awarded a peerage in 1981. Hugh Thomas is the author of *The Spanish Civil War*, which won the Somerset Maugham Prize; *Cuba: The Pursuit of Freedom*; *An Unfinished History of the World*; *Armed Truce: The Beginnings of the Cold War*; *Conquest: Montezuma, Cortés, and the Fall of Old Mexico*; and *The Slave Trade*. He won the Nonino prize and the Boccaccio prize in Italy in 2009, the Gabarron prize and the Calvo Serer prize in Spain in 2006 and 2009, and the PEN prize in Mexico in 2011. He has the Grand Cross of the Order of Isabel the Catholic in Spain and the Order of the Aztec Eagle in Mexico, and is a Commander of the Order of Arts and Letters in France.

## ABOUT THE TYPE

This book was set in Sabon, a typeface designed by the well-known German typographer Jan Tschichold (1902–74). Sabon's design is based upon the original letter forms of sixteenth-century French type designer Claude Garamond and was created specifically to be used for three sources: foundry type for hand composition, Linotype, and Monotype. Tschichold named his typeface for the famous Frankfurt typefounder Jacques Sabon (c. 1520–80).